This volume is sponsored by
The Center for Japanese Studies
University of California, Berkeley

Liberalism in Modern Japan

Liberalism in Modern Japan

Ishibashi Tanzan and
His Teachers, 1905–1960

SHARON H. NOLTE

UNIVERSITY OF CALIFORNIA PRESS

Berkeley   Los Angeles   London

University of California Press
Berkeley and Los Angeles, California

University of California Press, Ltd.
London, England

© 1987 by
The Regents of the University of California

Printed in the United States of America

1   2   3   4   5   6   7   8   9

Library of Congress Cataloging-in-Publication Data

Nolte, Sharon H.
Liberalism in modern Japan.

Bibliography: p.
Includes index.
1. Japan—Intellectual life—20th century.
2. Liberalism—Japan. 3. Japan—History—Taishō period,
1912–1926. 4. Ishibashi, Tanzan, 1884–1973. 5. Tanaka,
Ōdō, 1867–1932. 6. Shimamura, Hōgetsu, 1871–1918.
DS822.4.N64   1986   952.03′2   85-21002
ISBN 0-520-05707-4 (alk. paper)

Contents

Preface

Liberalism was a cluster of ideas in prewar Japan. It defies simple definition, in part because it was intellectually pluralistic and diffuse, and in part because many of its central and local proponents and organizers have not yet received scholarly analysis. However, the major figures in this study—Tanaka Ōdō, Ishibashi Tanzan, and, to a lesser extent, Shimamura Hōgetsu—constituted three of its most united and coherent voices. They consistently upheld the dignity of the individual, freedom of expression, the equality of the sexes, the legitimacy of popular participation in cultural creation and in politics, progressive social engineering, and decolonization. Although many of their ideas will be familiar to present-day Western readers, others might seem bizarre. In either case the patterns and relationships among ideas reveal a distinct historical context.

An undergraduate student of modern Japanese history aptly illustrated the difficulties of inducing relationships among discrete phenomena. Impressed by media accounts of Japanese hard work, frugality, and strong family bonds, he remarked, "They have real values—I'll bet they don't waste money on designer labels and status symbols like we do." Few comments could seem more ludicrous to anyone who has visited Japan, yet the student was no dullard. Without much information about Japan, he drew upon American culture to elicit a mythical paradigm in which low divorce and crime rates were linked with plain living. His naive blunder highlights the necessity of empirical study of the historical, cultural, and social links among ideas that may have no logically necessary relationship. The necessity of course arises in any historical inquiry, but it is particularly urgent in the case of modern Japan since its analysts, whether foreign or Japanese, are almost without exception profoundly steeped in Western culture and theory.

The problem of Japanese liberalism is, I believe, intrinsically interesting, but it is also part of a much broader network of related questions. The most obvious of these is how liberalism, a Western import, existed and adapted in the context of Japanese society. Beginning in the late nineteenth century, Japanese reformers introduced German, British, French, and American political theory while searching for indigenous precedents for their intellectual innovation. At the same time their own context posed problems—especially the threat of Western domination epitomized in the unequal treaties, which followed the Perry Expedition—for which Western thinkers offered no ready answers. Domestic well-being was always linked to some assessment of Japan's place in the world, although those assessments would differ remarkably. The tensions of shifting foreign relations and rapid development militated against continuity in democratic thought, and twentieth-century liberals compounded their problems of adaptation by developing a definite sense of distance from nineteenth-century advocates of laissez-faire and natural rights, and from earlier Japanese protests such as the Popular Rights movement of the 1880s. An examination of who twentieth-century liberals were, how they used imported ideas and to what ends, and how they were connected with one another in institutions and trends reveals a great deal about the transformation of modern Japan.

The problem of evaluating liberalism is rendered more difficult by the disarray among specialists regarding Japan's place in modern world history. Japan resists interpretation in terms of two of our major paradigms of non-Western nations, the colonial/postcolonial and the revolutionary. At the turn of the century, when this study begins, certain aspects of social and intellectual life were more closely parallel to those of China than to those of any Western nation. Chinese intellectual and cultural influence was still powerful; the narrow political elite had a strongly bureaucratic character and no landed base; mercantile and industrial interests lacked political independence; the working class was minuscule and the population overwhelmingly rural; the patriarchal stem family dominated youth and women by managing property and arranging marriages. Yet since Japan already had a large and advanced sector of heavy industry plus an overseas empire by the time of World War I, comparisons with the West have been more common. An older scholarship emphasizing parallels to Germany—an authoritarian constitutional monarchy supplanted by fascism—is waning in influence, while controversial recent work suggests parallels with Great Britain, Sweden, and the United States. Meanwhile, influential Japanese scholars continue to use interpretive principles that defy comparative analysis: the emperor-state, the vertical society, the anatomy of dependence. However, no suggestion of Japanese uniqueness ought to be tolerated unless its nature can be specified.

Japan must be located in broader paradigms according to specific aspects of its modern experience, their parallels or lack of parallels in other nations, and, most important, the patterns and clusters of analytically discrete phenomena. A study of liberals, who clearly accepted some Western ideas but wielded them in a distinct political arena, is one step toward this end. Liberals developed a paradigm of modern Japanese history as essentially Western in its institutional structure of constitutional monarchy and industrial capitalism, but non-Western in its culture and social organization. Their attention to a cleavage between institutional "form" and cultural "spirit" was informed by the most advanced historical theory of their day, as well as by an acute and detached understanding of their own society. Their interpretations are a starting point for reconsidering Japan's place in the world, a problem of intense concern throughout modern Japanese thought.[1]

1. David Titus advocates comparisons with Great Britain and the United States in "Political Parties and Nonissues in Taishō Democracy," in Harry Wray and Hilary Conroy, eds., *Japan Examined: Perspectives on Modern Japanese History*, 181–90; and Mitani Taiichirō cites the United States as the most influential foreign source of culture in "Taishō demokurashii to Amerika," in Saitō Makoto et al., eds., *Nihon to Amerika: Hikaku bunka ron.* Carl Mosk stresses the demographic similarity to Sweden from the mid-nineteenth century in *Patriarchy and Fertility: Japan and Sweden, 1880–1960,* 207–23. Also citing nineteenth-century developments, such as economic bureaucracy, political equality, and anti-bourgeois culture, Yasuke Murakami describes contemporary Japan as a variant of a "Franco-Italian-type political system" in "The Age of New Middle-Mass Politics: The Case of Japan," *JJS* 8 (1982): 34–35, 53. For a critique of Japanese interpretations of fascism and the emperor-state see Itō Takashi, *Shōwaki no seiji,* 3–30.

Scholarship depends on cooperation, and I welcome the chance to acknowledge the greatest of many debts that I have incurred in the course of this work. Professor James B. Crowley, who advised the dissertation on which the first half of the book is based, has continually stimulated my thinking about modern Japan and served as a wise mentor and friend. Hugh Patrick was an inspired teacher and remains a supportive critic.

In Japan, Professors Mitani Taiichirō and Itō Takashi were generous with their time and ideas; Professor Hanzawa Hiroshi kindly shared his copies of Tanaka's letters from the United States. Tanaka Miki and Ishibashi Tan'ichi deserve special thanks for sharing memories of their fathers. Satō Yoshimaru of the Waseda University Daigakushi Henshūjo was most helpful in finding documentary material on Tanaka; Tani Kazushi of *Tōyō keizai shinpō* was indefatigable with encouragement and introductions. I was greatly assisted by several staff members of the Stanford Inter-University Center, the Tokyo University libraries, and the National Diet Library, where my friends Yamaguchi Miyoko and Edamatsu Sakae were ever ready with good cheer and good advice.

The University of Chicago archives, Palo Alto High School, and Stanford University all shared their records. Katharine Lockwood at the Center for Dewey Studies, Southern Illinois University at Carbondale, helped me find relevant letters from Tanaka, Dewey, and Paul Carus. Roscoe M. Pierson at Lexington Theological Seminary showed the true joy of an inspired archivist in tracing Tanaka's career there. Marlene Mayo and Fred Pernell were indispensable guides to the National Archives. Hideo Kaneko of Yale and Emiko Moffitt of the Hoover Institution were generous with their vast knowledge of sources.

The work would have been impossible without generous financial support from the Social Science Research Council, the Stanford Inter-University Center, a Yale University Sumitomo Fellowship, the Northeast Asia Council of Association for Asian Studies, and the Japan Foundation.

Kathleen Triplett has labored valiantly for years over various drafts, while Susie Moore and Sue Mahoney prepared the final version, with support from the Faculty Development Committee at DePauw. A special thanks must go to Bob Newton.

Portions were first published in *Journal of the History of Ideas* and *Journal of Asian Studies*.

Barbara Metcalf and Phyllis Killen at the University of California Press have shown the highest standards of professionalism and combined their rigor with warmth and humor. The readers deserve credit for great improvement in the manuscript. Eiji Sekine and George Elison of Indiana University helped me to verify the transliterations. Many thanks too for the editing by Sally Serafim.

I am also grateful to the many colleagues and friends who read and commented on all or part of the manuscript at one stage or another: John Whitney Hall, Frank Baumer, Byron Marshall, Marius Jansen, Bill Hoover, Akira Iriye, Richard Mitchell, Jim Huffman, Miles Fletcher, Richard Smethurst, John Campbell, Hugh Patrick, and Shank Gilkeson. And the most heartfelt appreciation for my friends Dennis Cordell, Sally Hastings, Don Niewyck, Anne Walthall, and Ann Waltner, who believed in me when I wasn't sure that I believed in myself. And of course, Reid and Lukacs.

The remaining problems are my responsibility.

Abbreviations

Introduction: Liberal Intellectuals and Their Institutional Context

The Taishō period (1912–26) was the crucible of Japanese modernity. In it, the authoritarian state crafted after the Meiji Restoration (1868–90) was found wanting, but reformers could not prevail. Much of Taishō conflict and Taishō culture survived World War II, but the traces are complex and subtle, sometimes elusive. The period is often defined in terms of the political, social, and intellectual movements conveniently summarized as "Taishō democracy," and thus dated from the various protests surrounding the Russo-Japanese War (1904–05) to the increased repression precipitated by the Manchurian Incident (1931).

A rich lode of Japanese scholarship on the Taishō democratic movement suggests a threefold division: First, efforts from the cabinet, ministries, and established political parties to expand political participation and guarantee a minimal level of social security through labor protection; aid to the aged, disabled, mothers and dependent children; health insurance, employment agencies, and other social reforms. Although much of the welfare legislation was enacted only in the thirties under pressure to unify the people for military ends, the bills reflected the demands of labor, tenant, and feminist movements during the twenties. Thus a second level of the democratic movement was the social organization of the disenfranchised. Reformist popular organizations represented important social change during the twenties but proved vulnerable to governmental and military cooptation during the thirties. A third level, and the primary interest here, was intellectual change and its relationship to the growth of edu-

1

cation, the media, and the urban new middle class. The interconnections of political movements, social transformations, and intellectual change are not yet clear. All of these trends affected the personnel and policies of the state in patterns that deserve further attention. However, the democratic movement could not transform the fundamental structure of Meiji institutions; in fact it was made possible by those institutions.

The Meiji Restoration of 1868 immediately abolished hereditary restrictions on occupation and residence, institutionalizing the slogan "rule by men of talent." Redefinition of the polity in terms of meritocracy had been one of the dominant themes of pre-Restoration discourse. H. D. Harootunian described the Restoration conception of authority as a "new program of knowledge and power that valorized merit, ability, and practicality over mere status ascription" and lost the communitarian themes of pre-Restoration thought.[1] In place of community came competition, unavoidably sanctioned by the ideal of meritocracy. The social effects of the Restoration were clear by 1900: the formation of new elites in a rationalized bureaucracy and a skilled business management based on civil service examinations and systematic recruitment of university graduates. Industrialization, mass literacy, urbanization, and the emergence of the nuclear family spawned new problems and new professions in education, the media, and social work. Professionals led a pluralistic questioning of traditional values, and debated the significance and desirability of social change in new general-interest journals.

In 1890 the Meiji government had promulgated Japan's first modern constitution, with a weak legislature responsible to men of substantial property, who constituted about 3 percent of the population. The Constitution would serve liberal politics as its legal basis and its ultimate limitation. Under its cryptic provisions the Meiji oligarchs perpetuated rule by local cliques of the warrior class and constructed a new imperial mythology to transform the basis of political legitimacy among the people. Thus individual mobility was walled within a newly

1. H. D. Harootunian, "Ideology as Conflict," in Tetsuo Najita and J. Victor Koschmann, eds., *Conflict in Modern Japanese History: The Neglected Tradition*, 61.

efficient, intrusive, and authoritarian state. However, the waves of social change set in motion by the Restoration beat against Meiji institutions and sapped the foundations of Meiji ideology.

The coalescence of an incomplete meritocracy marred by class divisions, regional cliques, gender segmentation, and repression sustained the Restoration ideal of meritocracy as an emancipating force. Taishō thinkers, by asking what constituted merit and who could judge it, explored the multiple tensions between meritocracy, participation, and freedom in a quest for fundamental human values. They crossed a bridge from the initial Meiji preoccupation with the relative merits and uses of things Japanese and things Western, to new concerns posed by an established state structure and a complex web of social institutions that could be labeled neither distinctively Western nor distinctively Japanese. They participated in an international cultural sphere.[2]

Taishō intellectuals also spoke to specifically Japanese conditions. Torn between admiration and reproach for the Meiji heritage, they reinterpreted their past according to their perceptions of the future spiritual and cultural requirements of the Japanese people. They called for a "Taishō Restoration" in order to fulfill the ideals of Meiji as well as new visions. Tanaka Ōdō (Kiichi) attributed the search for a Taishō Restoration to "equal parts inspiration and despair"—the inspiration of Meiji patriotism and the despair over the Meiji legacy of social unrest and moral confusion.[3] Restoration is a sorely inadequate translation for the *ishin* achieved in Meiji and sought in Taishō and again in Shōwa (1926–) Japan, for it never referred to concrete institutional arrangements of the recent past. In its Meiji and Shōwa variants, *ishin* meant direct imperial rule, a mythical state of affairs. Thus the term indirectly addressed the imperative of creating new forms and values. The Taishō *ishin* sought by contemporary writers meant the democratization of existing institutions but also the

---

2. Minami Hiroshi, *Taishō bunka*, 1–39; Iida Taizō, "Taishō chishikijin no seiritsu to seiji shisō: Bunmei hihyōka o chūshin ni."
3. Tanaka Ōdō, "Hiratsuka Raichō Shi ni ataete Shi no fujinkan o ronzu," *CK* 30, special issue on "Taishō shin kiun" (July 1915): 107.

transformation of culture and social relations. The power of the *ishin* in all three eras stemmed from its relevance to creating a modern Japanese society rather than modeling one on either the past or the West.

The Meiji reforms did not create a liberal state and society, but they did form a pluralistic institutional and cultural context in which liberalism was possible. Cultural pluralism, defined as a product of ethnic and religious diversity, has not been emphasized in studies of Japan. However, long-term borrowing from China and modern borrowing from the West did differentiate the customs and attitudes of the elite from those of commoners, since recent imports tended to be the monopoly of an elite. The premodern political order was remarkably pluralistic, consisting of independent vertical hierarchies linked only by formal authority at the top, and the Meiji Constitution perpetuated this pattern even while vastly increasing the power of the central government. Interagency competition mitigated authoritarianism, especially during the 1920s, when the numbers of political actors increased while their ideologies diverged. Meanwhile the state encouraged or at least tolerated other competing institutions such as private business, education, and the media. A pluralistic framework of institutions and, to a lesser extent, culture created the environment in which liberal thought could emerge.[4]

The social basis of Taishō liberalism was the urban new professional and managerial middle class. Its members were not all liberals, nor did they owe their beliefs to a single relationship with the means of production. Rather they shared a dependent and yet restless relationship with the state. The creation rather than creator of the Meiji state, the new middle class was numerically small and politically fragile. Its members relied on state initiative to sustain industrialization, national independence, and the social order that rewarded middle class skills and professions; however, they resented the exceedingly narrow basis of state power. The writers in this study, although

---

4. Peggy Reeves Sanday, "Cultural and Structural Pluralism in the United States," in Sanday, ed., *Anthropology and the Public Interest*; R. P. G. Stevens notes that "pluralism was a natural consequence of definite structural characteristics of the Meiji Constitution," in "Hybrid Constitutionalism in Prewar Japan," *JJS* 3 (1977): 99.

their liberal opinions were in the minority, had strong links with broader trends in urban middle class culture.

THE WRITERS

Philosopher Tanaka Ōdō, literary critic and drama director Shimamura Hōgetsu, and political economist Ishibashi Tanzan enjoyed an influence in their own day that has been almost wholly overlooked by scholars. The neglect is peculiar since Ishibashi defended his liberal views through the Pacific War (1931–45) and stepped forth as minister of finance, minister of international trade and industry, and finally prime minister during the first postwar decade. He is the most prominent test case for the central historical question of whether or not the Taishō democratic movement had a postwar legacy. Tanaka and Shimamura were more minor figures, but they were Ishibashi's teachers at Waseda University and his confidants until they died. Together, the three writers illustrate how philosophy and literature informed social, economic, and political theories in the Taishō era. They taught in a private university and wrote in middlebrow magazines and the business journal *Tōyō keizai shinpō* (Oriental economist), all more likely homes for liberalism than the imperial universities or the leftist movements that until recently have absorbed the interest of most scholars of Taishō thought.[5]

The writers broke ground in the semipopular, general-interest journals. All three published widely, believing that journalism was essential to a society based on both expertise and mass participation. Preferring serious but general-interest periodicals such as *Chūō kōron* (Central review) over narrowly academic journals, they wrote about personal experience and popular culture: lecture societies and avant-garde theater, new

5. A rediscovery of Ishibashi began with the publication of his complete works in 1970–72. Watanabe Tōru described *Tōyō keizai shinpō* under Ishibashi's editorship as the most unified and coherent voice of the Taishō democratic movement; "Sōron," in Inoue Kiyoshi and Watanabe, eds., *Taishōki no kyūshinteki jiyūshugi: 'Tōyō keizai shinpō' o chūshin toshite*, 1. Matsuo Takayoshi and Masuda Hiroshi have worked on Ishibashi, while Kano Masanao has included him in a more general account of the era; see bibliography. *JS* (no. 33, Sept. 1984) commemorated the hundredth anniversary of Ishibashi's birth and included articles on Tanaka and Shimamura; the issue was widely remarked in the newspapers and may spark a second "rediscovery."

fashions in housing, furniture, clothing, and food, and the advent of department stores, movie theaters, encyclopedias, airplanes, and aviatrices. Viewing themselves as leaders of a rising individual self-consciousness, the three writers articulated their social function as independent artists and intellectuals. Skeptical of the Meiji success ethic, which welded individual upward mobility to the national interest, they incorporated self-expression and self-discovery in their notions of achievement. They also castigated governmental censorship, which perpetuated the ignorance of the people and menaced the professional ethics and livelihood of writers. In spite of their critical spirit they were optimistic gradualists, vigorous in affirming the potential of industrial society to liberate individuality.[6]

The writers always compared Japan with the West, most often with Great Britain and the United States. Tanaka spent a decade in the United States studying progressive thought, particularly John Dewey's instrumentalism. Shimamura studied in England and Germany, discovering the individual character, which he identified as the focus of all modern Western and Russian literature. Ishibashi admired Tanaka's philosophy, which he later embellished with the ideas that he drew from the British Bloomsbury circle and the German left-wing Social Democrats, especially Wilhelm Liebnecht and Karl Bebel. Thus the three are correctly interpreted as an Anglo-American current in Taishō thought even though their outlook was more broadly eclectic, critical, and cosmopolitan. They did not believe that the Anglo-American nations were superior in all respects, nor that Japan would become a part of Western civilization. They condemned the United States and Great Britain for racism, imperialism, and cultural arrogance but still viewed the two countries as exemplars of desirable trends such as high industrial production, individual freedom, public political participation, and nonviolent evolutionary change. Some of these ideals already had institutional and social bases in Japan. Oth-

6. Tanaka Ōdō, "Jiyū shisōka no rinrikan," in *Shosai yori gaitō ni*; Ishibashi Tanzan, *Ishibashi Tanzan zenshū*, 1:224–25, 516; 2:32–38, 322, 331; Shimamura Hōgetsu, *Kindai bungei no kenkyū*, 471–72.

ers could be realized by Japanese adaptation and reform. Thus the writers emphasized comparison for the sake of uplift, avoiding reference to other countries that they considered as backward as Japan or even worse. They read Japanese history through Western history, and non-Western history through Japanese history; for example, Ishibashi judged that the Russian and Chinese revolutions would form integrated and independent national states, as Japan's Meiji Restoration had already done.

The writers' similar backgrounds encouraged their commonalities in thinking. Each came from a family belonging to what Thomas Huber has characterized as the service intelligentsia: Tanaka's father was a small landlord, Shimamura's an ironworks manager, and Ishibashi's a Nichiren priest. Before the Meiji Restoration these groups had possessed special skills and knowledge, but they had been barred from high office by their hereditary status. They had been highly receptive to the idea of a meritocracy. Moreover, Confucian education had taught them a strong sense of responsibility for the welfare of the whole society.[7] Their Taishō heirs also chafed at the narrow base of governmental power and challenged it, not by seeking power themselves, but by groping toward a new order that would permit full popular participation in political decisions and cultural creation.

Each of the writers lost a parent in childhood, and each left home in his early teens. Tanaka's mother died during his infancy, and his father sent him out for adoption by a neighboring family in his adolescence, but he ran away to study in Tokyo. Shimamura's mother, a chronic invalid, and his father, a bankrupt alcoholic, had both died before he reached the age of ten; he was adopted by a local official. Ishibashi lived with his mother at some distance from his father's temple, and from the age of ten was entrusted to a disciple who supervised his education while his father departed to a new and distant temple. Distance and disruption in their families encouraged the writers to question traditional values and to hope that free

7. Thomas Huber, *The Revolutionary Origins of Modern Japan*, 52–59, 211–17.

choice in marriage by men and women equal in education,
income, power, and status might enhance family solidarity.

None of the writers was a Christian, despite the significant
role Christianity played in inspiring other late Meiji and Taishō
reformers. Tanaka, like many other Meiji youths, converted
to Christianity but later renounced the faith. After studying
with John Dewey he, like Dewey, retained a strong philosophical commitment to individual and collective human dignity
but distrusted organized religion. Ishibashi grew up in the
highly reformist Nichiren ethos of the late nineteenth century,
when Buddhists tried to compete with Christian missionaries
by sponsoring mass education, proselytizing, and advocating
secular reforms. Shimamura was abstractly interested in both
Buddhism and Christianity but was not a worshiper.[8]

Finally, none of the writers conformed easily to highly structured modern institutions, even to universities. Shimamura
eventually abandoned his professorship and his academic writing in order to found a modern theater. Tanaka attended four
missionary academies in Japan, graduating from none, before
earning his B.S. at the University of Chicago; handicapped by
his lack of a Japanese degree, he failed to reach the rank of
full professor until he was sixty-one years old, three years before his death. Ishibashi, who began primary school two years
younger than his classmates, twice failed the entrance examinations for both middle school and Tokyo First Higher
School. Family background, religion, and education inclined
the writers toward analytical detachment, nonconformity, and
an inquiry into values apart from the day-to-day mechanics of
society and institutions. Their intellectual independence was
sustained by a relatively autonomous private university, a

8. On the relationship between Christianity and reform see Irwin Scheiner, *Chris-
tian Converts and Social Protest in Meiji Japan*; Kiyoko Takeda, "Japanese Christianity:
Between Orthodoxy and Heterodoxy," in J. Victor Koschmann, ed., *Authority and the
Individual in Japan: Citizen Protest in Historical Perspective*; Nobuya Bamba and John F.
Howes, eds., *Pacifism in Japan: The Christian and Socialist Tradition*; and Peter Duus,
"Yoshino Sakuzō: The Christian as Political Critic," *JAS* 4 (1978): 301–25. Recently
the reformist impulse in Buddhism has received more attention; see Kathleen M.
Staggs, "'Defend the Nation and Love the Truth': Inoue Enryō and the Revival of
Meiji Buddhism," *MN* 38 (1983): 251–82; and Stephen Large, "Buddhism and Polit-
ical Renovation in Prewar Japan: The Case of Akamatsu Katsumaro," *JJS* 9 (1983):
33–66.

boom of journals and journal readers, and a compromising but critical relationship with the state.

WASEDA UNIVERSITY

The writers could not have existed apart from Waseda University. Founded in 1882 by Ōkuma Shigenobu and Ono Azusa, Waseda commands a reputation as the alma mater of such eminent reformist politicians as Ōyama Ikuo, Ozaki Yukio, Tagawa Daikichirō, and Nagai Ryūtarō. Waseda claimed fifty-three alumni in the House of Commons in 1924, second only to Tokyo Imperial University; these men were overwhelmingly affiliated with the relatively progressive Kenseikai (Constitutional Government party). Sir George Sansom found at Waseda a "freedom of thought and expression" that was "none too palatable to the government."[9] Freedom nurtured several of the major political and intellectual movements of the Taishō era. In 1901 four of the six founding members of the Social Democratic party (Shakai minshutō) were associated with Waseda.[10] American pragmatist philosophy, the naturalist movement in literature, and feminism also flourished at Waseda. The faculty were an unusually disparate lot with a high proportion, like Tanaka, lacking Waseda degrees and contributing to a climate of nonconformity.[11] Although many were left of center, Kita Ikki's younger brother Kita Reikichi, a devout partisan of divine imperial rule, also taught there. The faculty reveled in open controversy, lambasting President Ōkuma himself for interference in personnel decisions in 1919.[12]

Waseda's pluralism prompted alumnus Kamitsukasa Shōken

9. Sir George Sansom, *The Western World and Japan: A Study in the Interaction of European and Asiatic Cultures*, 459–60; on Waseda graduates in the political parties see Ozaki Moriteru, *Nihon shūshoku shi*, 164.

10. Cyril F. Powles, "Abe Isoo," in Nobuya Bamba and John F. Howes, eds., *Pacifism in Japan: The Christian and Socialist Tradition*, 156.

11. *ITZ* 15:46.

12. On the campaign against Ōkuma known as the Waseda uprising (*sōdō*), see Tanaka Ōdō, "Gakumon no dokuritsu no igi to han'i to junjo to o ronzu," *CK* 33, no. 1 (Jan. 1918): 64–92; *ITZ* 15:245–49. For more general information on Waseda see Ozaki Shirō, *Waseda Daigaku*; and Nakanishi Keijirō, *Waseda Daigaku hachijūnen shi*.

to conclude: "There is no Waseda faction. In this free age, having attended the same university is an even more shallow connection than having ridden the same streetcar."[13] Kamitsukasa exaggerated. Diverse opinions were linked by a thread of resentment against the bureaucracy and its preparatory school, Tokyo Imperial University. Moreover, Waseda faculty were dedicated to enlightening the people, a mission that embroiled the university in public controversy from the time of the Russo-Japanese War, and they were strongly committed to publishing in general-interest journals and newspapers rather than academic periodicals. Students' relations with faculty tended to be more informal than the prevailing etiquette at the imperial universities. Waseda upheld a humanistic quest for value distinct from either state service or utilitarian technology.[14]

Waseda also drew a more diverse group of students than the imperial universities. Admissions were based on different criteria, for Waseda had a two-semester preparatory course with an entrance examination stressing reasoning ability, whereas tests in the state system required rote mastery of specific materials and held students responsible for their own preparation.[15] The Waseda examination offered a great advantage to bright and questioning students from public primary and middle schools, especially in the provinces, where nineteenth-century education was quite uneven in quality. Tuition and living costs were about twenty yen per month at the time of the Russo-Japanese War, about half what a typical graduate could earn as a starting salary as a middle school teacher in the provinces, where pay was higher to lure educated youth away from the excitements of the capital.[16] A new graduate would earn an average monthly starting salary of ten to fifteen yen in banking, twenty-five to forty yen in the civil service.[17] A literary career exacted further sacrifices: Shima-

---

13. Kamitsukasa Shōken, "Shimamura Hōgetsu ron: Bundan no gaimu daijin," *CK* 26, no. 7 (July 1911): 100–02.
14. Masamune Hakuchō, "Shimamura Hōgetsu ron," *CK* 26, no. 7 (July 1911): 95–96.
15. Shimura Hidetarō, *Ishibashi Tanzan*, 15; *ITZ* 15:24–28.
16. Shimura, 54–56, 70.
17. Earl H. Kinmonth, *The Self-Made Man in Meiji Japanese Thought*, 222.

mura earned only fifteen yen a month as editor of *Waseda bungaku* (Waseda letters), and Ishibashi started at eighteen yen a month at *Tōyō keizai shinpō* in 1911 despite several years of journalistic experience.[18]

The relatively high costs and uncertain rewards of a Waseda education certainly must have discouraged the children of workers and tenant farmers. On the other hand, Waseda students by no means displayed the affluence of their counterparts at Tokyo or Keiō University. Most Waseda students lacked the cash for the regulation Western-style uniform and attended classes in threadbare cotton *hakama* and *haori* (traditional men's formal dress), in contrast to the Keiō image, which required a silk jacket. Typically Waseda students received only part of their expenses from their families, scraping together the remainder by means of tutoring, delivering newspapers or milk (three to four yen a month), clerking in shops, or even pulling rickshaws.[19]

No student of twentieth-century literature can ignore the preeminent position of Waseda faculty and alumni—Shimamura, his students Honma Hisao, Sōma Gyōfū, and Chikamatsu Shūkō, and Tanaka's students Kimura Ki, Ishimaru Gohei, and Masamune Hakuchō—in small but distinguished literary magazines such as *Waseda bungaku*, *Myōjō* (Morning star), and *Bunshō sekai* (World of letters). In a feminist journal such as *Fujin kōron* (Woman's review), too, Waseda was prominently represented by its founder, Shimanaka Yūsaku (a student of Tanaka and later editor of *Chūō kōron*), as well as Abe Isoo, Honma Hisao, and Hoashi Riichirō.[20] Abe, Tagawa Daikichirō, Shimada Saburō, and Ozaki Yukio wrote for *Fujin no tomo* (Woman's friend). Tagawa denounced the traditional family system in *Tōyō jiron* (Oriental review) under Ishibashi's editorship, and he and Abe both introduced women's suffrage bills in the House of Commons during the 1920s and 1930s; the Waseda ethos mingled journalism and politics. Shimanaka was only one of several Waseda faculty and graduates to found

18. Shimura, 94; Yoshida Seiichi, *Kindai bungei hyōron shi*, vol. 1, 729, 743.
19. Shimura, 54–56.
20. Sotani Hiromi, "*Fujin kōron* no shisō," in Kindai Joseishi Kenkyūkai, ed., *Onnatachi no kindai*, 171–78.

their own magazines. Ubukata Toshirō, a student of Tanaka and writer for *Waseda bungaku* under Shimamura's editorship, later worked for *Chūō kōron* and founded two magazines of his own.

Waseda commanded the business journals as well. President Masada Giichi of Jitsugyō no Nihon publishing company was a Waseda graduate, as were the heads of the political, social, Japanese culture, and Japanese economic bureaus at *Chūgai shōgyō shinpō* (Foreign and domestic business).[21] At *Tōyō keizai shinpō* the Waseda presence was overwhelming. Amano Tameyuki, a Waseda professor, succeeded Machida Chūji as editor shortly after the journal was founded, presiding until 1907 when he left to head the Waseda business school; he remained in close contact with editorial and managerial concerns into the 1930s. The third and fourth editors, Uematsu Hisaaki and Miura Tetsutarō, were his students. The fifth was Ishibashi Tanzan.[22]

Waseda alumni were also prominent in the daily newspapers. Shimamura edited the *Yomiuri* Sunday supplement before his departure for Europe in 1902, and Ishibashi contributed occasional pieces throughout the prewar period. In 1924, the *Yomiuri* bureau chiefs for economics, Tokyo politics and finance, and culture were all Waseda alumni. When Ishibashi joined the *Tōkyō mainichi* staff in 1909 his senior classmates there included editor Seki Kazutomo, social bureau chief Takasu Baikei, Tanaka Suiseki, and Kuratsuji Hakuda. This *Tōkyō mainichi* was purchased by the *Hōchi* in 1908 and is not related to the present-day *Mainichi*, whose 1924 head editor, Kuratsuji Akiyoshi, and local, social, and English bureau chiefs were also Waseda graduates. The strong performance of Waseda graduates in journalism has continued in the postwar era.[23] Waseda taught its students the writing, speaking, and intellectual flexibility essential to success in politics and the media; it prepared them less well for the more highly structured office environments of the bureaucracy and large corporations.

21. Ozaki Moriteru, 164–65.
22. Ibid., and Ono Hideo, *Nihon shinbun hattatsu shi*, 164–65; Watanabe Tōru, "Sōron," 26–27.
23. Shimura, 74–76; Young C. Kim, *Japanese Journalists and Their World*, 27–32.

THE JOURNALS

During the first three decades of the twentieth century, journalism developed the corporate organization, personnel, structure of information, and ethos that would form its basic character into the postwar era. Tanaka, Shimamura, and Ishibashi played significant roles in this process, and journalism in turn provided them with a forum, an income, and an audience. Especially in the Taishō era, a boom in the circulation and in the intellectual quality of the periodicals indicated an increasingly pluralistic and sophisticated society.[24]

Often new ideas and trends were expressed first in little magazines (*kojin zasshi*), small vehicles for the tastes and opinions of the editor. If the ideas sparked interest, they would soon be taken up by the general-interest journals (*sōgō zasshi*), and eventually by mass-circulation publications.[25] For example, naturalist literature and theory made its debut in *Waseda bungaku*, under Shimamura's editorship, with a circulation of about two thousand copies, but by 1908 naturalism had become a leading topic in *Chūō kōron*. The women's literary magazine *Seitō* (Bluestocking) printed only one thousand copies of its first issue in 1911, but it received three thousand letters in reply, mainly submitting manuscripts and asking for marital advice or staff positions on the magazine.[26] Editors of the two leading general-interest journals, *Chūō kōron* and *Taiyō* (The sun), quickly remarked on *Seitō*'s impact and devoted entire issues to "the woman question" in 1913. Magazines were commonly passed from hand to hand, especially in the country and among students.[27] Families also shared and discussed reading material; a Tokyo survey of primary school students in 1920 found that from 60 to 70 percent of those polled had

24. The boom in twentieth-century journalism is discussed in Kuwabara Takeo et al., "Jaanarizumu no shisōteki yakuwari," in Kuno Osamu and Sumiya Mikio, eds., *Shidōsha to taishū*, Kindai Nihon shisōshi kōza, vol. 5. For treatments of the late nineteenth-century press see James L. Huffman, *Politics of the Meiji Press: The Life of Fukuchi Gen'ichirō*; John D. Pierson, *Tokutomi Sohō, 1863–1957: A Journalist for Modern Japan*; and Kenneth Pyle, *The New Generation in Meiji Japan*.

25. Haruhara Akihiko, *Nihon shinbun tsūshi*, 90–91.

26. Murakami Nobuhiko, "Fujin mondai to fujin kaihō undō," in Iwanami Kōza, *Nihon rekishi*, vol. 18, 229–30.

27. Tsurumi Shunsuke, "*Chūō kōron* no rekishi," SS, no. 476 (Feb. 1964): 121–29; Robert J. Smith and Ella Lury Wiswell, *The Women of Suye Mura*, 11, 13–14.

a rudimentary grasp of the terms socialism, democracy, strike, sabotage, labor problem, universal suffrage, class victory, reform, freedom, equality, individualism, and the woman problem, with 53 percent citing newspapers, magazines, or books as the source of their information.[28]

In both circulation and impact, *Chūō kōron* led the general-interest journals of the Taishō era, outpacing a host of imitators such as *Taiyō* and *Shin Nihon* (New Japan) but falling behind latecomer *Bungei shunjū* (Spring and autumn letters) a few years after its founding in 1923. *Chūō kōron*, though more venerable, was a distinctly modern phenomenon. Founded as *Hanseikai zasshi* (Moral Reflection Society journal) in 1887 under the auspices of Nishi Honganji priest Ōtani Kōson in Kyoto, it initially urged temperance and other forms of individual moral responsibility. By the turn of the century, it had moved its office to Tokyo and changed both its name and its editorial philosophy.

The title *Chūō kōron*, suggested by religious scholar Kōnan Junjirō, evoked the Western tradition of a city forum for debating public issues. No such forum existed in Tokyo, but *Chūō kōron* moved boldly to create one by publishing studies of social problems such as Kawakami Hajime's early investigations of poverty. Editorial policy was eclectic, including columns on current events, literature, the arts, and leading academic theories of the day. Between 1907 and 1919 the monthly also featured reviews of the career, opinions, and personal character of a leading bureaucrat, politician, scholar, or writer. By 1919, at the high tide of the Taishō democratic movement, the editors jettisoned reviews of elite public figures in a change that staffer Shirayanagi Shūko dubbed "from the hero line to the mass line."[29] By that time circulation had boomed, from only five thousand copies during the Russo-Japanese War to 120,000 copies, while the sister *Fujin kōron* printed 70,000 copies.

28. Ōtsuki Ken, *Gakkō to minshū no rekishi*, 186–87.
29. Shirayanagi Shūko, "Eiyūsen kara minshūsen e," *CK* 33, no. 10 (Oct. 1918): 15–35; for more general information on *Chūō kōron* see Chūō Koron, ed., *Chūō kōron nanajūnen shi*; Sugimori Hisahide, *Takida Chōin: Aru henshūsha no shōgai*.

The impact of *Chūō kōron* and other general-interest journals was first of all evident in the sincerest form of flattery, imitation. The more polemical socialist magazines of the twenties such as *Kaizō* (Reconstruction) mirrored the format and broad cultural perspective of the generals. The daily newspapers founded their own weekly editions such as *Shūkan asahi* and *Sandee mainichi* (offspring of the Sunday supplement that Shimamura had once edited) in 1922. Business magazines also mimicked the generals in theoretical editorials that ranged well beyond economic and financial issues. The business journals were the first large-scale publications to advocate universal suffrage; *Tōyō keizai shinpō* demanded the enfranchisement of all adult men from 1907, and women from 1911.[30]

Tōyō keizai shinpō was founded in 1895 by Machida Chūji, later president of the Minseitō (Democratic party), minister of commerce and industry, and a pivotal figure in Ishibashi's transition into government consulting during the thirties. In founding the *Shinpō*, Machida expressed his admiration for the London *Economist* and his hopes for a liberal economic system. After two years, however, he left the journal to begin his political career, placing Waseda professor Amano Tameyuki in charge as managing editor. Under Amano's direction, *Shinpō* continued its paeans to free enterprise and began to support the role of political parties in the government and freedom of expression. Editorials also criticized the land tax for permitting nonproducers (landlords) to shift the tax burden onto producers. In foreign policy, *Shinpō* criticized wasteful armaments expenditures but demanded a strong Japanese presence in Asia and governmental development of Korean and Manchurian resources. Imperialism, however, was tempered with the recommendation of an open door in Korea and the warning that the economic benefits of the Russo-Japanese War would be offset by increased defense costs, whereas the gains of the war would not meet the people's aroused expectations.[31]

30. Uematsu Hisaaki, "Giin kaikaku," and "Futsū senkyoan no shōsoku ika," *TKS*, 5 Apr. 1907 and 25 Feb. 1911; Kuwabara et al., 158; Shimura, 100–01.
31. "Honshi sōkan no shimei to kongo," *TKS* 14 Nov. 1925; Matsuo Takayoshi, "Kyūshinteki jiyūshugi no seiritsu katei," in Inoue and Watanabe, eds., *Taishōki no kyūshinteki jiyūshugi*, 33–34, 39, 41–42.

Although *Shinpō* published the various viewpoints of its individual staffers and outside writers, its editorial policy was more unified than that of *Chūō kōron*. The Russo-Japanese War was a turning point in *Shinpō*'s policy and in the nation at large as well. During the war social democrats protested poverty, high taxes, and the government's high-handed command. Tokyo people of all classes rioted against the peace terms in front of the imperial palace at Hibiya Park; and naturalist literature revealed a new and harsh image of a conformist and repressive society. Less conscious forces of change are also clear in retrospect. Inflation doubled the electorate, which was based on a qualifying sum of tax payment, and exacerbated budgetary and financial problems, which were to explode in the Taishō political crisis of 1911–12. At this time, too, Japan acquired its special treaty rights and interests in Manchuria; they would later be defended at the expense of democratic gains.[32]

As the new editor of *Shinpō*, Uematsu was in a position to respond to changes brought by the war. Amano, before departing to head the Waseda business school, had turned joint managerial authority over to Uematsu, Miura, and two other staff members. *Shinpō* was reorganized as a joint stock company, with Uematsu as president and 1,386 of its 1,400 shares held in the name of the president and chief editor. Editorial and financial independence allowed Uematsu and his successors to take some unpopular positions. Under Uematsu, *Shinpō* continued its support for parliamentary parties and freedom of expression and took up the cause of suffrage. Uematsu believed that the contemporary political modus vivendi, in which the political parties sought power through compromise with the Meiji oligarchs and bureaucracy, was a temporary state of affairs that would eventually be supplanted by a true parliamentary system in which the parties would represent the whole people and control the state by means of majority-party cabinets. In foreign policy, *Shinpō* continued to criticize arm-

32. Matsuo, "Kyūshinteki jiyūshugi," 32–43; Shumpei Okamoto, "The Emperor and the Crowd: The Historical Significance of the Hibiya Riot," and Yoshitake Oka, "Generational Conflict after the Russo-Japanese War," both in Najita and Koschmann, eds., *Conflict in Modern Japanese History.*

aments budgets, but it also urged Japanese emigration, even at the risk of war, and colonization of the Asian mainland.[33]

When Uematsu died in 1912, his successor Miura signaled an epochal change in *Shinpō*'s foreign policy recommendations. He reproached his people for condescension toward China and intrigue in the 1911 revolution and urged Japan to abandon its treaty rights and interests in Manchuria. He reasoned pragmatically that outraged Chinese would one day make dangerous neighbors, and that the benefits of an exclusive position in Manchuria were less than the costs of defending the region from Chinese nationalism, Russian depredations, and American capital. Territorial expansion was no longer possible in Asia or elsewhere except by means of war with the great powers, a war that would cramp financial and industrial development, burden the people, provoke the powers, and complicate diplomacy. Placing domestic welfare first, Miura and Ishibashi during the next two decades renounced economic laissez-faire and attacked state policies that coddled industry and commerce at the expense of workers and peasants.[34]

As editorial policy changed between 1907 and 1913, so the journal's content broadened. *Shinpō*, which during the Russo-Japanese War had about the same circulation as *Chūō kōron*, did not expand as rapidly. Uematsu decided to expand *Shinpō*'s coverage from economics and politics to include society, culture, and education. Miura, too, recognized the demand for breadth and depth but was shackled by *Shinpō*'s small size and frequency of printing; the journal came out every ten days until 1919, and every week thereafter, since it reported on the financial markets and other rapidly outdated business news.

In 1911, when *Shinpō* founded its own monthly, *Tōyō jiron*, Ishibashi was hired to edit it with socialist Katayama Sen. *Jiron*

---

33. Watanabe Tōru, "Sōron," 9; Matsuo, "Kyūshinteki jiyūshugi," 50–57. On party-bureaucratic compromise see Tetsuo Najita, *Hara Kei in the Politics of Compromise.*
34. "Shina osorubeshi," *TKS*, 5 Apr. 1910; Miura Tetsutarō, "Sangyōjō no daini ishin," *TKS* 25 Aug. 1912, and "Manshū hōki ka gunbi kakuchō ka," *TKS* 5 Jan.–5 Mar. 1913; Yamamoto Shirō, "Chūgoku mondai ron," in Inoue and Watanabe, eds., *Taishōki no kyūshinteki jiyūshugi*, 109–13; Matsuo Takayoshi, *Taishō demokurashii*, 81–92; Shumpei Okamoto, "Ishibashi Tanzan and the Twenty-one Demands," in Akira Iriye, ed., *The Chinese and the Japanese: Essays in Political and Cultural Interaction.*

invited essays from prominent writers and political figures including Tanaka, Ishizawa Kyūgorō, Uehara Etsujirō, and Tagawa Daikichirō, all of whom called for a new society that would liberate individualism. *Jiron* focused on such social and cultural problems as the reform of the family system and the emancipation of women, contrasting the rational organization of modern industry with the military virtues of preindustrial Japan. The monthly encouraged freedom of speech and religion, protested governmental suppression of naturalist and socialist literature, and sneered at the revived emphasis on ancestor worship and Shinto in the public schools that followed the treason trial of Kōtoku Shūsui. However, *Jiron* failed to capture a viable share of the market from the established general-interest journals and lost money when two entire issues were confiscated by the police. It folded after Uematsu died in 1912, but *Shinpō* absorbed *Jiron*'s social, intellectual, and cultural themes and also expanded the length and range of its editorials throughout the twenties. *Jiron*'s writers formed the Liberal Lecture Society (Jiyū Shisō Kōenkai) in 1914. The society ceased public lectures when Uehara was jailed for an incautious speech against the Terauchi cabinet in 1916 but continued to meet as a discussion society until disrupted by the Great Kantō Earthquake of 1923.[35]

Many small journals like *Jiron* sustained controversial and eccentric writers. The relatively low break-even circulation for a general-interest journal, around three thousand copies in 1911, allowed new viewpoints to reach the public. Despite Ishibashi's close identification with *Shinpō* during his three decades of full-time work there, he also contributed to *Yomiuri, Kaizō, Chūgai shōgyō shinpō, Jiji shinpō* (Daily news), and *Fujin no tomo*. Shimamura was most renowned for editing *Waseda bungaku*, but he also worked on *Yomiuri* and wrote an annual article or two for *Chūō kōron*. Tanaka at the peak of his career appeared in twenty-odd monthlies and three or four newspapers during one year. Editors paid two to four yen for a contribution from a well-known figure, making it possible for

---

35. Matsuo, "Kyūshinteki jiyūshugi," 57–67; *ITZ* 15:90–92; Watanabe Tōru, "Sō-ron," 31–32.

a writer to subsist entirely on free-lance essays were one not too demanding of creature comforts or elegance of expression. Taishō journalism presented a yeasty ferment of views and visions, perhaps even more than the media of postwar Japan, in which the sheer scale of capitalization and markets tends to overshadow or absorb independent figures.[36]

Writers expanded their influence beyond the journals in several ways. Tanaka, Shimamura, and Ishibashi lectured at business, labor, and community organizations as well as public and private primary and secondary schools. All three published books as well; their sales figures are not available, but during the twenties a work such as Kawakami Hajime's *Shakai mondai kenkyū* (On the social problem) sold 120,000 copies immediately, and Takabatake Motoyuki's *Marukusu shihonshugi kaisetsu* (Marx on capitalism) sold 200,000. Other activities also drew public attention. Shimamura's theater production of Leo Tolstoy's *Resurrection* drew three thousand viewers in Kyoto in only two days. Ishibashi founded the Japan Economic Club (Nihon Keizai Kurabu), which by 1942 had twenty-nine regional branches, where staffers frequently journeyed to lecture. The writers' activities were extensively reported in the daily newspapers, which had a circulation of 1,630,000 in 1905. For a population of forty-five million with an average household size of five, this meant that one household in six received a daily paper. By 1924 total daily circulation was 6,250,000 for a population of fifty-nine million. By 1931, there were ten million copies for a population of sixty-five million, marking nearly universal coverage. The writers' sideline activities—lectures, books, theater, clubs, and the resulting news stories—enhanced their impact, especially since Tanaka, Shimamura, and Ishibashi shared a common ethos with other Taishō journalists.[37]

---

36. Kisaki Masaru, *Kisaki nikki*, 320; Shimura, 93–103; Yamamoto Taketoshi, *Shinbun to minshū*, 79–98.

37. Yoshida Seiichi, *Shizenshugi no kenkyū*, vol. 1, 729; Shimura, 193–95; Tsutoi Kiyotada, "Nihon ni okeru taishū shakai to hyōjunka," *SS*, no. 688 (Oct. 1981): 178–200; Uchikawa Yoshimi, "Shinbun dokusha no hensen," *Shinbun kenkyū*, no. 20 (July 1960): 19; Ōtsuki, 188; Shūichi Katō, "The Mass Media, Japan," in Robert E. Ward and Dankwart A. Rustow, eds., *Political Modernization in Japan and Turkey*.

JOURNALISTIC ETHOS

A disparate lot of essayists subscribed to standards of cultural criticism (*bunmei hihyō* or *hyōron*) and impartiality (*fuhen futō*). Cultural criticism was the definitive genre of the Taishō era. Its masters belonged to the generation born during the first twenty years of the Meiji era; thus Tanaka, born in 1867, was one of the oldest, and Ishibashi, born in 1884, one of the youngest.[38] All writers in this generation struggled to find their role in transforming their society, but it was Takayama Chogyū who coined the term *bunmei hihyō* (a translation of *kulturkritik*) in a 1901 *Taiyō* article that demanded a new critical spirit from intellectuals.

Why, Takayama demanded, were there in Japan no critics of the caliber of Friedrich Nietzsche, Matthew Arnold, Walt Whitman, Leo Tolstoy, Emile Zola, Emile Rousseau, and Henrik Ibsen? Takayama believed that these model critics shared an unwavering inner vision that enabled them to challenge their own generation and nation: "Cultural critics will not yield save to their own beliefs, and for the sake of consistency in their beliefs, they will not turn back from battling the enmity of the whole world."[39] Cultural critics confronted the spirit of their time, now voicing it, now analyzing, now opposing. They redefined an intellectual heritage and milieu, recasting its myths, tensions, and ambiguities in a dialectical renewal of society's moral order. Yet Japan lacked cultural critics, and its people waited in vain for the words that would illuminate the meaning of their daily experience. Contemporary Japanese intellectuals "have ears, but do not hear the voice of the folk (*minshū*); they have eyes but do not see the spirit of the age."[40]

Takayama was and is a revered figure in Japanese letters, and many Taishō intellectuals responded to and reiterated his challenge. Historian Iida Taizō lists some two hundred writers who did all or part of their work in the genre of cultural criticism, among whom the most famous were Natsume Sōseki,

38. Iida Taizō, "Taishōki bunmei hihyōka chosaku ichiran," *Hōgaku shirin* (Hōsei University) 80 (1982): 179–211.

39. Takayama Chogyū, "Bunmei hihyōka toshite no bungakusha," in *Gendai Nihon bungaku zenshū*, vol. 59, 62.

40. Ibid., 64.

Tokutomi Roka, Tokutomi Sohō, Nishida Kitarō, Tayama Katai, Kōtoku Shūsui, Anezaki Masaharu, Minobe Tatsukichi, Hasegawa Nyozekan, Arishima Takeo, Yosano Akiko, Yoshino Sakuzō, Kawakami Hajime, Ōyama Ikuo, Abe Isoo, Ōsugi Sakae, Tanizaki Jun'ichirō, and Hiratsuka Raichō. It is difficult to name a Taishō intellectual who did not work in this genre.[41]

Tanaka Ōdō elaborated the rationale for cultural criticism, offering a more sociological formulation than Takayama under the rubric *jinsei hyōron* (criticism of life). By changing terms he hoped, even more than Takayama, to differentiate this genre from literary pastimes, without losing Takayama's sense of the integrity of culture. He found his model critics in the Meiji enlightenment (Fukuzawa Yukichi), the British philosophic radicals (John Stuart Mill), and the American pragmatists (William James and John Dewey). These thinkers won Tanaka's admiration because each had welcomed the rapid change of his society while searching for fundamental human values by which to guide that change. Ishibashi would accept Tanaka's conception of cultural criticism and bring it to bear on concrete questions of politics and economics.[42]

Tanaka's whole generation was perplexed about the relationship between the various parts of society and its whole. The era was one of academic specialization, in which new disciplines were cut off from old ones by scholars such as Onozuka Kiheiji at Tokyo University, who distinguished political science from law. Philosophy was a subdivision of literature at Waseda, and ground-breaking thinkers such as Sugimori Kōjirō in sociology and Ishibashi in economics began their inquiries in Tanaka's classes because there was no one else to teach them. The general-interest journals expressed and defended the realm of unified intellectual experience.

Taishō writers also expressed another ideal, impartiality. It emerged in the daily newspapers, especially the *Asahi*, around the time of the Sino-Japanese War (1894–95). Like cultural

41. Iida, "Taishōki bunmei hihyōka chosaku ichiran," 181–82.
42. Tanaka Ōdō, "Jinsei hyōron no igi to jinsei hyōronka no shikaku," *CK* 25, no. 7 (July 1910): 33; cf. *ITZ* 1:130–41, 182–94.

criticism, impartiality was a reaction against the journalistic heritage of the mid-Meiji period, but for different reasons. Proponents of impartiality accused the political parties' organ papers of having distorted facts and failed to gain a mass audience during the Popular Rights movement of the 1880s. They explicitly described periodicals as a commodity (*shōbaihin*) and readers as an impersonal market. Thus they stressed the scientific, technological character of the information system, in contrast to the unwavering individual vision celebrated by Takayama. Impartiality could degenerate into a mere pandering to popular appetites, but in its more sophisticated versions it acknowledged that the information media are part of a social totality and not discrete mechanisms for transmitting random facts or eternal verities.[43]

Again and again Taishō essayists invoked the ideal of impartiality. Upon becoming chief editor of *Shinpō* in 1924, Ishibashi wrote: "Our task is the sacred one of leading the general public, for the greatest happiness and well-being of all mankind; truly it must be unbiased and nonpartisan. Thus it is most regrettable to publish the opinions of one party, zaibatsu, or company. [Impartiality] is the sole life of our organization, and our duty to society."[44] Ishibashi was one of the most lucid and uncompromising of cultural critics, but he followed the sanctioned style of impartiality. He always began editorials by conceding that the opposition's case did not utterly lack merit in theory or under certain hypothetical circumstances of utter irrelevance to the case at hand. Tanaka also opened essays with lengthy and deferential acknowledgments of the position he would criticize, and Shimamura offered pained apologies for his inability to transcend his personal experience. The writers' intentions become intelligible only when the conventions of contemporary journalism are taken into account.

Impartiality evolved into a journalistic convention amid the tensions between the modern press and the state. Impartial administration that balanced the interests of the whole nation

    43. Yamamoto Taketoshi, 140.
    44. Ishibashi, quoted by Watanabe Tōru, "Sōron," 8; see also Yamamoto Taketoshi, 100–30.

was a central prop of bureaucratic legitimacy.[45] To the extent that bureaucrats could depict the press as a self-interested faction, journalists would be left without social utility except as mere reporters of events. The pioneer generation of modern intellectuals and journalists thirsted for a truer sense of service, a grander mission. They retaliated by exposing bureaucrats as self-interested regional, military, and financial cliques, and by styling themselves as the voices of sober and disinterested vision.

In another sense impartiality described the world in which its proponents worked. Writers reached their audience through stylistic merit and persuasive power. Authority and social status were also important for those who were professors at prestigious universities, but formal position could not assure continuing influence in the vigorously competitive press. Cultural critics challenged one another; indeed, reviews constituted a large portion of the genre. Criticism could be blistering even between colleagues or friends; for example, Iwano Hōmei described Tanaka's philosophy as "a plate of dry bones," but after a hiatus of two years the two continued to dine together.[46] Although not all Taishō writers sanctioned this spirit of debate, they lived within it, comprising an open universe of discourse that minimized hierarchy and admitted their readers. Tanaka, Shimamura, and Ishibashi all articulated a concept that Oliver Wendell Holmes called "the free market of ideas." They insisted that society benefited from contention in which the best proposals would ultimately win assent. Nonetheless, their optimism was tinged with fear of repression and reaction. They cloaked their demands in the mantle of impartiality and hoped that self-restraint would strengthen their claims against external restraint. Inspired by their ideals of cultural criticism and impartiality, they left the mid-Meiji world behind, in search of a new relationship between author and audience.

45. On the bureaucratic ideology see Bernard S. Silberman, "The Bureaucratic State in Japan: The Problem of Authority and Legitimacy," in Najita and Koschmann, eds., *Conflict in Modern Japanese History*. On the ethos of impartiality in the postwar press see Jōji Watanuki, *Politics in Postwar Japanese Society*, 26–27.

46. Iwano Hōmei, "Wakamiya, Tanaka hikaku ron," *CK* 32, no. 12 (Dec. 1917): 70–74.

THE AUDIENCE

Taishō periodicals, except for the little magazines, were commerical concerns dependent on the readers' response. Circulation was volatile, and substantial capital was invested: fifty thousand yen in *Tōyō keizai shinpō* in 1921, and three times as much in a major daily newspaper, the *Ōsaka mainichi*, in 1919. Periodical circulation doubled between the Sino- and Russo-Japanese wars because of advances in technology, managerial rationality, and advertising revenue as well as an increase in the size and sophistication of the reading public. Advertising revenue also became important after the Russo-Japanese War. Advertisers distinguished various publications by the number and social status of the readers, running pitches for financial services and office supplies in *Tōyō keizai shinpō*, for books in *Chūō kōron*, and for mass-market goods such as liquor and patent medicines in all the publications.[47]

Who read the general-interest journals? Japanese scholars stress the media influence on elite opinion leaders and decision makers but also assert that even a fairly abstruse journal like *Chūō kōron* could be seen in the hands of a worker or farmer during the Taishō era. The hypothesis of mass influence can neither be proven nor rejected with the evidence presently at hand. Periodicals were inexpensive: forty to fifty *sen* for a monthly newspaper subscription in the last decade of Meiji, twelve *sen* for a copy of *Tōyō keizai shinpō*, and thirty-seven *sen* for *Chūō kōron*. By this time large cities had established milk halls and reading rooms for free and convenient access to periodicals. Periodicals were also seen in many barber shops and waiting rooms. The elite who wrote and managed the periodicals were consciously aiming at an integrated national audience, and accordingly they were reluctant to acknowledge class and other distinctions between readers and nonreaders. A pronounced individual and national drive for upward mobility favored the formation of a relatively homogeneous society.[48]

47. Shimura, 192–93; Kuwabara et al., 152–53; Ono, 343, 481–82; Haruhara, 90–91.
48. Minami, 51–63, 181; Murakami, 223–54; Kuwabara et al., 153; Ono, 343; Yamamoto Taketoshi, 135.

The few surviving collections of journals' reader survey cards indicate an audience developing among, but not limited to, the urban new middle class. The collections, never more than a few hundred cards, may even overrepresent the higher status and more literate readers. Between 1898 and 1900 all the major dailies were popular among merchants and shop-clerks, with 25 to 52 percent of the respondents identifying themselves as such. (The higher figure is for Fukuzawa Yu-kichi's *Jiji shinpō*, which stressed business news.) In contrast, few respondents identified themselves as businessmen (*jitsu-gyōsha*, *kaishain*) or bankers, perhaps because the terms indicate positions in large, modern institutions, which were just devel-oping at the turn of the century. *Yomiuri*, with a strongly in-tellectual orientation, found that 41 percent of its respondents were students and 3 percent teachers. Of all the newspapers surveyed *Yorozu* (All things considered) had the greatest re-sponse from factory workers, 15 percent. Neither farmers nor officials constituted more than 8 percent of the respondents to any newspaper, nor soldiers more than 14 percent.[49]

The doubling of newspaper and journal circulation between the Sino- and Russo-Japanese wars predated the conspicuous debut of the new middle class, and newspaper surveys during that time showed a preponderance of merchants, shopclerks, and students. Since during this decade the newspapers them-selves improved dramatically in style, lucidity, coverage, and printing quality, the boom probably reflected the growth of media habits among the old, propertied middle class with their families and employees in city and country. At the end of the decade the general-interest journals still had few subscribers, but their staff and free-lance writers were part of the new middle class and were influential beyond their numbers.[50]

Taishō figures suggest the vigorous growth of a market for periodicals among the urban new middle class of professionals, managers, and their families. *Fujin no tomo* readers who re-quested budget-planning assistance from the magazine in 1912–13 included the wives of corporate employees, bankers,

49. Yamamoto Taketoshi, 138.
50. Yamamoto Fumio et al., eds., *Nihon masu komyunikeeshon shi*, 138.

bureaucrats, teachers, doctors, and soldiers, with incomes of from 30 to 180 yen per month.[51] *Fujin kōron* targeted the middle class in explicit editorials on the stabilizing role that the middle class played in society.[52] The journal's success in identifying with its audience was acknowledged by the Social Bureau of the City of Tokyo, which requested *Fujin kōron*'s assistance in its 1923 attempt to identify and count the middle class. Both women's magazines expressed a managerial conception of the home, encouraged the housewife's expertise in budgeting, product selection, sanitation, health, and family psychology. They catered to urban nuclear families who had emancipated themselves from the customs of the older generation.

Tōyō keizai shinpō had a much clearer and narrower corporate audience due to its financial reporting. A 1931 survey of readers drew a mere 215 responses but confirmed the modern, cosmopolitan corporate audience that the journal's content suggested. Seventy-two percent of the respondents were corporate employees, bankers, stockbrokers, or accountants; another 4 percent worked in typically large, high-technology industries such as steel and fertilizer. Eleven percent were in typically smaller and more traditional industries like textiles and sake brewing.[53] Ishibashi noted that earlier the *Shinpō* had been popular with students, but only 5 percent of the 1931 respondents were students or reporters.[54] Ishibashi also reached a more diverse set of readers with articles in *Yomiuri*, which had a circulation of 120,000 in 1930.[55]

Language usage also suggests the social position of a journal's readers. *Chūō kōron* employed a highly abstract and sinified vocabulary. Nonetheless it tried to reach graduates of rural higher elementary and middle schools, whose formal education gave them an influence beyond that of their urban counterparts; they were the rural new middle class. Grappling with change, *Chūō kōron* joined other journals in a movement

51. Saitō Michiko, "Hani Motoko no shisō," in Kindai Joseishi Kenkyūkai, ed., *Onnatachi no kindai*, 160.
52. Sotani, 178.
53. Watanabe Tōru, "Sōron," 30.
54. *ITZ* 15:131–44.
55. Y. Takenobu, *The Japan Yearbook, 1930*.

to develop a standardized writing style closer to the vernacular (*genbun itchi*). Shimamura was one of the leaders in the movement, which reached from the small literary magazines to the daily newspapers. Despite broad support for its objectives, the movement took years because many older scholars could write only in the archaic literary style (*kanbun*). Tanaka's student Ubukata Toshirō, after his graduation from Waseda, earned more by writing vernacular translations for established scholars than by composing his own essays. Even renowned liberal Yoshino Sakuzō needed an amanuensis for his early ventures in journalism until he mastered the new style in 1922. Despite efforts at simplification, *Chūō kōron*'s language was more difficult than that of other general-interest journals that employed phonetic notation (*furigana*) to simplify the reading of abstract terms and proper names. Since *furigana* indicated only pronunciation and not meaning, Ishibashi persuaded *Tōyō keizai shinpō* to assist its readers by more direct methods: precision, economy of expression, and a fairly standardized vernacular vocabulary and style from the outset of the Taishō period. As the period ended fifteen years later, use of the vernacular had become universal in journalism.[56]

Scattered surveys and journal content suggest that members of the urban new middle class, who had left their provincial homes to follow new dreams, were most likely to respond to the general-interest journals. Various sets of statistics date a dramatic increase in the numbers of the new middle class between 1904 and 1920, corresponding rather precisely with the definitive intellectual impact of *Chūō kōron*. Shibamura Atsuki estimated the number of independent professionals (medical employees, educators, shrine and temple officials, technicians, office workers, and professionals) at 926,700 in 1925, 147 on the 1909 index. Commercial and industrial employment, 1,128,200 at 182.4 of the 1909 index, excluded capitalists, workers, and owner-managers of shops too small to pay taxes; thus it approximated white-collar employment in commerce and industry. Government employees (below the rank of *hannin* but excluding clerks [*kakyū kōmuin*] and laborers) num-

56. Yamamoto Taketoshi, 140; Tsurumi Shunsuke; *ITZ* 15:348, 64–65.

bered 325,000, 206.2 on the 1909 index. The figures would place the new middle class at some 10 percent of the non-agricultural work force. Estimates of a white-collar group of double that size have been advanced, but the more conservative estimates define a group with a fair degree of responsibility who might have been more receptive to the perspective of the general-interest journals.[57]

Its rate of increase and prominence in new occupations let the urban new middle class set the tone for Taishō culture. Enrollments in higher education also escalated, as graduates of middle and girls' higher schools rose from 2.9 percent of the age cohort in 1910 to 4.2 percent in 1920 and 10 percent in 1930. College and university graduates were still a small minority but increased from .3 percent of the age cohort in 1910 to .6 percent in 1920 to 1.9 percent in 1930.[58] Especially in Tokyo, success became more and more dependent on education rather than family status or connections. The population of Tokyo grew much faster than that of the nation as a whole, doubling from two to four million between 1900 and 1920 while the national population increased by only 22 percent.[59] Urban concentration encouraged the new middle class in Tokyo to regard itself as the intellectual and cultural arbiter for the nation as a whole.

Why was the new middle class drawn to the media? Its members earned a living from skills and knowledge acquired in modern formal education. Attuned to the relationship between information and success, they relied on the media to continue education during adult life. Broad interests were encouraged by lifetime employment, job rotation, and in-house training in large, high-technology corporations, which struggled to retain their skilled labor force during the 1920s. Since lifetime employment militates against narrow specialization, it

57. Shibamura Atsuki, "Dai toshi ni okeru kenryoku to minshū no kōdō," in Koyama Hitoshi, ed., *Taishōki no kenryoku to minshū*, 48–56; Gotō Yasushi, "Kindai tennōsei ron," in Rekishigaku Kenkyūkai, Nihonshi Kenkyūkai, ed., *Kōza Nihonshi*, vol. 9, 191–214.

58. Robert E. Cole and Ken'ichi Tominaga, "Japan's Changing Occupational Structure and Its Significance," in Hugh T. Patrick, ed., *Japanese Industrialization and Its Social Consequences*, 66–67.

59. James W. White, "Internal Migration in Prewar Japan," *JJS* 4 (1978): 82–123.

afforded an occupational basis for the continuing interest in the art of free-ranging punditry.[60] At the same time, theories of marketing and scientific management prodded business-men to investigate the wide range of evidence and views set forth by the general-interest journals. Journals also offered insight into the strategies of the workplace through interviews with the famous and powerful.

Journals suggested new outlooks suited to the cities. Employment in Tokyo meant attenuated family ties in the provinces and adaptation to a new environment lacking in tradition and precedent. Members of the new middle class, whose skills and education made them relatively autonomous, were neglected in the hierarchical state ideology, and they turned elsewhere for comprehension of their place in a larger whole.[61] More concretely, urban areas suffered from political weakness and poor services. Progressive historian Charles Beard marveled at the endurance of Tokyoites who would flock to lectures on academic topics even though they had to slog home in the dark through six inches of mud.[62] The general-interest journals proposed improvement in articles on city administration and services. The media offered a kind of psychic mobility, an opportunity to test new definitions of reality mentally and emotionally. Finally, the journalistic ethos of cultural criticism and impartiality expressed a quest for equity rooted in the ambivalent relationship of the urban new middle class with the state.

THE STATE

The Meiji state had created the new middle class by abolishing hereditary restrictions on occupation and residence and sponsoring industrialization. New managerial and professional positions opened and partially fulfilled the Restoration ideal of meritocracy. Meritocracy won broad adherence among the new middle class, especially Taishō journalists. The overwhelming

60. Watanuki, 9.
61. Carol N. Gluck, "Japan's Modern Myth: Ideology in the Late Meiji Period," 9.
62. Charles A. Beard, *The Administration and Politics of Tokyo—A Survey and Opinions*; Kuwabara et al., 169.

majority of even reformist writers affirmed the Meiji settlement as vastly preferable to Tokugawa rule. Very few launched
systematic structural critiques of the Meiji state and society. In
their view Meiji institutions did not merit rejection but required completion in a Taishō Restoration.

The Meiji state narrowly restricted access to political power,
proffered an ideology of hierarchy and submission, and censored fundamental dissent. The bureaucracy was widely resented as the bastion of the new rulers from the leading
Restoration domains of Satsuma and Chōshū. The franchise,
based on an annual property tax qualification of ten yen in
1902 and encompassing a mere 980,000 men, excluded most
of the salaried new middle class. The tax qualification was
reduced to three yen by 1920 and eliminated by 1926, but
women were excluded until 1945.[63] The most liberal wing of
journalists (including Tanaka, Shimamura, and Ishibashi, who
lived with cultivated professional women) chafed under the
last restriction. Moreover, under the Meiji Constitution even a
universal franchise could not have ensured the accountability
of powerful independent governmental organs such as the
House of Peers, the military, and the Privy Council.

Political discourse also had to address a comprehensive state
ideology. Meiji state ideology, two decades in the making, crystallized in the Constitution and the Imperial Rescript on Education of 1890. Both the Constitution and the Rescript justified political authority by the divinity of Japan's imperial line,
unbroken for ages eternal. Both clearly stressed the obligations
of subjects more than the limitations on state power. Since
most of the rights of subjects existed within the limits of the
law—and could be abridged by law—state authority could be
interpreted as absolute.[64] In contrast, liberal interpreters such
as Minobe Tatsukichi envisioned the Meiji state in more flexible and pluralistic terms, under which the emperor and legislature shared power as organs of the state.[65]

63. Isomura Eiichi, ed., *Gyōsei saishin mondai jiten*, 705.
64. Richard Minear, *Japanese Tradition and Western Law: Emperor, State, and Law in
the Thought of Hozumi Yatsuka.*
65. Frank O. Miller, *Minobe Tatsukichi: Interpreter of Constitutionalism in Japan*, 62–
65.

A parallel division of opinion arose regarding the Imperial Rescript on Education, which enjoined the moral cultivation of Japanese subjects and prescribed the eternal harmony of the emperor and the Japanese people: "Our imperial Ancestors have founded Our Empire on a basis broad and everlasting, and have deeply and firmly implanted virtue; Our subjects ever united in loyalty and filial piety have from generation to generation illustrated the beauty thereof."[66] In this spirit scholars steeped in the Japanese past, such as Inoue Tetsujirō, welcomed the Rescript as a holistic and absolute ethic for modern Japan, a scripture to be read in fundamentalist terms.[67]

Other scholars struggled to minimize the impact of state ideology, first in philosophy, then in politics. Philosopher Ōnishi Hajime, Tanaka's predecessor at Waseda, demanded freedom of inquiry in ethics and denounced Inoue: "It is cowardly for contenders in the field of ethical theory to use the Imperial Rescript as their shield."[68] Ōnishi's imagery anticipated by twenty years Ozaki Yukio's famous denunciation of Prime Minister Katsura's forces who attempted to "destroy their enemies by using the throne as a parapet and imperial rescripts as bullets" during the Taishō political crisis.[69] Ōnishi pinpointed the dilemma of prewar philosophers: how to distinguish ethics, a legitimate area of inquiry, from the moral behavior prescribed by the Imperial Rescript on Education. Later Yoshino Sakuzō investigated the dilemma of prewar liberals: how to wrest the sanctity of the throne away from oligarchs and bureaucrats and enlist it in the democratic cause.[70] Just as Yoshino's distinction of political processes from the locus of sovereignty became the keystone of democratic politics,

66. Tsunoda Ryusaku, Wm. Theodore de Bary, and Donald Keene, eds., *Sources of Japanese Tradition*, vol. 2, 139–40.

67. Pyle, *The New Generation in Meiji Japan*, 122–40; and Nakauchi Toshio, *Kindai Nihon kyōiku shisōshi*, 39–51.

68. Ōnishi Hajime, "Kyōiku chokugo to rinri," in *Ōnishi Hajime zenshū*, vol. 6, 55–59; for a translation and commentary see my "National Morality and Universal Ethics: Ōnishi Hajime and the Imperial Rescript on Education," *MN* 38 (1983): 283–94.

69. Ozaki is quoted by Najita, *Hara Kei in the Politics of Compromise*, 147.

70. Yoshino's definitive exposition of his democratic theory was "Kensei no hongi o toite sono yūshū no bi o nasu no michi o ronzu," in Ōta Masao, ed., *Shiryō: Taishō demokurashii ronsō shi*, vol. 1.

Ōnishi's distinction of ethical theory from moral behavior became the keystone of arguments on behalf of academic freedom during the Taishō period.

To question so comprehensive a state ideology required an integrated paradigm of society, culture, history, and psychology as well as politics. Many shied away from the challenge; in Tatsuo Arima's account: "The hybrid and inarticulate nature of the new system's political symbols made it extremely difficult for the individual either to embrace or to reject its social manifestation."[71] Privatism was one response to the ambivalence of state symbols. But another was vigorous competition to capture those symbols and invest them with new meanings. Like most modern intellectuals, Tanaka, Shimamura, and Ishibashi seldom wholly repudiated or wholly accepted the symbols and institutions of their society. The broad and complex middle ground was the center of interest in the Taishō era. State power lent an aura of unity to all forms of protest against authority. Defiance ranged from Shimamura's aesthetic interest in the individual to Ishibashi's defense of Russian and Japanese communists. Before the mid-1920s the Taishō democratic movement was strongly nonsectarian, welcoming almost any form of disassociation from the state.

Although the writers struggled toward a constructive middle ground of gradual reform, they did not escape censorship. Two issues of Ishibashi's *Tōyō jiron* were confiscated, and several of his articles were deleted from *Tōyō keizai shinpō*. Tanaka and Ishibashi disbanded their Liberal Lecture Society when their colleague Tagawa was jailed. Shimamura's theater production of *Magda* was closed by the Home Ministry pending mandatory revisions. Ishibashi reported numerous searches of the homes of *Shinpō* staff members and felt compelled to burn his letters from Katayama Sen about the Russian Revolution.

---

71. Tatsuo Arima, *The Failure of Freedom: A Portrait of Modern Japanese Intellectuals*, 4. For other significant interpretations of privatism among intellectuals see Kano Masanao, "Atarashii kokuminzō no keisei," in Hashikawa Bunsō and Matsumoto Sannosuke, eds., *Kindai Nihon seiji shisōshi*, vol. 1, Kindai Nihon shisōshi taikei, vol. 3; and H. D. Harootunian, "Between Politics and Culture: Authority and the Ambiguities of Intellectual Choice in Imperial Japan," in Bernard S. Silberman and Harootunian, eds., *Japan in Crisis: Essays in Taishō Democracy*.

All the writers protested censorship on general principles and in specific instances. Nonetheless they moderated their rhetoric to avoid direct confrontation, believing that their efforts to propound a new sense of popular assertion and participation would force change within the system.[72]

Throughout the Taishō period, censorship was authorized by the Newspaper Law of 1909 and justified by elastic, sometimes fantastical, notions of public peace and morals, the dignity of the imperial house, the legitimacy of the political status quo, and, after 1926, the sanctity of private property. Usually the police initiated censorship under Home Ministry direction, but other ministries also employed it, and in wartime the military issued blanket edicts. In peacetime, administrators used censorship not to suppress all criticism but to constrict the public influence of dissent.[73] Early in the Taishō period, censors confiscated the entire press run of a journal issue or book after publication, but publishers lost so much money that they sought and won a system of prepublication advising.[74] Prepublication warnings implicitly threatened lost sales and even fines or imprisonment. Nonetheless, in 1932 Ishibashi wrote that he received warnings (*kiji sashitomi meirei*) daily but usually ignored them since they were too vague to follow.[75]

Censorship by public opinion was another menace. Rightist agitator Mitsui Kōshi labeled Tanaka an anti-Japanese and treasonous republican a decade and a half before Mitsui's more famous attack on Minobe.[76] Popular reaction could provoke police action or even lead to murder as in the case of Diet member Yamamoto Senji, who was assassinated for criticizing the Peace Preservation Law of 1926.[77] Many Japanese also risked being fired for political or social criticism. For ex-

72. *ITZ* 15:150–52, 87–90.
73. For fuller accounts see Richard H. Mitchell, *Censorship in Imperial Japan*, esp. 141, 224, 236–37; and Jay Rubin, *Injurious to Public Morals: Writers and the Meiji State*; Elise Tipton, "The Civil Police in the Suppression of the Prewar Japanese Left."
74. Fumiko H. Coyne, "Censorship of Publishing in Japan, 1868–1945."
75. Watanabe Tōru, "Sōron," 9.
76. Mitsui Kōshi, "Kuwaki Hakushi to Tanaka Ōdō Shi no sansō o shitekisu," *Shin Nihon*, May 1918, 7–9.
77. Mitchell, 103; Robert J. Lifton et al., *Six Lives, Six Deaths: Portraits from Modern Japan*, 158.

ample, Katayama Sen's wife, Nobuko, divorced him in 1923 because she feared that his Communist activities in the Soviet Union would provoke her dismissal from a teaching position at a country girls' school.[78] For writers, notoriety could enhance sales, but during the 1930s blacklists banned dissidents from the major publications.

Taishō liberals believed that continuing to publish, even while compromising with the censors, could transform the Japanese polity from within by awakening the people. Yet arbitrary and vacillating censors made it impossible to gauge the risk of a particular statement. On the other hand writers who said too much were often censored but seldom fined or jailed. They devised strategies to express fundamental criticism within the ordinary boundaries of permissible discourse. First among these strategies was the omission of information.

Kosugi Tengai's journal *Mumei tsūshin* (Anonymous report) published some of Ishibashi's early essays, but it concealed the identities of all authors. It quickly collapsed under police surveillance, since editors, publishers, and printers as well as authors shared responsibility for seditious content. In a different tactic, which had been used since the mid-Meiji period, editors deleted inflammatory terms such as "revolution," replacing them with meaningless symbols.[79] The major newspapers printed editions half filled with blank pages after the rice riots of 1918 to protest the government's news blackout.[80] More often, information was omitted in editorials, where phrases such as "recent trends in our country" substituted for precise description. Contemporary readers understood the political context; in fact, even the police acquiesced in the tactic of vagueness and reprimanded Ishibashi for a 1932 editorial (on financial uncertainty in Chungking) that was "just a little too concrete."[81] (Disturbance of the financial world was one of the informal criteria for censorship.)[82]

78. *ITZ* 15:89.
79. Jō Ichirō, *Hakkinbon hyakunen*, 73–110; Hatanaka Shigeo, *Shōwa shuppan dan'atsu shi*, 171–81; Mitchell, 99, 163–64. Hatanaka was editor of *Chūō kōron* from 1941 to 1943.
80. Ono, 150.
81. Watanabe Tōru, "Sōron," 9; Ono, 378–87.
82. Mitchell, 265.

Writers also juxtaposed textual passages to express more criticism than they dared to make explicit. Maejima Toyotarō was arrested in 1881 for juxtaposing references to the Emperor Jinmu and Hachisuka Koroku, a scheming sixteenth-century warlord. Another form of juxtaposition was to inject a formidable thicket of obscure Chinese characters in a semi-popular work. Nakae Chōmin had used the tactic as early as 1881, and Tanaka employed it to signal particularly daring statements. The unfamiliar words probably confused many readers as well as the unscholarly censors.[83] Nevertheless, rhetorical and stylistic techniques of dissent were known to generations of writers and officials, and were conventions of the literate culture.

Ishibashi juxtaposed examples to question the imperial ideology in a 1912 essay that opened by summarizing the European parable of the emperor's new clothes. Of course he used the general monarchical reference *ōsama*, not the sacrosanct term *tennō*. Camouflaged as a mere raconteur, he began to stalk his target, suggesting that the parable's theme of blind servility applied to many Japanese beliefs such as morality (*dō-toku*) and ethics (*shūshin*). The beliefs were closely associated with the emperor cult but were still conventional objects of moderate criticism. Next he appeared to change topics, mentioning a recent imperial visit to a women's college. The visit had been preceded by weeks of frantic preparation, but a student complained that it would have been better had His Majesty seen the usual poor and dirty place. Ishibashi's final vignette contrasted an alert American-educated Japanese with a docile and foolish product of the Meiji system; most Japanese youth, Ishibashi concluded, were too subservient. By juxtaposing a series of anecdotes that, taken separately, were fairly innocuous, he made clear his preference for rational social analysis over imperial mythology. Confident that he had made his point, he concluded by reassuring his readers, inside and outside the police force, that the import of the examples was the penetrating vision of children. The censors were probably not fooled, but they had to consider the political risks of pros-

83. Mitchell, 76; Lifton et al., 135–36.

ecuting cautious forms of criticism. Writers and police jock-
eyed in ritualized patterns to spread or restrict new values.[84]

The writers often published complaints about censorship.
Ishibashi decided to print verbatim an army warning about his
editorials on the Siberian intervention. Clause by clause he
dissected the army's vague, pompous, and menacing missive
in the next issue of *Shinpō*. Few editors were as courageous as
Ishibashi, but readers had other ways to see past the censors.
Some banned publications did circulate due to police inefficiency, and some heavily censored radical groups relied on
handbills and private printing. In the thirties the police forbade editors to substitute symbols (*fuseji*) for inflammatory
words on the grounds that readers could supply the omissions.
Certainly X X X X X appearing suddenly in a line of type
would catch the eye and trigger curiosity, while the absence
of a journal issue on the newsstand would provoke comment.
Three issues of *Chūō kōron* were banned during the last decade
of Meiji, but each time sales of the subsequent number
jumped. Writers who defied regulation had an avid audience.[85]

Meiji policies aimed at building national wealth and strength
rather than allowing individual liberty or self-fulfillment; accordingly, new avenues of political participation were coupled
with indoctrination and censorship. The urban new middle
class, created by planned industrialization under a centralizing
state, lacked a political and organizational base, and its more
articulate members were inclined to regard the remnants of
local power—the base of the political parties—as even more
benighted than the national bureaucracy. Local political, clan,
and religious organizations were weak compared with those in
China or the West, and they were identified with the world
the writers had left behind in their search for modernity. The
absence of an urban middle class power base strengthened the
statist tendencies in Taishō democracy.

Tanaka, Shimamura, and Ishibashi channeled their writings
within state-sanctioned boundaries because they accepted the

---

84. *ITZ* 1:479–80.
85. Mitchell, 166–71, 243, 280–81; Tsurumi Shunsuke; Jō, 73–110.

Restoration ideal of meritocracy. The rewards of talent loomed large for the writers, each of whom was more famous and higher in status than his father. The writers sustained an esprit of their own intellectual and cultural leadership, but they contrasted their open realm of public debate with the closed corridors of the governmental bureaucracy. Pluralism was sustained by an institutional base at Waseda and in the media. The writers' efforts succeeded because of a general consensus among the intelligentsia that modern Japan required new values. As state-sanctioned institutions and elite discourse absorbed iconoclasm, the political system grew ever more innovative and sophisticated. The social forces unleashed by the Restoration could never be channeled wholly within Meiji state bounds; the state could survive only through change.

1

Ethics: Tanaka Ōdō and John Dewey

John Dewey had perhaps the greatest global influence of any American philosopher, and Japan was the earliest and most vigorous assimilator of Western thought in the non-Western world. Moreover, Dewey's ideas accorded with a pragmatic tendency in the temperament of the Japanese people, and a tradition of philosophic instrumentalism from Ogyū Sorai (1666–1728), who had described institutions and values as the artifacts of changing society. Sorai's philosophy, however, had been enmeshed in his justification of the samurai right to rule.[1] In contrast twentieth-century Japanese intellectuals debated the ideas of John Dewey as part of a conscious national effort to design a new participatory and meritocratic industrial society. The first and foremost proponent of instrumentalism in Japan was Tanaka Ōdō, who studied at the University of Chicago between 1892 and 1897. Waseda became a center of the study of American pragmatism through the efforts of Tanaka, his students such as Ueda Seiji and Nieda Rokusaburō, and younger colleagues such as Hoashi Riichirō—an orientation which continues today.[2]

AN AMERICAN EDUCATION

When Tanaka met John Dewey he was twenty-six years old, imbued with the intellectual currents and national goals of late

1. On Ogyū Sorai see, for example, Masao Maruyama, *Studies in the Intellectual History of Tokugawa Japan*, trans. Mikiso Hane; Tetsuo Najita and Irwin Scheiner, eds., *Japanese Thought in the Tokugawa Period, 1600–1868*.
2. Recent scholarship has qualified but not vitiated distinctions between the respective intellectual climates of public and private universities; see Byron K. Marshall, "Professors and Politics: The Meiji Academic Elite," *JJS* 3 (1977): 71–98; James Bartholomew, "Japanese Modernization and the Imperial Universities, 1876–1920," *JAS* 37 (1978): 251–72.

nineteenth-century Japan. He resembled many other intelligent and ambitious young men of the 1880s who were resolved to learn from the West in order to aid their country's transition to the modern world. Born in 1867 in the village of Nakatomu just outside Tokyo, Tanaka was the second son of a well-to-do landlord family. He attended four missionary schools in four years, searching for a method to reconstruct Japanese society.[3] He admired the comprehensive vision of the Confucian sages but rejected their insistence on social hierarchy and disparaged the prevailing limited, utilitarian approach to Western learning. Men of learning, he instructed his elder brother, should move beyond the Confucian sages and the limited, utilitarian study of Western scholarship to conceive a new all-encompassing philosophy, "even knowing that it is impossible in modern society."[4]

Summoned home for his army draft physical examination in 1887, Tanaka briefly labored on the family farm. The next year he fled to a translating and English-teaching job with the American missionary Eugene Snodgrass (Disciples of Christ) in Tsuruoka, Yamagata Prefecture. Snodgrass succeeded, where four years of missionary schooling had failed, in converting Tanaka to baptism in March of 1889. Snodgrass capitalized on the Disciples' antisectarian claims, his own high repute as a biblical scholar, and the lure of an American education. Tanaka boarded a steamship for San Francisco in August of 1889, and attended Snodgrass's alma mater, the College of the Bible (Lexington Theological Seminary) for three years.[5]

3. Tanaka attended Dōjinsha (Nakamura Keiu's academy), Tokyo Eiwa Gakkō (Aoyama Gakuin), Tokyo Senmon Gakkō (Waseda University), and Dōshisha University in Kyoto. Tanaka Kiichi, "Rirekisho" (1899), Waseda University Daigakushi Henshūjo, Tokyo, "Bungakubu ni kansuru shorui." His childhood and family were described by his daughter Tanaka Miki in an interview (3 Apr. 1976).

4. Tanaka Kiichi to Tanaka Keiji, 20 Apr. 1889, letters in the private collection of Professor Hanzawa Hiroshi, Tokyo Kōgyō University and in the Archives of Lexington Theological Seminary, Lexington, Kentucky.

5. Tanaka's baptism is recorded in Eugene Snodgrass, Diary, Snodgrass Papers, Archives of Lexington Theological Seminary; Tanaka Kiichi to Tanaka Keiji, 20 Apr. 1889. The United States was the most popular destination of Japanese students. During the last third of the nineteenth century there were perhaps one thousand Japanese college, university, and seminary students in the United States. The United States was favored because of its relative proximity and cheaper cost of living compared with Europe, a Japanese sense of identification with the newness and achievements of the

He appreciated the exceptional kindness and financial support that he received from American missionaries in Japan
and in Kentucky at the College of the Bible. Still, he did not
form any discernible lasting friendships with his missionary
teachers. He was outraged at those insular Americans who
thought that Japan was a colony of some great power or a
province of China. Christian sectarianism, as well as racial and
national bigotry, turned many young men of Tanaka's generation against Christianity and the West, and John W. Mc-
Garvey, who taught Tanaka and headed the college, was
denounced for puritanical intolerance in James Lane Allen's
classic *The Reign of Law* (1900).[6]

Extraordinarily reticent about his personal life and intellectual development, Tanaka left no explanation of his transfer
to the University of Chicago in 1892. Most probably he was
introduced to the Disciples of Christ leaders at Chicago—Edward Scribner Ames, William Lloyd Garrison, or H. S. Hil-
lett—whose religion was diffuse and largely submerged in
social consciousness. He left the Chicago Divinity House after
living there for one year, a move paralleled by his shift to the
rigorously secular classrooms of the Chicago pragmatists:
James Tufts (history of philosophy), George Herbert Mead
(logic and the methodology of psychology), James R. Angell
(experimental psychology), and John Dewey (history of logic
and logic of ethics).[7]

The search for a comprehensive, philosophic vision of modern Japanese society and ethics informed Tanaka's attraction
to, then rejection of, both Confucianism and Christianity; he
was a consistent nationalist but not a chauvinist. Speaking to
a group of Japanese students at the University of Chicago in
1894 (before he began his studies with Dewey), Tanaka defiantly honored the emperor's birthday by decrying the pa-

---

United States, and the influence of American missionaries, according to James T.
Conte, "Overseas Study in the Meiji Period: Japanese Students in America, 1867–
1902," 28–35.

6. Tanaka Kiichi to Tanaka Keiji, 20 Apr. 1889.

7. Tanaka's course of study at Chicago is recorded in *Register of the University
of Chicago*, 1894–98, and *Instructor's Reports*, University of Chicago Archives,
Chicago.

triotic frenzy that attended the Sino-Japanese War. The real progress of Japan, he claimed, lay in education, not in a military victory over China. Distinguishing his unhappiness with Japanese imperialism from socialist critiques, he added that the rule of any one class was arbitrary and unnecessary. At the outset of his studies with the Chicago pragmatists, he already condemned jingoistic nationalism, advocated the selective use of technological advances for humanistic goals, rejected class struggle, and believed in the resolution of complex social issues through education. These orientations could only be strengthened in the classrooms of Dewey, Mead, Tufts, and Angell.[8]

Whatever Tanaka's motives, he was singularly fortunate in entering the most creative intellectual milieu in the United States at that time. The Chicago group's innovation appealed to Tanaka, a young man of the Meiji era concerned with constructing a new Japan. Dewey, Mead, Angell, and Tufts "were deliberately breaking with traditions of thought and scholarship, opening new paths, challenging intellectual and academic habits, devising new ideas and terminologies."[9] Behind the originality and even idiosyncrasy of their individual styles, the men shared a rare sense of intellectual community and cross-fertilization within a common frame of reference.

Tanaka was also fortunate in attracting the personal support of John Dewey (then a junior assistant professor) for the doctoral program, but no fellowship was forthcoming. Since Dewey's assiduous efforts to get funds by finding translation jobs for Tanaka met with only partial success, Tanaka returned to Tokyo with his bachelor's degree and a letter of recommendation from a philosopher then better known than John Dewey, Paul Carus (editor of the *Monist*). Carus expressed his hope for Tanaka's success in "his aspirations of discretely adapting Western scholarship to the needs of the Japanese people."[10] Tanaka apparently had no further contact with

8. Tanaka Kiichi to his family, 23 Sep. 1894. Tanaka's professors at Chicago, Dewey, Mead, Angell, and Tufts, have been described as "the nucleus of the Chicago school of pragmatism" and are discussed in detail in Egbert Darnell Rucker, *The Chicago Pragmatists*.

9. William James, *The Letters of William James*, vol. 2, 201–02; Rucker, ii.

10. John Dewey to Paul Carus, 11 May, 30 May, and 26 July 1896, Dewey Papers,

Dewey until Dewey visited Japan in 1919. By that time Tanaka and other early interpreters had made Dewey's general views well known to Japanese intellectuals.

INSTRUMENTALISM

Although all contemporary reviews labeled Tanaka a disciple of Dewey, Tanaka himself hesitated. His only explicit discussion of Dewey emphasized the relevance of Dewey's democratic ideals to the acute problems of American industrialization:

> John Dewey's philosophy is the philosophy of an American. . . . [His] is the philosophy of industrial democracy. All the defects we can see in contemporary America, the arrogance, vacuity, contradiction, and weakening spiritual power, come from a single root. That is, that the laws and morals stemming from the society of seventeenth-century and eighteenth-century Europe, transmitted [to Americans] by their ancestors and still honored, are inadequate to fulfill the real needs of their present life. . . . This is the aim of the philosophy of John Dewey.[11]

Tanaka saw Dewey as he saw himself, a debunker of outmoded beliefs and systems, a prophet of the new order, a spokesman for industrial democracy. He also found America similar to Japan, outgrowing old systems and values and searching for new ones. Despite these similarities he understood the need to adapt Dewey's insights to Japanese conditions. Demanding a modern, individualistic Japanese culture, he berated his colleagues for their reverence toward foreign scholars and their tendency to divide into exclusive, competitive schools rather than to engage in the exchange of ideas. His aversion to unassimilated imported ideas and intellectual labeling may explain his reluctance to acknowledge his debt to Dewey. Nevertheless, his entire writing career bore the imprint of

---

Morris Library, University of Southern Illinois, Carbondale; Kiichi Tanaka to Paul Carus, 21 May and 24 June 1896, and 27 May and 30 Sept. 1897. Paul Carus *re* Tanaka, 27 May 1897, Archives of the Open Court Publishing Company, Morris Library.

11. Tanaka Ōdō, "Jon Juui [*sic*] no tetsugaku" in *Sōzō to kyōraku*, 244–45.

Dewey's instrumentalism, especially in his conceptions of evolution, psychology, and the relationship of the individual to society.

The theory of evolution, especially in the form of Social Darwinism developed by Herbert Spencer, was extremely popular in Japan at the turn of the century, as it was in the United States, though Japanese theorists were more inclined to stress the idea of survival of the fittest among nations rather than among individuals. Tanaka assumed that it was "impossible to explain the workings of any system, custom, or thought, apart from the conditions of adaptation to the environment."[12] A continuous and indeterminate process of human interaction with the environment precluded any institution, custom, value, or philosophy from being considered final or definitive. Societies were evolving organisms which could not be reduced to social scientific laws, and scholars should not mechanically extend the insights of biological and physical sciences to social problems. Tanaka, like the Chicago pragmatists, emphasized the scientific method, not scientific laws.

Dewey had little use for the allegedly scientific social laws of Auguste Comte and Herbert Spencer and stressed instead the experimental and undogmatic nature of scientific method:

> As natural science found its outlet by admitting no idea, no theory, as fixed by itself, demanding of every idea that it must become fruitful in experiment, so must ethical science purge itself of all conceptions, of all ideals, save those which are developed within and for the sake of practice.[13]

Refuting the idea that "scientific laws" dictated particular social policies or modes of behavior, Dewey regarded the scientific method as an instrument of progressive, experimental, and liberating human activity.

Tanaka sanctioned the definition of scientific method as a point of departure from which to develop a monistic method in philosophy that would comprehend all human activity, including scientific research itself. Like his teachers he criticized

12. Tanaka, *Fukuzawa Yukichi*, Ōdō senshu, vol. 2, ed. Sugimori Kōjirō, 64.
13. John Dewey, "Self-Realization as a Moral Ideal," in *The Early Works of John Dewey*, vol. 4, ed. Jo Ann Boydston, 53.

William James's dualism, which distinguished between "the principles of science and the principles of religion,"[14] and also distanced himself from Japanese neo-Kantians, who located humanistic inquiry on a different and higher plane of value than the natural sciences. He regarded the natural scientist as a specialist concerned exclusively with the natural world, and he assigned to philosophers the responsibility for explaining the historical, cultural, and logical aspects of the natural scientist's activity as an inquirer. Philosophy was to guide human conduct, including that of natural scientists, by articulating the human interests and the socio-cultural conditions that inspired, permeated, and maintained all human activity.

Applying his monistic method to human behavior, from physiological functions through the highest artistic and intellectual achievements, Tanaka followed the Chicago pragmatists in a new psychology. He credited William James with orienting psychology in a new direction by "replacing atomistic rationalism and crude empiricism with a fresh and elegant functionalism."[15] Although he embraced James's concept of "impulse" (*shōdō*) as more fruitful than the old stimulus/response paradigm,[16] he felt that the vocabulary of psychology was still inadequate to express the complexities of human behavior: "For the lower animals with their instincts, life is a *datum*; for human beings with their impulses, life is a *problem*."[17] The statement, a literal quotation from Dewey's *The Study of Ethics: A Syllabus*, recurred frequently in Tanaka's writings, with the italicized words in English.[18] Tanaka postulated a complex and integrated psychology in which a whole range of responses to any situation—physical, emotional, mental—were linked with each other, with past experience, with the situation itself, and with its resolution in behavior. His psychology re-

14. Tanaka, "Ko Kyōju Uiriamu Jiemusu [*sic*] o tsuiokusu," in *Tetsujinshugi*, vol. 1, 32. On the criticism of James's idea of the soul by Chicago pragmatists, see Wayne R. Leys, Introduction to *The Early Works of John Dewey*, in 4: xxiii.
15. Tanaka, "Shōdō to shisō," in *Gendai bunka no honshitsu*, 4.
16. "Jiyū shisōka no rinrikan," 242–43.
17. "Shōdō to shisō," 6.
18. Dewey, *The Study of Ethics: A Syllabus*, in *The Early Works of John Dewey*, 4:236. During the 1890s this study was "a scripture, treasured in those years' dearth of systematic writing from Professor Dewey's hand," according to Henry W. Stuart, "Dewey's Ethical Theory," in Paul A. Schilpp, ed., *The Philosophy of John Dewey*, note to 314.

jected a sharp dualism between stimulus and response, between organism and environment.

The Chicago pragmatists aggressively developed the new psychology of experience to challenge such traditional philosophical dualisms as mind and matter, ideal and real, subject and object. An organism's impulse toward its environment could not be determined by the inherent nature of external surroundings, but neither could it be located solely in the mind of the organism. Even the lower animals created their environments in some sense, as well as being shaped by them. Mead illustrated this point by reference to the emergence of a grass-eating animal. Grass, as food, was neither a product of the animal's mind nor a reality that existed in the world before the animal evolved into being; it was the result of a process of interaction and development.[19] In a similar vein, Dewey sardonically likened the idealist/realist feud in philosophy to a debate over whether the world was constituted solely of eaters or solely of food.[20]

Tanaka heartily applauded their conclusion that philosophers who abstracted concepts such as "mind" and "matter" ought to admit that they were dealing in intellectual constructs for specific and conscious purposes. The socio-cultural effects of those purposes then afforded the criteria to judge the validity of the abstractions.[21] Tanaka believed that the clarification of philosophers' social and cultural impact, and the dissolution of traditional philosophical abstractions and dualisms, would profoundly alter human ethics and social relationships. Traditional authority, Tanaka believed, was buttressed by philosophies of hierarchical dualism that ranked spirit higher than matter, ideals higher than desires, reason higher than feeling.[22]

Lacking idealistic or traditional principles of ethics, Tanaka was especially sensitive to, and eager to refute, the charges of

19. Mead, cited in Rucker, 28.
20. Dewey, *Essays in Experimental Logic*, 270.
21. Tanaka, "Tōzai bunmei yūgō no igi oyobi keika o ronzu," in *Shosai yori gaitō ni*, 123–24.
22. Tanaka, "Kaihōsha Uiriamu Jiemusu [sic]," *WB*, ser. 2, no. 118 (Sept. 1915): 6; see also idem, "Yokubō no risōka, hōritsuka," in *Tettei kojinshugi*, 142–43; and idem, "Shōdō to shisō," 7–8.

subjectivism, especially from neo-Kantian critics such as Kuwaki Genyoku and Nishida Kitarō. The construction of a similar defense was a general concern of the Chicago pragmatists,
who were vexed by the critical outcry over certain of William
James's less fortunate choices of language. Whereas James had
presented pragmatism as the cash-value of ideas, Dewey's ex-
plorations of logical theory disassociated his philosophy from
James's voluntarism. Dewey recognized that his

> theory may be called pragmatism. But it is a type of pragmatism
> quite free from dependence upon a voluntaristic psychology. It is
> not complicated by reference to emotional satisfactions or the play
> of desires.[23]

Tanaka, like Dewey, denied that pragmatism meant the defense of any bizarre notion that someone happened to find
useful or pleasant. Pragmatism, in their perspective, viewed
knowledge, including ethical knowledge, with respect to its underlying and motivating purpose, not its immediate use or
satisfaction.

For Tanaka, the goodness of an act should be considered
only in relation to its entire context of past experience and
present environment:

> Past experience attaches meaning and value to competing im-
> pulses; the choice is one of better, not best. In human action one
> effect gives rise to another and one relation depends on another,
> in an endless web; one merely calculates the relative values in the
> process. One might think that there is no choice but to fly into a
> sort of skeptical madness. But such an idea is merely an illusion,
> departing from, or disregarding, life.[24]

Tanaka, in short, claimed it was perfectly possible, in theory
and in practice, to make valid or sound ethical choices without
taking refuge in idealist philosophy or foundering in limitless
subjectivism. The self-conscious experimental method was the
best instrument for the constant reconstruction of society.

Tanaka's experimental method enlisted the insights of the
Chicago pragmatists to explain change and the dynamics of

23. Dewey, *Essays in Experimental Logic*, 347.
24. Tanaka, "Yokubō no risōka, hōritsuka," 142–43.

reform. He saw organized groups of persons, such as nations or subgroups within them, as entities that historically had developed certain accepted ways of performing essential tasks in adaptation to their particular environments. His notion of environment, with its reference to history and culture, differed from the natural environment of biology. It postulated a social environment, which was created by the institutions, beliefs, customs, and material achievements of the group's ancestors and contemporaries. To change the social environment gradually, individuals had to study and conserve their heritage because society and culture contained the heritage of earlier successful adaptation. Though Tanaka assumed that the accelerated change of modern societies required a high degree of flexibility and innovation, he remained scornful of those who ignored and spurned the past.[25]

Tanaka's critical engagement with the past bore Dewey's imprint. John H. Randall, Jr., has perceptively emphasized that Dewey's erudition and intense engagement with past philosophy made him "the greatest traditionalist among the leading philosophical minds of today."[26] Dewey, Randall noted, differed from other twentieth-century philosophers, especially logical positivists, in his belief that past philosophy was still worthy of study. At the same time, Dewey's method of social and historical criticism had a revolutionary impact. Tanaka extolled the pragmatism of the rural innovator Ninomiya Sontoku (1787–1856) and the Westernizer Fukuzawa Yukichi (1835–1901) but excoriated traditional Japanese politics and religion as subjectively idealistic and socially repressive.

TOWARD A DEMOCRATIC ETHICS

Returning to Japan in 1897, Tanaka faced a spectrum of social, cultural, and intellectual issues quite different from those that preoccupied young John Dewey in Chicago. Tanaka encountered the government's aggressive measures to centralize the educational system—through textbook standardization, control over teacher qualification, attempts to suppress indepen-

25. Tanaka, "Shōdō to shisō," 7–8.
26. John H. Randall, "Dewey's Interpretation of the History of Philosophy," in Schilpp, 81, 93.

dent private academies, and press censorship. These policies, along with patriarchal values that required obedience and self-abnegation from youth and women, constituted the central issues in Tanaka's writings.

Tanaka articulated a social philosophy directed at the reconstruction of society in the particular context of modern Japan, and accordingly he differed from Dewey in several respects. Dewey avoided postulating the nation as a primary determinant of thought. He neither called on philosophy to adapt itself to special American circumstances, nor identified himself as an American philosopher, nor decried the preponderance of European thought in American universities, nor alleged that American philosophers had failed to assimilate the ideas of foreigners. Assuming the relationship between European and American culture and thought, Dewey tended to wince at parochialism and to minimize the distinctive imprint of American culture on his thought. In contrast, Tanaka ceaselessly demanded a new *Japanese* philosophy and castigated the inability of Japanese scholars to critique foreign thought, culture, and institutions. Neither he nor his contemporaries could ever forget the national and cultural differentiation from the West that colored every aspect of debate over domestic issues and social philosophy.

Assimilating Western ethics was the purpose of the Teiyū Ethical Society (Teiyū Rinrikai), the first scholarly group that Tanaka joined after his return to Japan. The society published its proceedings in a monthly journal, and its members included such eminent philosophical and literary pundits as Kuwaki Genyoku, Anezaki Masaharu, Nakashima Tokuzō, Takayama Chogyū, Ukita Kazutami, Motoora Yujirō, Tomonaga Sanjūrō, and Ōnishi Hajime. Their writings challenged the ethical claims of the Imperial Rescript on Education, groped for intellectual standards that offered progress without treason, and evidenced some of the ambiguities of dissent under censorship.

The society spelled out its ambition to articulate a new, more individualistic and assertive ethic for the new Japan:

Although our country's civilization has made great strides since the Restoration, for too long now the root of morality has been left unattended. On the one hand, the submissive morality that was customary in the feudal age still controls the greater part of the people's hearts and minds; on the other hand, the complementary ideals of utilitarianism and rights received from Western tradition have already imparted a new direction to the people's moral concepts. . . . The disharmony of old and new brings chaos in social morality. . . . Even if loyalty to the sovereign and patriotism are necessary, their activity will have no life unless they strike the people's hearts; they must be rooted in fundamental human nature, and foster enlightenment.[27]

Rejecting the idea that the state was best served by docile and passive imperial subjects, the manifesto questioned the necessity of "loyalty to the sovereign and patriotism," and it demanded new answers to the unattended problem of an appropriate ethic for modern Japan.

Members of the Teiyū Ethical Society naturally differed in their specific prescriptions for the new morality, but they disclaimed any political motivation in their description of "utilitarianism and rights" as moral concepts that were "complementary" to "feudal . . . submissive morality." Anezaki Masaharu, for example, described the society as "a group without an 'ism' " that existed solely for the purpose of "research and debate entirely free from any presuppositions."[28] Affirming no particular ethical theory and opposing none, the society rejected the "dogmatism very prevalent in Japanese education" that idealized "state supremacy" and "single-minded patriotism." It proposed to foster individual "ethical cultivation" (*rinriteki kyōyō*), which meant "ethical freedom of spirit, and the development of human value."[29]

Tanaka illustrated the group's pluralism by criticizing precisely the type of self-cultivation that distinguished the Teiyū Ethical Society's statement of purpose. To Tanaka, the excessive emphasis on ethical self-cultivation led to subjectivism and mysticism, thereby thwarting progress toward the resolution of objective social problems and toward the fulfillment of con-

27. Teiyū Rinrikai, "Teiyū Konwakai setsuritsu no shui," *Rinri kōenshū*, no. 1 (1900): 1.
28. Anezaki Masaharu, "Kaikai no shi," *Rinri kōenshū*, no. 1 (1900): 2–3.
29. Ibid.

crete human needs. The preoccupation with individual self-cultivation, as much as the ongoing efforts to revive Confucianism and Bushido, demonstrated the contemporary malaise of intellectuals who failed to appreciate the new type of society evolving under the impact of modern science and technology.[30]

Tanaka bemoaned those Japanese "scholars, administrators, and educators" who propagated ethical formulas inimical to the development of industrial society and to the development of complementary forms of politics, education, ethics, art, and culture. Apropos the popular reaction to Japan's gains in power and prestige after the Russo-Japanese War, he judged:

> It is not surprising that the Russo-Japanese War, in which our country's power leaped from second or third class to first class, gave rise to a sort of religious spirit and fervor. It was at this time that the self-styled gods and prophets stepped forth. But however great Japan becomes, however rapidly, we are still human beings and will not likely find ourselves turned into gods. In any case the flattery of foreigners, and our own narcissism about the victory, have clearly caused a portion of our countrymen to lose all self-control and power of reflection.[31]

Tanaka felt that this type of national hubris impeded Japan's progress, and he launched a similar charge against the revival of outmoded institutions that he called "restorationism," the outlook that "does not understand the unique features of today's society, and despises and fears the present."[32]

Tanaka's hostility to the mystical patriotism and national self-worship surrounding the Russo-Japanese War failed to dampen his optimism about Japan's progress. He welcomed the unprecedented material wealth of his age, and scorned those who claimed this prosperity had caused a decline in morality:

> My opinion is that on the contrary our morality is undergoing unprecedented progress. . . . The reform of laws, the consolidation of constitutional government, the spread of education, the

30. Tanaka, "Jiyū shisōka no rinrikan," 149–233.
31. Ibid., 188–89.
32. Ibid., 201.

advance of learning, the rise of technology, and the expansion of colonies, all demonstrate the health of our national morality.[33]

In the immediate aftermath of the Russo-Japanese War, he saw constitutional government, industrialization, and colonization as being firmly linked together in the march of progress, a judgment he would not revise until the beginning of the Taishō era. He easily resigned himself to the casualties of Japan's unprecedented progress:

> In an age of rapid change, naturally old customs cannot immediately be reconciled with new demands, and we lapse into the miseries of bankruptcy, insanity, and suicide. . . . But from the viewpoint of society as a whole, these are minor points. . . . That these few should be fated to suffer these miseries, for the sake of the increase of all our wisdom and spirit, cannot be called a decline in morality.[34]

Rejecting the Social Darwinist outlook, which allotted the miseries of progress to the unfit, and the socialist view, which traced these miseries to the class struggle, Tanaka regarded the signs of social and individual tensions as rather random products of an age of abrupt discontinuity and international competition.

Tanaka, along with the vast majority of his contemporaries, viewed Japan's ability to compete with the West in industry, and to guarantee its national security, as desirable and necessary goals that were yet to be achieved. Nevertheless he labored to avoid a one-sided and irresponsible preoccupation with national power. The great task was the creation of a new Japanese personality, a new citizenry that could maintain and develop modern society.[35] The Japanese government, as Tanaka saw it, was thwarting the emergence of a more assertive, informed, and capable citizenry through censorship and indoctrination, which expressed a paternalistic insistence on loyalty and obedience. He did not deny the crucial role of the state in the reconstruction of society, but thought that the government must strike a balance between laissez-faire and inter-

33. Ibid., 228–29.
34. Ibid.
35. Ibid., 169, 171.

ventionist policies. The specific form and measures of government could never be proclaimed according to abstract or universal principles,

> but however the forms and measures change, there is one thing that must be the purpose of government: that is to increase the power and wisdom of the people. As for increasing their happiness, of course that should be the principal intent of all governments; but in the final analysis that happiness is, and must be, their power and wisdom. This is why paternalism is the enemy of the people's happiness.[36]

The Japanese state ought to intervene in society to encourage the people's political education rather than to suppress new ideas.

Tanaka's critique of paternalism challenged the conservative axiom that, while democracy might be an ideal form of government, it was entirely beyond the capacities of the Japanese people in the foreseeable future. Tanaka, like many liberals, urged the government to be more representative even though he held strong reservations about his countrymen's ability to understand the complexities of foreign and domestic affairs. He thought that participation would educate the public, and that the government was perversely enforcing ignorance:

> Recently books have often been proscribed. Not all books display high standards, or are written by great persons. I realize that some must be proscribed for the sake of prevailing customs and public security. But among those proscribed by administrators are some that proclaim the spirit of the age. These cannot be suppressed by mere administrative measures. For example, even the most unfair form of expression is the faithful testimony of some individual, and it is the duty of governors to tolerate such things. Why? Because humanity, in the needs of its existence, avoids extremes and seeks the middle road; an extreme opinion is opposed by a fair opinion.[37]

Much of what government censors deemed "dangerous thought," Tanaka concluded, was the innocuous personal testimony of some individual, which most people would not find

36. Ibid., 213.
37. Ibid., 215.

convincing. Yet the most shocking or outrageous opinion might be useful in some way. The duty of the governors was to tolerate individual self-expression for the sake of the continuing advance of society by means of what Oliver Wendell Holmes called "the free market of ideas," a concept far more appealing to Tanaka than a free market in economics.

Tanaka was unruffled by the degenerate youth who distressed other writers and provoked the official guardians of public morality. He severely criticized the rash of decrees and maxims by which the Ministry of Education proposed to restore proper morality after the Russo-Japanese War:

> The admonitions which forbid luxury and license, or visits to the theater and the reading of novels, all aim at imposing external restrictions on the students' behavior. . . . Not only are these admonitions useless, but pernicious.[38]

Students needed to cultivate reason rather than sentiment, and to develop individual judgment. The continuous stream of edicts from the Ministry of Education was just one aspect of an oppressive governmental paternalism. Far from remedying whatever shortcomings the people might display, paternalism merely perpetuated and exacerbated those shortcomings.

A more central issue was the substantive content of the primary school ethics courses (shūshin). Tanaka treated the concept of loyalty, the core of ethical instruction, as an outmoded appeal to sentiment rather than an exercise of reason appropriate to modern society:

> The love of a retainer for his lord was originally a relationship of interest in which the lord bestowed his protection. The submission of the follower to his lord to the point of throwing away his life appears to utterly nullify his original aim in entering into the relationship. . . . It is very illogical . . . but the original idea of self-interest has not been destroyed but rather transformed into something greater. Externally directed patriotism, or martyrdom, arises from the same type of motive, and advances by the same process. This phenomenon may be the most beautiful and majestic in

38. Ibid., 218.

moral life, but it is not reached by intellectual standards. It results
from the workings of emotional valuation.[39]

This passage, written during the tense year of Kōtoku Shūsui's
trial for treason, left considerable doubt as to the value of self-
denying loyalty in the present. However, Tanaka hoped that
loyalty, externally directed patriotism, and martyrdom would
gradually decline in the future.

Several years later, Tanaka held forth more boldly. Granting
the necessity for a balance of rational and emotional activity
in individual life, he claimed that any social ethic based on
emotional valuation tended to become separated from its original historical basis in human interest, and to resist reasonable
and necessary change:

> I believe it is perfectly well to abandon or alter a minor interest
> for a major one, but dangerous to transcend the idea of self-
> interest entirely. This is the behavior of a fanatic, and it is ex-
> ceedingly dangerous. . . . These emotional moralities, since they
> have no direct objective standard, cannot be changed and recon-
> structed to fit the situation. One must simply choose between
> abandoning them completely or preserving them intact forever.
> . . . If we do not get away from a devotion close to superstition in
> moral situations, we cannot advance our welfare.[40]

Primary school ethics courses were utterly incompatible with
modern science. The attempt to teach science and *shūshin* together would, he predicted, produce graduates who were in-
capable of either ethical behavior or scientific inquiry.[41]

In one sense, Tanaka's flexible and gradualistic social philosophy mirrored the eclectic construction of a modern state
and its industrial base in nineteenth-century Japan. In another
sense, he implicitly challenged the ideology of the Meiji Restoration, which was founded on the concept of the *kokutai* (national polity). As conservatives elaborated the *kokutai* at the
outset of the Taishō period, it acquired several implications
hostile to democracy. First, individualism was incompatible

39. Ibid., 245–46.
40. Tanaka Ōdō, "Rinri shisō kaihō no yōkyū," *TJ* 3, no. 7 (1912): 940–41.
41. Tanaka Ōdō, "Ichi no rikai to shiryoku o kakeru Nihon," *Chūgai* 2, no. 1 (Jan. 1918): 46–47; idem, "Wakaki josei no tame ni gakusei no igi o kōzu," in *Ōdō joseikan,* Bungei tetsugaku kōza, no. 5, 41.

with the emperor system, which demanded absolute loyalty
and obedience. Second, any possible harmonization of the two
derived from imperial benevolence and the unity of monarch
and people unique to an unflawed and inimitable Japanese
history. Finally, the corporate imperial state transcended not
only individual interests but the whole people, extending from
past to future. The ideology was repugnant to Tanaka because
of its hauteur toward concrete social situations, and its isolation
of Japan and the Japanese on a higher moral plane than other
nations. He called for a new national ethos that would self-
consciously adapt to social and technological change. Direct
denunciation of the imperial ideology, however, left a writer
subject to publication bans, harassment, loss of employment,
imprisonment, or execution. Hence Tanaka propounded an
alternative, "radical individualism," which denied that state
and moral aims could be conceived except on a basis of ever-
changing individual interests. Inspired by William James's *The
Will to Believe*, which distinguished James's radical empiricism
from previous empiricisms, Tanaka's radical individualism
proposed to remedy the defects of previous individualisms,
not by discarding them and seeking out new principles, but
rather by developing individualism to its ultimate meaning.[42]

Tanaka blamed the old, individualistic political philosophies
for assuming that "the individual's happiness necessarily collides with the culture of the past and with the interests of other
individuals."[43] In real life, he saw conflicting desires within one
individual, and conflicts among different individuals, tending
to work themselves out over time. Solutions were possible
through reflection, debate, and evolutionary change in self
and society. Tanaka examined this process of societal debate
and resolution from an individual, rather than a social, viewpoint. Instead of viewing cooperation in terms of an individual's submission to some abstract conception such as the
"common good," Tanaka saw cooperation in terms of the in-

42. Tanaka, "Tettei kojinshugi," in *Tettei kojinshugi* (1918). For some early Taishō
interpretations of the *kokutai* as antithetical to individualism, see Oda Yorozu, "Kokutai
to minsei," Inoue Tetsujirō, "Kokumin shisō no mujun," and Uesugi Shinkichi, "Minponshugi to minshushugi," all in Ōta Masao, ed., *Shiryō: Taishō demokurashii ronsō shi*,
vol. 1.
43. "Tettei kojinshugi," 28–29.

dividual's internalization of the habits and opinions of his social group. The individual could reconstruct these habits and customs to suit his own temperament and interests:

> Throughout his life the individual constructs a variety of means with which to express himself, but at first he must use existing forms. In his scrutiny and appreciation of these existing forms, he gradually creates anew those forms appropriate to his self-expression. . . . What is called imitation is actually for him a type of creation, the early stage of creation.[44]

As Japan's imitation of Western ways matured into autonomous creation, so Japanese citizens could recreate their politics and culture, stripping authority of its mystique.

> Who can plan, consider, and accomplish changes in the law? There is no one other than the individuals who are charged with respecting the law. . . . Rather than law-abiding, we must become law-creating.[45]

The description of all citizens as law-creating was a bold assertion in a country where the Constitution was considered not a contract or an expression of subjects' rights, but a gift from the divine emperor. Where suffrage was limited to male property owners and women were forbidden to attend political meetings, Tanaka advocated woman suffrage, a rare position even with the democratic movement.

Tanaka's "radical individualism" located society's potential for communication and cooperation within the experience of individuals who internalized and then reconstructed existing institutions:

> The individual carries on his life together with other individuals who are continuing the culture of the past. This is the only way he can preserve and develop his own life. If necessary he can cultivate "public morality"; he can admire "universal feelings"; he can build "eternal laws"; and it is possible, to the extent that these views can be adapted to the life and ideals of other individuals, that "objectivity" can be discovered. But at bottom, from start to finish, these generalities depend on the individual's acquiescence,

44. Ibid., 31–32.
45. Ibid., 32–33.

with his experience as its basis, from the standpoint of his individuality.[46]

All values, laws, moralities, as well as notions of "the state" or "society," that claimed to transcend individual experience were merely empty abstractions, metaphysical entities.

Tanaka's radical individualism was firmly rooted in his analysis of Japan's history and the contemporary democratic movement, and thus it differed from the Chicago pragmatism. Dewey, for example, assigned equal importance to examining human activity from the point of view of individuals and that of society, insisting that either viewpoint described the same process:

> All ethical theory is two faced. Society is always a society of individuals, and the individual is always a social individual. . . . But we can state one and the same process (as, for example, telling the truth) either from the standpoint of what it effects in society as a whole or with reference to the particular individual concerned.[47]

Similarly, Mead posited the group as prior to the formation of the individual self through the medium of language, and he also noted that any institution (such as science) could be described as the activities of individual persons making discoveries, sharing and communicating them.[48] Thus the Chicago school presented the choice of the social or individual viewpoint as a matter of intellectual method.

The profound differences between the social and intellectual environment of Japan and that of the United States in the early twentieth century readily explain the different emphases of Dewey's and Tanaka's instrumentalism. Dewey, brought up in the Vermont home of a small merchant of Congregationalist faith, saw little need to convince his readers of the virtues of personal independence. He intended to combat the evils of laissez-faire capitalism with his assertion of a co-

46. Ibid., 17–18.
47. Dewey, "Ethical Principles Underlying Education," in *The Early Works of John Dewey*, vol. 5, 55–56.
48. George H. Mead, *Movements of Thought in the Nineteenth Century*, ed. Merritt H. Moore, 405–06.

operative new individualism that permitted experiments in social engineering. Tanaka, disenchanted with the social engineering of the Meiji state and its deliberate revamping of outmoded hierarchical and authoritarian values, seized upon individualism as the more essential value. Both men denied any fundamental or inherent contradiction between the individual and society, and each stressed that facet of human activity, individualism or cooperativism, which he found weakest in his own society. Their freedom to choose concepts appropriate to their social circumstances was explicit and fundamental in their instrumentalist philosophy.[49]

The flexibility of Dewey's instrumentalism afforded it an impact in Japan beyond that of nineteenth-century liberal philosophies. Whereas laissez-faire economic individualism and Social Darwinism transmuted untrammeled self-interest into general welfare by means of universal laws, Japanese thinkers tended to locate the wellsprings of human progress in deliberate and conscious action rather than abstract mechanisms. Thus Dewey's pragmatic liberalism was far more palatable than laissez-faire or natural rights. Freedom of action, however, in Japan was the exclusive prerogative of the state; in fact it was the most theocratic version of state ideology that afforded the greatest freedom of action, as evidenced in the institutional iconoclasm of the Meiji state-builders. To reform a state possessed of such a claim, Tanaka believed, there was no means other than an aroused and self-conscious people.

Tanaka's insistence on individual psychology and education as the seedbed of political reform gained credence after the end of World War I, as liberals became frustrated by the failure of legislative victories to bring about social and cultural change. The government of party leader Hara Kei in 1918, initially viewed as a democratic triumph, actually tightened state control over education and renewed the state onslaught against so-called dangerous ideas. At this point the reform of education, and the creation of a new citizenry capable of transforming society and politics, became a major theme within the democratic movement.

49. Dewey, *Individualism Old and New*, 85.

Two of Tanaka's colleagues in the Taishō democratic movement, Anezaki Masaharu of the Teiyū Ethical Society and journalist Kimura Kyūichi, a Waseda professor, directed their
attention to the archaic and despotic mentality cultivated in
public education. Castigating the repressive nature of the Japanese educational system, Anezaki equated the emerging
movement on behalf of the rights of workers and women with
a societal demand that individuals should be treated as ends
in themselves rather than as means to strengthen the state.[50]
Kimura Kyūichi rejected governmental paternalism in favor
of government *by* the people, using the biological analogy that,
in citizens as in all living creatures, potentialities atrophy if not
used. Kimura propounded the Montessori method in education, which encouraged children to develop by means of their
own spontaneous impulses, and he connected this form of education to the development of democracy in Taishō Japan, and
ultimately to the "liberation of mankind."[51]

The editorials of *Tōyō keizai shinpō*, crafted by Tanaka's student Ishibashi Tanzan and other graduates of Waseda University, argued that the greatest barrier to Japanese democracy
was the government's continuing propagation of values and
social relationships inherited from the age of feudalism and
despotism. The demand for a new education for the freedom
and enlightenment of individuals, especially youth and
women, who would transform society and politics was embla-
zoned throughout the short-lived monthly *Tōyō jiron*. The *Jiron*
staff constituted the nucleus of the Liberal Lecture Society,
which, as Ishibashi recalled, stressed above all "the reform of
Japanese education."[52]

Japanese liberals were more courageous than naive in their
optimism. In 1919 Dewey, too, was cautiously optimistic,
prophetically judging that "unless the world overtly and on a
large scale goes back on democracy, Japan will move steadily

50. Anezaki Masaharu, "Jinponshugi to jikkō," in Ōta Masao, ed., *Shiryō: Taishō
demokurashii ronsō shi*, vol. 1.
51. Kimura Kyūichi, "Demokurashii no shinri," in ibid.
52. Ishibashi Tanzan, quoted in Inoue and Watanabe, eds., *Taishōki no kyūshinteki
jiyūshugi*, 8.

towards democracy."[53] (Dewey met with Tanaka, Anezaki, and other liberals, raising the question of whether the agreement resulted from his influence on their philosophy or from theirs on his view of Japan.) Faith in the liberating influences of education was fundamental to the Chicago school of pragmatism. Dewey's progressive educational theory relied heavily on George Herbert Mead's conception of the social self, which recognized the extent to which the self was formed by society and suggested that a new type of individual who would remold the larger society could be nurtured by control of the society of young children, especially in schools. According to Darnell Rucker, however,

> what has kept [Mead's] thought in the forefront of modern social science, however, are the clinical and even sinister implications of the socializing mechanisms he wrote about: we are fascinated by how thoroughly we are conditioned by our social environment, how little we are creatures of ourselves.[54]

If many Japanese advocates of educational and social reform shared Mead's optimism, they were stymied rather than fascinated by how thoroughly we are conditioned by our social environment. Anezaki, Kimura, Ishibashi, and Tanaka were all too aware of the manipulative uses of education and the media. They confronted phalanxes of pedagogues and politicians who asserted democracy and liberalism were socially destructive. The critics of democracy, for example Yoshida Kumaji, effectively captured the social self on behalf of an educational system that denigrated democracy and idealized the state.

Randolph Bourne and others criticized "an unhappy ambiguity in Dewey's philosophy as to just how values were created."[55] Similarly Tanaka's critics, especially idealist philos-

53. Dewey, "Liberalism in Japan," in *Characters and Events*, ed. Joseph Ratner, vol. 1, 169; see also "Japan Revisited: Two Years Later," in ibid.

54. Rucker, 149–50. Another American progressive optimistic about Japanese democracy, Charles Beard, judged in 1922 that "gradually the psychology of the people will adjust to the new facts of economic life," in *The Administration and Politics of Tokyo*, 149. Mead's *Mind, Self, and Society* was published in Japan in 1941 as part of a series on "Theories of Totalitarianism" according to Yasushi Adachi, "Aspects of Pragmatism in Japan," 29.

55. Randolph Bourne, "Twilight of the Idols," *Journal of the Seven Arts* 2 (1917): 696–97.

ophers such as Nishida Kitarō and defenders of the emperor's
transcendent divinity such as Mitsui Kōshi, demanded that Tanaka explain how he derived his ethics. Tanaka's instrumentalist position, that values rightly and properly emerged from
particular persons and particular temporal, social, and cultural
contexts, was distinct from his historical and ethical judgment
that individualism and democracy represented the dominant
and most suitable political values of modern, industrial society.
Both positions served him well during the first two decades
of the twentieth century, when philosophy, art, literature, and
the women's movement exalted the individual, and gains in
representative government appeared to prelude political democracy. During the Great Depression his vision of a peaceful
world of nations engaged in voluntary cultural exchange
would be overshadowed by the contention of mutually exclusive and belligerent national goals. In this context Tanaka
would be confronted with the dilemma of choosing between
those values that he thought ought to emerge from modern
industrial society, and those contrary values actually emerging
in Japan. He would reaffirm his cosmopolitan individualism
and lose the vast majority of his reading audience. Ishibashi
Tanzan would write the epitaph that, in 1932, marked Tanaka
as a lonely man: "A liberal in the true sense, a Japanist in the
true sense."[56]

56. *ITZ*, 2:254.

2

Literature: Shimamura Hōgetsu's Naturalism and Its Liberal Critics

The naturalist movement, flourishing for only a few years after the Russo-Japanese War (1904–05), marked the birth of a modern Japanese literature. The complex movement was united and unambiguous on certain points. The new literature was to be modern, which meant conversant with the latest Western styles; it was to be a source of national pride, though not the vehicle of chauvinism. It was to be Japanese, though the naturalists were profoundly ambivalent about their own aesthetic traditions. The national character of the new literature lay in a new relationship with its audience. Adoption of the vernacular style (*genbun itchi*), coupled with the mass literacy of the early twentieth century, created a national market. Plots and characters evinced far greater geographic and social mobility than there had been in the aristocratic palaces of the *Genji monogatari* or the townsmen's world within walls of the Tokugawa era. Moreover, naturalist writers were deeply concerned about their public influence, a concern they struggled to express and to reconcile with the personal quality of their creative impulses. In addressing the issue, they abandoned the Confucian ideal of learning in service to the state, and struggled to justify their existence as independent artists and professionals, engaging the attention of virtually all intellectuals.

New experiences, especially in modern education and geographic and social mobility, led to doubts about the meaning of individual experience. "The person who does not feel them may be lucky," observed Shimamura Hōgetsu.[1] He admired

1. Shimamura, *Kindai bungei*, 489.

poet and novelist Tokutomi Roka for his description of "the misery of victory" after the Russo-Japanese War. Culture and values had failed to keep pace with material and political change. Individualism and imported Western ideas had played a destructive role, inviting nativist and religious countercurrents and, according to Tokutomi, the "annihilation of the individual."[2] The quest for personal meaning was tortuous. Shimamura in one breath proclaimed the triumph of "self-love and self-life," yet in another speculated that "perhaps life is no more than a gray heart under a gray sky, lonely and desolate."[3] Tokutomi and Shimamura articulated the malaise of their generation of professionals, moved from predominantly rural origins to seek Western education and success in the capital.

Naturalist goals were social as well as aesthetic. The movement is often credited with having introduced the modern concept of the autonomous self (*kindai jiga*), a judgment that may surprise readers of French naturalist novels, especially those of Émile Zola, in which characters are the helpless prey of deterministic social and biological forces. Zola and his small coterie of followers, the core of Western naturalism in its most restricted sense, aimed to prompt reform by a rigorously materialist and scientific depiction of human subjugation. Japanese naturalists shared the technique of relentless description of the physical world; they felt the conditioning effects of society on individual behavior; they also shared the tone of protest and the aim of reform. Tayama Katai wrote on the dismay and horror of ordinary people during the Russo-Japanese War, Shimazaki Tōson sympathetically treated the plight of an outcaste, and many naturalist writers reveled in sexual passion, in both their highly publicized private lives and their literary works. Their chief target was the traditional family system. In the patriarchal stem family, the eldest male usually managed property and arranged marriages, younger members were subordinate to older ones, females to males, and the historical continuity of the household itself greatly outweighed any individual concerns of its members, especially the young. As portrayed by Shimazaki and Tayama, the family system forced

2. Ibid., 514.
3. Ibid., 7, 9.

strangers to live as husband and wife; it shackled talented young men to mundane pursuits in order to support their unwanted wives and children; it encouraged the parasitism of selfish and shiftless relatives on the talented and ambitious. Sometimes the demands of family loyalty even destroyed the household itself in a new society of individual competition.[4]

The concept of the individual hardly existed before the Meiji Restoration; until then, proper behavior was defined by class status and gender. In political thought, the public sphere (*kō* or *ōyake*) was identified with the imperial house and the bureaucratic functions of officials of talent and ability. Thus commoners were barred from politics (at least in theory), and their lives were irrelevant to higher culture. The private sphere (*shi* or *watakushi*, the standard term for "I") was defined negatively as behavior that failed to fulfill public ideals. The Japanese naturalists brought to their own society the discovery that individual experience and character were of the highest aesthetic and ethical significance. What linked Zola's seamy determinism with Henrik Ibsen's symbolic and metaphysical emancipation was their sympathy toward the individual lives of ordinary people, the assumption that such lives ought to be at the center of public and artistic attention. The discovery, despite its generality and lack of prescriptive import, marked "the emancipation of post-Restoration literature from unproductive dependence on extraneous models, both Western and Japanese," and defined the intellectual climate of the early twentieth century.[5]

Since the naturalists sought a means of individual escape from custom and convention, contemporary critics and later historians (such as Tatsuo Arima) charged them with blind adulation of physical instinct. All the naturalist writers and critics except Iwano Hōmei flatly denied this charge. (As will be shown, although Iwano did advocate unbridled instinct, he perversely identified instinct with social phenomena such as self-sacrifice in war and emperor worship.) Moreover, natu-

---

4. Katai Tayama, *The Quilt and Other Stories*, trans. Kenneth G. Henshall; Tōson Shimazaki, *The Family*, trans. Cecilia Segawa Seigle; Murakami, 229–30.
5. William F. Sibley, "Naturalism in Japanese Literature," *Harvard Journal of Asiatic Studies* 28 (1968): 169; Harootunian, "Between Politics and Culture."

ralist fiction, though permeated with sexual longing, unmistakably indicated the particular social origins of frustration. For example, Tayama's hero in *Futon* (The quilt) prefers his student, a lively and intellectual modern woman, over his passive, traditional wife, and Shimazaki's protagonist in *Ie* (The family) cannot forget that his wife has been coerced into the marriage by her parents. The characters' sexual frustration was inextricably connected to changing ideals and institutions; the social gave form to the biological.[6]

The subjective, often autobiographical character of the naturalist movement has prompted historians such as Arima to deny that it comprehended any significant elements of protest or defiance, and to conclude that it readily accepted the social and political status quo.[7] This interpretation ignores the movement's intellectual and political context. Three distinct groups in early twentieth-century Japan deemed naturalism a force for change, subversive or progressive. Governmental censors and quasi-official moralists repressed and condemned naturalism as destructive to the social order. Critics of the state such as Ishikawa Takuboku, Tanaka Ōdō, and Ishibashi Tanzan included the new literature among the allies of the common man even while attacking the movement's theoretical inadequacies. The naturalists themselves, especially Shimamura Hōgetsu, published essays opposing censorship, the traditional family system, and the subjugation of women. It seems more cogent to explain why naturalism in its own context expressed themes of protest and defiance that may be obscure to hindsight than to explain why contemporaries across the political spectrum were deluded as to the historic character of the movement.

First, the naturalists demanded a new morality predicated on the realities of human experience. For example, the explicit portrayal of sexual passion and frustration was an implicit argument for the reform, or abolition, of the existing marriage and family system in law and society. As Hasegawa Tenkei put it, naturalists sought the replacement of "authority" by "real-

6. Arima, 78.
7. Ibid. Certain censorship cases as well as the views of naturalists and liberals are elaborated below.

ity."[8] Scrupulous depiction of the lives and miseries of ordinary people was itself a recognized form of protest, echoing a rich tradition of peasant petition that Anne Walthall has called "the language of hardship."[9] In this tradition peasants narrated the rigors of livelihood in order to justify demands such as tax reduction and administrative reorganization. They appealed to the rulers' claims of benevolence and tested the government's legitimacy. The more intrusive Meiji state contracted the sphere of personal autonomy at the same time that Western intellectual imports justified self-assertion in an entirely new way and linked it with the well-being of society as a whole. Naturalism and Christian socialist protests against the Russo-Japanese War sprang up simultaneously, and both emphasized the constrained lives of the common people.[10]

Second, state ideology and censorship confirmed the rebellious character of naturalist literature. In the Imperial Rescript on Education of 1890, the Ministry of Education had reaffirmed the state's traditional commitment to defining and regulating morality, especially the virtues of loyalty and filial piety. The political meaning of filial piety was gradually developed with the concept of the family-state (*kazoku kokka*). As the divine ancestry of the emperor was the foundation of the national polity, so patriarchy was the foundation of the family. Meiji ideology held that family harmony, based on a hierarchy of age and sex, was not merely useful to the well-ordered state but was its microcosmic image, its organic component. In this context the value of filial piety could be construed as regulating an exceedingly wide range of personal behavior; in fact it was so construed. While school-children were drilled in models of obedience and service to family and state, literature was censored not only for "pornography," but for themes of domination, exploitation, and defiance within the family. Thus the

8. Hasegawa Tenkei, "Shizenha ni taisuru gokai," in *Meiji bungaku zenshū*, vol. 43, 187.

9. Anne Walthall, "The Ethics of Protest by Commoners in Late Eighteenth-Century Japan," 64–69. See also Irwin Scheiner, "Benevolent Lords and Honorable Peasants: Rebellion and Peasant Consciousness in Tokugawa Japan," in Najita and Scheiner, eds., *Japanese Thought in the Tokugawa Period*.

10. Matsumoto Kappei, *Nihon shingeki shi*, 56; Sannosuke Matsumoto, "The Roots of Political Disillusionment: 'Public' and 'Private' in Japan," in J. Victor Koschmann, ed., *Authority and the Individual in Japan: Citizen Protest in Historical Perspective*.

state upheld the naturalists' conviction that their personal experiences were of public significance. The naturalists' characters, utterly unconcerned with loyalty and filial piety, were
the reverse images of the state's model citizen, alike in their
fusion of public and private roles.

Finally, the structure of early twentieth-century society afforded a degree of generality to the naturalists' portrayal of
their own experience. While industrialization clearly defined
a new ruling class of high officials and great industrialists and
devastated some tenant farmers and traditional enterprises,
the middle ranks of society were yet inchoate. The old orders
of samurai, peasant, artisan, and townsman were fragmented
by considerable mobility both up and down the social scale,
but new industrial classes were barely born. The permanent,
male industrial workers in heavy industry constituted a small
minority, and unmarried country girls predominated in the
textile mills. Pioneers of the professional and managerial middle class generated and sustained naturalist literature. In this
society, both more traditional and more homogeneous than
the contemporary West, the naturalists, despite their autobiographical limits, treated three social issues of broad relevance:
the domination of the patriarchal stem family, the subordination of women, and the tension between the rural community and urban upward mobility."[11]

Popular reaction to the new literature is difficult to gauge,
but some naturalist novels were serialized in general-interest
journals such as *Chūō kōron*, or even in the major daily newspapers.[12] Periodicals were customarily passed from hand to
hand, especially in the provinces and among students. The
Ministry of Education acknowledged the influence of novels
in its continual injunctions against frivolous reading. Moralism, however, could not prevail against the public's appetite
for vicarious personal experience. Shimamura Hōgetsu observed:

> In the political parties and among the elder statesmen, in finance,
> foreign relations, and all matters, the public is most interested in

11. Sibley, 165.
12. Tsurumi Shunsuke, 121–29; Haruhara, 90–91.

persons. The center of interest is the yet undiscovered individual character. It is a kind of hero worship. It is the demand to become fulfilled and living beings.[13]

In Shimamura's view, the modern Japanese public scrutinized celebrities in the media in order to explore their own individual possibilities. The new citizenry also demanded greater fulfillment in work and family.

TOWARD A MODERN CULTURE

Shimamura was acutely conscious of his public responsibility as a writer. Although his fiction had little lasting impact, he profoundly influenced a generation of educated youth in his unsparing pursuit of an aesthetic philosophy for modern society. His student Ishibashi Tanzan wrote, "I am following the same road as Shimamura," but perceptively noted the greatest difference between them.[14] Unlike Shimamura, Ishibashi was certain life was intelligible. Superficially the two men could not have been more opposite in temperament and thought; while Ishibashi maintained a cool, occasionally cynical rationalism, Shimamura passionately grasped opposing concepts that could be reconciled only by flights of mysticism or poetry. It was his integrity in confronting his intellectual contradictions that left so profound an impression.

That literature and thought grew from personal experience was an article of faith among naturalists, as among philosophical pragmatists; yet Shimamura longed for a higher level of generality. Literature and literary theory, he wrote, required an integrated view of human nature, but philosophical certainty was possible only for the complacent, who had not experienced a life of struggle. His own trials as an orphan, groping for survival from the age of ten or eleven, had undermined his artistic and intellectual efforts:

> How could my ramshackle soul, now nearing forty, entertain a coherent philosophy? With my heart like an abandoned house, I am busy trying to hang onto a bed and a roof that doesn't leak.[15]

13. Shimamura, *Kindai bungei*, 487.
14. *ITZ* 1:16.
15. Shimamura, *Kindai bungei*, 2.

Certainly his childhood had been dreary. He was born Sasa-
yama Rōtarō in Iwami province (Shimane Prefecture) in 1871,
the eldest of four children of a formerly prosperous ironworks
manager ruined by foreign trade after the Restoration. After
the death of his mother, a chronic invalid, he managed to
study English while supporting himself by working in a hospital and a law court. Apparently his brothers and sisters also
left home while still young, for soon his father died, alone and
drunk, in a fire. Luckily a local official, Shimamura Bunkō,
recognized the talent of the young orphan and adopted him.
Sent up to Tokyo in 1890, Shimamura soon enrolled in the
political science department of Tokyo Senmon Gakkō (Waseda
University), and the following year transferred to the literature and philosophy department, where he worked with Ōnishi Hajime and Tsubouchi Shōyō. Upon graduation he began
editing and writing criticism for *Waseda bungaku*, which had a
circulation of two thousand copies and earned its editor fifteen yen a month, less than half the salary of a provincial
school teacher. The prestige exceeded the salary.[16] *Waseda bungaku* was "the center of the literary world of the naturalist era,"
and Shimamura soon became "the most influential of the Waseda literati" with broad impact in aesthetics and rhetoric, criticism and translation, and instrumental in the founding of
colloquial free verse and modern theater.[17] Shortly thereafter
he married his adopted father's niece, Shimamura Ichiko, who
would bear him four sons and three daughters.

His new family, who remained in Shimane while he pursued
his literary career in Tokyo and Europe, afforded little compensation for his lonely and bitter childhood. After he began
teaching at Waseda (hired with Tanaka to replace Ōnishi Hajime, who was in Europe), he formed warm and enduring relationships with his students, encouraging their visits to his
home and using his growing eminence to win them employment and publication opportunities. No concern of his students was too trivial: Ishibashi Tanzan recalled that Shimamura chided him that laced shoes were unsuitable apparel for

16. Yoshida, *Kindai bungei hyōron shi*, vol. 1, 729, 743; Yoshie Okazaki, *Japanese
Literature in the Meiji Era*, trans. H. Viglielmo, 71.
17. Robert Rolf, *Masamune Hakuchō*, 22.

a newspaper reporter, who had to remove his shoes upon entering a home for an interview. The host might be antagonized by the extra time the reporter took in relacing his shoes to depart! Though Ishibashi characteristically added that the extra time could be used to advantage, he was deeply touched by Shimamura's extraordinary solicitude.[18]

The turning point of Shimamura's intellectual life, as for so many writers of his generation, was his sojourn in Europe, between 1902 and 1905. At Oxford University he continued his study of aesthetics and psychology, attempted to grasp the historic and social context of Western literature, and enthusiastically attended the London theater. After eighteen months he transferred to the University of Berlin, where he continued to work in aesthetics and art history. While he was abroad Shimamura, like Tanaka, was overwhelmed with admiration for the achievements of Western technology and culture, but bitter toward Western arrogance and racism. In England at the outbreak of the Russo-Japanese War, he wrote:

> Formerly Europe, in its high-handed judgment of Orientals, Russians, and backward peoples, was accustomed to write off Asiatics as a loss in descriptions such as deceitful, cunning, brutal, and mean. The phrases Oriental treachery, Oriental cruelty, and Oriental servility were often heard. . . . Formerly Japanese shared the ill repute of China. Since the Sino-Japanese War, some persons understand that Japan is different from China, but that war could not win recognition of our country's position from the man in the street. For example, I am often asked when Japan became independent.[19]

For Shimamura the enemy in these two wars was neither China nor Russia, but Western hegemony. After his return to Japan, however, he never again addressed patriotic themes.

His fresh cultural perspective and familiarity with recent Western literary styles rapidly propelled him to prominence in criticism and drama. He resumed teaching at Waseda and editing *Waseda bungaku*, became the most definitive critic and theoretician of the naturalist movement, and joined Tsubouchi

18. *ITZ* 15:45, 59–60.
19. Ozaki Hirotsugu, *Shimamura Hōgetsu*, 24.

Shōyō's Bungei Kyōkai (Literary Society) for the study and
production of Western drama. Under Shimamura's direction
the group produced two of the most sensational events of early
Taishō culture, productions of Henrik Ibsen's *A Doll's House*
and Hermann Sudermann's *Magda*.

Shimamura heralded strong and individualistic heroines
like Nora and Magda as the dominant trend of modern society
and literature, and both characters were avidly discussed by
the fledgling feminist movement and its opponents. Meanwhile the lead actress in both productions, Matsui Sumako,
became Shimamura's lover. Tsubouchi, whose iconoclasm was
limited to literature, was appalled. He sent Shimamura traveling to Japan's ancient capitals, Kyoto and Nara, doubtless
hoping that a revitalized sense of the national past would restore him to honor, duty, and family, while Matsui was kept
in Tokyo for moral admonition. Failing to break up the relationship, Tsubouchi expelled the two from the Bungei Kyōkai, which dissolved as eminent writers and critics, formerly
of the naturalist movement, followed Shimamura and Matsui.
Personal and political concerns fused in the exodus, for the
celebrated Matsui resented her low pay, whereas Shimamura
and other dramatists discovered a new social realism in works
such as those of Gerhardt Hauptmann and dismissed Tsubouchi's favored individualistic heroes and heroines from the
new frontier of the avant-garde. Ishibashi described the fundamental issue as "democracy in art."[20] The new theater, the
Geijutsuza, was devoted to performing drama since Ibsen and
to awakening social consciousness. A still more spectacular
scandal followed Shimamura's death by influenza in 1918,
when Matsui hanged herself in the theater during a performance of *Carmen*, leaving as her last request that she be buried
with him, presumably in the Shimamura family plot with his
adoptive father, legal wife, and children. (Her request was
denied.)[21]

20. *ITZ* 1:507–09.
21. *ITZ* 1:509; Yoshida, *Kindai bungei hyōron shi* 1:801–04; Brian Powell, "Matsui
Sumako, Actress and Woman," in W. G. Beasley, ed., *Modern Japan: Aspects of History,
Society, and Literature*.

For a subordinate to follow a superior in death was a classic theme of the old warrior culture, and Matsui was clearly conscious of the tradition when she noted that Shimamura was her teacher (*sensei*) as well as her lover—a revered figure whose authority gave meaning to her own life. Such an attachment was remarkable in a woman celebrated as the ultimate symbol of liberation and Westernization in her time: the first actress in a society where men traditionally played women's roles, a relentless career woman who had left behind two husbands and several lovers in pursuit of her art. Matsui had earned her own living and defied public censure, played notoriously aggressive Western women in Western clothes and settings, and even possessed a Caucasian nose (by plastic surgery) and a buxom "Western" figure. Some contemporary journalists denounced her suicide as a final exercise in hysterical self-indulgence, but others compared her to the epitome of the old virtues, the stern General Nogi Maresuke, who had chosen to follow the Meiji Emperor in death in 1912.[22]

Shimamura's aesthetic theory, like Matsui's life, revealed traditional themes beneath its explicit preoccupation with the West. The first inspiration of his naturalism had been Jean-Jacques Rousseau's injunction to return to individual instinct as opposed to the artificial strictures of civilization. Yet instinct alone was uninspiring to Shimamura. He also mentioned Friedrich Nietzsche, Ivan Turgenev, and Leo Tolstoy as having inspired his literary goals: "the scrupulous depiction of the reality of life, and the positive hero."[23] Shimamura, like Turgenev and Tolstoy, was torn between the demands of art and the needs of society. Rejecting contemporary society and the mere realistic description of its frustrated victims, and also rejecting the tedium of reformist politics, he called for a literature of mystic vision, in which the "surface of extreme realism is lined with a sharply removed substance of absolute inexpli-

22. Nakayama Shinpei, Nakamura Kichizō, and Ihara Seiseien, "Hōgetsu—Sumako gōshi no ki," *CK* 34, no. 2 (Feb. 1919): 42–73; Kuwaki Genyoku et al., "Matsui Sumako no shi ni tsuite," *WB*, ser. 2, no. 159 (Feb. 1919): 27–34.

23. Shimamura, *Kindai bungei*, 12–13; see also Rufus W. Matthewson, *The Positive Hero in Russian Literature*, 111.

cability."[24] The nuances of emotional experience, and the mystery of life, had been among the dominant values of Japanese literature since at least the eleventh century, exemplified in the impressionistic and episodic character of Japanese poetry and poetic prose, and inspired by the Zen Buddhist quest for the ideal in daily reality through intuitive perception. Though some contemporary writers such as Nagai Kafū experimented with naturalism and then dismissed it as "Western literature . . . written in the Japanese language,"[25] scholars have noted continuities from the aesthetic and emotional individualism of late Tokugawa fiction and the traditional ideal—expression of the human heart—articulated by Murasaki Shikibu and Motoori Norinaga.[26] Hasegawa Nyozekan cogently expressed a syncretism akin to Shimamura's when he defined the *Genji monogatari* as a work of naturalism, urging that "civilization embraces not only 'the old' of one's own tradition, but equally 'the old' of foreign inheritance."[27]

It was in Western literature, especially in Ibsen, that Shimamura found powerful individual heroes and heroines who explicitly challenged social custom and convention. He described Ibsen's cultural milieu in terms that evoked the intellectual problems of contemporary Japan: "Among the pessimistic, a pure, passive contemplation was spreading; the only alternatives were activity or morality, and the main point was that Ibsen was in the latter camp."[28] For Shimamura, "activity" meant the utilitarian study of Western science and technology, the practical eclecticism of the Meiji state, the preoccupation of Meiji youth with material success and high status—in short, an escape from the broader issues of the human condition addressed by "morality." Shimamura looked to Ibsen for a sense of morality distinct from either unprincipled activity or passive contemplation.

24. Shimamura, *Kindai bungei*, 105–06.
25. Nagai Kafū, quoted in Mitsuo Nakamura, *Modern Japanese Fiction: 1868–1926*, 6 (see also 35–41).
26. Jun Etō, "Modern Japanese Literary Criticism," *Japan Quarterly* 12 (1965): 186; J. Thomas Rimer, *Modern Japanese Fiction and Its Traditions: An Introduction*, 16.
27. Nyozekan Hasegawa, *The Educational and Cultural Background of the Japanese People*, 16–17.
28. Shimamura, *Kindai bungei*, 332–33.

Morality, Shimamura believed, was the assertion of one's personal experience and inherent sense of truth. It permitted no compromise with contemporary society. Again he used Ibsen to prove his point:

> One can see the truth and portray its collision with contemporary society, or one can portray the ruin of truth itself. This is the root of Ibsen's pessimism. The strong individuality of the hero of *Brand* will not let him succeed, and he is destroyed. . . . Necessarily, the truth-tellers are always tragic; great heroes, but hopeless in their anguished efforts.[29]

Here the pessimism was more Shimamura's than Ibsen's. Ibsen dramatized an enormous transformative potential in everyday lives, such as that of the housewife Nora in *A Doll's House*. Ibsen's heroes, while winning few definitive secular victories (how is Nora to live after leaving her husband?), invoke triumphant vision and mysterious possibility, more than despair.[30]

A sense of victimization, pervasive in modern Japanese literature, stemmed in part from the writers' efforts to straddle two civilizations and cope with rapid change. "Victims," exclaimed one of Dazai Osamu's characters in the aftermath of World War II, "Victims of a transitional period of morality."[31] Later, Nobel Prize winner Kawabata Yasunari explained,

> Even after the beginning of the Meiji period in 1868, great men of letters appeared . . . but they had to spend their youthful time and energy in the study and introduction of Western literature. Many . . . were unable to reach maturity in their own creation grounded in the Japanese and Oriental traditions. Thus I tend to think they were victims of their age.[32]

Dazai and Kawabata expressed the dilemma of Japanese writers convinced that they must master Western literature, yet uncertain of its relation to their own creativity and culture. Shimamura's sense of alienation, however, was political and social as well as aesthetic.

---

29. Ibid.
30. Rolf Fjelde, trans., *Ibsen: The Complete Major Prose Plays*, 121.
31. Osamu Dazai, *The Setting Sun*, trans. Donald Keene, 187.
32. Yasunari Kawabata, *The Existence and Discovery of Beauty*, trans. H. Viglielmo, 42–44.

Governmental censorship goaded Shimamura to articulate his rationale for modern literature and to distinguish the good of society from the will of the rulers. Banning books (such as Kosugi Tengai's naturalist *Makaze koikaze* [Demon wind of love], serialized in the *Yomiuri* in 1903) was "not only an insult to the authors, but an injury to literature and an oppression of freedom of thought." Challenging the government's contention that censorship decisions were matters of law rather than the judgments of thought or morality, Shimamura noted that Kosugi's case had been settled not by law but by the administrative fiat of the Home Ministry:

> The legal right of self-defense has not been implemented; it is an instance of preventative interference. It is just like a school principal's decision, an educational attitude born of old-womanish solicitude. It is indeed a matter of thought and morality.[33]

Correctly noting the managerial character of Japanese censorship, Shimamura concluded that it stifled the creative development of art and society. He espoused the same argument as Tanaka, that individual self-expression served the best interests of society and culture as a whole. Though one particular writer or work might be pernicious and perverse, creativity and public enlightenment advanced through the process of free choice and open debate—the "free market of ideas."

Shimamura's protest against censorship was compromised when he joined the Bungei Iinkai (Committee on Literature), a governmentally sponsored effort at literary guidance formed in 1910 after the Kōtoku trial. The trial, resulting in stricter censorship and indoctrination in schools and community organizations, was a wrenching experience for contemporary intellectuals. As Nagai Kafū wrote after renouncing naturalism,

> of all the public incidents I had witnessed or heard of, none had filled me with such loathing. I could not, as a man of letters, remain silent in this matter of principle. Had not the novelist Zola, pleading the truth in the Dreyfus case, had to leave his country? But I, along with the other writers of my land, said nothing.[34]

33. Shimamura, *Kindai bungei*, 471–72.
34. Nagai Kafū, quoted by Edward Seidensticker, *Kafū the Scribbler: The Life and Writings of Nagai Kafū, 1879–1959*, 46.

For Nagai, the state's power to frame and execute Kōtoku was a bitter indictment of the new literature's search for public influence. During that year Shimamura, grappling with the same problem, courageously met with socialist Katayama Sen and anarchist Ōsugi Sakae, who were then the targets of severe police harassment, to discuss topics such as "art and practice."[35] He doubtless joined the Committee on Literature hoping to play a moderate and compromising role, and to bring standards of aesthetic quality to bear against governmental censorship.[36] Nevertheless, here he displayed more of the practical, Meiji success ethic than the transcendent morality he had earlier admired in Ibsen. Tanaka and Ishibashi supported the formation of the Committee on Literature on the similar grounds that it could inject an artistic perspective into governmental organization.[37]

Shimamura demanded a "practical morality" of "self-love and self-life,"[38] the free and responsible development of an individual's highest potential rather than either satisfaction of instinct or adherence to convention. For example, the relationship between men and women should be one of the "love of free individuals."[39] His new morality, of course, was quite as shocking to traditionalists as no morality at all, especially when those like Shimamura who were already married by the arrangement of their families flaunted the doctrine of free choice in love affairs. When his practical morality was berated for fracturing the social order, Shimamura retorted:

> Since naturalism is modern and destructive of traditionalism, it is naturally relevant to individualism and the social problem. . . . The two efforts of naturalism are to define society and to liberate the individual.[40]

35. Matsumoto Kappei, 57–60.
36. Nakajima Kotō, "Bungei Iin toshite tekitō na hito," *CK* 26, no. 7 (July 1911): 104; for an excellent account of the Committee on Literature see Rubin, *Injurious to Public Morals*, especially 113, 198, 200, 207, and 210 on Shimamura's role.
37. *ITZ* 1:73–75; Tanaka, "Bungei hogo mondai," *CK* 25, no. 4 (Apr. 1910): 140–42.
38. Shimamura, *Kindai bungei*, 7–8.
39. Shimamura, "Kindai bungei to fujin mondai," *CK* 28, special issue on "Fujin mondai" (July 1913): 9–10.
40. Shimamura, *Kindai bungei*, 67.

The collapse of the hierarchical status system and its concomitant ethos precipitated the need for an internal, self-generated morality:

> One will not penetrate the meaning of morality apart from the central gist of one's own life. When one opens one's eyes, one faces not a god or Buddha, but oneself. Thus the self is a god and a Buddha.[41]

Individual moral transformation, and not state paternalism, was to be the true wellspring of social reform.

The radical distancing of selfhood from culture and custom in naturalist theory made it difficult to discover the content of the self. Shimamura was unable to conduct his own life according to new, internal principles; he "often capitulated to conventional morality"[42] because he was "easily defeated by sympathy and pity (*nasake-make*)."[43] More bluntly, "It is all very well to be autonomous, but it is hard to be away from one's wife and children."[44] While it was the strong individuality of Ibsen's heroes that doomed them to tragedy, Shimamura suggested, his own emotional susceptibility to custom and personal ties jarred with his individualistic art and thought. His confessional essays recall the Japanese tragic hero—loyal and sincere but unable to act decisively in a world of manipulative corruption, acquiescing passively in his inevitable destruction—rather than the positive hero of the Russian radicals or the individualistic hero of Western tragedy.[45]

The naturalists, revolting against the traditional family and community, and rejecting unassimilated Western theories, found that the very nature of personal experience eluded them. One means of investigation was the "I-novel" (*watakushi shōsetsu*); naturalists "frequently restricted the viewpoint in their narrative to a single alter ego . . . [and] renounced the author's prerogative to recreate his own wider vision of reality."[46] With the viewpoint restricted to the momentary impres-

41. Ibid., 8.
42. Ibid., 5.
43. Ibid.
44. Ibid., 4.
45. See Ivan Morris, *The Nobility of Failure: Tragic Heroes in the History of Japan.*
46. Sibley, 163.

sions of a single protagonist, the social forces affecting the individual—which emerged with excruciating clarity in European naturalism—took on the nebulous shading of a Japanese ink painting. The I-novel was rooted in the peculiarly momentary and inchoate character of the naturalists' definition of experience, which, as Shimamura defined it, excluded all abstractions such as "individualism, socialism, instinctualism, even nihilism" because such ideas "all attempt to foresee an end to the process of destruction and reconstruction."[47] Of course Shimamura rejected the more blatant sort of ideological literature, praising Ibsen's social drama for artistic quality in contrast to "those problem plays that can be mistaken for an exercise in arithmetic."[48] While eulogizing the self, he was apologetic about the intrusion of thought: "As an individual one thinks about society, and science; choosing these as means, one resolves to portray the materials before one's own eyes; one cannot help defending the ground of one's ideas."[49] The tentative admission of thought to literature marks Shimamura's partial escape from the Tokugawa intellectual universe in which thought was objective and universal, belonging to the public realm of the rulers; feeling was subjective, constricted within the private realm of commoners and artists—to what remained after the removal of all public affairs.

Since Shimamura would not abandon the moral and social purpose of literature but was reluctant to articulate that purpose, he finally had to invoke a contemplative mysticism in order to state the relationship between the private and public realms:

> When we finish and set the book aside, we are inspired by a sort of contemplative mood, and cannot help reflecting on various human problems. . . . This may be called the religious mood that succeeds the arts. If it becomes resolved, it becomes a new religion or a new morality. Thus naturalism leads us to the gates of religion.[50]

47. Shimamura, *Kindai bungei*, 97.
48. Shimamura, "*Ningyō no ie* to Ipusen no sakugeki jutsu," *CK* 28 (Spring supplement, Apr. 1913): 128.
49. Shimamura, *Kindai bungei*, 94.
50. Ibid., 106.

The specifics of moral or social purpose—the forms that these might take if "resolved"—were outside the sphere of the artist, who served to envision infinite possibility. In Shimamura's pluralistic and open-ended vision, the reader was autonomous, free to form his or her own conclusions. The artist might serve as the eyes of the public, or even its conscience, but not its mind.

Shimamura's founding of the Geijutsuza with Matsui Sumako in 1913 defined a new dynamic of selfhood and public influence. The affair that led to their expulsion from the Bungei Kyōkai had begun when Shimamura was deeply depressed; he had been ill, and his wife (still living apart from him in Shimane after eighteen years of marriage, seven births, and two infant deaths) was said to have had hysterical tendencies.[51] His personal assessment of his impressive literary career was doleful:

> I'm forty-two, an unlucky age of biological and spiritual crisis. Until now I've been most ambitious, studying, disciplining myself, and working hard to achieve some measure of success, but I've accomplished nothing. The human span is a mere fifty years. When I wonder how much I'll be able to realize my own will in my last few years, my past life seems tiresome indeed. I'm planning a great revolution in my life—trying out my own desires.[52]

To the extent that such a passage can be taken at face value, Shimamura's eulogies of the self in the naturalist movement had been an intellectual commitment, perhaps a career strategy, rather than a personal plan of action. Upon founding the Geijutsuza he resigned his teaching position at Waseda, abandoned his academic writing, and devoted himself completely to the new theater and the popularization of a new culture.[53]

The Geijutsuza was to be the center of an ongoing festival of art:

> To my way of thinking, this theater is not a luxury. I would like the building to be a kind of club, ultra-modern in style, with a most approachable feeling to it. I would like to have a cafe, a

51. Matsumoto Kappei, 56–57.
52. Quoted by Yoshida, *Kindai bungei hyōron shi* 1:801.
53. Ōzaki Hirotsugu, 29–30.

clean and bright dining hall, and an occasional musical performance, or a very few individual exhibitions of painting or sculp-
ture, among the tables. It could be a romantic place with poets
writing and pasting their work on the walls, and people singing
along with mandolins. Literary people, bankers and businessmen,
officials and students, would all stop on their way home from
work, refreshing themselves amid all the arts. Diners would be
able to get a pass for the adjoining theater and go on in, with a
different impression from the usual mercantile management of
theater ticket counters.[54]

In fact "mercantile management" and the elite élan of Shimamura's vision were critical in actually reaching the public.
Partners in the theater were the literati Ihara Seiseien, Nakamura Kichizō, and Nakayama Shinpei, with many smaller con-
tributors.[55] Ishibashi Tanzan joined the theater's advisory
board and enthusiastically sent a list of twenty-nine subscribers, probably from *Tōyō keizai shinpō*.[56] Admission averaged one
yen (three *sen* for third balcony seats), postponing financial
success despite sell-out crowds and prompting the famous ac-
tor Sakamoto Gurendō to tell Shimamura he was too honest
to run a theater. Still the Geijutsuza benefited from the enormous publicity and popularity that had attended Shimamura's
last two productions with the Bungei Kyōkai, Ibsen's *A Doll's
House* and Sudermann's *The Home*. Rave reviews of Matsui's
performances, her release of Japan's first hit record, and of
course the added attraction of scandal all supported the new
venture. Attendance figures are difficult to obtain, but Shimamura recorded three thousand people in only three days
at a later production of Tolstoy's *Resurrection* in Kyoto; most
productions toured widely in the provinces, and even went to
Korea, Manchuria, Taiwan, and Vladivostok. Thus Shimamura
reached a much wider audience than he had as professor and
editor of *Waseda bungaku*. Financial success, and proof of his
definitive role in the popularization of modern drama, came
on the eve of his sudden death in November, 1918.[57]

54. Quoted in ibid., 30.
55. Ibid., 40.
56. *ITZ* 15:350–51; Shimura, 118.
57. Yoshida, *Kindai bungei hyōron shi* 1:803–04; Matsumoto Kappei, 70, 85–87, 90;
Ozaki Hirotsugu, 42.

NATURALISM, THE STATE, AND SOCIETY

Because of its self-conscious quest for public influence, naturalist literature from its beginning attracted the attention of commentators on politics and society. Several of the most acute analysts charged that naturalism failed to fulfill the promise inherent in its vernacular language, its appealing personal themes, and its claims of social relevance. Most notably, poet and essayist Ishikawa Takuboku and Tanaka Ōdō sympathized with the naturalists' rejection of traditional morality but criticized the movement's ambivalence toward state and society and its paucity of serious analysis. Tanaka observed that the experience the naturalists sought to portray was in fact dominated by "customary morality and paternalistic ideas"; echoing Marx, he urged that the point was not to portray reality, but to change it.[58] Ishikawa charged that the naturalists indirectly challenged the state, which legislated and indoctrinated custom and paternalism, but failed to make that challenge explicit. Under the influence of naturalism, "young men laugh at those who think seriously about the state, just as they laugh at faithful wives or husbands, or those who are not excessively sensitive."[59] Thus the movement was "not merely contradictory at first glance, but more and more contradictory the longer one looks."[60] It evaded the state's demands without rejecting them at the theoretical level or creating alternatives. Still he credited naturalism with a liberating impact on modern Japanese thought, recalling that young men of Meiji had turned to religion in search of their individuality, until "naturalism turned science from our enemy into our ally."[61]

Both naturalism and pragmatism regarded science as a means to the emancipation of the self, in contrast with the early Meiji sponsorship of science for state ends. Naturalism and pragmatism, both strongly influenced by Darwin, viewed evolutionary change as an opportunity for the assertion of human will rather than a sentence of subjugation to blind natural

58. Tanaka, "Waga kuni ni okeru shizenshugi o ronzu," *Myōjō* (Aug. 1908): 82.
59. Ishikawa Takuboku, *Takuboku zenshū*, vol. 10, 3–6.
60. Ishikawa, "Jidai heisoku no genjō," in *Gendai Nihon bungaku zenshū*, vol. 32, 205–10.
61. Ibid., 210.

law. There were other points of congruence between pragmatist philosophy and the naturalists' literary theory: a polemical attack against abstraction and over-intellectualization, a
quest for the nature of humanity in actual experience, and a
rejection of old religions and moralities. Tanaka conceded that
he shared three basic assertions with the naturalist movement:

1. That humanity should place value on the present alone.
2. That human activity ought in essence to be unitary and
   indivisible.
3. That individuals ought to have as their sole purpose the
   satisfaction of their desires.[62]

The commonalities were unsurprising, since Waseda University was the center of both naturalism and pragmatism. As
Tanaka went on to express his disagreements with the naturalists, he dubbed his colleague Shimamura his "most worthy
foe" among the naturalist theorists.[63]

Tanaka particularly took exception to the naturalists' division of reality into human nature, on the one hand, and custom or convention on the other, and to their exaltation of
human nature over custom in their stress on *jikkan* or true
experience. Drawing on his Western psychological theory, Tanaka argued that *jikkan* might mean "emotion," or "sensation,"
and that, in any case, *jikkan* constituted but one part of the
whole of human experience, which always included a logical
and reflective function as well.[64] By slighting intellect the naturalists obscured the unique and definitive features of human
experience. Also rejecting the idea that "true" perception or
experience demanded a complete break with custom and convention, Tanaka denied that such a break was conceivable for
human beings, who, from birth, assimilated the experience of
others—their parents, siblings, friends, and teachers—and the
written and oral traditions of their society.[65] To Tanaka, in-

62. Tanaka, "Iwano Hōmei Shi no geijutsukan to jinseikan to o ronzu," *CK* 24,
no. 9 (Sept. 1909): 21.
63. Tanaka, "Waga kuni ni okeru shizenshugi o ronzu," 58.
64. Ibid., 13–15.
65. Ibid.

dividual and personal experience was also communicable because it derived from language, culture, and society.

Tanaka detected the "birth pangs of the thought of the future" in the naturalists' insistence on the obsolescence of old religions and moralities, and on the need for new visions.[66] Admitting that the naturalists' position was arbitrary and extreme, he apologetically pointed to their ample provocation in the nature of existing society. Certainly he found their passionate quest for a new morality vastly preferable to the contemporary attempts to revive Confucianism and Bushido, and he distinguished his criticisms from those of governmental censors and defenders of conventional morality, who found "naturalism to be a complete error that ought, insofar as possible, to be repressed."[67] Censors and moralists misread Japanese society and history, which the naturalists merely ignored; and Tanaka agreed with Shimamura that the government's censors were under a far greater obligation of balance and restraint than were individual naturalist writers.

Tanaka quarreled with the naturalists over the means by which they hoped to inspire a new social morality, especially their impressionistic accounts of their own experience in the I-novel. Effective reform had to begin with existing social reality, not with abstract or hypothetical notions of "true experience." The state upheld the familial concept of human nature; the naturalists (he believed) overemphasized extremes of individual sexual desire. Both views failed to show a spirit of experimental inquiry about society and history, and proved, Tanaka exclaimed, "how unpropitious is the air of our country for the generation of criticism!"[68] Thus he coupled his praise for the naturalists' advocacy of a new social morality with his criticism of their inability to relate how the new morality would evolve from existing society.

Tanaka's reservations proved well-founded when poet and essayist Iwano Hōmei developed a blend of "extreme individualism and extreme statism,"[69] which found total identification

66. Ibid., 3–4.
67. Tanaka, "Bungei hogo mondai," 140–42.
68. Tanaka, "Kinsei bundan ni okeru hyōron no kachi," in *Shosai yori gaitō ni*, 13–14.
69. Iwano, *Hōmei zenshū*, vol. 15, 373–74.

between the self and the emperor. Naturalism, to Iwano, meant the denial of all human ideals and purposes, religions and philosophies:

> Real humanity... is without ideals. It is without purpose. Ideals, purpose, resolution, are created from the presupposition of something as opposed to something else. Thus the autonomous self that absolutely forbids the existence of other things is, from start to finish, unresolved.[70]

The Japanese imperial institution, Iwano insisted, transcended human ideals and purposes, religions and philosophies:

> The organization of our imperial household and our people is a felicitous fusing of extreme individualism and extreme statism. Relative individualism, at the same time it asserts the individual's rights, recognizes the rights of others; it is based on erroneous notions like egalitarianism. But absolute individualism sets no hypotheses within the self's power (and thus his rights). . . . It does not conflict with the imperial house in the least.[71]

Following the views of German-trained constitutional scholars such as Hozumi Yatsuka, Iwano contrasted Western relative individualism with Japanese absolute individualism, in which the emperor was identified with the people. The unique characteristic of the emperor's personality was to be wholly benevolent, "public" in contrast to the "private" character of his subjects. Inclusion of the whole people in the imperial will freed the people from all limitations: "In our national polity the individual is the state, and the state is the absolute individual."[72] Giving a surprising twist to the conventional analogy of the state and the family, Iwano also held that in sexual relations, "the soul is absolutely embodied, and the body is absolutely ensouled."[73] He portrayed the individual as the vehicle of overwhelmingly powerful instincts, but the direction of those instincts was unclear. Defying the conventional family-

70. Ibid.
71. Ibid.
72. Ibid.; on Hozumi see Minear, *Japanese Tradition and Western Law*, 57–59, 79–83, 91–94, 187.
73. Takehiko Nochi, "Love and Death in the Early Modern Novel," in Albert M. Craig, ed., *Japan: A Comparative View*, 173.

state morality in his three marriages and innumerable scandals, Iwano took pains to reintegrate state and individual in his analysis of the Russo-Japanese War:

> It is said that our countrymen died in battle for the sake of the state, but in truth there is no other explanation than that their deaths were brought about by the instinctive character of individuals. What are called Japanese spirit and Bushido are in fact no more than the unadorned activities of individuals acting according to their instincts.[74]

In basing the state on the "instinct" of the "absolute individual"—the emperor and Japanese subject as one—Iwano disdained the constraints of law, society, and custom, and asserted that the ultimate reality of all social relationships was power. Government exemplified the personal expression of power: "What I call the superior man governs by means of his whole and unique personality, and has no time to think of his subjects, or of benevolence, justice, or international conditions."[75] The personal conception of the imperial will cast off conservative Confucian values such as benevolence and social harmony, generating a more modern, almost fascist vision of unbridled state power ruling a Darwinian society.

Iwano's tirade provoked Tanaka into writing one of his rare discussions of the state per se. In lieu of his usual denial of inherent dualisms, Tanaka accented the persistent tension between state and individual and dryly predicted that Iwano's fusion of "absolute individualism and absolute statism" would never be achieved in reality, "at least until the dawn of the golden age dreamed of by prophets and philosophers of old, in which the lambs can lie down in safety with the lions."[76] Tanaka scoffed at Iwano's insistence that the relationship of the individual and the state was a matter of instinct:

> The individual instinctively works to realize his own desires, and the age in which those fuse with the policies of the state is yet far off. As long as human nature is what it is, there will probably never be such an age.[77]

74. Iwano 15:373.
75. Ibid., 447.
76. Tanaka, "Iwano Hōmei Shi no geijutsukan to jinseikan to o ronzu," 67–68.
77. Ibid.

However, a harmonious adjustment was possible:

> By reflection on both sides, when the state resolves to respect in-
> dividual demands, and the individual resolves to rely on state pol-
> icies, then alone are individual rights fused with the life of the
> state.[78]

Tanaka cited England as an exemplary country that had
achieved the proper balance between individual demands and
state structure. Because of this balance, the English had
avoided the malaise of skepticism and despair that prevailed
among the youth and intellectuals of France, Russia, and Japan.[79] In contrast the imbalance of state and individual in Japan was due to the rapid development of the past few decades,
which had produced a sharp cleavage between state and the
social order.

The naturalist movement quickly peaked and dissipated in
the closing years of the Meiji era. A movement to protect the
Constitution keynoted the ensuing Taishō era as one of political activism, which had languished since the Popular Rights
movement in the 1880s. From this vantage point Ishibashi
Tanzan, relegating the naturalists to history, criticized the naturalists' lack of political and social theory but also judged that

> the naturalist literature movement gave a great stimulus to reform
> in Japanese moral concepts, far more than most people supposed.
> It was the age of overthrow of the family-state, and the beckoning
> light of individualism, democracy, and liberalism.[80]

The naturalists' sense of human diversity and contradiction,
their dreams and desires, remained with Ishibashi throughout
his life, enhancing his commitment to a free and pluralistic
society and meliorating his drive toward political and economic
rationality. In rejecting repressive laws and customs, Shimamura, Tanaka, and Ishibashi drew from the West, where industrialization appeared to afford the material basis for the
unprecedented assertion that the political and social world
might be ordered for the purpose of human happiness. Their

78. Ibid.
79. Tanaka, "Bungei no shōka," *TJ* 2 (July 1911): 976–77.
80. *ITZ* 2:174.

relationship was reminiscent of the Bloomsbury circle, which also attacked estrangement of the sexes, deadening social custom and convention, and public intolerance toward the creative artist. Both groups of writers were convinced that their frustration as artists stemmed from the entire social world. Thus, as Raymond Williams has judged, "the extreme subjectivism of, for example, the novels of Virginia Woolf, belongs within the same formation as the economic interventionism of Keynes."[81] The parallel to Shimamura's mysticism and Ishibashi's later Keynesian finance is a striking one. Shimamura and Ishibashi, as well as Tanaka, perceived themselves as allies in the transformation of an irrational socio-political order.

By demanding that literature lead moral consciousness, the naturalists encroached on a preserve the state considered its own. And their starting point was at the opposite pole from the state, the constrained daily lives of the common people rather than the national needs of wealth and power as perceived by the authorities. Such a challenge was in continual danger of either suppression or incorporation by the state; Shimamura's efforts were both censored (especially his production of *Magda*, discussed in the following chapter) and incorporated (in the Committee on Literature). The naturalists were vulnerable to manipulation because they had deliberately preserved ambiguity in their discussion of the relationship of art and society, rebelling against Confucian notions of literature that served state and society, yet unable as pioneers in a reborn profession to abandon claims of social relevance altogether. In their view a clearer declaration of political and social ends would have vitiated their commitment to confront the contradictions of their age, and to reveal the actual experience of ordinary humanity. Unable to generalize save at Shimamura's mystical level of "absolute inexplicability," many naturalists fell back on their own, autobiographical experience in the I-novel or confessional essay. To present their troubled private lives as the means to social transformation was to accept, in reverse, the state's identification of public and private. Nei-

81. Raymond Williams, *The Sociology of Culture*, 81.

ther naturalists nor state ideologues gave credence to a private realm irrelevant to public values.

Neither the naturalists nor any other group in prewar Japan circumvented the dilemma between compliance and irrelevance; nor could they create a popular alternative to state authority. But they did create a new national literature of enduring popularity, thereby diffusing assertions of the significance of individual experience and self-discovery. The achievement itself made the naturalist movement obsolete. It raised a host of aesthetic and psychological, philosophical and religious, social and political questions, which were to be pursued by others in a context of increasing specialization. Progressive differentiation of labor and skills fragmented the relatively traditional and homogeneous society in which the naturalists' discovery of the self had seemed novel, even shocking.

Naturalists also attacked the traditional family system and censorship. Political liberals agreed that these two constraints on individual development stifled democracy; yet neither they nor the naturalists envisioned any means of progress apart from raising public consciousness. While correctly noting the state's suppression of individuality, the naturalists and liberals greatly overstressed the converse relationship between self-discovery and political reform. More often, introspection starkly revealed the helplessness of the individual. Nonetheless, a connection between consciousness and action is discernible in the early feminist movement, greatly influenced by the naturalists.

3

The Woman Problem: Shimamura, Tanaka, and Ishibashi Tanzan

Women were excluded from the quest for success and self-discovery enjoyed by urban middle-class men. Exclusion reflected the economic and political demands of the industrializing state. Japanese capitalism utilized the preexisting rural household economy by dispersing factories widely in the countryside and recruiting girls and single women, whose labor was under the patriarchal authority of their household head. Female labor was essential to the success of Japanese industrialization, especially in textiles. At the turn of the century textiles constituted about 40 percent of manufacturing output and 60 percent of the critical export commodities that permitted the import of raw materials and advanced technology. The textile labor force was 60 to 80 percent female, much higher than in Western nations at any stage of development. In 1900 the Home Ministry promulgated the Public Peace Police Law, which banned unions and strikes and barred women from joining political organizations and attending political meetings. Control of the labor force—well over half female until World War I, sequestered in dormitories, and subject to parental authority—left only two alternatives for industrial reform: governmental paternalism, or dismantling the family system.[1]

The denial of public rights was paralleled by the denial of private rights in the Civil Code of 1898, which emphasized the

1. Yasue Aoki Kidd, "Women Workers in the Japanese Cotton Mills, 1880–1920"; Gary R. Saxonhouse, "Country Girls and Communication among Competitors in the Japanese Cotton-Spinning Industry," and William V. Rapp, "Firm Size and Japan's Export Structure: A Microview of Japan's Export Competitiveness since Meiji," in Hugh T. Patrick, ed., *Japanese Industrialization and Its Social Consequences*; Sheila Matsumoto, "Women in Factories," in Joyce Lebra et al., eds., *Women in Changing Japan*; and Inoue Kiyoshi, *Nihon joseishi*, 205–17.

authority of the household head to manage family members' property, determine their place of residence, and approve or disapprove the marriages of men under thirty and women under twenty-five. Although a woman could become a household head, men were preferred. Although a woman could own property, if she married she was required to obtain her husband's consent in financial and legal transactions. Women were also excluded from all higher education except a handful of women's colleges and specialized academies during the first decade of the twentieth century, though opportunity increased thereafter. Educational deprivation was especially damaging in an age when new professions defined greater opportunities for ambitious young men.[2]

As the Meiji elite avidly imported Western technology, institutions, and thought, there was a widespread fear that women might be resistant to the new influences, infectious carriers of Japan's backwardness. Hence the national interest required the transformation of women's skills and values. Feminist Hiratsuka Raichō recalled that her mother, wife of a high government official, had during the 1880s "dutifully followed her husband's suggestions on modernizing their home-life: she obtained Western-style clothes for herself and her children, drank milk daily for her health, and attended classes. . . ."[3] The theme of modern, scientific, and rational home management continued in the mass-circulation women's magazines of the 1890s. The Japanese elite recognized, as Tanaka Ōdō's future wife, (Takanashi) Takako, wrote in 1918, that "in the interests of the home and for the sake of future generations, something must be done to carry the women forward into a position more in harmony with what the nation is reaching for in other directions."[4] Coeducational primary schools, which taught world geography, mathematics, and science along with patriotism and obedience, aimed at enhancing the role of Japanese women in bringing up scientifically

2. *The Civil Code of Japan*, trans. W. J. Sebald, 2–5, 168–69, 178–89, 227; Wakamori Tarō and Yamamoto Fujie, *Nihon no joseishi*, vol. 6, 286.

3. Nancy Andrews, "The Seitōsha: An Early Japanese Women's Organization, 1911–1916," 50–51.

4. Taka Takanashi (Tanaka Takako), "The Change in the Status of Women under the Modern Conditions of Japanese Life," 63.

minded and patriotic children. The modern, educated mother who contributed to the state by preparing children for citizenship was an ideal that received wide support from the contemporary West and from missionary schools. By the turn of the century, the ideal was widely accepted among intellectuals, journalists, and the staffs of women's schools.[5]

Thus the new feminine ideal of the Meiji era was the "good wife, wise mother" (*ryōsai kenbo*). It was a definite departure from tradition before it became the pillar of orthodoxy in the twentieth century. Traditional elite standards of female behavior (such as the mid-seventeenth century *Onna daigaku* [Greater learning for women] by Kaibara Ekken) had indeed demanded obedience to the husband, but they had placed duties to the parents-in-law even higher and had not discussed the processes of child rearing. In contrast, the ideal of wise mother reflected the emergence of the nuclear family and the educational needs of the modern Japanese nation. Her skills in budgeting and assisting the children's education both aided and displayed the family's upward mobility. The good wife, wise mother of the Taishō era incorporated elements of education and expertise. The ideal was the first step toward the professional housewife of post–World War II Japan, whose role is to manage all domestic concerns through rational methods in budgeting, consumption, and human relations. The role of good wife, wise mother, though restricted in scope, required new autonomy and initiative, and encouraged women to develop new skills and interests that could not always be confined within the home.[6]

Gradually the increasingly impersonal labor market began to differentiate among women according to their class and

5. H. von Straelen, *The Japanese Woman Looking Forward*, 12, 84, 121. Prewar education is discussed in Takashi Koyama, *The Changing Social Position of Women in Japan*, 18. The American ideal of educated motherhood is discussed in Sheila Rothman, *Woman's Proper Place*, 97–134.

6. Ekken Kaibara, *The Way of Contentment and the Greater Learning for Women*, trans. Ken Hoshino. Sharon L. Sievers analyzes the "revolutionary" change in the ideals of womanhood during the Meiji era in "Feminist Criticism in Japanese Politics in the 1880s," *Signs* 6 (1981): 602–03; see also Katano Masako, "Ryōsai kenboshugi no genryū," in Kindai Joseishi Kenkyūkai, ed., *Onnatachi no kindai*, 34–42. On postwar women see Suzanne H. Vogel, "The Professional Housewife," International Group for the Study of Women, *Proceedings of the Tokyo Symposium on Women*, 150–55.

skills. Yet, as Ishibashi Tanzan cogently observed, social, educational, and legal definition of women as good wives and wise mothers shackled their competitive potential. The primary school enrollment and attendance of females lagged well behind those of males until the twentieth century. Even restricted access to education, however, opened new careers. The rapid expansion of education created a huge demand for new teachers, and by 1908 one-quarter of the public primary school teachers were women. Few other professional opportunities existed. Women were first permitted to take national qualifying examinations in medicine as early as 1884, but in law not until 1933. However, the most prominent professional women of the Taishō era were writers and journalists, and often activists as well: Yamataka Shigeri of *Kokumin shinbun* and *Shufu no tomo*, Oku Mumeo, Hiratsuka Raichō, Ichikawa Fusae of *Nagoya shinbun*, Yosano Akiko and Hani Motoko of *Fujin no tomo*. As writers they were relatively free from the wrenching social demands of specialized training or integration into a complex office hierarchy, and they communicated their experience and views to the public.[7]

Journalism by and about women played a critical role in raising consciousness. The last full year of the Meiji era, 1911, was a symbolic turning point in public attention to the woman question. Hiratsuka Raichō founded the women's literary society Seitōsha (Bluestockings) and began publishing *Seitō*, the first journal in Japan that was written and published entirely by women. Shimamura presented his production of Henrik Ibsen's *A Doll's House*. Both events were much discussed in the newspapers, and the general-interest journals followed *Seitō*'s lead by inviting more women essayists and devoting entire issues to the women's question: *Shin Nihon* in January 1913 and three times more during the decade, *Taiyō* in June 1913, and *Chūō kōron* in July 1913. During the first year of the Taishō era, Shimamura opened another play that debunked the pa-

7. *ITZ* 1:274–75; Elizabeth Knipe Mouer, "Women in Teaching," in Joyce Lebra et al., eds., *Women in Changing Japan*, 160–69; Lois Dilatush, "Women in the Professions," in Joyce Lebra et al., eds., *Women in Changing Japan*; von Straelen, 103; Kathleen Molony, "One Woman Who Dared: Ichikawa Fusae and the Japanese Women's Suffrage Movement," 53, 60–61, 105, 188; *Japanese Women* (Tokyo, ed. Ichikawa Fusae) 1, no. 6 (Nov. 1938):4; Andrews, 48, 54.

triarchal family, Hermann Sudermann's *Magda*. The general-
interest journals also began to carry advice columns devoted
largely to family problems. Ishibashi cited one from the Teiyū
Rinrikai's *Rinri kōenshū* in 1912, Ichikawa Fusae worked on one
at *Rikugō* (Universe) before becoming a leader of the women's
suffrage movement, and Tanaka Takako wrote one after 1931.

Although some of the reporting and advice was reactionary,
the media were the message in the sense that never before
had questions of family and sex roles been argued in a national
forum. The media's impact on women was assumed by feminist leaders after World War I. For example, supporters of
women's right to attend political meetings argued that to deny
this right was meaningless since women were already informed
about politics from reading newspapers and journals. Japanese
women finally gained the right to attend political meetings in
an amendment to the Public Peace Police Law which passed
the Diet in 1922.[8]

As the woman question drew public attention, avant-garde
writers of both sexes began to view women in terms of the
ongoing debate over the meaning of selfhood and society.
Three new ideals arose in considerable tension with the ideal
of the good wife, wise mother. The first was self-discovery and
self-fulfillment, with roots in the missionary schools and the
naturalist literature movement; this was the predominant
theme of the early Seitōsha. The second was full citizenship
and equal participation in all areas of national life, articulated
by liberals such as Tanaka and Ishibashi. The third new ideal,
inspired by American progressive women and suffragists, was
the transformation of the larger society through the special
nurturing capacities of women. Tanaka Takako, who held a
master's degree in social work from the University of Chicago,
expressed the third ideal in journal articles and activities on
behalf of women workers, mothers, and children. Thus vocation as self, as citizen, as mother or reformer became an
urgent question for middle-class women as it had been for
middle-class men, though women's choices were narrower. The
new ideals met considerable opposition in public opinion as

8. Shinobu Seizaburō, *Taishō seiji shi*, 810.

well as repression by the state, which broke up women's meetings under the Public Peace Police Law and confiscated feminist publications.

NATURALISM AND WOMEN

The naturalist writers intuitively grasped the weight of oppression on Japanese women; however, they were unable to include women in their movement or to capture women's experience in their fiction. No woman of their generation succeeded in using a Western literary form such as the novel, though a few flourished in traditional genre. Japanese naturalists created no Emma Bovary or Anna Karenina. Their failure to delineate complex and credible female characters mirrored the larger realities of their society rather than their individual lack of sympathy, for Shimazaki Tōson raised possibilities unimaginable to most of his peers when he wrote, "Just try being a woman. See how you like it."[9]

Psychic estrangement between the sexes paralleled political, legal, and educational segregation and was increased by arranged marriage, often to a virtual stranger. The naturalist movement in literature denounced the traditional family system, especially parentally arranged marriage, but from a male viewpoint. Coerced into marriage by his adopted father, who was sponsoring his schooling, Shimamura in 1895 portrayed women as shackles binding ambitious young men: "Woman is a vain incarnation. She hopes for wealth in a rich household, or honor with a scholar. Then she discovers the poverty and chill of the study."[10] Tayama Katai expressed a similar view: "Now I've fallen into the trap of life. A wife is an encumbrance enough to me, and yet now there's a child too. Things are hopeless now—now I'll never be able to get out from this trap, this frightening, horrifying trap of life."[11] Shimamura and Tayama resented the wives forced upon them by the older generation, but they did understand that women too were victims of the patriarchal family system. Tayama's protagonist Tokio

---

9. Shimazaki, *The Family*.
10. Quoted in Yoshida, *Kindai bungei hyōron shi* 1:743–44.
11. Tayama, 10.

in *Futon*, despairing over his conventional wife, urged his female student Yoshiko to become a modern woman without lover or husband:

> Once a woman gave herself physically to a man her freedom was unmistakably destroyed; . . . modern Western women well understood such things and so never got into difficulties in their affairs with the other sex, and . . . modern Japanese women most certainly had to do likewise.[12]

For Tayama celibacy was contrary to human nature. Therefore, independent women could not exist in the context of Japanese society.

Psychic estrangement between the sexes was also engendered by the greater social mobility of men in comparison with women. Successful men left behind the brides of their youth. In *Futon*:

> To Tokio nothing was more regrettable than his having contented himself with his wife, who had nothing more to offer than her old-fashioned round-chignon hairstyle, waddling walk, and chastity and submissiveness. When he compared the young, modern wife—beautiful and radiant as she strolled the streets with her husband, talking readily and eloquently at his side when they visited friends—with his own wife—who not only didn't read the novels he took such pains to write but was completely pig-ignorant about her husband's torment and anguish, and was happy as long as she could raise the children satisfactorily—then he felt like screaming his loneliness out loud.[13]

In life as well as literature many Taishō intellectuals were estranged from their domestically preoccupied wives and attracted to an actress or writer such as Matsui Sumako, Hiratsuka Raichō, Kamichika Ichiko, or Itō Noe. A few dramatic cases appeared in the media. Ishibashi Tanzan in 1912 cited a newspaper account of a poor and humble couple whose hard work had educated the husband to win a prestigious post in the regional bureaucracy. Their subsequent separation was attributed to "different levels of culture and refinement." Ishi-

12. Ibid., 70.
13. Ibid., 42.

bashi concluded that "she should not have sacrificed her development for his."[14]

LITERARY FEMINISM

Certain women close to the naturalists developed a powerful drive to write and publish their own literature. The very name of the Bluestockings is one evidence of its close ties with the naturalist movement. Hiratsuka's mentor, Ikuta Chōkō, a well-known naturalist critic, had told her about the term of ridicule applied to the women of Elizabeth Montague's London salon. Hiratsuka defiantly chose the name for her group, commenting, "I know well what other feelings are hidden under that laugh of ridicule, so I am not at all afraid."[15] Iwano Hōmei's wife, Kiyo, who had earlier demonstrated for women's rights in the Diet chamber with a group of Social Democrats, was a charter member. Shimamura frequently lectured to the society, and Tanaka, acquainted with the Iwano couple and Hiratsuka, sympathetically reviewed the group's journal.

The original aim of *Seitō* was self-expression rather than activism: it was to be a journal of, by, and for women, conveying their special experiences in their own words. The distinction, however, could not readily be preserved in the face of their exclusion from public affairs.[16] Hiratsuka's opening editorial was a compelling plea for personal autonomy: "In the beginning, woman was the sun. She was an authentic person. Today she is the moon. She lives by others, shines with the light of others; she is the moon with the pallid face of an invalid. . . . We must restore our hidden sun."[17] Hiratsuka's sense of individual identity shines through her career and her prose. She also wrote, responding to derisive media attacks on the new woman, "I am a new woman. At least, day by day I pray and struggle to be a new woman."[18] Her appeal to ancient traditions was equally clear. The sun that once was woman is

14. *ITZ* 1:285–89; see also 497–500 on the emergence of white-collar women.
15. Quoted in Andrews, 56.
16. Andrews, 50–53; Wakamori and Yamamoto 6:297.
17. Hiratsuka Raichō, *Genshi, josei wa taiyō de atta*, vol. 1, 328.
18. Quoted by Tanaka Ōdō, "Hiratsuka Raichō Shi ni ataete Shi no fujinkan o ronzu," 114–15.

of course the goddess Amaterasu, greatest in the Shinto pantheon, and mother of the divine imperial line. There is no escaping Hiratsuka's implication that the patriarchal state and the patriarchal family had been built with a missing keystone, the power of women.

The first issue, printed in a run of one thousand copies, attracted an astonishing three thousand letters in reply, some submitting manuscripts, most requesting advice on marriage problems or staff positions on the journal. Gradually the group attracted younger women of less distinguished social backgrounds, mainly writers and teachers, who swelled the membership to a maximum of two or three hundred. New members effected a shift from literature to the woman question in early 1913, so that by September the group's charter was rewritten to omit all mention of literature, and the journal began to publish translations from the works of Swedish feminist Ellen Key, British psychologist Havelock Ellis, and American anarchist Emma Goldman. Despite the critical role the Seitōsha played in inspiring debate, their translations and not original writings contained the most specific discussions of new roles for women. Translations were somewhat safer from repression, and certainly censorship played a role in *Seitō*'s reticence: three issues were confiscated, and three others interfered with, for themes such as eroticism, denunciation of the traditional family system, the betrayal or trivialization of women by men, and socialism. But fear of the police was not the only reason *Seitō* lacked a political program.[19]

Hiratsuka, attracted to Zen Buddhism since her schooldays, rejected rational thought in her quest for a new selfhood:

> We reach for knowledge in order to liberate ourselves and escape from the abyss of ignorance and darkness. Yet is not the knowledge of the amoeba, after all, merely that of wiping its eyes and discovering its shell? In order to escape that shell there is no means other than to struggle. All thought obscures our true wisdom.[20]

19. Murakami, 229–30; Andrews, 49, 56–62; Pauline C. Reich et al., "Japan's Literary Feminists: The *Seitō* Group," *Signs* 2 (1976): 284–85; Ken Miyamoto, "Itō Noe and the Bluestockings," *Japan Interpreter* 10 (1975): 197.

20. Hiratsuka, quoted by Tanaka in "Hiratsuka Raichō Shi ni ataete Shi no fujinkan o ronzu," 114–15.

Like Shimamura, Hiratsuka was committed to a subjective and impressionistic rendering of experience in order to stimulate the imaginations of her readers. The two also agreed that the ultimate meaning of life was love, but while he stressed the free relationship of spouses, she emphasized the mother-child bond. Her studies in Buddhism and her interpretation of Christianity led her to seek self-realization in self-sacrifice, in the voluntary but absolute devotion of motherhood. While noting that "outside of marriage, women's way of life should have limitless possibilities," and sanctioning birth control, she devoted her later career to the needs of women within marriage: protective legislation for mothers and children.[21]

Mothers were the heroines in Shimamura's productions of *A Doll's House* and *Magda*. In *A Doll's House* Nora, who left her husband and three children to educate herself, was played to rave reviews by Matsui Sumako. How did the play work in Japanese? Shimamura's translation was fairly faithful to the English version, yet played well and was selected from a host of competitors by Hijikata Yoshi of the new theater movement after World War II. Shimamura elaborated Nora's final judgment that her husband was a stranger into *mizu shirazu no tanin* ("a never-seen, never-known other"),[22] a hand-grenade of a phrase lobbed amid Japanese familial and communitarian sensibilities, and one that exploded the earlier and milder portrayals of estrangement in naturalist literature. Shimamura, minutely preoccupied with the set and unable to sleep for months before opening night, decided to use Western costumes and settings along with the original characters' names but, somewhat contradictorily, wanted to portray Nora as an ordinary Japanese woman "who wasn't capable of reading foreign languages, and knew nothing about Western women."[23]

By all accounts, audiences exited debating the characters as if they were real persons. According to one report by a Sei-

21. Quoted in Reich et al., 289. Hiratsuka's commitment to absolute love later prompted her to admiration of Matsui Sumako's suicide after Shimamura's death; see Kuwaki et al., "Matsui Sumako," 18–36.

22. Shimamura, trans., *Ningyō no ie*, WB, ser. 2, no. 50 (Jan. 1910): 145; for an account of the performance see Yoshida, *Kindai bungei hyōron shi* 1:797–98.

23. Ozaki Hirotsugu, 17; Nakamura Kichizō et al., "Matsui Sumako to Shibata Kan," *CK* 27, no. 7 (July 1912): 126.

tōsha member who attended the performance on tour in Osaka, audiences condemned Nora and sympathized with her husband, Torvald. A young married woman considered the housewife's role as separate but equal: "I feel sorry for Torvald to have to live for seven years with a woman who had no respect for herself as a wife or as a mother."[24] In contrast most Seitōsha women neither misunderstood nor rejected Nora's behavior, but they interpreted the play's insistence on self-development as a precondition for family responsibilities.

Ueno Yōko, a teacher at Josei Kōtō Shihan Gakkō (Women's Higher Normal School), regarded Nora's break with her family as a symbol for the mental and spiritual liberation of all women. "Nora's enlightenment is the enlightenment of all women, or should be. . . . She has hitherto been kept in idleness, and untrue to herself. . . . She must develop as a conscious self. . . . All true human beings must follow Nora. Nora's future is our future as women."[25] However, Ueno chose to interpret the play in strictly symbolic rather than social terms. The true meaning of Nora's departure was not her physical escape, but her psychic awakening. Inner transformation would liberate wives and mothers from "subservience" and "fulfill their true natures."[26] Ueno also believed that there were alternatives to family roles: "Some women may devote themselves to scholarship or the arts, or be economically or otherwise unable to marry."[27] She hoped for acceptance of a plurality of female roles, including careers chosen by either vocation or necessity, but she said little about the possibility of combining family and career.

The one wholly unsympathetic review was by Hiratsuka herself, who denounced Nora's abandonment of her home. No true freedom or self-discovery could possibly come from so wanton an act of selfishness. Hiratsuka claimed that Japanese women, who were relatively independent in household affairs, could scarcely believe that even a girl of fourteen or fifteen could be so blindly instinctive as Nora. Paralleling the natu-

24. Quoted in Ide Fumiko, *Seitō no onnatachi*, 71–72.
25. Ueno Yōko, "*Ningyō no ie* yori josei mondai e," *ST* 2 (Jan. 1912): 89.
26. Ibid., 90–91.
27. Ibid., 108.

ralists' dichotomy between instinct and society Hiratsuka viewed self-interest as instinctive, and motherhood as part of a social network of obligation and duty permeated with altruistic religious values. Her contrast of instinctive selfishness with a humane society in which "real human beings sacrifice flesh and blood for each other" was aimed at Nora rather than at her husband.[28] Still, Hiratsuka, like all other *Seitō* reviewers of *A Doll's House*, agreed on the necessity of transforming social consciousness.

Shimamura Hōgetsu and Matsui Sumako, interviewed for their interpretations of the play by *Seitō* and a host of other publications, echoed the theme of consciousness raising but also demanded that the family be reconstructed. Matsui concluded that it was necessary to "tear down the doll house [*ningyō no ie*] and build a house of human beings [*ningen no ie*]."[29] Shimamura understood that reconstruction of the home would demand a reordering of the entire society:

> Woman cannot be herself in today's society, which is man's society; the laws are made by men, and women's behavior is decided by male judgment. . . . Oppressed by spiritual confusion and faith in authority, woman loses confidence in her moral right and ability to rear her own children.[30]

For Shimamura, the central motif of the play was Nora's conclusion that her ignorant passivity made her an unfit mother. The women's movement must liberate individuality, but an individuality that was different from that of men. The functions of men and women were distinct, but morally and socially equal. Shimamura sanctioned educational, occupational, legal, and social equality, but he placed greatest emphasis on the spiritual dimension of the problem: "The woman problem is the problem of humanity, the problem of the philosophy of love."[31] For him as for Hiratsuka, concrete reform was a mere

28. Hiratsuka, "Nora-san ni," *ST* 2 (Jan. 1912): 140.
29. Matsui Sumako, "Nora to Maguda ni tsuite," *CK* 28 (Special issue on "Fujin mondai," July 1913): 101.
30. Shimamura, "*Ningyō no ie* to Ipusen no sakugeki jutsu," *CK* 28 (Spring supplement, Apr. 1913): 129–30.
31. Shimamura, "Kindai bungei to fujin mondai," 22; see also his "Kindai fujin no jikaku no naiyō," in *Taishō dai zasshi*, 90–98.

means to spiritual freedom. Shimamura and the Seitōsha
women sought women's self-fulfillment but were reluctant to
sanction self-interest. They resolved this dilemma by giving
priority to inner mental and psychic transformation, and, in
demands for institutional change, by citing the needs of altruistic mothers and the future of the whole society.

In contrast, Ishibashi Tanzan frankly sanctioned women's
self-interest. Echoing Shimamura's theme of the helplessness
of the housewife in a male-dominated society, he noted that
industrialization and urbanization had usurped many of her
traditional productive functions. The housewife was a parasite,
and a defenseless parasite. Subject to the vicissitudes of competitive capitalism, she was deprived of the means to compete
in higher education, gainful employment, and political rights.
He urged that the solution to the women's question was self-
interest, not self-sacrifice. He defended Nora's desertion of
her family because she was searching for "a transformation of
reality, and a standard of judgment about reality."[32] In his view
Japanese society, especially the family, resisted transformation
because of the persistence of "medieval despotism."[33]

A Doll's House escaped censorship but Shimamura's next
production, *Magda,* suffered from revisions mandated by the
Home Ministry. Shimamura sardonically remarked that the
term "woman question" (*fujin mondai*) was in danger of becoming confused in the public mind with "publication banned"
(*hatsubai kinshi*).[34] In *Magda* the heroine defied her father
rather than a husband, a more serious breach of traditional
Japanese morality, but, more important, the rising public
interest in *A Doll's House* and *Seitō* prompted the government
to interfere, after an initial term of caution. One Home Ministry official commented that many parts of *Magda* threatened
"loyalty and filial piety, Japan's essential virtues," and Matsui
was "so bewitching that I myself felt her appeal."[35] The script
version had been printed in *Waseda bungaku* two months earlier

32. *ITZ* 1:47.
33. Ibid.
34. Shimamura, "Kindai bungei to fujin mondai," 3.
35. Quoted in Ide Fumiko, *Seitō,* 61–62.

and had circulated freely, a double standard that Ishibashi lampooned.[36]

Magda, like *A Doll's House*, concerns the home and a woman's independence. Seventeen-year-old Magda had been driven out of her home for refusing her father's choice of suitor, a fairly common situation in Taishō newspapers. The play opens twelve years later when a traveling music festival visits Magda's provincial hometown, and the glamorous "Italian" opera-singer turns out to be none other than the long-lost daughter, accompanied by her child, whose father is revealed as the paternally sanctioned suitor. The powerful pull of blood ties has survived, along with the patterns of overt authority and submission, and covert emotional manipulation. The suitor agrees to marry Magda, provided that the child be banished to a discreet distance under an assumed name. Magda refuses honor and respectability, and demands not freedom for her art, but rather the elements of physical and emotional survival that the patriarchal family denies to the individual:

> Leave art out of the question. Consider me nothing more than the seamstress or the servant-maid who seeks, among strangers, the little food and the little love she needs. See how much the family with its morality demands from us! It throws us on our own resources, it gives us neither shelter nor happiness, and yet, in our loneliness, we must live according to the laws which it has planned for itself alone.[37]

Her argument with her father ends with his fatal stroke, leaving the family pastor to suggest that Magda will atone for her conduct with prayers on her father's grave.

The Home Ministry Police Bureau was not satisfied with prayers, and it forbade presentation of the play until Shimamura added a closing soliloquy in which Magda declared, "I am to blame for everything."[38] Magda's apology was necessary in order to show that she had reflected upon conduct that

36. *ITZ* 1:215.
37. Hermann Sudermann, *The Old Home*, trans. Charles Winslow Homer, 157.
38. Imai Seiichi, "Taishō demokurashii," in *Nihon no rekishi*, vol. 23, 110–11.

violated the precept of filial piety as set forth in the Imperial Rescript on Education. Shimamura told Ishibashi that he would have preferred to close down the production rather than to submit to censorship, but theater finances and the dependence of employees disallowed defiance. Despite (or because of) the controversy over the mandated revisions, *Magda* was even more popular than *A Doll's House*, and toured in Osaka, Kyoto, and Nagoya.[39]

Whereas Nora abandoned her offspring, Magda sacrificed respectability for hers, a choice that made her much more appealing to Japanese women. In fact, the two plays afford a kind of litmus test for sentiments about the maternal role. Reviewers naturally compared Nora and Magda, generally feeling more empathy for Magda's prolonged vacillation than for Nora's radical transformation of consciousness. Matsui Sumako and Hiratsuka Raichō both advanced the peculiar interpretation that Magda had placed her child before her art. In Hiratsuka's interpretation, Magda had become a great singer only in order to care for her child. As a celebrity, Magda had encountered new ideas of self-realization but still longed for her old home. Her rejection of the past brought disaster rather than liberation. "Old and new thought cannot be reconciled, and by the defeat of old thought, will new thought gradually triumph? I don't think so."[40] Even the woman who sought independence for altruistic ends, to benefit her child, was likely to be destroyed by her lingering loyalty to traditional beliefs and feelings. The only answer Hiratsuka could suggest was, again, religion. The power of prayers by her father's grave could move Magda's heart outside herself.

The Seitōsha women failed to mention the censorship of *Magda*, which for Ishibashi was paramount. He dismissed Magda as an ordinary old-fashioned woman, who had developed the sense of confidence and pride that naturally accompanied paid employment but quickly capitulated to conventional human feelings. Though uninhibited in criticizing his teacher's production, Ishibashi upheld Shimamura by de-

39. *ITZ* 1:224–25; Yoshida, *Kindai bungei hyōron shū* 1:800.
40. Hiratsuka, "Yonda *Maguda*," *ST* 2 (June 1912): 7.

crying the paternalistic and managerial character of censorship, as Shimamura had earlier. The Home Ministry had interfered without reference to law or the Constitution. Ishibashi proffered popular government, based on universal suffrage and party cabinets, as the only solution to bureaucratic high-handedness. Nonetheless he acknowledged the importance of Shimamura's work in raising consciousness and pointed to the need for more literature and journalism of advanced thought.[41]

LIBERAL FEMINISM: TANAKA ŌDŌ

Tanaka and Ishibashi were unresponsive to themes that greatly interested the Seitōsha women: the emotional pull of the old traditions, the expression of women's personal experience, and the protection of motherhood. They attempted to justify women's full participation in all areas of public life, downplaying both inherent and acquired differences based on gender, and urging enhanced opportunity. Both tried to use the publicity generated by the Seitōsha and avant-garde theater in order to promote women's equality in education, work, law, and politics.

As early as February 1910, Tanaka had urged that the goals of girls' education should be the same as boys'. In that year the Ministry of Education recognized home economics as part of the official course of study in girls' high schools, responding to demands for practical education raised in the writings of Otatake Iwazō, Yoshida Kumaji, and Sawayanagi Masatarō. Practicality for these educational theorists meant acceptance of the social hierarchy and, for women, acknowledgment of their innate limitations and reliance on male authority. A few months before the ministry's edict, Tanaka advanced a different version of practical education for young women, arguing that the central task of high schools was to take students as they were, already shaped and molded by their homes and their society, and "in five years to change and reform them as far as possible."[42] He disparaged educators who "try to teach

41. *ITZ* 1:220–23; see also 101–06 and 462.
42. Tanaka, "Joshi kyōiku zakkan," *Rinri kōenshū*, no. 90 (Feb. 1910): 52.

etiquette, or cooking, or prate about the nature of the home."[43] The domestic arts were rather remote from the experience of high school girls, who could easily learn them later if the need arose. Accepting a plurality of roles for women, he regarded girls' need for domestic skills as problematic. His ideal curriculum for girls' schools included English, physics, chemistry, history, and ethics, all "taught in a spirit of experiment."[44] Tanaka placed politics and economics first, however: "It is indeed regrettable that our young women are so ignorant and indifferent regarding events in society and the trend of national development."[45] More than a decade before women gained the legal right even to attend political meetings, Tanaka considered the role of girls as homemakers secondary to their role as citizens of modern Japan.

Tanaka reviewed *Seitō* from the same perspective. He welcomed Hiratsuka to the ranks of "the allies of enlightenment and happiness, and the foes of darkness and infamy."[46] Compliments duly paid, he criticized Hiratsuka's subjective emphasis on inner awakening, which overstressed the development of personal character (*shūyō, kakugo*) and ignored the historical conditions that had determined women's status. Hiratsuka's metaphorical and radical attacks on the station of women in present society posed a serious intellectual problem. The meaning of knowledge was the crux of the debate between Tanaka and Hiratsuka. Whereas she had derided the knowledge of the amoeba "wiping its eyes and discovering its shell," he retorted: "The most manifold and powerful forces with which to destroy the shell one has built for oneself are those of knowledge."[47] Tanaka censured Hiratsuka's mystical anti-intellectualism, just as he had taken issue with the anti-intellectualism of naturalist writers. Despite his rare lack of condescension toward the women's movement, he grossly underestimated the urgency behind *Seitō*'s original aim, the opportunity for women to express themselves in their own words and in their own journal. Nevertheless he correctly rec-

43. Ibid., 54.
44. Ibid., 59.
45. Ibid., 58.
46. Tanaka, "Hiratsuka Raichō Shi ni ataete Shi no fujinkan o ronzu," 108.
47. Ibid., 116–19.

ognized the mystical, anti-intellectual limitations of Hiratsuka's thought that led her to eulogize self-abnegation and self-sacrifice. Her psychic and his social perspective ought to have been complementary.

Gradually, Tanaka became more specific in his support of political and economic goals for women. An advocate of women's suffrage, Tanaka applauded the success achieved by "women of advanced consciousness" (*fujin no senkakusha*) in 1922 in winning the right to participate in political meetings.[48] Despite his concern that women's suffrage might result in only formal rather than real political participation, Tanaka thought it "better they should have the right than not" and believed that the grave ills that had afflicted Japanese society since the Restoration—especially militarism and imperialism—were of particular concern to women: "When we used Western civilization militarily rather than culturally we were all the losers, but were not the greatest losers the women?"[49]

Tanaka related the women's movement to individualism and democracy but found classical theorists of democracy deficient in their discussions of the family. Although he assumed that family relations could not remain stagnant while modern industry transformed all other aspects of Japanese life, he admitted that "the most fundamental and central parts of life are hardest to change."[50] At one point he tentatively suggested some form of cooperative child-rearing, which could free Japanese children from the class prejudices of their parents:

> The home cannot be abolished, but insofar as possible to emancipate children from the home, to leave behind the background of the home, and to treat them simply as children born into cooperative life, having them play and travel together, would develop in them the spirit of sympathy and mutual assistance.[51]

He suspected that the dramatic public successes of a few exceptional women would not prove beneficial to the average woman, who could not immediately escape the anonymous

48. Tanaka, "Wakaki josei no tame ni gakusei no igi o kōzu," 29–31.
49. Ibid., 42–43.
50. Tanaka, "Tettei kojinshugisha no ren'aikan, kekkonkan," in *Sukui wa hansei yori*, 354.
51. Ibid., 369–70.

tedium of bearing and raising children at home: "The time
and efforts that women devote to children and the household
must be kept within reasonable bounds."[52] All women should
have "the opportunity and motive for education, economic independence, and the authority to reform political, social, and
legal institutions."[53] He did not, however, suggest how the reduction of household burdens might be achieved.

LIBERAL FEMINISM: ISHIBASHI TANZAN

In contrast to Tanaka, Ishibashi Tanzan was unimpressed by
the Seitōsha. He condescended to the group because of the
elite social origins of its most famous members: "They represent the old-style woman who can happily amuse herself and
eat."[54] Ishibashi's jibe, contrasted with Tanaka's painstaking
tribute, reveals the great differences between the two men in
generation and attitudes, for both were in complete agreement
on the goals of political, legal, social, and economic equality
for women. Both, too, regarded women's equality as only one
aspect of an emerging modern Japanese citizenry, in sharp
contrast to Hiratsuka's preoccupation with feminine experience and self-expression.

Ishibashi was seventeen years younger than Tanaka, Tanaka's student in the philosophy department at Waseda during
the Russo-Japanese War. His later writings were to typify the
collective concerns of that era: efficient economic management, the social dislocations due to advancing industrialization, and the birth of a social democratic party. The social
problem, he wrote, had displaced both the Meiji Popular
Rights movement and naturalist literature. Ishibashi tended to
explain political problems in terms of the economic, class, and
status structure of society a decade before Marxism became
the definitive stamp of a large segment of Japanese intellectuals. He judged Marx's materialism an error "but with much

52. Ibid., 371.
53. Ibid., 372.
54. *ITZ* 1: 292; see also 191–92, 462, 497–500. Despite his derision Ishibashi
criticized the Ōkuma cabinet's suppression of *Seitō* issues; 1:541–42.

truth" and was influenced by German socialist Karl Bebel's *Women under Socialism* as well as by English liberal John Stuart Mill's earlier *The Subjection of Women*.[55]

Although both men belonged to a small liberal minority, Ishibashi developed the support to become prime minister in 1956 whereas Tanaka died in relative obscurity in 1932. The difference in their fates was very much a matter of occupation and style rather than fundamental difference of purpose. First, as a financial journalist, Ishibashi translated Tanaka's highly abstract instrumentalism into specific responses to contemporary political, social, and economic issues. Second, he adroitly performed customary social roles and enjoyed a broad and warm acquaintance despite his aggressive individuality of opinion. The personal difference between Tanaka and Ishibashi is well illustrated in their relationship with Waseda professor Kaneko Umaji, a German-inspired idealist notably hostile to the Anglo-American currents represented by Tanaka and Ishibashi. Whereas Kaneko literally could not bear the sight of Tanaka, he relied on Ishibashi's services in arranging his daughter's wedding. Tanaka never performed such favors, and it was not Tanaka, the major adviser, but Shimamura who arranged Ishibashi's employment after graduation. Nevertheless Ishibashi never hinted a criticism of Tanaka, though he freely derided others among his teachers, a fact evidencing both Ishibashi's loyalty and Tanaka's intellectual power.[56]

Ishibashi learned personal integrity in his childhood. His father Sugita Nippu (Tansei) was born in 1855 into a long line of Nichiren laymen in Yamanashi Prefecture, but was adopted in childhood by the priest Higuchi Nichiju. Sugita kept his original family name although his household was bankrupt. He became a professor at the sect's Daikyōin (later Risshō University) in Tokyo, where he married Ishibashi Kin according to the couple's free choice, not by parental arrangement. Kin was descended from an old lineage of Nichiren laymen who had supplied tatami to Edo castle, an eminent position with

55. *ITZ* 1:58; see also 62–63 and 15:349.
56. Hattori Bennosuke et al., "Tanaka Ōdō no hito to shisō o kataru," *JS*, no. 7 (Nov. 1977): 1–27.

quasi-samurai status. Although the Ishibashi family had hoped for an adopted son-in-law in Kin's marriage, Sugita could not and would not abandon his priesthood.

Subsequently there was some confusion as to which household Ishibashi would succeed. He was born Sugita Seizō (in 1884) but took the religious name Tanzan upon graduating from middle school, an indication that he would succeed his father, who had become abbot of Shōfukuji in Masuho, Yamanashi, in 1888. However, he was not close to his father and spent his childhood with his mother outside the temple in the nearby city of Kōfu according to Nichiren custom. After taking the name Tanzan he saw even less of his father; Sugita Nippu was transferred to Honkakuji in Shizuoka in 1894 and entrusted his son's education to disciple Mochizuki Nikken at Jōonji in Kagaminakajō, where Ishibashi would later return to study a tenants' movement. In 1906 Tanzan was formally designated the Ishibashi heir, but he was ordained as a Nichiren priest in 1909 after he had already begun his career in journalism. His interest in new definitions of the family was doubtless encouraged by his parents' free choice in their marriage, their ambivalence about his future, and his distance from his father.[57]

Sugita Nippu and Mochizuki Nikken both belonged to the reformist faction of Nichiren, and they gave Ishibashi, by his own account, a classical Chinese education with an "extremely progressive cast," stressing proselytism and social reform.[58] Sugita was a stern and even eccentric personality who accosted strangers on the street with aphorisms concerning honesty, diligence in study, and the faith that could move mountains. He required Ishibashi as a child to sit for hours memorizing texts, and he imparted something of the iconoclasm and personal independence traditional to the Nichiren sect, as well as the spirit of reform that was sweeping the intelligentsia in early Meiji. Sugita, like Tanaka Ōdō, was deeply interested in Western thought but derisive of those who cited it in a superficial

57. *ITZ* 15:3–6, 341–47; Shimura, 4, 15–19; Kawamura Kōshō, *Meiji Taishō Nichiren monka Bukka jinmei jiten*, 258–59.

58. *ITZ* 1:622–24; Hattori et al., 21. On Sugita's and Mochizuki's position in the Nichiren sect see Tokoro Shigemoto, *Kindai shakai to Nichirenshugi*, 137.

manner, and claimed that audiences responded with wondering admiration when he cited the theories of the famous Western scholars "Mr. Table" and "Professor Biscuit." Sugita founded a magazine of popular enlightenment, *Kyōyū zasshi* (Journal of the friends of education), and also founded two schools, the Keimō Gakusha in Masuho and the Yamanashi Normal School, during the late 1880s. Both schools were open to all children and emphasized independence from the government. Sugita was politically committed enough to invite speakers from the Popular Rights movement to Shōfukuji, where young Ishibashi gained a certain reputation for his mimicry of their orations. Later Sugita served as national leader of the Nichiren sect. Mochizuki Nikken became abbot of Kuonji, where Nichiren had died in exile after castigating the Kamakura government and predicting Japan's destruction in the Mongol invasions. Ishibashi began to quote Nichiren's warnings of doom during the late 1930s. During the preceding three decades his writings revealed his religious heritage only by their emphasis on rigorous study and freedom in defying convention.

Ishibashi attended the Yamanashi Prefectural Middle School, where his principals were first Shidehara Tan, elder brother of the renowned moderate foreign minister of the twenties, Shidehara Kijūrō, and later Ōshima Shōken, a devoted disciple of the American missionary William Smith Clark at Sapporo Agricultural College. Impatient of academic formality, Ishibashi twice failed the notoriously abstruse entrance examinations to Tokyo First Higher School, the inside track to the prestigious Tokyo Imperial University. Only the suggestion of a teacher that he take the Waseda examination rescued him from "idling aimlessly" and perhaps "dying somewhere near Port Arthur" when the Russo-Japanese War broke out.[59]

A variety of progressive and iconoclastic influences, from reformist Nichiren Buddhism to the Popular Rights movement and American missions, prepared Ishibashi for critical scrutiny of society and history at Waseda. It was Tanaka Ōdō's instru-

59. *ITZ* 15:6–25, 59–65; Shimura, 34–35.

mentalism, however, that supplied a logical framework for his critical insight. After graduation he served his compulsory two years as a foot soldier and officer candidate in 1909–10, finding military life not as bad as he had expected even though he was suspected of socialist tendencies and closely watched. In 1911 Ishibashi was hired by *Tōyō keizai shinpō* editor Miura Tetsutarō to edit a new monthly on society and culture, *Tōyō jiron*, which emphasized the repressive nature of the traditional family system. In 1914 he married Iwai Umeko, a friend of Miura's wife and descendant of the elders of Yonezawa *han* (domain) whose traditional upbringing required her to seek the consent of both her father and elder brother to the match. Though Umeko was no activist, she worked as a primary school teacher during the first few years of her marriage to Ishibashi.[60]

Women could not realize their individual potential, Ishibashi believed, without rigorous technical and theoretical education as well as economic, legal, and political rights including suffrage and candidacy for public office. To compete in the professions women needed an independent ethos of personal achievement (*risshin shusse*) comparable to the ideas that had spread among ambitious young men during the late nineteenth century. Educational reform was necessary at all levels. Like Tanaka, Ishibashi was concerned that girls' schools bred "narrow perception and weak judgment," and he preferred coeducation.[61] All universities should be open to women. Spotlighting the first woman to enter Tōhoku Imperial University through the regular examination system in 1914, Ishibashi pointedly asked why the supposedly more progressive private schools (such as Waseda, which did not admit women until 1939) were lagging on this point.[62]

Ishibashi understood that unequal education mirrored society's segregated roles for men and women. To provoke his readers into considering the disparity between their expectations of men and of women, he habitually applied the clichés

60. Ishibashi Tan'ichi, "Katei de no chichi no danmen," in Chō Yukio, ed., *Ishibashi Tanzan: Hito to shisō*, 229; Shimura, 114; Ishibashi Umeko, "Omoide no ki," *Ishibashi Tanzan zenshū geppō*, no. 15 (1972): 4–11.

61. *ITZ* 2:341.

62. Ibid.; see also 1:514–15, and *Japanese Women* 2, no. 3 (May 1939): 4.

of each sex to the other. On good wives and wise mothers, he intoned: "Certainly girls should be educated to be good wives and wise mothers, just as boys should be brought up to be good husbands and wise fathers [*ryōfu kenpu*]. The question is, what does this mean?"[63] When Osaka high school girls went on strike over the peremptory dismissal of favorite teachers and, according to a newspaper account, "directly petitioned the prefectural governor in a manner most unbecoming to little ladies," he dryly commented that he had little sympathy with student agitation but failed to see why girls should not indulge in it as long as boys did so routinely.[64]

Why was it so difficult to judge men and women by the same standards? Women had been kept behind in the despotic family system during the national transition from household production to mass production and individual competition.

> In social history, the family is an economic unit. But today, the household has lost its economic basis. Today, that basis is the individual; thus, just as past customs and relationships were needed to protect family enterprise, today individual character must be developed.[65]

Since society discouraged women's development of individual character even more than men's, women who had lost their household economic functions were divided into two groups according to class: the most oppressed of workers or the idlest of consumers.

The vanguard women of the new industrial society were workers. Women textile workers were essential to Japan's industrial strength:

> It was recently argued, in terms of the prospect of war with the United States [over the immigration question and Taft-Knox proposals for the internationalization of Manchurian railroads] that we could not afford to lose our market for thread. From this perspective we should respect our women who produce thread, along with the Americans who buy it.[66]

63. *ITZ* 1:173–74.
64. Ibid.
65. *ITZ* 1:250.
66. *ITZ* 1:282.

Women workers were at the mercy of market changes even
more than men. The Japanese employment system of lifetime
security and abundant fringe benefits emerged only during
the shortage of highly skilled labor consequent on the boom
of heavy industry during and after World War I. Moreover,
that system did not (and does not) apply to women, whose
employment was automatically defined as part-time or temporary. "In my view," Ishibashi concluded, "the problem is not
whether women have such-and-such a nature, but how they
are to eat."[67] All women risked the economic and social consequences of their weak position in the labor market: "Necessity falls on women who believe their main aim is marriage."[68]
In addition, the attempt to confine women within a vanishing
household economy damaged the nation, vitiating the potential productive contributions of fully half the population.

Ishibashi regarded the corporate household as a bastion of
class privilege. The Ministry of Education's new primary
school textbooks after the Kōtoku trial included lessons such
as "compiling your family's genealogy and history" and "priz-
ing legacies and respecting your home's treasures." Ishibashi
was furious. Most commoners had no genealogy or history before the Meiji era, and no property to speak of; some had no
hope of property. Such lessons were damaging to poor students' self-respect, which could be enhanced by lessons on
"why Japan has changed so much from the past, and why the
people wanted change."[69]

Ishibashi clearly understood the interplay of state policy, education, and poverty and how it discouraged women workers
from respecting themselves or demanding improvement in
conditions. The ideology of "good wives, wise mothers" was
propagated by national leaders and opinion-makers of the upper classes.

67. *ITZ* 1:290–91; on the gradual emergence of paternalism and lifetime employment for men in large, modern companies see Byron Marshall, *Capitalism and
Nationalism in Prewar Japan*; Koji Taira, *Economic Development and the Labor Market in
Japan*, 97–127; Thomas O. Wilkinson, *The Urbanization of Japanese Labor, 1868–1945*,
103–05.
68. *ITZ* 1:60.
69. *ITZ* 1:171.

Most of the wives and daughters of these educators, scholars, and politicians are consumers supported by men's incomes, and submissive. But these men should not make their wives and daughters the standard for all Japanese education, social service, and political authority.[70]

The mass media mirrored the upper-class definition of women as consumers rather than producers. Examining nine women's magazines, Ishibashi found that one month's photographs included two of factories and eight of schools, along with nineteen of styles, thirteen of homes, and one hundred and thirty-three of models and women. Women's magazines—and their entire image of women as a collectivity with special needs, functions, and interests—merely reinforced the segregation of women from the mainstream of Japanese life.[71]

Equalization of employment would democratize the family and was inseparable from the reform of state structure.

Familialism is a reaction against worldwide democratic trends, just as are statism and bureaucratism. Family despotism is political in nature, but without elections or legislatures. The family, however, has the potential for the kind of direct democracy practiced in ancient Greece, of which the state representative system is a mirror.[72]

Patriarchy was despotic, and despotism was masculine (*otoko rashii*).[73] Indeed, for Ishibashi as for conservatives, the family was a microcosm of the state. Seeking a more democratic state, he pursued the vision of Dewey and the American progressives, that families and schools could be training-grounds for participatory politics, and he noted a similar concern with the democratization of home life in the writings of German Social Democrat Wilhelm Liebknecht.[74]

Drama mingling sex and politics vividly confirmed the relationship of family and state. In 1916 Ishibashi defended the portrayal of a woman who had an abortion in *Shin ningen* (New

70. *ITZ* 1:283.
71. *ITZ* 1:260–61.
72. *ITZ* 2:471–73; see also 341.
73. *ITZ* 3:25.
74. *ITZ* 1:58–60.

humanity) by Nakamura Kichizō, Shimamura's associate in the
Geijutsuza. The play was based on an actual instance in which
the widow of a soldier killed in the Russo-Japanese War became pregnant during an affair with a former boyfriend and
was imprisoned after her illegal abortion. Nakamura's challenge to statist morality was hammered in by the identity of
the unfortunate woman's accusers, who were politically ambitious officers of the Army Reserve. She embraced imprisonment for the sake of freedom greater than she enjoyed in
society. Her authentic humanity clashed head-on with state law
and ethos. The Home Ministry intervened, but after considerable revision the play was permitted to open: the characters'
names were changed, the woman's deceased husband was cast
as an Alaskan explorer rather than a soldier, and the word
abortion was not spoken. On the other hand, the egotistical
machinations of the Army Reserve officers were uncut. Ishibashi prudently avoided defending abortion outright but
shared information about the original script and its revision
with his readers. He urged the merits of the play in promoting
moral reflection and chastised its suppression at the hands of
"stupid lower bureaucrats."[75] Such works continued the naturalist attempt to confront public policies in terms of their effects on the private lives of individuals. Meanwhile, Ishibashi
and other liberals labored to translate private self-expression
into political principles.

Deliberately avoiding the orthodox role of women as wives
and mothers, Ishibashi had little to say on what would happen
to the family as women moved toward full equality in public
life. Naturally Ishibashi rejected arranged marriage. It was
predictable that such marriages left the spouses estranged and
frustrated; hence, Ishibashi and other reformist intellectuals
tended to accept a relationship such as that of Shimamura
Hōgetsu and Matsui Sumako as the equivalent of a marriage
of free choice, even though Shimamura was already legally
married. The serious journals were extremely restrained about
discussing sexual relationships, and Ishibashi was unusually
frank in condoning premarital unchastity for women and ad-

75. *ITZ* 2:419–20.

vocating sex education.[76] There is no indication that he or most other reformist intellectuals envisioned any arrangement other than permanent and exclusive monogamy based on free choice, with divorce a rare and tragic exception. Nevertheless he stressed individual relations in the family and downplayed the corporate character of the household, even insisting that children were not an essential part of marriage and that the customary insistence on an heir was demeaning to women.[77] He offered lukewarm support to proponents of birth control, which he viewed mainly in economic terms, as a means for poor families to regulate their expenses, but contended that birth control was a mere palliative for the real problem, "the unequal distribution of wealth in society."[78] He was somewhat more specific than Tanaka in advocating a more efficient living environment, applauding the 1915 Ueno exhibition of modern housing. The people's daily life had been neglected in the Meiji Restoration, and the nation's industrial accomplishments ought to be brought home, literally. Ishibashi deplored traditional Japanese housing as too costly and inconvenient, with unworkable kitchens and unhygienic toilets. The diet was poor in nutrients and ought to be supplemented by Western, Chinese, and Korean food adapted to Japanese conditions. Western clothing was simpler than kimono and thus could liberate women, but it was too expensive, partly because women were reluctant to buy the wider bolts of cloth needed to make it; the small market for Western costume made it an expensive luxury item. All aspects of home life ought to be analyzed with special attention to the working class's need for efficiency and economy.[79] He also urged the formation of urban consumer cooperatives, with revisions in the Civil Code to permit women autonomous commercial activity without the consent of their husbands, and he was active in organizing cooperatives in Kamakura after the Great Kantō Earthquake of 1923.[80] Although concerned with the ration-

76. *ITZ* 1:274–79, 2:327.
77. *ITZ* 1:279–80.
78. *ITZ* 8:524–26.
79. *ITZ* 2:428–31, 543–48.
80. *ITZ* 5:34–36; Shimura, 41–42.

alization of home life, he never assigned this responsibility exclusively to women.

Ishibashi glossed over the mother-child bond that was so
central to Hiratsuka as well as contemporary conservatives. If
children were born he vaguely suggested they be entrusted to
"the public"; he was especially optimistic about the educational
roles that could be played by "farmers and intellectuals."[81]
Viewing the family as a collection of individuals rather than a
corporate body, he emphasized the external productive functions of its members rather than its internal functions, which
he viewed as largely consumptive. His analysis, however, overlooked the nurturing character of the parent-child relationship, which was not a voluntary association of compatible
personalities freely chosen. Moreover, in viewing women in
public as producers and women in the home as consumers, he
failed to allow for the productive and uncompensated contribution of child care to national well-being. While groping to
legitimize women's right to education, employment equality,
and participation in the public sphere, he inadvertently constructed a paradigm that disallowed their claims as mothers,
a new cleavage of public and private. His brief—indeed, cav-
alier—dismissals of the significance and magnitude of the
problem of child care were to be the Achilles' heel of his highly
progressive vision of women's equality.

SOCIAL FEMINISM: TANAKA TAKAKO

Tanaka's wife Takako stressed precisely those family and nurturing roles that Ishibashi neglected, believing that the emancipation of women's tenderness in the public sphere could
create a more benign and equitable society. Her articulate self-
definition as a social worker illustrated the increasing specialization typical of urban middle-class men and women during the 1920s. She admired but did not participate in the
philosophical quest for self-discovery characteristic of the naturalists and Seitōsha women. Neither was she adept in Tanaka's and Ishibashi's style of political and social analysis.

81. *ITZ* 1:97.

Instead, she devoted most of her public activity to solving practical problems for women workers, mothers, and children. She also sought to bridge the gap between the few middle-class women seeking vocations and the many ordinary women whose first concern was their family's well-being. In doing so she evidenced yet another of the pluralistic modes of Taishō feminism, setting a rare example as a married professional woman with a child and reaching a mass audience through family counseling and the media.

Takanashi Takako (1888–1966) was born the third daughter of a Noda soy brewer and former lower samurai, Takanashi Chūi. Her mother, Yuki, was the daughter of a Mito official (*kanjōyaku*) and niece of the second wife of eminent entrepreneurial pioneer Shibusawa Eiichi (1841–1931). This connection was to bring her both opportunity and burdens due to Shibusawa's singular wealth and prominence. Son of a prosperous peasant descended from the demobilized samurai of the sixteenth century (*gōnō*), Shibusawa briefly served in the Finance Ministry but withdrew to manage the first national bank, playing a definitive role in the founding of modern currency and trust systems and subsequently founding over five hundred private corporations. Long a premier spokesman of industrial and financial interests, he devoted his later years to social services and education.[82]

Takako graduated from Japan Women's College, Hiratsuka Raichō's alma mater, and entered the English faculty there until joining Shibusawa and his wife when he headed an economic delegation to the United States in 1909. She remained in the United States until 1918, graduating from Palo Alto High School and earning a bachelor's degree in English from Stanford in 1917 and a master's degree in social work from the University of Chicago in 1918 before she returned to teach English and sociology at Japan Women's College. So lengthy a foreign education was exceedingly rare among Japanese women in this period. She was over thirty when she returned

82. The most complete biography of Takanashi Takako (Tanaka Takako) is in Ichiyama Morio, *Noda no rekishi*, 268–69; see also her memoir, *Tōyō*, 236. On Shibusawa see William Chambliss, *Chiraijima Village*; and Marshall, *Capitalism and Nationalism in Prewar Japan*, especially 78–85.

home, far too old, well educated, and independent for a conventional marriage. Like many feminists she dropped the last syllable of her personal name (*ko*, meaning child), but later reattached it. Shibusawa again played a decisive role in Takako's life when he sponsored John Dewey's lectures at Tokyo University in 1919, and Takako met Tanaka, who had organized a dinner party in Dewey's honor. Takako attended the party without bringing cash to cover her share of the expenses, and Tanaka called at her home a few days later to rectify this excess of gentility and to end the isolation of these two eccentric personalities.[83]

Doubtless the two were of like mind on many contemporary issues. Takako had studied with W. I. Thomas, Earnest W. Burgess, Albion W. Small, and Edith Abbott, all clearly within the pragmatic tradition that stressed the importance of social education in gradual progress. For Takako, their assumptions made it possible to analyze Meiji Japan in terms of a general and universal theory of social progress:

> Human progress is carried on by two conflicting forces: one, which tries to maintain existing conditions and resists any change; and the other, which tends to reject the old and bring out innovation. . . . Both of them contribute to the promotion of social welfare. . . . Generally this transformation in conditions of life is the result of an evolutionary rather than a revolutionary process. Therefore, when changes occur very suddenly, not gradually, and artificially, not naturally, they involve always great confusion and sometimes severe conflict.[84]

Her analysis of how sudden and externally prompted industrialization had affected Japanese women revealed her own ambivalence.

Takako was generally complacent about the pace of change for upper-class women. She defended the elite custom of pa-

83. Archives of Stanford University and the University of Chicago. Shibusawa's role in arranging Dewey's visit to Japan is mentioned in George Dykhuizen, *The Life and Mind of John Dewey*, 186; Tanaka Takako, "Fujin no shakai jigyō," *Katei shūhō*, no. 520 (13 June 1919): 3; Interview, Tanaka Miki, 3 Apr. 1976.
84. Takanashi, 1. Her academic records are in the University of Chicago Archives. The relationship of the sociology department at Chicago with Dewey's earlier development of pragmatism there is discussed in C. Wright Mills, *Sociology and Pragmatism*, 448.

rentally arranged marriage as a constraint on the ill-regulated passions of youth. Women's family difficulties, she believed, derived mainly from the occasional excesses of the old conventions—domination by in-laws, inability to earn a living if disaster struck the male breadwinner, extreme self-abnegation and chastity such as that of a young woman who committed suicide upon the death of her fiancé. In contrast, she cited several examples of dutiful traditional women who were beloved, respected, and fulfilled. Progress had been made; it would continue, but there was much to be admired and preserved in the gracious yet disciplined feminine character of the old upper classes.[85]

Takako did not read *Seitō* while studying in the United States, though she could hardly have escaped hearing of Hiratsuka's abortive elopement while she was at Japan Women's College. Disgusted by newspaper reports of two trivial but notorious episodes in which Bluestockings drank "five-colored *sake*" (a liqueur mixture) at a public cafe and visited the Yoshiwara pleasure quarter for research, she censured, "Unfortunately the conduct of those women was outrageously radical, entering into men's fields, even on the vicious side, so that they became repugnant to all members of society."[86] Nevertheless, Takako, true to her even-handed insistence on the positive role of both convention and innovation, continued: "It is unjust to condemn this group of women without understanding that their actions are the outbursts of the repressed impulses of women, who suffered a long servitude under the old regime."[87] Takako was confused by her conservative upbringing and limited knowledge of Japanese society, her desire for change, and her nationalistic attraction toward those Americans who portrayed the Japanese status quo in a favorable light.

No such ambivalence clouded Takako's indictment of factory conditions. She had been awakened to the plight of Japanese women workers by an American evangelist who had visited Japan and lectured at Stanford. Takako was "stunned";

85. Takanashi, 23, 25–28, 39–40.
86. Ibid., 50–51.
87. Ibid.

"I vowed to devote my whole life to helping such people."[88]
Her study of sociology at Chicago introduced her to problems
she had never seen: confined conditions, thirteen- to sixteen-
hour days, child labor, night work, runaways, disease, and
death. She also believed that her efforts on behalf of women
workers would resolve her own problems of vocation, for elite
leadership was needed since the labor movement was yet weak
and recent factory legislation owed more to elite initiative than
to popular demands. Upper-class women's maternal nurturing
instinct could be harnessed and would transform the social
order by championing the protection of the weak and helpless.
The maternal cure for social ills, which Takako learned from
American progressives and suffragists, was a useful argument
against traditionalists, who were appalled by the prospect of
women rendered masculine by higher education and public
participation—instead, the society would be rendered feminine.

After her return to Japan in 1919, Takako was chosen as a
government adviser on women workers in Japan's delegation
to the first International Labor Organization (ILO) convention in Washington in October 1919. Thus she became embroiled in the controversy surrounding the so-called labor
delegate Matsumoto Uhei, a highly paid chief engineer who
had no connection with the budding union movement and had
been selected by the Home Ministry. At the first lecture meeting for Japanese women workers, sponsored by the Yūaikai
(Friendly Society) Women's Bureau under Ichikawa Fusae, Takako was heckled as "bourgeois" before a crowd of some fifteen hundred people. Takako, however, had just completed a
crash tour of Japanese factories and made an unexpectedly
positive impression, speaking beautifully after Ichikawa qui-
eted the hecklers.[89] In Washington she delivered a scathing

    88. Tanaka Takako, *Tōyō*, 209; idem, "Fujin no shakai jigyō," 3; Takanashi, 35–
36. On American views of maternal instinct and social reform see Charles H. Cooley,
Social Organization, 363–64; and Rothman, 97–134.
    89. Ichikawa Fusae, *Watakushi no fujin undō*, 47; Wakamori and Yamamoto 6:281–
83; Molony, 85–87; Yamanouchi Mina, *Yamanouchi Mina jiden*, 53–54. For a general
account of the first ILO Conference and Japanese labor see Iwao F. Ayusawa, *A History
of Labor in Modern Japan*, 121–26; and Marshall, *Capitalism and Nationalism in Prewar
Japan*, 78–85.

indictment of the plight of Japanese working women as "slaves of the capitalists, mentally and physically."[90] So unexpected a statement from one of her background is in fact quite typical of the shocks accompanying Taishō feminism.

Takako's role as a woman activist meant a considerable defiance of convention. Soon she provoked another controversy by marrying Tanaka Ōdō and giving birth to their first child five months after the wedding. Publicly renouncing her earlier defense of arranged marriage, she defended their courtship as a mutual protest against the custom. She also expressed the novel opinion that her marital choice had been influenced by her professional judgment, and ought to strengthen her vocation in social work: "My attitude toward my work, and toward the position of the family in society, was that only love marriages could succeed. And I chose him as a guide in my work, as well as a personal companion."[91] Subsequently she was elected a trustee and served as a speaker in the New Woman's Society (Shin Fujin Kyōkai) founded in 1919 by Ichikawa Fusae and the "outrageously radical" Hiratsuka Raichō.[92]

The goals of the New Woman's Society were the free development of women's ability; public recognition of the equal value of men and women, and relationships of cooperation based on respect for the differences between the two; clarification of the social significance of the home, and protection and promotion of the rights and interests of women, mothers, and children. Though these goals stressed woman's separate sphere, Ichikawa understood that they could not be achieved without political rights. Most significantly, the group determined to seek amendment of Article 5 of the Public Peace Police Law of 1900, which barred women from joining political organizations or attending political meetings. Opinion was shifting in favor of women's rights in principle, with opponents increasingly stressing gradualism. Takako, Ichikawa, and Hiratsuka along with other leading members lobbied Diet representatives until the ban on attending political meetings was

90. Quoted in Arthur Morgan Young, *The Socialist and Labour Movement in Japan*, 91–93.

91. Tanaka Takako, *Tōyō*, 246.

92. Ichikawa, *Watakushi no fujin undō*, 10, 26; Fukushima Shirō, *Fujinkai sanjūgo-nen*, 1147–53; Ide Fumiko and Esashi Akiko, *Taishō demokurashii to josei*, 90–95.

revoked in 1922. The minor victory in politics reflected far deeper changes in consciousness, for example in journalism, which was generally more respectful than it had been toward the Seitōsha a decade earlier.[93]

The New Woman's Society disbanded in 1921 when Hiratsuka transferred her primary emphasis from political rights to protective legislation for wives and mothers. Ichikawa, after a brief sojourn in the United States that included study of social work at the University of Chicago, continued the struggle for political rights, while former Seitō member Yamakawa Kikue denounced both women for failing to understand the priority of socialist revolution in emancipating Japanese working women. In addition to diverging ideologies, personal problems played a role in the group's collapse and certainly explained Takako's sabbatical from public affairs.[94]

Married professional and activist women experienced unprecedented conflicts of loyalties and considerable physical strain. During the first five years of her marriage Takako, in her early thirties, endured four births, three infant deaths, and the total destruction of her home in the Great Kantō Earthquake of 1923. Her surviving daughter was named Miki ("the age that is yet to come"), bearing Takako's "hopes for a society not yet born, in which women are free to make their contribution in work against misery and injustice."[95] Miki remembers Takako as a cheerful and decisive mother, but Takako described herself as "weak and nervous, fearful of earthquakes, tidal waves, and dark streets, fluttery over the children's illnesses."[96] She hoped that Miki would develop more "logic, correct thinking, and conceptual powers," and "choose a work full of love for the world."[97] Tanaka Miki never married and is a teacher at Shiraume Junior College who specializes in education for the handicapped.

---

93. Ishizuki Shizue, "Fujin undō no tenkai," in Koyama Hitoshi, *Taishōki no kenryoku to minshū*, 163; Molony, 101, 110, 114, 155–56; Inoue Kiyoshi, *Nihon joseishi*, 242–55.
94. Molony, 134–35, 138–39, 270.
95. Tanaka Takako, *Tōyō*, 242–44, 261.
96. Interview with Tanaka Miki, 3 Apr. 1976; and Tanaka Takako, *Tōyō*, 242.
97. Ibid., 243–44.

The marriage of Tanaka Ōdō and Tanaka Takako was, by all accounts, exceptionally close and happy, a model of companionship characterized by "much discussing and critiquing together" and "a mutual interest in the welfare of society," rather than a more conventional marriage based on functional division of labor.[98] Gradually, however, Takako was drawn into the role of the traditional, self-abnegating upper-class woman whom she had always admired. Neither husband nor wife could sustain the relationship of equality to which both were intellectually committed. When Takako learned that her husband preferred to dictate his journal articles, she eagerly became his scribe:

> I was defeated by him, and as in olden times the vanquished became the slave of the victor. But I was a willing slave. As I lived with him, more and more, I felt the transcendence of his talent and the greatness of his work. I found a greater value in aiding his work than in fulfilling my trivial self. And soon it ceased to be a sacrifice. In the life of a serving-woman, I found the value of living.[99]

Such sentiments from a genuine member of the feminist avant-garde give some indication of the barriers facing Taishō women. Genteel poverty aggravated the tension between the two Tanakas' careers, for he adamantly refused to accept money from her relatives. As their debts mounted during his final illness he demanded that she sell his library, but she secretly sought aid from family and friends, and after his death in 1932 donated the library to Waseda University as a memorial.[100]

Journalism was a vocation that Takako could pursue while a homemaker; and her occasional article for *Fujin no tomo*, *Fujin kōron*, and *Shufu no tomo* doubtless contributed to the family budget. Her intense domestic preoccupation probably afforded her a rapport with women readers beyond that of the naturalists, the Seitōsha, or the liberals. She also had a larger

98. Ibid., 216–17.
99. Ibid., 262.
100. Tanaka Takako, "Ko Tanaka Ōdō no zōsho ni tsuite," *Shobutsu tenbō* (Dec. 1932): 54–56; Ichiyama, 268–69.

audience. Women's domestic magazines had circulated in the hundreds of thousands as early as the 1890s. *Fujin no tomo*, founded in 1903 with a printing of ten thousand copies, reached a circulation of three million by 1935, and was popular even in remote rural areas, where copies of it were passed from household to household. It favored modern and scientific approaches to a wide range of women's interests, from household management and family relations to career guidance and political rights. In it Takako discussed egalitarian marriage, while Shibusawa contributed articles on increasing family income. Ichikawa and Ishibashi shared their concern with the daily life of the average woman, cooperating in economic lectures for the Young Women's Christian Association (Nihon Kirisutokyō Joshi Seinenkai) and the Women's Suffrage League (Fusen Dōmei) at women's schools and the offices of *Tōyō keizai shinpō* during the 1920s and 1930s. *Fujin no tomo* founder Hani Motoko would campaign for Ishibashi in the election of 1946.[101] Their sense of shared purpose in helping women blurred aims that are analytically distinct in retrospect. Frugality and rational home management served state ends by increasing the savings rate while providing for young, old, and ailing family members and sparing state welfare budgets, but they also realized personal goals within existing institutional constraints. Moreover, all of the writers went beyond home management to urge the development of women's individual characters, sometimes in functional separation but moral equality vis-à-vis men, sometimes in full public participation. Their discourse during the 1920s was characterized by a fusion of the aims of aiding women under present conditions and gradually transforming those conditions.

After Tanaka's death, Takako resumed her career in social work. She became a member of the Child Protection Society (Jidō Hogo Kyōkai), and, in 1933, head of the first public marriage counseling center (Tōkyō-shi Kekkon Sōdansho), es-

101. Tanaka Sumiko, ed., *Josei kaihō no shisō to kōdō*, vol. 1, 224–25; Murakami, 235–36; 606; *ITZ* 15:73, 388, 51; Saitō Michiko, 152; Arase Yutaka, "Taishō kankaku to shuppan jōtai: Senkanki Nihon ni okeru," *SS*, no. 689 (Nov. 1981): 192–200.

tablished by the Social Bureau of the Tokyo city government. She also lobbied on behalf of the Personal Conciliation Law (Jinji Chōtei Hō), which passed the Diet in 1939 and established arbitration boards chosen by local judges in every ward in the nation. Anticipating that family matters would constitute the bulk of the boards' work, Legal Minister Shiono Suehiko hoped for women arbitrators, but few were actually selected. Of the first 150 board members in Tokyo only twenty-five were women, including Takako as well as two other Taishō journalists and feminists, Hani Motoko and Yamada Waka. The arbitration boards were made part of the family court system in 1947, and, by 1979, 40 percent of their counselors were women. In such instances change in social policy and social life continued through the wartime period while the movement for political rights was held in abeyance.[102]

Takako continued in these positions until 1963, publishing five books on modern marriage, writing her memoirs, and producing a newspaper advice column. Takako's columns resoundingly denounced feudal superstition, including assumptions of the inferiority of women. Still, her advice was more pragmatic than ideological. To a woman whose husband beat her, and who had no blood relatives of her own who might shelter her, Takako advised attempting to calm the man by gentle kindness and perhaps the tactful intervention of a neighbor; in the depths of the Great Depression, "you will never be able to support your three children alone."[103] Takako also compromised with wartime policies, mildly but pointedly complaining in 1943 that the marriage counseling office had become a means of "increasing strength through population" and had thus "lost its function of social education."[104] Apart from that cryptic comment she avoided the war in her memoirs, and further details about her activities must await new studies of social welfare and the women's movement. Still, it is clear that she retained her official position, attempting to

102. Tanaka Takako, *Tōyō*, 271–72; Ichiyama, 268–69; von Straelen, 146; *Fujo shinbun*, no. 1713 (9 Apr. 1933): 2; on the Jinji Chōtei Hō see Kodama Katsuko, *Fujin sanseiken undō shōshi*, 285.
103. Tanaka Takako, *Tōyō*, appendix.
104. Ibid., 211.

aid women and children within the confines of military authority.

CONCLUSION

By the early 1930s, cracks had formed in the walls excluding women from public affairs. Literary women had begun to engage each other and their male counterparts in the media. A few urban middle-class women took more active roles in society as teachers, journalists, and social workers, while white-collar service employment increased among single women. Several leading state and private universities had begun to admit women. One minor political right, the right to attend meetings, had been won, and full participation had been widely debated. Although the patriarchal Civil Code remained in force until 1945, its fundamental premises had been called into question, and courts began to uphold the rights of women in bringing suit for breach of promise, divorcing an adulterous husband, and managing their own property. The introduction of rationalized home management techniques increased the housewife's independence from her mother and particularly from her mother-in-law. Smaller and upwardly mobile urban nuclear families opened new opportunities. Finally, journalism played a definitive role in communicating all these new experiences and possibilities to a mass audience.

To a limited extent women shared in the evolving pluralism of Taishō society and culture. As the prewar women's movement moved from self-discovery to reform, it debated nearly all possibilities of improving women's condition: self-expression, marital equality and social support for motherhood, quality private or public child care, working conditions, educational and employment opportunity, and political rights. The one exception, rarely discussed, was sexual freedom. Birth control was advocated by some members of the Seitōsha and New Woman's Society, but only as a means to maternal health, quality child care, and household economic betterment. The inattention to sexual self-expression is curious considering the feminists' roots in the naturalist literature movement, which was preoccupied with desire to the point of obsession. However, as the more repressive feminine roles of the elite filtered downward in society, license was equated with the poor and backward, while feminists' restraint in discussing sexuality enhanced their status and widened their audience. For women, admission to new opportunities was often at the price of sexual and biological functions.

Public life and private life were polarized in thought because they were polarized in society. The upwardly mobile, urban nuclear family increased the responsibilities of married women, especially in supervising their children's education. The private sphere, the central reality of most women's lives, tended to absorb the demands for psychic awakening and self-fulfillment that had been posed by Shimamura and the Seitōsha women, who tried but failed to place personal experience on the agenda of public discourse. Ultimately their proposals for social reform aimed at enhancing women's separate sphere in the home. They acknowledged woman's special biological and social functions and struggled to envision her sphere as separate but equal, but vision lapsed into mysticism.

Tanaka and Ishibashi correctly perceived that women could achieve equality in public life only by acceding to a male standard, the Meiji success ethic. Hence they rejected the concept of a separate sphere and regarded the ambivalent self-expression of a Hiratsuka or a Magda as a problem to be surmounted by equal education and democratic reform, not as a different mode of experience or a source of reformist insight. Yet women's experience was the key to the problem, for most professional women, like Tanaka Takako, learned that individual competition did not allow for marriage and child care, as long as marriage and child care were not acknowledged by the developing meritocracy. In this sense the psychic estrangement of the sexes persisted even in the efforts of dedicated reformers, and most women continued to be excluded from the educational and bureaucratic meritocracy.[105]

105. For a present-day account of the separation of public and private functions, and the position of women in recruitment by examination, see Takie Sugiyama Lebra,

Tanaka Takako's career illustrates another constraint on urban middle class women, for they, even more than their male counterparts, were dependent on the industrializing state. The Japanese government selected her as an ILO delegate. The Tokyo city government employed her as a family counselor. In utilizing official channels for her professional energies she was typical of the vast majority of women professionals in teaching and social service, for these professions were either created or quickly absorbed by the state. Although women in these professions did organize for purposes of raising professional standards or improving working conditions, their lack of independence militated against broader social and political demands. Women journalists enjoyed somewhat greater independence, but they were subject to censorship. State domination and altruistic values channeled the vast majority of educated women into service or patriotic activities. Welfare work for mothers and children, by acceding in state policies, continued gradual development through the Pacific War era.

From the Meiji through the Taishō era, the interdependence of family and state continued but changed in form, as women were needed less in the factories and more in the services and the home. Taishō feminists grasped the interdependence but failed to overcome it. None surmounted the social and psychological division of labor to detail a comprehensive and practical program for a society of equality between the sexes. Their effects were as polarized as the society in which they lived: on the one hand, the public success of a few exceptional and usually single professional women, and on the other, an increasing recognition of the social necessity of educated motherhood, which was to become the nucleus of the postwar professional housewife's role.

"Japanese Women in Male Dominant Careers: Cultural Barriers and Accommodations for Sex-Role Transcendence," *Ethnology* 20 (1981): 300.

4

History as Taishō Politics: Tanaka and Ishibashi

History was a weapon in the acute political competition of the late Meiji and Taishō eras. Tanaka and Ishibashi constructed interpretations of the Japanese past, especially of the nineteenth century, that they believed would forward desirable Taishō trends such as democracy. Simultaneously, an academic and purportedly scientific historiography emerged at the imperial universities, while the Ministry of Education staked its own claim by sponsoring projects in Meiji history and controlling historical instruction in the public school textbooks. Symbols of the national past were ambivalent and multifaceted, encouraging contending factions to seize them and invest them with desired meanings. At issue were distinct visions of Japan's place in the world and of its domestic society, culture, and polity.

As internationalists, Tanaka and Ishibashi criticized both the Perry Expedition that had brought Western civilization to Japan under the threat of armed force and the imperial ideology that distinguished Japan from all other nations. Rejecting both Westernization and nativism, Tanaka searched for an indigenous bent toward pragmatic reform in his interpretation of Ninomiya Sontoku, and revived Fukuzawa Yukichi's thesis of Japan's authoritarian political culture. Subsequently Ishibashi applied Tanaka's paradigm of *bakumatsu*-Meiji history to the Russian and Chinese revolutions, concluding that Japan should encourage international economic cooperation and cultural exchange while abstaining from military intervention. Their writings on history and foreign policy not only illuminate an important theme in the Taishō democratic movement

131

but also are the most widely studied of their works in Japan today.

The Ministry of Education dominated the people's understanding of national history during the early twentieth century. Primary school textbooks portrayed benign and far-sighted rulers, especially the Meiji Emperor and his loyal advisers, and self-sacrificing subjects such as Ninomiya Sontoku (whom Tanaka was to cast in a quite different light). Of course the Ministry of Education also built Tokyo Imperial University as the sine qua non of scholarship in history and other fields, and, after 1904, directed the publication of documents in the history of the Meiji Restoration (*Ishin shiryō kōyō*) and interpretive studies (*Ishinshi*). Although ministerial projects covered a broad range of topics and interpretations, popular writers outside the government discerned an attempt to make national history a bureaucratic monopoly.

Meanwhile, history as an academic discipline had developed at Tokyo Imperial University under Ludwig Riess, an enthusiastic disciple of Leopold von Ranke. The Rankean model— scrupulous fidelity to primary sources and sensitivity to judging past epochs by their own standards of value—engendered a highly philological orientation in Japanese academic history. Led by the renowned Kuroita Katsumi, professional historians upheld the study of Japan's past for its own sake. Professedly independent of contemporary issues, they confined history (*rekishi*) to the pre-Meiji era. Everything after 1868 was defined as current events, which belonged to the domain of journalists and not scholars. Kuroita's famous *Shintei zōho kokushi taikei* (Revised and expanded outline of national history) exemplified Japanese academic history at the beginning of the Taishō era in its presumptions that Japan was an independent culture and that careful philological research produced a scientific representation of pre-Meiji Japanese history.[1]

Meanwhile, critics of the government such as Tokutomi Sohō and Takekoshi Yosaburō unabashedly tried to promote public enlightenment through popularized history. They established the tradition that has prevailed in journalism and the

---

1. Haga Noboru, *Kindai Nihon shigaku shisōshi*, 53–105.

private universities, the discussion of contemporary events in terms of Japan's cultural history (*bunmeishi*). From the outset, Japanese cultural historians eulogized the folk as the source of creativity and vitality. Popular historians during the 1880s and 1890s fit ancient and medieval Japan into their portraits of the present, often charting Japanese history along Western outlines of universal laws or stages of civilization. On this basis, they took sides on such issues as the Popular Rights (*jiyū minken*) movement of the 1880s, and the relevance of the Japanese polity (*kokutai*) and the national essence (*kokusui*) to the Meiji Constitution.[2]

Supporters of the Taishō democratic movement turned to the past, too, but rarely to the pre-Meiji past, to marshal history behind the struggle for freedom against tyranny. Tanaka Ōdō accented the discontinuity of modern Japanese history, the revolutionary impact of the collision with Western power and Western civilization that had brought about the Meiji Restoration. Skeptical of transcendental laws of civilization, Tanaka considered the development of human freedom and individualism to be the distinctive trend of modern world history. The development and progress of democracy in Japan, in his outlook, required no legitimation in the continuities of Japan's history, in the eternal verities of the national polity or the national essence. If Japanese history was neither unique nor Western, what then were its landmarks that might guide the present and future democratic movement?

Along with many other Taishō liberals, Tanaka often turned to the Charter Oath of 1868 for historical legitimation of the contemporary democratic movement. Tanaka, Ishibashi, Yoshino Sakuzō, and many of their compatriots repeatedly cited two clauses of the oath that they believed sanctioned their ideals of democracy and cosmopolitanism:

1. Deliberative assemblies shall be widely established and all matters decided by public discussion.
5. Knowledge shall be sought throughout the world so as to strengthen the foundations of imperial rule.[3]

2. Ienaga Saburō, "Keimō shigaku"; Peter Duus, "Whig History, Japanese Style: The Minyūsha Historians and the Meiji Restoration," *JAS* 33 (1974): 415–36.
3. The Charter Oath is translated in Tsunoda, de Bary, and Keene, eds., *Sources*

Of course Taishō liberals were quite in error in insisting that the oath proclaimed an official policy of liberal cosmopolitanism. Philological investigation has demonstrated that the framers intended "public discussion" in the first clause to mean rebalancing the political relationships of the rulers. The fifth clause is explicitly ambiguous, and such foreign beliefs as Christianity which cast doubt on imperial rule risked suppression from the Restoration through the Taishō period. The misreading was deliberate. Taishō liberals did not regard the intentions of the oath's framers as binding. Instead, they challenged the narrow concentration of power that the Meiji statesmen had designed. They chose to interpret public discussion to mean the political and civil rights of all adult Japanese, including women. They echoed the Popular Rights movement of the 1880s, which had also invoked the Charter Oath to claim that Japan was already committed to a democratic polity, with merely its details and timing at issue.

Taishō liberals regarded the Popular Rights movement with ambivalence, criticizing from within the tradition, just as reformers after World War II were highly critical of the Taishō democratic movement because it had achieved only a small portion of its aims. Tanaka stressed the samurai heritage and values of the Popular Rights movement leaders and preferred Ninomiya Sontoku and Fukuzawa, who had devoted themselves to changing peasant life and public opinion rather than to seizing power. Ishibashi, too, criticized the movement's leaders as little different from the government that they opposed, but his preference for the oppositionist wing of the Meiji elite was unmistakable. He had emulated its orators during his childhood in Kōfu; he named Itagaki Taisuke as one of the four great thinkers of Meiji Japan, along with Fukuzawa, Shimamura, and Tsubouchi Shōyō; and he interpreted the attempted assassinations of Itagaki and Ōkuma Shigenobu as instances of martyrdom for new ideas, like the assassinations of Ōmura Masujirō, Ōkubo Toshimichi, Mori Arinori, and

---

of Japanese Tradition, vol. 2, 137. Tanaka, "Hiratsuka Raichō Shi ni ataete Shi no fujinkan o ronzu," 108; *ITZ* 1:231–32; 15:98–99, 104–05; Tetsuo Najita, *The Intellectual Foundations of Modern Japan*, 41; see also Robert Spaulding, "The Intent of the Charter Oath."

Hara Kei. Despite Ishibashi's obvious admiration for the Popular Rights movement he discussed it but little, focusing instead on the broader problem of why a democratic system had not been realized in the Meiji era.[4]

Yoshino Sakuzō took up the same problem, and advanced a highly critical interpretation of the Popular Rights movement. Associating the movement with outbreaks of violence such as the Satsuma Rebellion, Yoshino praised the Meiji oligarchy for having consolidated authority. Yet his historical studies, which comprised half of his life's work and merit as much attention as his better known constitutional theory, aimed to support the Taishō democratic movement. He attempted to make democracy legitimate by means of a relativistic scheme of historical evolution, in which Meiji authority had served a purpose in its own time by creating a stable and unified national system. Now the Meiji order could serve as the springboard to Taishō democracy. Cutting across the dualistic cleavage of Taishō from Meiji history, Yoshino idealized constitutional monarchy as the highest form of government.[5]

In contrast, Tanaka and Ishibashi accepted the Meiji state on a more pragmatic basis, believing that it had indeed consolidated order and initiated industrialization and ought not to be rejected wholesale in favor of untested abstractions. On the other hand neither man dreamed of idealizing constitutional monarchy in general or the Meiji state in particular. Tanaka derided the worship of Restoration leaders as national heroes:

> The root of the Restoration was the collusion of, on the one hand, factions formed to advance private interests, and on the other, scholars wallowing in trivia, forgetting their public responsibilities. Together they sought to foster a return to the past. . . . How much has our country lost through the collaboration of crafty politicians and idiotic pedants, engaged in a useless and meaningless attempt at reaction?[6]

4. *ITZ* 4:93–95; 15:102–05; 1:231–32, 61.
5. On Yoshino Sakuzō's views of Meiji history see Mitani Taiichirō, *Taishō demokurashii ron*, 197–213.
6. Tanaka, *Fukuzawa Yukichi*, Ōdō senshū, vol. 2, ed. Sugimori Kōjirō (1948), 255–56.

Ishibashi likewise attacked the Restoration for perpetuating regional, bureaucratic, military, and financial cliques, concluding that the real reason for the frustration of democratic forces lay in the strength of the state, and not in the weakness of its opponents. Their colleague in the Liberal Lecture Society, Uehara Etsujirō, interpreted Japanese constitutionalism more as a response to foreign pressure than as a domestic movement, but nonetheless saw real strengths in the democratic forces.[7]

Despite numerous and sharp disagreements among Tanaka, Ishibashi, Yoshino, and Uehara, all agreed that historical inquiry ought to serve an indigenous democracy. All rejected the academic and purportedly neutral historiography developing in the imperial universities, as well as a different style of historical politics, the Ministry of Education's glorification of inspired rulers and selfless subjects. Each in his own way looked to premodern popular culture in his effort to discern the wellsprings of creativity and reform in Japanese society, though none was fully successful in articulating these themes and linking them to Taishō democracy. Neither did they regard the Popular Rights movement as a prescription to cure the ills of Taishō Japan. Rather in their historical studies they sought new ways to understand and transform the relationship between the state and the people.

FUKUZAWA YUKICHI AND NINOMIYA SONTOKU

Tanaka's historical assessments of Ninomiya Sontoku (1911) and Fukuzawa Yukichi (1915) must be considered in the context of the contending claims on the Meiji past. The two prominent figures had been incorporated into the statist ideology of the *shūshin* primary school ethics courses to glorify national wealth and power. Nevertheless both had been private citizens remote from the government: Ninomiya (1757–1856) was a peasant whose rural improvement projects predated his receiving modest official rank, while Fukuzawa (1835–1901) was a journalist and educator who trumpeted his aversion to bu-

---

7. Uehara Etsujirō, *Hachijūji no omoide*, 34.

reaucratic service. If Tanaka could succeed in his reinterpretations of the two thinkers, he would surely win followers, for Ninomiya and Fukuzawa are still numbered among the best-known and most admired personalities in modern Japan. Journal polls of readers consistently have counted Fukuzawa high among the great men in Japanese history. Ninomiya's maxims of personal behavior were widely propagated in prewar Japan, making him the Benjamin Franklin of the Meiji and Taishō eras. Tanaka hoped to enlist the two popular figures in his own cause of a pragmatic and individualistic society.[8]

Tanaka's biographies were militantly revisionist. At the end of Meiji Japan, Ninomiya Sontoku was remembered and revered as a sage who expressed the orthodox virtues attributed to the Japanese peasant class: hard work and morality, hierarchy and order, cooperation and self-abnegation. The distinguished Christian philosopher Uchimura Kanzō eulogized Ninomiya's teachings, comparing them with Christian altruism. The Education Ministry elevated Ninomiya to an exemplar of the virtues taught in *shūshin* ethics courses. The Hōtoku Societies, who literally worshiped Ninomiya's teachings, enjoined an archaic communalism symptomatic of social discontent with urbanization and capitalist industrialization. According to Tanaka, each of these images of Ninomiya (as Christian altruist, moralistic patriot, and prophet of pastoral virtues) had badly misinterpreted his teachings, which were predicated on a concept of legitimate self-interest. By ignoring Ninomiya's concrete and immediate material goals, Tanaka argued, Ninomiya's would-be followers had transformed his teachings from an agrarian self-help venture into a transcendental matrix of moral relationships.[9]

The preface to Tanaka's *Fukuzawa Yukichi* signaled his revisionism too, volunteering that Fukuzawa was greatly admired and almost never read. At the turn of the century, reformist intellectuals such as Tokutomi Sohō, Kuga Katsunan, Kinoshita Naoe, and Miyake Setsurei remembered and criticized

---

8. Ichimura Hiromasa, ed., *Ronshū: Fukuzawa Yukichi e no shiten*, 206.

9. Tanaka, "Ayamaretaru Ninomiya Sontoku," *TJ* 2, no. 7 (Aug. 1911): 91–94; Kanzō Uchimura, "Ninomiya Sontoku—A Peasant Saint," in Tadaatsu Ishiguro, ed., *Ninomiya Sontoku*; *ITZ* 13:583–86.

the older Fukuzawa for anachronistic materialism, inconsistency, blind imitation of Western thought, worship of high bureaucrats and successful capitalists, and contempt for the Japanese commoner. By 1915, Fukuzawa was virtually the exclusive historical property of the opponents of liberalism.[10] A concurrent biography, for example, portrayed Fukuzawa as a militant Meiji advocate of the "spirit that makes a state a state," and an exemplary believer in the "preservation of the national essence."[11]

Rescuing Fukuzawa from nativists, Tanaka persuasively represented "Fukuzawa as a *hyōronka*"—a cultural critic and remarkably original thinker who had provided a masterful methodology for contemporary essayists who were concerned with promoting individualism and democracy. Tanaka's interpretation anticipated the views of such well-known scholars as Hani Gorō, Maruyama Masao, and Ishida Takeshi. All later cited Tanaka's judgment that Fukuzawa "was by no means an imitator or adapter; he was the creator of a new civilization and a new learning."[12] Tanaka's biography made Fukuzawa Yukichi the most significant thinker of Meiji Japan, and postwar interpretations confirm the assessment.

Tanaka regarded his two biographies as complementary, one stressing improvements in the livelihood of the peasant class, and the other highlighting individual upward mobility, which could blur class distinctions. In Ninomiya's emphasis on increased village and regional productivity, Tanaka found the nucleus of a capitalist ethos, but one with greater cooperative potential than Western Protestantism and liberalism.[13]

10. Ichimura, ed., 208–21. Tokutomi Sohō had earlier treated Ninomiya and Fukuzawa as representatives of the Meiji people's spirit, but Tanaka departed from Tokutomi's interpretation, which separated material from spiritual culture, linking Fukuzawa with the former and Ninomiya with the latter. Tanaka was also angered by Tokutomi's enthusiasm for empire; see Tanaka,"Hyōronka toshite no Tokutomi Sohō," *Shin Nihon* 7, no. 5 (1917): 89–105.
11. Ichimura, ed., 228; Tanaka, *Fukuzawa Yukichi* (1948), 50.
12. Hani Gorō, "Taikeiteki tetsugakusha *Systematiker* toshite no Fukuzawa Sensei," in Ichimura, ed., 61–62; Ishida Takeshi, "Kaisetsu," in *Fukuzawa Yukichi shū*, Kindai Nihon shisō taikei, vol. 2, 581. Maruyama Masao also stresses Fukuzawa's independence as a thinker, and mentions Tanaka's interpretation, in "Fukuzawa Yukichi no tetsugaku," in *Gendai Nihon shisō taikei*, vol. 34. Different interpretations of Fukuzawa continue, for example in Kinmonth, "Fukuzawa Reconsidered," 677–98.
13. Tanaka's interpretation of Ninomiya anticipated Robert Bellah, *Tokugawa Re-*

Tanaka contended that Ninomiya made man, rather than nature or God, the source of morality. Ninomiya had observed that "the theory of good and evil is . . . a matter of the way of man, derived from the self of the first human being. . . . Thus we say that it is good to reclaim barren land, and evil to lay waste to our fields."[14] Tanaka developed Ninomiya's ethic more rigorously:

> If good and evil are distinctions established by human beings, on the basis of human interest [*rigai*], then good and evil are made purely social, and moral relationships are set in congruence with interests; moreover good and evil are restricted to beings with a common consciousness—in short, to humanity.[15]

Ninomiya denounced reliance on authority in favor of human ingenuity, which could manipulate the laws of nature in the social interest.[16] He supported concrete rural improvement by means of reclamation and other projects.

Tanaka preferred to stress Ninomiya's secularism over that of Ogyū Sorai (1666–1728), whose instrumentalist approach to power has received far more attention. Ninomiya was interested in the welfare of the peasantry, not the stability of the ruling class. Ninomiya, Tanaka argued, was a peasant who had raised himself to the attention of the rulers "by his personal qualities alone."[17] Ogyū and Ninomiya had both accepted the Tokugawa distinction between the rulers and the ruled, but Ninomiya had set out to improve the people's welfare, without any ambition of joining the ruling class. Ogyū had devoted his efforts to promoting the efficiency of the ruling class, treating the peasants as a means to that end.

Since Tanaka believed that the Tokugawa legacy of ethical distinction between ruler and ruled was a formidable impediment to individualism and democracy, his preference for Ninomiya was hardly surprising. Indeed, Tanaka discerned that

---

ligion: The Values of Preindustrial Japan, which also found a Japanese analogue to the Protestant ethic.

14. Ninomiya Sontoku, quoted in Tanaka, *Ninomiya Sontoku,* 43–44.

15. Tanaka, in ibid., 47.

16. Ibid., 85–86.

17. Ibid., 157; see also 18.

commoners still engaged in politics in order to join the ruling class, just as they had in the past. Since the sixteenth century, even lords of peasant origins such as Toyotomi Hideyoshi had been

> not prompted by the motive of leading the class to which they belonged, raising its position and changing the distribution of power. They left the class to which they belonged in its original condition and merely split themselves off into a different class.[18]

Ninomiya was an exception, whose efforts to mitigate antagonism by means of cooperative economic development could inspire reform of the imbalanced relations in Meiji–Taishō Japan.

Tanaka contrasted Western social classes, formed by a more advanced level of capitalism under an ideology of unshackled self-interest, with Japanese classes, molded by feudal hierarchy. No ideology of laissez-faire would arise from Ninomiya's frame of reference, which entailed no Protestant sense of individuality, no personal power and responsibility to divine and forward God's plan through capitalist enterprise. The weakness of individualism in premodern Japanese thought, Tanaka believed, had encouraged submission to authority, but it had also played a positive role in denying legitimacy to destructive greed. In that sense Ninomiya had been more prescient than economic thinkers in the contemporary West, because he had stressed the integrated social framework of production and ethics:

> Adam Smith, while attempting to explain the principle of morality entirely by altruism, interpreted the principle of economics as self-interest. Thus the two principles separate into absolute opposites, and no exchange between them is possible.... [Ninomiya] Sontoku saw economics and morality as the most intimately connected matters, and tried to reform both at the same time, bringing them into interaction with each other.[19]

Ninomiya's generation and class had circumscribed his thinking. Modern methods to integrate economics and morality, in-

18. Ibid.
19. Ibid., 166–67.

cluding credit cooperatives and health insurance, had been beyond Ninomiya's purview. With limited means by which to improve the lot of the peasantry, Ninomiya had ultimately retreated to ascetic altruism. Nevertheless Tanaka believed that Ninomiya's bent toward a secular and humanistic ethos, along with his dedication to the material and moral life of his own class, had planted the indigenous seed of a modern industrial ethos. Ishibashi would sanction Tanaka's interpretation of Ninomiya and develop further the quest for an integration of economics and social morality.[20]

Tanaka's profile of Fukuzawa Yukichi also illustrated his vision of socially responsible self-interest. Fukuzawa's method of analysis conditionally accepted existing society while exposing it by the light of critical reason, balancing conservative and progressive impulses in order to achieve gradual reform. Tanaka's rapport with Fukuzawa's intellectual method offset his rejection of Fukuzawa's political and social prescriptions, for Tanaka viewed Fukuzawa as a product of his times who must be interpreted in his historical context.

The Meiji generation, including Fukuzawa, had shared the crisis engendered by confrontation with the West. Commodore Perry had called into question Japan's historic closed-door policy, but his seemingly innocuous demands for trade and treaty ports also had been "lined with ambition." Tanaka lamented Perry's methods as fervently as he supported Japan's opening: "Of course, it is foolish to avoid trade without proper grounds, since it is more often mutually profitable than not, but what right does one country have to force another into it?"[21] Superior Western power had led to the unequal treaties, which in turn had severely handicapped the development of Japanese commerce and industry.

The more contact we had with the West, the more we were overwhelmed by superior military power; this fact explains our prof-

20. Ibid., 194. See also Tanaka, "Sekai heiwa no risō ni chinamite shoka no bunkashugi o kentōsu (1)," *CK* 37, special issue on "Sekai heiwa to jinruiai" (July 1922): 45; and idem, *Sōzō to kyōraku*, 48. For Ishibashi see *ITZ* 11:523; 13:512, 583; 14:521, 523; and Hattori Bennosuke, "Jiyū shisōka Ninomiya Sontoku to Ishibashi Tanzan," *JS*, no. 5 (Apr. 1977): 34–40.

21. Tanaka, *Fukuzawa Yukichi* (1948), 84–85.

itless trade. . . . Like today, at that time in the international sphere
there was no morality or reciprocity. Only an appropriate degree
of economic and military power could be relied on to support a
nation's prestige and independence.[22]

The only possible response had been the single-minded Meiji
focus on national power and independence. The Meiji generation had used the goals of national strength and independence as the sole criteria for sweeping reforms of state and
society. Given the Meiji imperatives, Tanaka believed, Fukuzawa Yukichi had been the most prescient of his generation.

While all of the Meiji generation had been preoccupied with
national independence and security, Fukuzawa had grasped
the integrity of Meiji life and culture. He had discerned the
crucial task of his and future generations, to carry Japan from
the adoption of the outward forms of Western civilization
(technology and industry) to self-criticism according to the underlying spirit of Western civilization—individualism, liberty,
and representative government. He had confronted the problem of how to absorb Western civilization, "without bringing
on bankruptcy in the present, or impediments for the future."[23] If Fukuzawa had provided no satisfactory answer, his
exploration of the issue had surpassed that of other Meiji
thinkers. In this respect, Tanaka added, Japan had still not
advanced much since Fukuzawa's time.

Fukuzawa had employed the spirit of Western civilization in
a critical theory of Japanese history in his *Bunmeiron no gairaku*
(Outline of a theory of civilization). Western comparisons high-
lighted the Japanese imbalance of power, which had produced
arbitrary rulers and obedient subjects. As Tanaka interpreted
Fukuzawa's discovery:

> When a country's power is concentrated in one class, the princi-
> ples of life are made simple, and civilization does not advance, or
> it declines; but when power is well distributed in all classes, the
> principles of life become differentiated and complex, and civili-
> zation tends to advance.[24]

22. Ibid., 8–9.
23. Ibid., 13.
24. Ibid., 152.

Western civilization could also inspire a critique of unrepresentative government and the hierarchical family system in Taishō Japan. Both Fukuzawa and Tanaka believed that Western societies and values rendered principles by which Japanese development could be advanced.

To explain why the psychic and social effects of the imbalance of power in premodern Japan had persisted in spite of the modern introduction of representative institutions, Tanaka employed Fukuzawa's distinction between the form and the spirit of a civilization. The spirit of despotism prevented new institutional forms from working effectively.

> The relationship between voters and representatives is still subject to those habits and emotions of despotism, just as before. Why do the voters elect representatives? What aspect of the voters do the representatives represent? There is no understanding or commitment between the two. Thus changes in the numbers of representatives [from the various political parties] have no effect whatsoever on policy. In spite of this the voters and the representatives fancy that they are a people with a fine representative system, and exercising representative government. Is this not remarkable?[25]

As long as the people treated their representatives with exaggerated respect, Tanaka reasoned, representative government could not function properly, and the so-called representatives of the people would act arbitrarily. Tanaka shared Fukuzawa's sense that politics was only one part of a socio-cultural whole, and could not advance independently.

Fukuzawa's distinction between the form and spirit of institutions was fundamental to Taishō discourse. Believing that rudimentary parliamentary institutions had preceded mass demand for them, Taishō democrats asked how an ethos to sustain and expand those institutions might be fostered. They acknowledged that institutions depended on some collective sense of values. How could a society that had abruptly abandoned a traditional ethos formulate a new one? Like Tanaka, Yoshino Sakuzō and Ōyama Ikuo argued that the spirit of democracy lagged behind its form in Taishō Japan, and urged

25. Ibid., 164.

the nurture of individual consciousness.[26] Kawata Shirō as well urged that new individual values were essential to consensus, defining consensus not as the absence of conflict but rather as the dynamic result of interaction and accommodation among diverse individual and social needs, and the voluntary commitment to certain restraints that were integral to the functioning of civilized society.[27] In their preference for spirit over form the democrats risked losing sight of the realities of power. They began with an acute insight into the political and social order, but tended to end in exhortations to individual awakening. Nevertheless, their accommodationist inquiry into the spirit of a progressive society and polity showed growth in intellectual and political flexibility.

The study of Fukuzawa Yukichi, with its bleak view of pre-modern political culture, stimulated Tanaka to contest the concept of a unique, immutable Japanese national policy (*kokutai*) by postulating in its place an evolving nationality (*kokuminsei*).

> Nationality is nothing more than a name for the continuity of behavior that a certain people, in the past, have developed while controlling and utilizing the stimuli that came from their environment. Thus if their environment changes, either materially or socially, and its stimuli change, then naturally the method of controlling and using them must change. Since nationality is no more than a name given to the continuity of behavior, one may say then that *a new nationality is born* [emphasis added].[28]

American imperialism, in the Perry expedition, had served as midwife to a new Japanese nationality that was neither traditional nor Western. In light of this history, Tanaka rejected the possibility of a universal model of development. He insisted on the centrality of particular circumstances to social ethics, and he saw the most powerful and significant set of circumstances in the development of the nation-state. Unable to deny the significance of nationality in the modern world, Tanaka

26. Yoshino Sakuzō quoted in Duus, "Yoshino Sakuzō," 85–86.
27. Kawata Shirō, "Minponshugi ni kansuru ichi kōsatsu," in Ōta, *Shiryō* 1:79.
28. Tanaka, *Fukuzawa Yukichi* (1915), 142–43. For a similar conception of Japanese nationality see Nyozekan Hasegawa, *Japanese Character and Culture*, trans. John Bester, 4–8, 91–92, 98, 103–04, 148. For one of the more logical expositions of the *kokutai*, Japan's unique virtues, and their relation to empire see Inoue Tetsujirō, "Kokumin shisō no mujun."

hoped for a flexible and cosmopolitan sense of nationality. In other words, the criteria by which Japanese nationality could be deemed valuable must similarly recognize the value of other nationalities, and the criteria were subject to constant evolutionary change.

Here Tanaka departed from Fukuzawa while still considering himself within Fukuzawa's tradition of critical inquiry and pragmatic adaptation. Whereas Fukuzawa had argued that individual independence and self-respect were necessary to national independence, Tanaka turned Fukuzawa on his head, deriving the value of nationalities and states from their utility in fulfilling the needs and desires of individual persons. Each person's nationality was a valuable heritage; moreover, respect for each people was essential to world peace: "Today coexistence with different peoples is a central and indispensable condition for individual values."[29] By describing the coexistence of nationalities as a means to fulfill the needs of persons, Tanaka denied that the state had any intrinsic right to exist that transcended the interests of either its own people or another people. By reversing Fukuzawa's reasoning, Tanaka simultaneously justified democracy and renounced imperialism.

At the height of public interest in the Twenty-One Demands against China in June 1915, Tanaka published "My Assertion of Nationalism," his most definitive statement on international relations. It defended a pluralistic world order of distinct peoples who maintained their political and cultural autonomy while freely and voluntarily assimilating foreign discoveries according to their own particular circumstances. He stressed the irreparable individual and cultural loss that accompanied the political subjugation of any nation, and emphasized the initiative and autonomy of each nation that must be the starting point of its development. He described imperialism as a crude, rapacious, and misguided pursuit of national interest, distinguished by transnational, universalistic ideology. He found prototypes for ideological imperialism in the French Revolution, which rationalized the Napoleonic Wars by the distorted ideal of fraternity, and in the perverted Social Darwinism that

29. Tanaka, "Yo ga kokuminshugi no shuchō," *CK* 30, no. 6 (June 1915): 28.

supported colonial empires in the late nineteenth century and early twentieth century. Universalistic imperialism looked down upon other peoples and could not conceive of international relations based on respect for the dissimilarities of nationalities and cultures.[30]

Tanaka firmly believed that some cultures were more backward than others; he could hardly argue otherwise in view of his disdain for premodern Japanese political culture. He also believed that certain universal trends were intrinsic to modernity: industrialization, individualism, and democracy. Nevertheless, the trends needed to be filtered and adapted through the particular history and culture of each people. His interpretation of Meiji history had made him acutely sensitive to the distorting role that foreign military superiority had played in his own country's attempt to adapt Western civilization. Thus he challenged imperialism while rejecting any notion of pure cultural relativism or egalitarianism.[31] The development of every nation, no matter how belated and confused, must be autonomous and voluntary, according to the will of its own people.[32]

Tanaka's affirmation of nationality challenged the most popular arguments used to justify Japanese hegemony over China—the pan-Asian claim of Japan's special cultural affinity with China, and the humanitarian contention that Japan's successful experience in assimilating Western civilization should guide and benefit China. However lofty the rationale, Tanaka insisted, intervention by one nation in another's political affairs entailed irreparable cultural loss for the victim, the perpetrator, and the entire world. He disavowed "empty humanism" in favor of a "realistic" conception of national self-interest, which, like individual self-interest, relied on the welfare of others.[33] Claiming that a nation ought to have the smallest military capable of maintaining its security, Tanaka interpreted national security very narrowly: "Great powers must realize that they are civilized only to the extent that their

30. Ibid.
31. Ibid.
32. Ibid., 28–29.
33. Ibid., 30.

national well-being can be reconciled with that of the human race."[34]

Tanaka offered a more abstract version of the "Little Japan" recommended by *Tōyō keizai shinpō*. Miura and Ishibashi assumed that empires were economic burdens rather than assets and viewed the maintenance and expansion of Japanese rights on the Asian continent as contrary to the enlightened national interest. Whereas Tanaka preferred a cultural critique of imperialism, *Shinpō* marshaled the economic arguments against imperialism.[35] Working from Tanaka's vision of a plurality of autonomous cultures, as well as *Shinpō*'s historic concern with the costs of armaments and colonial administration, Ishibashi analyzed the Chinese and Russian revolutions and Japan's place in a new world order consequent on the first world war.

ISHIBASHI'S ANTI-IMPERIALISM

Nakamura Kōichi wrote that "modern Japanese history is the history of failure to comprehend China."[36] Japan was not alone in its failure to conceive and implement constructive policies toward its strife-torn neighbor, for the European, Russian, and American records in China were at best ambivalent. Yet Ishibashi was emphatic in pointing out that the Japanese record was the worst from the Twenty-One Demands of 1915 through the China Incident of 1937. Japan's blatant disregard for Chinese life, property, and national aspirations, its consistent propensity to strengthen and encourage the forces of terror, reaction, and disintegration, belied an ideology of racial and cultural solidarity. In Ishibashi's view blindness to China's demand for national autonomy contrasted with Japan's relatively constructive adaptation to the Western world order.

His daring demand that Japan abandon its empire won few adherents in his own generation, but he bequeathed a rigor-

---

34. Ibid., 34; see also 32.
35. Matsuo, "Kyūshinteki jiyūshugi," Yamamoto Shirō, "Chūgoku mondai ron," and Inoue Kiyoshi, "Nihon teikokushugi hihan," all in Inoue and Watanabe, eds., *Taishōki no kyūshinteki jiyūshugi*.
36. Nakamura Kōichi, "Tairiku mondai no imeeji to jittai," in Hashikawa Bunsō and Matsumoto Sannosuke, eds., *Kindai Nihon seiji shisōshi*, vol. 2, Kindai Nihon shisōshi taikei, vol. 4, 52.

ously integrated conception of how a culturally autonomous
Japan might relate to a pluralistic and interactive world, one
resolution of the tension between nationalism and internationalism that has been and is one of the central themes of
modern Japanese thought.[37]

For Ishibashi, as for Tanaka, the Twenty-One Demands of
1915 were a watershed in Japan's relations with China. The
demands, designed to give Japan political, military, and economic hegemony over the Chinese government, invited so
much Chinese hatred and Western suspicion that they shadowed Japanese diplomacy for decades to come. During the
1930s Ishibashi would argue that Japan had so damaged its
image in China by making the demands that subsequent conflict was inevitable unless Japan assumed the responsibility for
proving itself in restraint and conciliation. As negotiations
about the demands were in progress, Ishibashi developed
Miura's argument that the Japanese empire did not justify its
military and political costs, and Tanaka's vision of the world
as a voluntary marketplace of cultural and economic exchange.

While many Japanese blustered that Chinese resistance
justified Japanese imperialism, Ishibashi's point was exactly
the reverse.[38] The only hope for an end to the anti-Japanese
movement in China was for Japan to renounce political and
military controls, renounce its claim to special rights and
interests in Manchuria and Mongolia, and return Shantung,
which it had captured from Germany. Ishibashi did not include trade and investment in his definition of imperialism;
indeed, he deemed China an appropriate area for Japanese
economic expansion. However, he insisted that all advanced
countries provide capital for Chinese development, and that
Japan renounce attempts at monopoly and cease coercing
China into economic treaties. Indeed he urged that Chinese
outrage over the demands was likely to diminish Japanese
markets, in a typical example of the economically counterproductive effects of militarism.

37. Shumpei Okamoto, "Ishibashi Tanzan and the Twenty-one Demands," 184–
85; Uesugi Mitsuhiko, "Taishōki jiyūshugisha no taigaikan: Ishibashi Tanzan o rei
toshite," *Takachiho ronsō* (Apr. 1980): 73–100; Masuda Hiroshi, ed., *Shō Nihonshugi:
Ishibashi Tanzan gaikō ronshū, 1913–1917.*
38. *ITZ* 1:331, 335, 411–15.

Ishibashi invoked the Meiji Restoration as a paradigm of China's contemporary history, particularly stressing the exclusionist trends (*jōi*) of the late Tokugawa period as an analogue to Chinese xenophobia. The historical perspective afforded several conclusions relevant to Japanese policy. First, Japanese ought to understand how they and other foreigners provoked Chinese violence. Second, China was moving toward a new and progressive national unity since the revolution of 1911. Rather than deploring China's tardiness in creating a viable national government that could sponsor industrialization and ensure peace and order, Ishibashi merely commented that China was far larger and more diverse than Japan, and thus the task of reorganization was slower. Consequently, a Japanese policy of patience and respect for Chinese autonomy would ultimately be rewarded in a relationship constructive for both nations.

Even as Yuan Shih-k'ai moved toward monarchical restoration while warlords made a mockery of the new republic, Ishibashi avoided the derision and contempt expressed by many Japanese commentators. Since Japanese critics of Yuan were often devout adherents of Japan's own emperor system, he admonished them with tongue in cheek: "Even if a republic is the better system, there is no help for it, if it is not suited to the Chinese people."[39] He was far from naive about China's political travails, relying on contemporary reporting from Uehara Etsujirō and other perceptive and experienced sources, but he preferred to stress the responsibility of Japanese for the destructive effects of their own country's policies. Consequently he concluded that Japan ought to interfere in China only in direct and immediate protection of Japanese life and property, avoid demands for political and military hegemony that spawned threats to that life and property, and negotiate against intervention by other countries.

Public opinion overwhelmingly supported the demands, and even well-known liberals divided. Okuma Shigenobu and Nagai Ryūtarō endorsed the demands[40] while Yoshino, who held a pessimistic view of the Chinese revolution and the in-

39. *ITZ* 2:402; see also 434–35; 1:410–11; 2:331–35; 5:156–58.
40. Sharon A. Minichiello, *Retreat from Reform: Patterns of Political Behavior in Interwar Japan*, 37–38.

roads of the Western powers at the time, described the demands as "minimal," and regretted Japan's abandonment of the "Group 5" political demands, which would have reduced China to a veritable Japanese puppet.[41] Yoshino had taught at Peking Law College and was genuinely sympathetic to Chinese development, but, like so many other contemporary Japanese, Yoshino convinced himself that development could proceed only under Japanese management, and he differed with Ishibashi's insistence that a people's autonomous choices constituted the only reliable basis for development.[42]

Still, Ishibashi was not alone. He cited two *Yomiuri* editorials opposing the demands and published an article by Tagawa Daikichirō that blamed the anti-Japanese movement on Japanese governmental policies and Japanese popular ignorance and racism. Tagawa, like Ishibashi, welcomed Chinese nationalism. Diet representatives Uehara Etsujirō and Motoda Hajime criticized the demands. Uehara was outraged by Japanese callousness toward Chinese workers. Ministry of Agriculture and Commerce Secretary Tsurumi Sakio deplored the exploitive treatment of Chinese students in Japan. Two legal scholars also supported Ishibashi's commitment to a Little Japan policy. Since 1912, Suehiro Shigeo of Kyoto University had called for the internationalization of Manchuria and favored Korean independence. Ariga Nagao, professor of international law at the Army War College, organized a movement to defend China while serving as an adviser to Chinese president Yuan Shih-k'ai. Ishibashi defended Ariga against calls for his resignation, and took advantage of the outcry in order to analyze the link between domestic reaction and foreign expansionism. He also denounced Japanese government and army attempts to suppress criticism in Chinese newspapers.[43]

41. Mitani, *Taishō demokurashii ron*, 190–91; Inoue Kiyoshi, "Nihon teikokushugi hihan," 141–45; Yoshino, "Shina ni taisuru nijūichi kajō," in Matsuo Takayoshi, ed., *Yoshino Sakuzō: Chūgoku Chōsen ron*, 23–30; Masuda Hiroshi, "Ishibashi Tanzan no Manshū hōki ron," *Kokusai seiji*, no. 71 (Aug. 1982): 76; Matsuo Takayoshi, "Profile of an Asian-Minded Man, 8: Sakuzō Yoshino," *The Developing Economies* 4 (1966): 391.
42. Yoshino Sakuzō, *Nisshi kōshō ron*, 228, 247.
43. The editorials "Kyōman o imashimeru" and "Tai-Shi mondai wa haruka ni kyoku o musubu no yūdan o nozomu," both in *Yomiuri shinbun*, 4 May 1915, are discussed in *ITZ* 2:344. Tagawa Daikichirō, "Shina manyū shokan," *TKS*, 15 and 25

Ishibashi welcomed the March 1 (Korean independence) movement in 1919 as signifying the beginning of the end of Japanese rule. As in his analysis of China, he emphasized the brutality of Japanese domination, under which "Koreans are robbed, and used like horses and dogs."[44] Yet the brutality or benevolence of foreign domination was not the issue. The Koreans had a distinct language and history, and without exception they disliked foreign governance, as any other people would. They would continue to oppose Japanese rule until achieving independence, and opposition would rise with education and self-consciousness. Japanese officials had long smothered any Korean initiative under the pretext that local autonomy would encourage the rape of Japanese women and other evil Korean customs. Korean police and officials had secretly aided the rioters. Japan's failure to grasp the inevitability of anticolonial movements could lead it to disaster, he concluded. In contrast Ishibashi took little note of the nationalistic May 4 movement of 1919 in China.

Earlier the Russian Revolution had afforded Ishibashi another opportunity to test his vision of national and cultural pluralism against political upheaval in a non-Western industrializing nation. For Ishibashi the revolution did not precipitate an abrupt and dramatic engagement with Marxism, as it did for so many other Japanese and Chinese intellectuals. Since his college days he had been well-read in the works of German Social Democrats such as Liebknecht and Bebel. Moreover, he implied that Russia and China were more backward than Japan by comparing their twentieth-century struggles with 1868. He avoided dwelling on Japan's advancement since that argument fit so readily into the arsenal of imperialism, and he preferred to chide his readers about Japan's deficiencies. Nevertheless, he dismissed Bolshevism as a model for Japan, and continued to study Marxism along with liberal and social democratic thought in an eclectic and critical spirit,

---

July 1915. On Uehara, Tsurumi, and Motoda see *ITZ* 1:408–09. Suehiro Shigeo, "Shin Nichiro kyōyaku ni tsukite," *Gaikō jihō*, no. 189 (15 Sept. 1912): 11–20; and *ITZ* 1:246. On Ariga see *ITZ* 2:351. On Japanese attempts to suppress criticism of the demands in Chinese newspapers see *ITZ* 2:331.

44. *ITZ* 3:78–80.

finding no serious challenge to his prior world view in the Russian Revolution. Its lessons fit within the themes that he had been developing: the overthrow of a monarchy due to the repressive nature of its bureaucratic administration, the irresistible demand of an awakening people for security of livelihood and a political voice, the folly of foreign intervention, and the priority of civil liberties. A Leninist party, on the other hand, seemed irrelevant to his quest for a more direct relation between government and people.

Ishibashi joined other liberals, including Yoshino and the *Ōsaka asahi* writers, in interpreting the February revolution as a monarchy destroyed by popular reaction against bureaucratic despotism.[45] With Japan in the midst of a general election, Ishibashi demanded the defeat of the repressive cabinet of General Terauchi Masatake in order to spare Japan a similar consequence: "Count Terauchi, his cabinet, and their bureaucrats have violated the people's right to be loyal to their sovereign and love their country [*chūkun aikoku*] by arbitrarily designating whatever doesn't suit them as lèse majesté and a crime. . . . They have perpetrated despotic oppression no better than that of the Russian bureaucracy. I speak freely from deep concern for the security of the throne, and hope that the bureaucrats, especially Prince Yamagata and Count Terauchi, will reflect."[46]

Ishibashi's profound devotion to the emperor surfaced only when he was taking particularly risky stands. Most reformers such as Yoshino and Hiratsuka routinely appealed to the imperial mythology to legitimize new programs, but Ishibashi usually avoided mentioning it altogether, preferring rational arguments of political and social utility. In this exceptional instance, he seized the moment to imply that bureaucratic arrogance might lead Japan where it had led Russia. Such a suggestion could be made only tangentially in an article on foreign affairs. Ishibashi's manipulative and strategic relationship with the prevailing framework of discourse makes it difficult to evaluate the sincerity of this editorial. The whole

45. Masuda Hiroshi, "Ishibashi Tanzan no Roshia kakumeikan: Yoshino Sakuzō to no hikaku kōsatsu," *JS*, no. 14 (Feb. 1980): 17; Asukai Masamichi, "Roshia kakumei to Nikō jiken," in Inoue and Watanabe, eds., *Taishōki no kyūshinteki jiyūshugi*, 266–69.
46. *ITZ* 2:4.

corpus of his Taishō writings suggests that, in fact, he saw no danger of revolution in Japan, where the people needed to become far more assertive to achieve even moderate reform, but he enjoyed taunting the power holders with the ultimate consequences of despotism.

Ishibashi went beyond most liberal opinion in discerning livelihood as the fundamental issue in the Russian Revolution. On this point he was joined by socialist Fukuda Tokuzō, but not by Yoshino, who clung to a narrow despotism/liberalism focus.[47] Receiving reports from the former *Shinpō* staffer and Communist Katayama Sen, first from America and then from Russia, Ishibashi graphically depicted the unendurable misery that war had heaped on workers and soldiers. Whereas Yoshino described radical Russian workers and soldiers as "even more debased than Japan's Seiyūkai [Society of Political Friends] and Kenseikai parties,"[48] Ishibashi interpreted Russian radicalism as an entirely rational response to wartime conditions. Yoshino emphasized the broader base of anti-Bolshevik factions, but Ishibashi insisted on the overwhelming popular appeal of Lenin's slogan, "peace, land, and bread." Ishibashi, although sympathetic to the Bolsheviks, avoided the rhetoric of class struggle and connived to force Bolshevism within his framework of enlightened individual self-interest. "The *self*-consciousness of Russian laborers and lower-rank soldiers is more highly developed than that of our peasant or even merchant classes. The peasantry is not the foundation of conservatism (as bureaucrats believe), but the wellspring of liberalism and socialism [emphasis added]."[49] Ishibashi surely romanticized the Russian Revolution, but his enthusiasm for popular movements contrasted with the fears widely expressed in 1920s Japan. He identified enlightened self-interest with democratic socialism, which he believed to be a rising trend in all advanced countries during World War I.

For the Russian revolution, as for the Chinese, Ishibashi's conceptual paradigm was Japan's *bakumatsu* period, the years preceding the Meiji Restoration marked by xenophobia, vio-

47. Fukuda Tokuzō, "Tadashii rikai o yōsu," in *Taishō dai zasshi*.
48. Yoshino Sakuzō [Furukawa Gakujin], "Roshia no kakumei," *CK* 32, no. 4 (Apr. 1917): 121.
49. *ITZ* 2:14.

lence, and even class struggle. Naturally the strife in Russia was more severe, endangering the unity of the country; yet the trials might well be a prelude to national integration and development. Accordingly Ishibashi concluded that foreign intervention would merely fan the flames, for military weakness was one of the original causes of the turmoil, as it had been for Japan. Thus "support for the counterrevolutionaries is tantamount to support for the *bakufu*," Japan's ancient regime.[50]

Lenin's separate peace with Germany was the most divisive issue for Taishō liberals, whose attitudes toward Japan's alliance with the democratic allies ranged from enthusiastic to benignly neutral. They were sympathetic to Woodrow Wilson's plan for public and legal international contracts, which revolutionary Russia appeared to be flouting. For example, the *Ōsaka asahi*, which initially had welcomed the February revolution very much in line with *Shinpō*, by May was predicting a complete German victory due to Russian capitulation and urging Japan to think of its Siberian interests; by December the *Asahi* resoundingly denounced the idea of a separate peace and labeled Lenin a despot and usurper. Nonetheless its editorials opposed the dispatch of Japanese troops. When the censors intervened, the *Asahi* feistily compared the Terauchi cabinet to the Bolsheviks.[51] Yoshino had cherished hopes from the beginning of the revolution that Russia would continue the war against Germany. Recalling his training as a legal scholar, he refused to acquiesce in Russia's right to break treaties. His stand on Japanese intervention was ambivalent: he agreed with Ishibashi that an expedition would win the hatred of the Russian people but sympathized with its claim to aid the Allies.[52]

In contrast, Ishibashi praised the separate peace for fulfilling the hopes of the Russian people. He had immediately predicted, in February 1917, that the Russian war effort would

50. *ITZ* 2:13, 33. Masuda stresses Ishibashi's grasp of the universality of the Russian revolution in "Ishibashi Tanzan no Roshia kakumeikan," 18–19. For contrasting contemporary interpretations stressing the peculiarity of Russian history see Fukuda, and Tōyama Sentarō, "Raidō o imashime," in *Taishō dai zasshi*.

51. Asukai, 276–79, 283.

52. Yoshino Sakuzō, "Tandoku wagi no kaishi ni yotte Rokoku wa nanimono o eran to suru," *CK* 33, no. 1 (Jan. 1918): 102; see also his "Roshia no kakumei," and "Iwayuru shuppei ron ni nan no gōriteki konkyo ariya," *CK* 33, no. 4 (Apr. 1918); Masuda, "Ishibashi Tanzan no Roshia kakumeikan," 18–22, 26–31.

collapse, a judgment prescient even by European standards, as journals such as *The New Statesman* anticipated Russia's reorganization for renewed battle against Germany. Aware of the magnitude of forces released in the Russian Revolution, Ishibashi lambasted Japanese intervention as unprincipled, dangerous, and at best futile. Intervention resembled the very Prussian-style militarism that the Allies were presumably fighting to destroy. Intervention would damage Japan's relations with the Allies, who were already suspicious of Japan's continental interests. Naturally Russians would regard Japanese troops as "murderous and militaristic invaders."[53] Japan's relationship with China would also suffer, since the Chinese government had moved troops into northern Manchuria and was suspicious of foreign intervention and fearful of expanded hostilities. Ishibashi warned: "What I particularly fear is making enemies of our neighbors, the one hundred and fifty million people of China and Russia, by our reckless dispatch of troops."[54] He anticipated the absence of reliable allies that would plague Japan during the 1930s. In his view, principle and pragmatism offered the same conclusion.

Since military intervention was destined to fail and to increase international tensions, what ought to be the Japanese policy? In what historian Asukai Masamichi termed his "most shocking" position, Ishibashi alone among liberal journalists advocated Japanese humanitarian aid to the Bolsheviks as early as March 1918.[55] Japanese aid would help Russia to combat famine and restore order, leading eventually to a profitable trade relationship with Japan. A weak Bolshevik government mired in foreign and civil war, on the other hand, would merely prolong the chaos and aid Germany. In addition, the restoration of peace would encourage Russian democracy, making Japan more secure. Japan's long-term interests, therefore, lay in aiding the most powerful faction, the Communists, to restore stability.[56]

53. *ITZ* 2:38; see also 7–8, 10.
54. *ITZ* 2:29. See also Asukai, 283; James W. Morley, *The Japanese Thrust into Siberia, 1918*, 110–12; Kikuchi Masanori, *Roshia kakumei to Nihonjin*, 245.
55. Asukai, 289–93.
56. *ITZ* 2:20–23, 31–33.

Opposition to Japan's intervention had a somewhat broader constituency than aid to the Communists. Ishibashi read Japanese public opinion as indignant over the separate peace but apathetic about a Japanese expeditionary force. General Machida Keiu agreed that public support for intervention was minimal. The government was also divided. Censorship was employed to present at least the facsimile of martial unity. The *Ōsaka asahi* moved to support for an expedition by March 1918, after its censorship the previous December. *Shinpō*'s criticism was tolerated longer, perhaps because the journal reported on essential financial news, but it received a warning notice from the army censors on July 18, 1918, the very date of imperial approval for the expedition. Upon public announcement of the decision two weeks later, some sixty papers were banned.[57]

Ishibashi's response to the army's warning was extraordinary: he printed and critiqued it in the next issue of *Shinpō*:

> Journalism prompting misunderstanding of the content of the Imperial Government's negotiations with the United States, Great Britain, and other Allies concerning the dispatch of troops to Siberia, causing interference or opposition to the mutual friendship of the Allies in relation to the Imperial Government's proposed attitude and measures and the like, or revealing concrete areas of operation (except Vladivostok), numbers of troops, or other military plans, will be subject to the banning of publication.[58]

The message, he announced, surpassed even the usual vagueness of censorship criteria. Although there might be some "clarity and reason" in the final clause regarding specific military operations, the overall import of the prohibitions was tantamount to "banning any discussion of the issue at all."[59] He defiantly reminded his readers that his unqualified opposition to intervention was already a matter of public record, "but what of the future?"[60] Despite pressure he periodically demanded a complete withdrawal of Japanese troops as long as

57. *ITZ* 2:12, 40. Mitchell, *Censorship in Imperial Japan*, 175–76.
58. *ITZ* 2:32–33.
59. Ibid.
60. Ibid.

the expedition continued.[61] The police restrained themselves, probably because interference with a respected business journal such as *Shinpō*, for the sake of an unpopular military venture, might have caused more trouble than it was worth, and because there was no active antiwar movement.

Before the end of the Siberian intervention, Ishibashi would revise his rosy image of the Russian Revolution and criticize its apologists as well as its demonologists. Bertrand Russell's account of revolutionary Russia was translated in Ōyama Ikuo and Hasegawa Nyozekan's *Warera* (We) in 1920. Ishibashi, who had read Russell's original article in *Nation*, informed his readers that *Warera* had omitted much of Russell's discussion of Bolshevik "excesses," including violations of civil liberties, interference in elections, minority despotism, military politics, and the emergence of government officials as a new nobility. Russia's food distribution was inadequate, with a soaring black market spawning profits higher than those under capitalism. Nonetheless determined not to mint ammunition for anticommunist crusaders, Ishibashi concluded that Bolshevik despotism stemmed from Russia's history of bureaucratic rigidity and victimization under foreign imperialism. The death of Lenin, he warned, might bring a second Napoleonic empire flaunting the same style of universalistic ideology that Tanaka had discerned in revolutionary France and in European colonialism.[62]

Ishibashi's outlook on foreign affairs had crystallized by the end of the first world war. Historically, he and Tanaka argued, Western civilization had benefited Japan, but the manner of its introduction under the guns of Commodore Perry's black ships had engendered militarism and perpetuated reactionary despotism. Economically, *Shinpō* had always been averse to high taxes and armaments spending. Philosophically, Tanaka and Ishibashi recognized the value of autonomous individual and national growth. Japanese intervention in the Chinese and Russian revolutions had confirmed Ishibashi's general sense that intervention boded no good, and that revolution was de-

61. *ITZ* 3:74, 98–99.
62. *ITZ* 3:522–24; see also 2:32–38, and Asukai, 293–306.

sirable only in the extremes of oppression and misery. In contrast, Meiji Japan, he concluded, had accomplished far too much to merit radical rejection, though its failures and flaws required relentless criticism to stimulate public education and participation. With these fixed opinions he turned to examine the postwar world order and Japan's relationship with the West.

The Versailles Conference bitterly disappointed Ishibashi and other Japanese intellectuals, most notably Prince Konoe, who castigated Western greed, racism and hypocrisy in his first step toward the new Asian order he would proclaim in 1938.[63] Ishibashi, dedicated to Wilsonian principles of self-determination and international cooperation, was disappointed in their betrayal at Versailles. He complained that a double standard applied to victors and vanquished: the self-determination of dependencies, demilitarization, and the prosecution of war crimes applied only to Germany and its allies but ought to apply to the victors as well. In particular, he decried the denial of Indian and Korean bids for independence.[64] He believed that a double standard prevailed within the victors' camp as well, especially in American demands that Japan return Germany's former leased territory in Shantung to China. No Western Ally lost territory: "Two countries were soundly defeated in the war: Germany and Japan."[65] He did not deny that Shantung should be Chinese, but he resented the selective way in which the principle of self-determination was applied. Racism was one component of Western hostility toward the Japanese empire, and Ishibashi regretted the League of Nations' failure to accept a Japanese proposal for racial equality that would have ended discrimination against Asians in North America, Australia, and Africa.[66]

Despite his disappointment with the West, Ishibashi never failed to point out Japan's often graver errors. Japan also practiced racial discrimination, prohibiting Chinese labor in Japan, restricting Korean and Taiwanese immigration, and banning

63. Yoshitake Oka, *Konoe Fumimaro: A Political Biography*, trans. Shumpei Okamoto, 14–15.
    64. *ITZ* 2:120.
    65. *ITZ* 3:87.
    66. *ITZ* 3:132–39.

foreign property ownership. With these examples Ishibashi hoped to combat the self-righteous indignation that most of his people felt toward Western discrimination. He conceded that the West had often treated Japan unfairly, but he demanded that Japan assume responsibility for its poor conduct, which had inflamed Western antagonism. Accordingly Ishibashi urged support for international cooperation in the League of Nations, even when the league failed to fulfill his hopes for arms limitation, freedom of the seas, an end to racial discrimination, and international democracy. He also joined the Japan League of Nations Association (Nihon Kokusai Renmei Kyōkai Kaigō).[67]

At the same time, Ishibashi would have appended economic functions to the league, as John M. Keynes suggested in *The Economic Consequences of the Peace*. Keynes deplored the debilitating effect of impossible Allied demands for German reparations, with Ishibashi's endorsement. More significantly, Keynes revealed the vulnerability of the entire world economic system on the following points: "instability of an excessive population dependent for its livelihood on a complicated and artificial organization, the psychological instability of the laboring and capitalist classes, and the instability of Europe's claim, coupled with the completeness of her dependence, on the food supplies of the new World."[68] Ishibashi shared Keynes's fears and would insist upon cooperative international economic planning, especially an international public debt for industrial development, after World War I and again after World War II. International funding for Chinese industrialization would supplement skimpy Chinese capital and be preferable to exploitation by the capitalist countries. It would also be preferable to the consortium loans organized by the powers, which in Ishibashi's view merely replaced monopoly spheres of influence with an oligopoly. The greed of the powers hampered the development of world resources, which ought to be under the League of Nations.[69] Empire ought to

67. On Japanese racial discrimination see *ITZ* 3:68–70. On the role of the league see *ITZ* 3:130, 174–76; and 15:365.
68. John Maynard Keynes, *The Economic Consequences of the Peace*, 25.
69. *ITZ* 3:174–76.

be replaced with a more equitable mechanism for the international transfer of capital, goods, and services.

Ishibashi's most definitive foreign policy statement heralded Japan's invitation to the Washington Conference in July 1921 and urged that the basis of the conference's discussions ought to be Japan's granting of independence to Korea and Taiwan and withdrawal from Karafuto, Siberia, and China. Most of his argument was devoted to Japan's economic self-interest according to two main propositions. First, trade outside the empire, especially with the United States and Great Britain, was greater than trade within it, and the rising political and military tensions of empire were not worth the potential sacrifice of Western relationships. Second, the Japanese empire did not in fact increase trade, nor did it protect vital Japanese economic interests.[70]

Ishibashi's arguments were more pragmatic than moral, but his moral commitments were abundantly clear in his denunciations of Japanese brutality and his converse assurance that each people did hold the potential for their own autonomous development. When he insisted that he was a realist and not an empty humanist, it is not always clear whether he spoke in conviction or strategy. Moral and practical themes coalesced in his arguments, a legacy from Tanaka and from the cultural orientation that Tanaka had discerned in Ninomiya Sontoku. His definition of Japan's national self-interest contained a hefty portion of idealism along with competition:

> If we were to give up Manchuria, give up Shantung, give up all pressure on China, what would happen? What if we freed Korea, Taiwan? England and the United States would be most put out. They would be unable to defend their claims to world moral leadership if Japan were to take so liberal a stance. China and all the poor weak countries would turn to rely on us. India, Egypt, Persia and Haiti, and all the colonies would agitate for their own independence. Our place in the world would ascend from the ninth hell to the ninth heaven, and the United States and Britain would be helpless to stop it.[71]

70. Ogura Masatarō, comp., '*Tōyō keizai shinpō' genron rokujūnen*, 70–73; Masuda, "Ishibashi Tanzan no Manshū hōki ron," 81. Ishibashi first took up the question of the independence of Korea and Taiwan in 1917; see *ITZ* 2:120.
71. *ITZ* 4:13–14.

Next Ishibashi disarmingly conceded that since some readers would not accept moral arguments, he would proceed to pragmatic economic and political analysis.

Ishibashi attacked what he counted as the two most rational arguments in favor of empire: first, that Japan's economy and national defense would be crippled or at least damaged by the loss of its empire, and second, that Japan's empire was as legitimate as those of the other great powers. More than the murky ideologies of pan-Asianism or imperial divinity, he feared the appeal of realistic claims for empire among educated and open-minded persons. Allegations of the economic necessity of empire drew the heaviest of his fire. Trade with the United States was among Japan's vital interests, and immigration disputes were unlikely to alienate the two. "But when China comes into the relationship, it changes the picture. Europe has now had enough of war, but not so Japan and the United States. Both countries are in a period of capitalist accumulation and under capitalist control, especially in war. . . . Both countries are now looking outward in imperialism for gain, and will collide in China."[72] Conflict was both irrational and probable.

Ishibashi appealed to reason by presenting figures on the aggregate value of combined imports and exports to various countries and territories in 1920:

Korea	312,493	(thousand yen)
Taiwan	292,857	
Kwantung	310,549	
United States	1,403,800	
India	587,000	
England	330,000[73]	

The total quantity of Japan's trade in its colonies and spheres of influence was slight in the global picture; Japan traded more with England than with any of the colonies, and more with the United States than with the whole empire. (Ishibashi did not examine balances of imports and exports with each

72. *ITZ* 3:109–10.
73. *ITZ* 4:15–16.

nation, but later as he developed his economic theory, he would argue that trade balances could be regulated by governmental fiscal, monetary, and industrial policy.) Contrary to popular belief, Japan was not dependent on the empire for essential materials such as raw cotton, which came mainly from the United States and India, or rice, which came from French Indochina and Siam, or iron and steel, which Japan imported from America in five times the quantity supplied by the empire. Sugar was the only important commodity for which the colonies and spheres of influence were the major source of supply. Finally, he compared the rates of increase in trade with China, India, and the United States over the past decade to show that military intervention at best availed nothing. In 1920 the American trade stood at 263 on the 1910 index, the China trade at 124. The rate of increase in trade with India was the same as that in trade with China.

Military intervention could indeed win small commercial victories, such as preventing the Chinese government from increasing its tax on imported thread, but in Ishibashi's view the gains were lost when Chinese resentment spawned boycotts and reduced trade. Trade was only one part of the entire relationship between the two peoples, which in the early twenties was reaching the final extremes of estrangement: "China would not hesitate to attack Japan today if only it had the power."[74] Yet an alternative economic policy, which attempted to work within the perceived needs of the Chinese government and people, would be immensely profitable, and less risky.

The utility of the empire in defense, Ishibashi held, was an illusion since it was the empire itself that required defense. The real danger of war lay in the colonies and in Japan's intervention in China and Siberia. China and revolutionary Russia were absorbed in their internal struggles, and Ishibashi believed that no other power would capture Taiwan or Korea if Japan granted them independence. The abandonment of the empire would greatly enhance Japan's security. "As for the home islands, if we were giving them away for free it would be hard to find takers."[75] Ishibashi correctly judged that in

74. *ITZ* 3:110.
75. *ITZ* 4:19; Asukai, 171.

1921 Japan was by far the best armed and most militant power in East Asia. He aimed to undercut widespread assertions of Japan's vulnerability before an alleged Anglo-American or Russian threat, and to prove that Japan was creating its own vulnerability by sowing hatred and suspicion through acts of aggression.

Other arguments for empire Ishibashi dismissed with some contempt. American maneuvers to exclude Orientals (which reached fruition in 1924) were abhorrent, but of little practical consequence; the real answer to poverty was not emigration but domestic economic growth coupled with an enlightened social welfare policy. The injustice of European empires was surely a legitimate point, but it was hardly a reason for Japan to follow in Western footsteps. Finally, the day of empire was past; cooperation with national independence movements would strengthen ties with those peoples, who would one day be free whether Japan's policy were to be assistance, neutrality, or outright resistance. In decolonization the moral policy and the practical policy were one and the same. Ishibashi would not compromise in this position until 1932, when he acquiesced in Japan's creation of a puppet state in Manchuria, and even after that time he would continue to espouse a conciliatory foreign policy that sought avenues of cooperation between Japan's interests and those of other peoples.[76]

Ishibashi noted that public reaction to the Washington Conference was generally negative, but he tried to combat doubt by encouraging liberal study groups on foreign policy. He publicized the National Policy Association (Kokusaku Kenkyūkai), Ozaki Yukio's organization of Tokyo University professors including Yoshino Sakuzō, and he served on the board of directors of the Arms Limitation Society (Gunbi Shukushō Dōshikai).[77] He also formed a Pacific Research Society (Taiheiyō Kenkyūkai) with Miura, Dietman Suzuki Umeshirō, and

76. For a more complete treatment of Ishibashi's lack of interest in Japanese emigration see Masuda Hiroshi, "Ishibashi Tanzan no tai-Bei imin fuyō ron," *JS*, no. 21 (Nov. 1981): 28–49. On Japanese emigration in 1913, see Matsuo Takayoshi, "Taishō demokurashii no ichi suimyaku: Ishibashi Tanzan to sono senkōshatachi," in Akamatsu Toshihide Kyōju Taikan Kinen Jigyōkai, ed., *Akamatsu Toshihide Kyōju taikan kinen: Kokushi ronshū*, 1173–74.

77. *ITZ* 4:10; 15:358.

former Liberal Lecture Society members Tagawa Daikichirō and Uehara Etsujirō. The group drafted a petition to the Diet that urged armaments limitation on the condition that all powers abandon imperialistic ambitions. Their proposal, however, was far less daring than Ishibashi's individual position, and contingent on the actions of the Western powers.

The Pacific Research Society demanded that all nations enjoy equal access to the world's resources and markets. The lofty principle was close to the actual position of the Japanese government. Moreover, the Pacific Research Society proposed the termination of Japanese intervention in Siberia and China, but not the relinquishment of Taiwan, Korea, or Manchuria, where an economic open door was advocated under, presumably, continued Japanese administration. In concession to a widespread Japanese sense of grievance against the West, the proposal demanded comparable Western concessions. Hence it was as impossible in global politics as Ishibashi's personal views were in Japanese politics. It also showed a strong bias toward advanced industrial countries by its demands:

    I. Elimination of the fundamental cause of international strife, imperialist ambition.

   II. Full implementation of global economic equality of opportunity.

 III. Full realization of a global economic open door.

     A. Removal of all restrictions on foreign property ownership and industry.

     B. Elimination of all protectionist taxes and tariffs, including preferential trade relations between colonies and their mother country.

     C. Removal of restrictions on coastal trade by foreign ships.

     D. Internationalization of the Panama Canal.

   IV. Absolute termination of intervention in China, Siberia, and Mexico.

    V. Full and free deliberation about the problems of imperialist struggle, without restriction of the agenda.[78]

The Pacific Research Society viewed imperialist struggle as

78. *ITZ* 4:55–59.

a problem among advanced industrial nations, and not between them and their colonies or spheres of influence. The
demand for equal economic access to Western colonies baldly
revealed the way that the rhetoric of peace could serve Japanese interests. Japanese were extraordinarily irritated at
American espousal of disarmament and an open door in Asia
while the United States retained its privileged sphere in Latin
America. The Washington Conference disappointed its strong-
est Japanese supporters and made liberals vulnerable to caricature as the flunkies of Anglo-American domination.[79] Yet
because of his alarm about Japanese and Western imperialism,
Ishibashi stuck to his pacifist guns, making tactical adaptations
to gain broader support.[80]

Tanaka, Miura and Ishibashi did not prevail in their recommendation that the Japanese empire be abandoned, but
some diffusion of their arguments was evident during the
1920s. For example Foreign Minister Shidehara Kijūrō in
1927 stressed the economic rationality of nonintervention:

> Even if China becomes a communist nation, foreigners could live
> and trade with China after a few years. . . . [A]fter the Russian
> Revolution, Japanese were allowed to live, trade, and do business
> in Russia without any particular danger.[81]

Shidehara had not taken up the Little Japan cause. Ishibashi
criticized the foreign minister for "refusing to give one inch
on Japan's rights and interests in South Manchuria,"[82] and he
damned Shidehara with the faint praise that he was "at least
not as reckless as [Seiyūkai Foreign Minister] Tanaka Giichi."[83]
Nevertheless, Shidehara's rhetoric of peaceful economic rationality indicates the diffusion of anti-imperialist thinking,
even as the defense and expansion of the Japanese empire
proceeded.

---

79. Toru Takemoto, *Failure of Liberalism in Japan: Shidehara Kijūrō's Encounter with Anti-Liberals*, 230.
80. For a detailed treatment of Ishibashi's critique of armaments spending see Andō Minoru, "Ishibashi Tanzan no gunjihi ron ni tsuite: 1920–1930 nendai no ron-setsu," in Tanaka Hiroshi, ed., *Kindai Nihon ni okeru jaanarizumu no seijiteki kinō.*
81. Shidehara quoted by Takemoto, 67.
82. *ITZ* 7:208.
83. *ITZ* 7:395.

CONCLUSION

Tanaka and Ishibashi conceived their interpretations of the Meiji Restoration while competing to capture national symbols for the democratic cause in the Taishō era. They were part of an heuristic popular historiography that set itself against detached academic inquiry, on the one hand, and state glorification of hierarchy and submission on the other. Though their purpose of public enlightenment and reform continued the traditions of the Meiji enlightenment and the Popular Rights movement, they departed from Meiji interpretations of Japanese history in order to explain the persistence of the strength of the state in the twentieth century. On this basis they declined to regard the Popular Rights movement as a model for Taishō democrats, and they postulated an abrupt discontinuity in Japan's history in the mid-nineteenth century, rather than attempting to find the roots of parliamentary democracy in ancient times. Of course their rejection of premodern society was not complete, for they did admire Ninomiya Sontoku's blend of economic rationality and social responsibility. Nevertheless, they believed that the West had brought more advanced systems and conceptions based on democracy and cosmopolitanism, which had been legitimized as Japan's national policy in the Charter Oath of 1868. Why, then, were these ideals still far from fulfillment in the 1910s?

The superiority of Western economic and military power, and its assertion on a global scale in nineteenth-century colonization, had sparked a crisis in Japan, when authoritarian political traditions had been recast to serve in the power struggle of the Meiji oligarchs. In their pessimistic evaluation of the Restoration, Tanaka and Ishibashi did not deny Meiji achievements, but they undercut the mystique of autocratic benevolence by stressing the self-interest of Meiji politicians, and by urging that the real virtues of the Meiji transformation—industrialization, cosmopolitanism, and democracy—might have been realized more fully without the distorting strain of militarism. A darker view of the Restoration led Ishibashi to a relatively brighter view of the Chinese and Russian revolutions than Yoshino held, and a stronger case against Japanese intervention therein. Confident that Chinese and Russians could form stable national governments, forward industrialization, and move toward peaceful and participatory ideals as Japan had already done, he warned that foreign intervention would merely delay and deform the healthy processes of national transformation. He was not oblivious to the profits of wartime growth and colonial exploitation; indeed, he cited profits as the probable cause of a future clash between the United States and Japan in China. Nevertheless, he believed that the fruits of domination were, in the long run, outweighed by their costs and risks in economic as well as human terms. His opinions were predicated on his interpretation of *bakumatsu*-Meiji history.

Despite negative evaluations of Japanese militarism and imperialism, Tanaka and Ishibashi tolerated the Meiji state on a pragmatic basis because they believed that its accomplishments were considerable if allowances were made for the circumstances under which it took form, and that its ills could be cured by gradual reform and persuasion. They did not launch a direct assault on the state ideology of imperial divinity, though they obviously deemed it but one of the weapons of the Meiji elite in its effort to monopolize political power. Tanaka countered the ideology of a divine, immutable, and uniquely Japanese national polity (*kokutai*) with an evolutionary, relativistic *kokuminsei*, which was no more or less valuable than the cultural autonomy and national independence of any other people. Ishibashi developed Tanaka's conception of international cultural pluralism along with a critique of the economic losses of imperialism. Both relied on pragmatic reasoning and largely avoided appeals to the imperial symbol.

Tanaka and Ishibashi were remarkable in the ways in which they linked foreign and domestic affairs. Tanaka attempted to show, through Ninomiya, that the Japanese people had indigenous traditions of practical eclecticism, in which the people asserted their needs and their culture in some independence from the rulers, and reformed institutions according to the trends of the times. Foreign military and economic pressure had provided an opportunity for the rulers to strengthen the other side of Japan's political culture, its traditions of authority and submission. Yet at the same time the West had brought fully elaborated ideologies and institutions of individualism and democracy, which Tanaka and Ishibashi believed would eventually prevail. Liberalism merely required time for absorption and adaptation to Japanese history and culture. Meanwhile, however, a new dynamic of foreign and domestic trends had arisen when Japanese militarism and imperialism thwarted the autonomous development of Koreans, Chinese, and Russians. Ishibashi noted that the Twenty-One Demands and the Siberian Intervention catalyzed restrictions of Japanese civil liberties, and also complained that armaments spending depleted social and industrial capital. He warned that militarism might generate further division among the Japanese people; for example, he rejected proposals for a mercenary force on the grounds that it would victimize the poor and dampen the protests against militarism.[84] He and Tanaka discerned two historical paths before Japan: mutually reinforcing democracy and pacifism, on the one hand, or mutually reinforcing repression and militarism on the other.

84. *ITZ* 3:70–73.

5

Taishō Democracy: Tanaka and Ishibashi

The Taishō democratic movement crested between World War I and the end of the Washington Conference in 1922. The temporal parameters highlight the interplay of foreign and domestic trends. Earlier intellectual and political trends reached maturity, while wartime economic conditions brought long-simmering labor, tenant, and consumer unrest to the boiling point. Japan's decision to side with the ultimately victorious Allies strengthened the hand of those who defined democracy as the ineluctable trend of world history, and it encouraged the diffusion of Woodrow Wilson's ideals of self-determination and a new equity in international organization. Marxism stimulated Japanese reformers to invest comprehensive views of the social order, already a strong theme in Japanese thought, with more precise analysis of social forces and institutional interests. Marxism was at first interpreted as part and parcel of the evolving democratic movement, a more extreme version of protest against arbitrary authority. At the end of World War I democrats still sustained a highly inclusive and syncretic character, defining themselves in terms of what they opposed.

Nearly all left-of-center intellectuals shared certain fundamental beliefs during the Taishō period. First, they were committed to developing an integrated and coherent vision of the social whole. Second, they stressed the individual's potential for new creative and productive activities and welcomed the increased political involvement of their compatriots. Finally, all liberals and a good many self-described Marxists believed in the possibility of a democratic society and polity under the Meiji Constitution by means of peaceful and legal change.

They demanded a complete restructuring of power and wealth (*kakushin*), but they either avoided the term revolution (*kaku-mei*), with its implications of physical violence, or employed *kakumei* in the same sense as *kakushin*. Shared beliefs, though highly general, challenged police repression and a state ideology of hierarchy and subordination.

Democratic unity was to be short-lived. Democrats' very sense of power, and its confirmation in minor victories, encouraged the emergence of more elaborate policy positions, which in turn increased sectarianism. Forces external to the movement itself were still more damaging. The state adroitly fragmented popular movements through a blend of concession and repression. A sluggish economy, and the Great Kantō earthquake of 1923, weighed most heavily on the disenfranchised. The earthquake levelled the older, eastern sections of Tokyo, killing more than one hundred thousand people in fires, drownings, and collapsing buildings, and spawning panic, riots against Koreans, and police attacks on radicals. The great world powers defied Wilsonian principles, especially after Chiang Kai-shek's establishment of the Nanking government in 1927 and the crash of the American stock market in 1929. Although the peak of the democratic movement was brief, it was extraordinarily interesting as an elaboration of earlier intellectual trends, a new quantity and quality of liberal organization, and an eventual framework of deliberation about reform under the Allied Occupation.

Historians conventionally place Tokyo University legal scholar Yoshino Sakuzō at the center of the democratic movement. Yoshino's academic background enabled him to legitimize democracy from the perspective of the Meiji Constitution and legal system, and to appeal to a generation of progressive administrators and party politicians. However, the lofty moral ideals that Yoshino attached to his notion of democracy weakened its political potential. As Tetsuo Najita has aptly summarized:

> He conceived of democracy as a pure metaphysical ideal, and it was idealism that led him, toward the end of his life, to deny in sweeping fashion the democratic potential of organized political

activity—a denial which a supporter of liberal or social democracy in the West at that time would have found difficult indeed to uphold.[1]

Yoshino idealized the creative development of the morally autonomous individual, and also idealized the national spirit of a people. He ultimately denied the utility of politicians and interest groups, placing "the burden of political change almost exclusively on the shoulders of autonomous and moral individuals stripped of their organizational links with the political world."[2] He contracted an incurable discontent with "the pragmatic manipulation of legal institutions to achieve concrete ends."[3] Alterations in the mechanisms of the institutional order became means to spiritual ideals.

A sense of fellowship in the democratic movement concealed fundamentally different philosophies. Yoshino's idealistic view of society as essentially moral was contested by Japanese Marxists. Tanaka Ōdō and Ishibashi Tanzan described themselves as closer to Marxists than idealists, insofar as they viewed conflict as central to social and political processes.[4] Nonetheless, they differed sharply in analyzing the nature of conflict. First, for Tanaka and Ishibashi class struggle was only one facet of modern society. Both saw the central cleavage in Taishō Japan as one of the rulers (who owed their power to gender, regional origins, and personal cliques as well as class) versus the ruled. In addition, Tanaka stressed conflicts among generations, cultures, and beliefs, whereas Ishibashi analyzed economic contradictions that lacked a clear class character such as urban versus rural, or importers versus exporters. Second, they believed that no conceivable form of social organization could or should terminate conflict; resolution and reconciliation were processes rather than results. Therefore they defended democratic institutions as mechanisms by which people could reduce social inequity, but not eliminate it, and advance individual self-development, but not perfect it. Their lack of

1. Tetsuo Najita, "Some Reflections on Idealism in the Political Thought of Yoshino Sakuzō," in Silberman and Harootunian, eds., *Japan in Crisis*, 31.
2. Ibid., 59.
3. Ibid., 47; see also 56–58 and Duus, "Yoshino Sakuzō," 315–16.
4. Tanaka, "Sekai heiwa no risō ni chinamite shoka no bunkashugi o kentōsu," part 2, *CK* 37, special issue on "Sekai heiwa to jinruiai" (Aug. 1922): 39.

interest in human perfectibility and their tolerance for ambiguity distanced them from both idealists and Japanese Marxists, despite shared political commitments to legislative redress for the disenfranchised.

The arguments between idealists, Marxists, and pragmatists were debated at a high level of abstraction. One of the most remarkable and difficult aspects of contemporary thought was its insistence that such issues as the nature of sovereignty or the validity of apriorities were directly linked to actual politics. Whereas a few pundits such as Tanaka's student Ubukata Toshirō ridiculed intellectuals' bids for public influence, Taishō democrats correctly judged that popular protest, to succeed, had to win legitimation under the hegemony of a state that was already armed with an elaborate political, ethical, and legal philosophy. It had to obtain general recognition of its claims or else resort to force of arms. For this reason intellectuals struggled to shake off the cobwebs of statist ideology and believed themselves to be but one step away from street demonstrations.

Tanaka and Ishibashi's philosophic justification of democracy was important for another reason as well. It encouraged Ishibashi to treat concrete issues in a way few other intellectuals could match. He shared his views in new organizational structures and alliances, where he encountered persons of various occupations and beliefs who might agree with him only on single issues. Hence the parts of his integrated pragmatic program reached far beyond its whole, interlocking with major interwar movements, planning systems, and reforms, and built a basis of support for his entry into postwar politics.

PHILOSOPHY

Tanaka and Ishibashi were hostile to the idealism that so heavily shadowed their intellectual context. Neither Tanaka nor Ishibashi ever addressed Yoshino directly, perhaps from reluctance to engage the theoretical legal and constitutional issues that loomed so large in Yoshino's thought. Their rebuttal of idealism emerges most clearly in Tanaka's critique of the philosophies of Nishida Kitarō and Sōda Kiichirō. Sōda and

Nishida led the neo-Kantians, who dominated Japanese academic philosophy during the 1920s and were Tanaka's most formidable opponents. They favored the Heidelberg school of Wilhelm Windelband and Heinrich Rickert and distinguished the human from the natural sciences, attempting to acknowledge the laws of modern science while preserving the moral autonomy of individuals. Sōda and Nishida admired the democratic trends of Taishō Japan, and both are conventionally described as political liberals. Through Nishida and Sōda, Tanaka addressed concepts that were also present in Yoshino's thinking: idealism and an idealized notion of the self. He showed the repressive potential of the concepts in his debate with Sōda concerning the suicide of Matsui Sumako.

Selfhood for Tanaka existed in a dynamic interrelationship with the natural and social environment. As Hasegawa Nyozekan noted, the self in Tanaka's individualism was not the pre-experiential, absolute, and abstract self of contemporary psychology and philosophy (*jiga*); it was rather a concrete and relative self (*jiko*): simply the "I" (*watakushi*) of everyday life.[5] In contrast Nishida postulated the "self-consciousness of the pre-experiential self," which, in reflection, "takes its own function as object" rather than "accidents appended from outside."[6] Tanaka retorted that he could not imagine why the pre-experiential self might reflect on its own function. Impatiently he judged that Nishida's brand of self-conscious reflection "might exist, and then again it might not"; "I myself think it is no more than a result of erroneous abstraction and generalization."[7] Tanaka defined individuals in terms of their concrete daily experience, whereas Nishida viewed them in terms of the higher levels of intellectual awareness. Hence the political implications of their respective notions of selfhood differed remarkably.

The ominous political possibilities of the ideal self were chillingly clear in Sōda Kiichirō's philosophy of value. As a member of the progressive Reimeikai with Yoshino, Sōda deemed

5. Hasegawa Nyozekan, preface to Tanaka, *Tettei kojinshugi* (1948).
6. Tanaka, "Nishida Hakushi no tetsugaku shisaku no tokuchō to kachi to o ronzu," *Waseda Daigaku shi* 2, no. 3 (Mar. 1969): 75; see also Nishida Kitarō, *Jikaku ni okeru chokkan to hansei*, preface and 188–222.
7. Tanaka, "Nishida," 75.

himself a supporter of the Taishō democratic movement, offering it a "right to intellectual recognition" in terms of the "philosophy of value."[8] Sōda dismissed "bureaucratism, conservatism, and militarism" but also rejected the dialectical antithesis that he discerned in "democracy, progressivism, and liberalism."[9] He developed his philosophy of culturalism (*bunkashugi*) as "an internal and transcendental perspective from which to consider both [sets of beliefs]."[10] Ikimatsu Keizō places Sōda in that current of the Taishō democratic movement which expressed "the ideology of the cultivated bourgeoisie."[11] If Sōda represented one group of the cultivated bourgeoisie, it is all the more important to recognize how different his goals were from those of Tanaka and Ishibashi.

Sōda disparaged representative government by postulating an inherent contradiction between two conceptions of individualism: the private fulfillment of individual talent, and the rule of the majority, which presupposed the numerical equality of individuals.[12] Formal political equality constrained individual freedom. Although Sōda proposed a dialectical resolution of the contradiction, his argument was heavily weighted against majority rule and in favor of the creative individual who contributed to the "process of realization of cultural value."[13]

Sōda equated majority rule with socialist programs of economic equity. The ideologies of majority rule, popular rights, and egalitarianism had been gaining ground since the eighteenth century, when the economic and social transformation brought by industrialization had threatened the "biological and cultural existence" of the "weak persons in society" (*shakaiteki jakusha*).[14] Sōda apparently referred to the socially disadvantaged rather than the biologically unfit, but his argument was strongly reminiscent of Social Darwinism: the biological will to survive had prompted the weak to demand a

---

8. Sōda, *Bunka kachi to kyokugen gainen*, 44.
9. Ikimatsu Keizō, *Taishōki no shisō to bunka*, 94.
10. Ibid.
11. Ibid.
12. Sōda, 6.
13. Ibid.
14. Ibid., 16–17.

"right to existence," and the demand had constituted the motive force of modern democratic political movements and labor movements.[15] Society's failure to meet this demand, in Sōda's view, would result in a brutal struggle for material survival.

For Sōda, the requirements of the social whole were the only possible justification for recognizing the right to existence of the weak. In economics, the people's right to existence was clearly subordinate to the needs of the state: "No one is likely to dispute recognition of the people's right of existence, and fulfillment of their material demands, as far as the state's finances permit."[16] In politics, majority rule was necessary in order to consolidate the social group, but detrimental to the creative individual: "There is no way other than majority rule to create a single mode of behavior, and consolidate group opinion, by departing from the individual; and majority rule can have no other logical basis."[17] Majority rule demeaned individuals by treating them as ciphers, "a motley array of headcovers on Hibiya Field," rather than as unique personalities with unique talents.[18] However, majority rule was permissible in order to realize such common interests as national unity and popular identification with the state. Sōda viewed the state as a defense against majority rule, rather than the reverse.

Sōda diminished majority rule to an "idealization of natural science" that merited a limited role in the mundane activities of economics and politics, and he contrasted these activities with a separate and higher sphere of "the culture of freedom."[19] In the culture of freedom, which was based on "historical philosophy" instead of natural science, "Human personality is not equal, but in some sense comprises a special and inalienable meaning within itself, and allows discrimination on the basis of value."[20] Sōda's culture of freedom assigned each individual an appropriate rank and position "from the perspective of transcendent cultural value," and the hierarchy per-

15. Ibid.
16. Ibid., 18.
17. Ibid., 8–9.
18. Ibid., 9.
19. Ibid., 10–11.
20. Ibid., 12.

mitted "the demand for the absolute submission or sacrifice of one personality for the sake of the perfection of another."[21] According to Sōda, only religion or metaphysics, which derived their logical basis from the philosophy of value, could legitimate this demand for absolute submission.

Tanaka retorted that majority rule had served as the weapon of "the people against the privileged minority" during the eighteenth and nineteenth centuries. It was an emancipating historical force and not merely, as Sōda would have it, the dreary alternative to a brutal struggle for material existence.[22] Industrialization and democracy had afforded more, not less, opportunity for the individual of superior talent; and majority rule was more effective than the old class and status systems in developing and utilizing individuals of superior potential. Like Sōda, Tanaka believed that democracy served the interests of the social whole, but he denied that it constricted the creative minority. Once the artificial barriers of status, class, and privilege were overcome, members of any group would spontaneously tend to recognize and accept the judgment of their most able cohorts. In this sense, Tanaka judged that effective leaders could be chosen "more directly and accurately under majority rule than under minority despotism."[23]

Sōda insisted that individuals' worth, and their very right to existence, were contingent on their place in a hierarchy of cultural value. The contingency was absolutely unacceptable to Tanaka, who derived value itself from cultures, or particular groups of human beings.[24] He stressed the process by which culture was formed in order to satisfy the needs of groups and individuals: "People create industry, art, learning, politics, and morality to solve problems. These things are certainly values for them, but why? Not for the sake of some 'culture' envisioned in the distant future, but as means to fulfill their desires for life, which is their primary value."[25] Culture and cooperative society, Tanaka insisted, came into being in order

21. Ibid., 12–13.
22. Tanaka, "Sekai heiwa no risō ni chinamite shoka no bunkashugi o kentōsu," part 2, 36.
23. Ibid.
24. Ibid., 33–34.
25. Ibid.

to realize the needs and interests of human beings. Thus social life, by its very nature, was contingent on the prior right of every individual—even an individual who never had and never could produce culture in Sōda's sense—to existence and self-development.

In effect, Tanaka turned Sōda on his head. Tanaka argued that advanced levels of culture existed only insofar as society acknowledged individual value. Sōda, charged Tanaka, derived the value of individuals from their function as group members and made them "the objects, not the subjects, of value."[26] Despite Sōda's contention that every individual had an appropriate place in the process of cultural creation, Sōda's premises inescapably excluded ordinary people from the realm of primary value. Tanaka defined culture as a human construction designed to fulfill individual needs in the present, and he felt Sōda's higher culture was a cruel teleological projection by which the needs of living individuals were perpetually sacrificed to the vague and fantastical aims of the distant future.[27]

Sōda and Tanaka completely disagreed about the meaning of Matsui Sumako's suicide. A few months after Shimamura's death in 1918, Matsui hanged herself in the Geijutsuza during a performance of *Carmen*. Public opinion divided about the morality of her action, and the journal *Waseda bungaku* solicited comments, mainly from colleagues and students of Shimamura at the Waseda literature and philosophy department. Among them were Hiratsuka Raichō, Kuwaki Genyoku, Miyata Shū, and Tanaka. Hiratsuka sympathized with Matsui's loss of the will to live without her teacher and lover, while Kuwaki Genyoku and Miyata Shū deplored the possible influence of the disreputable affair on impressionable young people.[28] Tanaka alone treated Matsui's suicide as a tragedy occasioned by Japan's benighted marriage and divorce laws. Since Matsui and Shimamura had been living together for some years before their deaths, Tanaka argued, surely either

26. Ibid., 32.
27. John Dewey, review of Lester Ward, *The Psychic Factors of Civilization*, in *The Early Works of John Dewey*, ed. Jo Ann Boydston, 4: 212.
28. Kuwaki Genyoku et al., "Matsui Sumako," 18–36.

Shimamura or his wife would have insisted on divorce under a more liberal legal system. Matsui had been driven to suicide by the repressive and anti-individualistic laws of Japan, and by the economic dependency of women, which combined to make divorce an object of scandal, shame, and horror.[29]

In contrast, Sōda described Matsui's death as a sublime expression of selfless devotion and compared it with other celebrated suicides such as those of General and Mrs. Nogi after the death of the Meiji Emperor: "Those suicides prompted by loyalty as a cultural *idée* . . . are an absolute assertion of individual character, which ought to be deemed the ultimate beauty of human life. They can be criticized in terms of their public influence . . . yet at the same time I cannot resist a boundless admiration and respect for these acts."[30] Sōda's boundless admiration confirmed Tanaka's charge that Sōda's sense of culture encouraged the sacrifice of living individuals for ideals. Sōda's creative individual found fulfillment only in acts of ultimate significance; concomitantly most people were not individuals in Sōda's sense. Sōda's lack of interest in ordinary human experience was inextricably linked to a rejection of politics as a means to ameliorate that existence. His blindness prompted Tanaka to reject idealism in toto: "The argument that for everything there is something higher, that each part takes its meaning from the whole, is the goose that laid the golden egg of absolutism."[31]

All of Tanaka's writings crusaded against transcendental philosophical positions—the rigid old moralities of Confucianism, Buddhism, or the rural Hōtoku Societies; the mysticism of the naturalist writers and Hiratsuka Raichō; the culture of Sōda Kiichirō; and the ideal self of Nishida Kitarō. Tanaka deemed all of these philosophies to be unacceptable abstractions that purported to work independently of, and dictate behavior to, actual human beings in concrete situations. They reminded Tanaka of Japan's statist ideology, the divine and unbroken imperial line, and the myth of Japan's unique, im-

29. Tanaka, in Kuwaki et al., "Matsui Sumako," 27–29.
30. Sōda, quoted in Baba Keinosuke, "Sōda Hakushi no tetsugaku shisō," in Sōda Hakushi Gojūnenki Kinenkai, comp., *Sōda tetsugaku e no kaisō*, 44.
31. Tanaka, "Nishida," 84–85.

mutable national polity, which transcended reason and human effort.

There was, however, an instrumental facet to Japan's emperor-state. Kuno Osamu and Tsurumi Shunsuke have described an "esoteric" version of the imperial ideology, which contrasted with the "exoteric" version of transcendence and sanctity. Whereas the exoteric version aimed at the masses through primary education, the esoteric version was commonplace in university education and among the elite.[32] The esoteric view appeared as early as the Meiji Restoration, when Ōkubo Toshimichi referred to capturing the imperial jewel, and later when Minobe Tatsukichi described the emperor as an organ of the state. Ōkubo and Minobe were instrumentalists in the sense that they unblushingly manipulated the legitimizing power of the imperial household, and the unbroken imperial line, as means to national progress.

Neither idealist nor instrumentalist thinkers solved the thorniest intellectual problem confronting Taishō democrats, imperial sovereignty. Imperial sovereignty was directly linked to a welter of nonrepresentative institutions: the cabinet, the armed forces, the Privy Council, the elder statesmen, and the House of Peers, all of whom held their positions by virtue of the imperial will, according to the Meiji Constitution. However, elected representatives could also make claims on the imperial will, permitting democratic gains to be legitimized provided that their practitioners could overcome the resistance of other active political institutions. Hence Tokyo University legal scholars Yoshino Sakuzō and Minobe Tatsukichi opted for the strategy of distinguishing a functionally democratic political system (*seitai*) from the historical and spiritual national polity (*kokutai*). Their works pointed toward a system pragmatic in its politics and transcendent in its ideology. Their strategy seemed a viable route to parliamentary politics between 1919 and 1931, when six of the nine cabinets formed were headed by the leader of the majority party in the lower house and Japan showed a genuine possibility of evolving toward an English-

32. Kuno Osamu and Tsurumi Shunsuke, *Gendai Nihon no shisō*; and Kuno, "The Meiji State, Minponshugi, and Ultra-Nationalism," in Koschmann, ed., *Authority and the Individual in Japan*, 60–80.

style system as Uematsu Hisaaki had predicted.[33] Yoshino's and Minobe's state theories were profoundly important for their role in proving to intellectuals and administrators that parliamentary politics could be legitimized in legal, even patriotic terms. However, the theories' highly abstract and administrative character certainly militated against mass appeal and obscured the political competition and social friction that were very much a part of the Taishō democratic movement.

In contrast, Ishibashi avoided the problem of sovereignty, limiting himself to the actual processes of politics, which formed only one side of Minobe's and Yoshino's theories. He differed from Yoshino, who described constitutional monarchy as the ideal form of government, in refusing to idealize any aspect of the existing state or to postulate a hypothetical ideal state; and he adamantly defined the state as a malleable instrument of changing social conditions and purposes. His pragmatic approach was evident in his few and cursory discussions of sovereignty in the abstract, his choices of language, and his conditional acceptance of the Meiji Constitution. Although he preferred to avoid the abstruse and perilous topic of sovereignty, in one early essay he judged that "originally, sovereignty resided in the whole people."[34] The hypothesis allowed him to pose the provocative question of why people acquiesced in their governments. All governments ultimately rested on the tacit consent of the governed, who would revolt under extreme oppression. Since the people's tolerance was essential to any government, the parliamentary system was a more efficient method by which to achieve it. The laborious line of reasoning blurred the distinction between imperial and popular sovereignty, but Ishibashi's language hinted at a preference for popular sovereignty, for he consistently employed the terms *minshushugi* ("the people as master"), *minshūshugi* (with strongly populist overtones of economic and social reform), and *demokurashii* (a direct transliteration).

33. Miura Tetsutarō, "Saikin seiken no shinsō," *TKS*, 5 July 1914.

34. *ITZ* 1:349. See also Matsuo, "Taishō demokurashii no ichi suimyaku," 1176; and idem, "Kokumin shuken ronsha Ishibashi Tanzan," *Ishibashi Tanzan zenshū geppō*, no. 5 (Mar. 1971): 4–6; Kisaka Jun'ichirō, "Taishōki no naisei kaikakuron," in Inoue and Watanabe, eds., *Taishōki no kyūshinteki jiyūshugi*, 225–27; Tanaka Ōdō, "Genka ni okeru shinwaka no genryū o kyūmeisu," in *Sukui wa hansei yori*, 39.

Language signaled Ishibashi's considerable distance from Yoshino, who adopted a term coined by conservative Uesugi Shinkichi, *minponshugi* ("government with the people as its basis"), in order to accommodate imperial sovereignty. Yoshino's theory of democracy was far more influential than Ishibashi's because it was an elaborate and explicit accommodation with the position of the emperor under the Meiji Constitution.[35] Still, some pundits such as Miura and Uehara Etsujirō shared Ishibashi's reluctance to sanction the monarchy. Uehara criticized Yoshino's *minponshugi* as abstruse, and weak in guaranteeing individual rights and party cabinets; he concluded that "democracy means that all are equally human."[36]

The most lucid indication of Ishibashi's views on sovereignty was the way that he qualified his acceptance of the Meiji constitutional order. He conditionally accepted the Meiji state because, first, it had created a nucleus of parliamentary institutions and, second, its authoritarian features derived from its historic context, particularly the need to fend off Western imperialism and to preserve national independence. The statism and bureaucratism that he abhorred in the twentieth century had been useful in the nineteenth to unite the nation and import foreign knowledge. Statism had mobilized the people around patriotic ideals, destroying ancient localism, while bureaucratic specialization had facilitated the absorption of Western institutions, ideas, and knowledge. Hence the Meiji state was legitimate only because it had fulfilled purposes essential to the continued independent development of the whole people. In the twentieth century it would be judged by how effectively it fulfilled changing purposes and new demands.

In the Taishō era, Meiji state ideology and structure were outmoded, Ishibashi believed, because Japan had already formed

35. Yoshino, "Kensei no hongi"; Uesugi Shinkichi, "Minponshugi to minshushugi"; Matsumoto Sannosuke, "Seiji to chishikijin," in Hashikawa and Matsumoto, eds., *Kindai Nihon seiji shisōshi*, vol. 2; Matsuo, "Kokumin shuken ronsha Ishibashi Tanzan," 5; Kisaka, 226–28; Bernard Silberman, "The Democracy Movement in Japan," 87–94.

36. Uehara Etsujirō, "Yoshino Hakushi no kenpōron to minponshugi," in Uehara Etsujirō Jūsankai Kikinen Shuppan Kankōkai, ed., *Uehara Etsujirō to Nihonkoku kenpō*, 94; see also his "Yoshino Hakushi no kenpōron o hyōsu."

a united nation and reached a level of industrialization that
was fairly competitive with the West. Now the problem was not
to create national unity but to permit free expression of the
people's diverse interests. The increase of political and social
tensions at home made it essential to decrease conflict over the
empire and trade abroad, in contrast to the Meiji era when
the foreign threat had been more urgent. The importation of
Western knowledge via bureaucratic management grew less
and less significant as the gap between levels of development
in the West and Japan began to close, and private institutions
such as business, the universities, and the media assumed expert functions in competition with the bureaucracy. Summon-
ing a future in which Japan's first priority would be to create
a system of socio-economic and political equity, a challenge no
nation had yet surmounted, Ishibashi urged that the guides
to future development would be neither bureaucrats nor foreigners, but the Japanese people themselves. The people who
could succeed in this task were not the romanticized folk of
the premodern community, but a modern people armed with
education, sophisticated methods of organization, and legal avenues of participation, yet drawing on a sense of equity that
had evolved from their traditions and culture.[37]

Well before Yoshino set forth his constitutional theory, Ishibashi had exposed the instrumental use of the imperial symbol
as pointedly as he dared. He had accused the functionaries
who were charged with preparations for the crown prince's
trip to Hokkaido, in 1911, of behaving with crass arrogance
toward the common people by requiring schoolgirls to procure
special shoes from Tokyo at considerable expense, disrupting
education and normal governmental functions, spending millions for road and building repairs and even bribing rickshaw
attendants to assure enough carriages, forbidding the use of
warning sirens during the imperial visit, and intercepting
travel "as if in revival of the old regime."[38] The people ought
to be treated with more respect. Conversely the imperial institution might be used for constructive social purposes such

37. *ITZ* 2:176–79; Furuya Tetsuo, "Fuashizumu zenya no seijiron," in Inoue and
Watanabe, eds., *Taishōki no kyūshinteki jiyūshugi*, 324.
38. *ITZ* 1:183–85.

as the sponsorship of a Nobel-style prize to encourage intellectual and artistic achievement, which would be a more fitting memorial to the Meiji Emperor than "foolish shrine construction," which encouraged "excessive national unity" and the "atrophy of individual judgment."[39] Aware of the contradiction inherent in manipulating the imperial cult to encourage individual autonomy, Ishibashi concluded that it would be best to confine debate to practical issues and to renounce "the worst trend in Japan, using the throne as a pretext [*kōshitsu o kuchi ni suru*]."[40] His comments passed the censors by avoiding challenge to the emperor system per se, yet they prodded the public toward a transformed political culture.

During the decade from 1917 to 1927 Ishibashi shifted from the abstract principles that he had learned from Tanaka to a host of concrete applications in representative government, freedom of expression, labor and tenant policy, and financial reform. In developing new policy positions he joined significant research/political associations, groups that typified the structure of Taishō liberalism and would serve as his springboard into postwar politics. The organizations addressed discrete issues, but his thought during these years was still distinguished by an integration of political, social, and economic themes in a comprehensive vision of a new kind of society. Nonetheless, politics will be treated first here, and the social problem subsequently, in order to emphasize the interaction of democratic thought and the Meiji state.

Ishibashi buttressed his conception of a new participatory political culture with a host of pragmatic reform proposals, the most important of which was universal suffrage. Circumstances conspired to raise the issue immediately after he joined the *Shinpō* staff: editor Uematsu had already come out in favor of suffrage for all adult men and women, universal manhood suffrage had passed the lower house in 1911, and the movement to protect the Constitution fought armaments spending and Prime Minister Katsura Tarō's use of imperial rescripts during the Taishō political crisis. Ishibashi was only one of many professionals, especially journalists, lawyers, and party

39. *ITZ* 1:487–90.
40. *ITZ* 2:446.

politicians, who lectured and wrote on behalf of democratic reform at this time, but his reasoning was distinguished by its firm espousal of self-interest. The single most important argument in favor of universal suffrage was to establish a relationship of material interest (*rigai kankei*) between the people and their representatives.[41]

In welcoming popular demands on the system, Ishibashi differed from essayists such as Sōda, Oda Yorozu, or Uesugi Shinkichi, who viewed suffrage primarily as a method of encouraging patriotism. He envisioned other positive effects from suffrage. First, it would discourage political corruption and encourage the political parties to take more responsible positions. Second, it would strengthen the power of the lower house in the government by enhancing its legitimacy. Finally, it would prevent revolution by abolishing the privileges of the upper class—the real reason that many of the elite opposed the measure under various pretexts. Questions about the political capability of the working class raised by commentators such as Nitobe Inazō and Ozaki Yukio were irrational, because the present system of tax qualification was not based on merit, only on wealth. Moreover, representative government did not require the voters to be political scientists, only to grasp the needs of their daily lives. Ordinary people were far more capable of judging their own interests than were their putative social and intellectual superiors, and they ought to do so at once.[42]

Few Japanese intellectuals shared Ishibashi's confidence in self-interest, and when universal manhood suffrage finally passed both houses of the legislature in 1926, its mainstream supporters were more interested in the mobilization of the people by the state than in the accountability of the state to the people. The prevailing climate of opinion even influenced Ishibashi, for in a single note in 1920 he would argue that he supported suffrage "not as a right, but for the security and welfare of the state."[43] Kisaka Jun'ichirō has singled out this

41. *ITZ* 1:464; Matsuo, "Taishō demokurashii no ichi suimyaku," 1170, 1177; Yamamoto Shirō, *Taishō seihen no kisoteki kenkyū*, 335–36.

42. Uesugi Shinkichi, "Minponshugi to minshushugi"; Oda, "Kokutai to minsei"; *ITZ* 1:516; 2:54–58, 324–25, 333, and 3:3–26.

43. *ITZ* 3:63; on the parliamentary movement for universal manhood suffrage

particular passage as "reactionary" compared with Uematsu Hisaaki's advocacy of universal suffrage as a natural human right fifteen years earlier.[44] Criticism of Taishō democrats for ignoring natural rights is widespread in scholarly accounts. However, Ishibashi's political and intellectual context accounts for the omission. Politically, he addressed a special session of the Diet that he hoped would finally pass universal suffrage after nearly a decade of frustration. Ishibashi wanted the swing votes, for minority support from the faithful had been settled for years and was unlikely to dissipate now in the Diet, although the suffrage movement was losing ground with labor and intellectuals due to its delays and frustrations. Immediate passage of universal manhood suffrage, Ishibashi hoped, would moderate popular anger at oligarchic government. Intellectually, he was reading the works of German Social Democrats, as well as John Maynard Keynes, all of whom regarded natural rights as an outmoded and metaphysical conception. Ishibashi, like the Western thinkers he admired, struggled to posit his political arguments as tenable theories of social reality, which could be confirmed by historical processes. The academic tone doubtless militated against mass appeal, yet an insistence on natural rights, which had far less foundation in Japanese culture than Ishibashi's perspective of rational social utility, would hardly have won mass commitment. As Ishibashi grappled for a socially scientific defense of parliamentary politics, he also advocated independent labor and tenant activism, making it clear that for him the people's assertion of their interests was the first priority, and the strengthening of state and society was to be a by-product.

Universal suffrage alone would not make Japan a publicly responsible parliamentary system, as Ishibashi realized, and he proposed a comprehensive set of other political reforms. Universal suffrage and party cabinets could not assure the accountability of the House of Peers, the army, or the elder statesmen. The House of Peers persistently vetoed and delayed

---

see Edward G. Griffin, "The Universal Suffrage Issue in Japanese Politics, 1918–1925," *JAS* 31 (1972): 275–90.

44. Kisaka, 244.

universal suffrage, women's rights, and other reformist measures. A series of constitutional amendments were necessary,
Ishibashi argued, to ensure that the popularly elected lower
house was paramount in the government. The assertion was
daring, since the Constitution was the sacrosanct gift of the
Meiji Emperor and only the emperor could amend it. Peers
ought to be subordinated to the House of Commons by a requirement that all government bills first be introduced in
Commons, and that Peers' powers be limited to the expedi-
tious amendment, passage, or rejection of bills forwarded
from the lower house. Nonetheless Ishibashi did intend to preserve a second chamber independent of the first. He was
interested in occupational representation in the upper house,
even though he was aware of British socialist Sidney Webb's
reservation that such a system always underrepresented labor.
Ishibashi hoped that strong union representation in an occupational system, and direct popular election of Commons,
could hold the capitalists at bay.[45] *Chūō kōron*, *Shin Nihon*, and
the Kenseikai party strongly supported the reform of the
House of Peers, and in 1925 the Diet passed a modest change
in that body's composition aimed toward broader representation.[46]

Ishibashi urged still other legislative and administrative revisions. Civilian military ministers and the prime minister
should command the army by eliminating the requirement
that the service ministers be officers, who were responsible to
the general staffs.[47] Popular accountability should be extended
to local government, first in the election of prefectural governors. Legal change could not affect the elder statesmen since
their role was informal, but Ishibashi could not restrain his
impatience, eulogizing the passing of Yamagata Aritomo with
the comment, "Even his death is a service to the nation," and
urging the two remaining *genrō*, Saionji Kinmochi and Matsukata Masayoshi, to renounce all their privileges.[48] The accountability of dominant institutions was already long overdue.

45. *ITZ* 5:45–48; Tanaka suggested abolishing the House of Peers in "Genka ni
okeru shinwaka no genryū o kyūmeisu," 40.
46. Satogami Ryūhei, "Taishō demokurashii to Kizokuin," in Inoue Kiyoshi, ed.,
Taishō no seiji to shakai, 261–69.
47. *ITZ* 4:111.
48. Quoted in Matsuo, "Taishō demokurashii no ichi suimyaku," 1175–76; see also

Freedom of expression and association were as important as universal suffrage in implementing a full-fledged parliamentary system, and conversely, representative government could curtail the arbitrary bureaucratic suppression of controversial ideas and movements. Ishibashi publicly denounced a great many instances of police interference with thought and action during the Taishō period, and suggested an independent agency to prevent use of the police for partisan political purposes. In countless editorials over the decades of his journalistic career, he also reiterated his theoretical rationale for liberty, echoing Tanaka's thesis that society required the constant generation and competition of new views and visions. Since Tanaka and Ishibashi justified freedom in terms of its benefits to society rather than in terms of absolute and unabridgeable individual rights, both conceded that the government might correctly restrict freedom of expression under certain rare circumstances. The only such circumstance that Ishibashi ever mentioned was the suppression of precise data concerning military maneuvers during the Siberian Intervention—and then he defended his right to criticize the purposes and effects of the expedition.

Ishibashi upheld the civil rights of the unpopular: the millenarian Ōmoto sect, anarchists, Koreans, and *burakumin* (outcastes).[49] In 1920, the police arrested members of the Ōmoto sect on charges of lèse majesté, and destroyed the group's major shrines. Although the sect was generally vilified in the press, Ishibashi upheld its members' rights and cautioned that such "superstitions" as the Ōmoto sect flourished only because of the "impotence of scholars and the government's restriction of expression."[50] Only Ishibashi and Yoshino Sakuzō criticized the government's action in major journals.[51] Ishibashi also decried the death of anarchist Ōsugi Sakae, who was strangled by the police in a jail cell in the panic and desperation which

---

idem, "Kokumin shuken ronsha Ishibashi Tanzan" for a brief summary of Ishibashi's reformist proposals.

49. On *burakumin* organization in the Suiheisha, which Ishibashi applauded, see *ITZ* 5:443. Ishibashi supported the Suiheisha on general principles and not from any particular familiarity with *burakumin* experience; hence his rather significant absence of prejudice is not explored in detail here.

50. *ITZ* 3:514.

51. Matsuo, "Taishō demokurashii no ichi suimyaku," 1178–79.

followed the Great Kantō Earthquake. In the wake of the disaster, most newspapers castigated the left for opportunism. Ishibashi countered that the public needed education in the purposes of the left; that the government encouraged antiradical hysteria; and that "the people may well fear the army, police, and officials more than earthquake and fire."[52] He again chastised the government and newspapers for fanning hysteria about the arrest of Korean anarchist Pak Ryul for an alleged plot to assassinate the emperor.[53] The lonely defense of unpopular views, cults, and minorities proved the consistency of Ishibashi's thought and the rigor of his commitment to social and intellectual pluralism. In other instances such as the case of Professor Morito Tatsuo, Ishibashi cooperated with numerous other intellectuals and writers to protest censorship and repression.

Notably missing from Ishibashi's political criticism was the disdain for the political parties that formed so central a strand in prewar political discourse. Ishibashi was quite generous in dispensing specific criticism to particular cabinets, individual politicians, and party policy and behavior across the political spectrum. The Ōkuma cabinet was repressive, the Yamamoto cabinet worse, and the Terauchi cabinet worst of all; the Hara cabinet was unethical and wrong-headed in its foreign policy, colonial administration, and commodity pricing policy; the Seiyūkai and Kenseikai were hypocritical in their poses of respect for elections.[54] In 1916 he even sneered that any one of the parties might call itself the Landlords' party, Plutocrats' party, Imperialist party, or Arms Expansion party, but on the whole he avoided attacking the political parties in general terms.[55] Most critics of the parties rejected partisan interests. In Ishibashi's view, the problem was not whether interest assertion was or was not legitimate, but rather whose interests were being served in political processes, and whose excluded. Condemnation of the parties per se led ineluctably in the direction of a nonparliamentary system. Although pained by the parties'

52. *ITZ* 5:474.
53. *ITZ* 5:532.
54. *ITZ* 3:25, 41, 53.
55. Kisaka, 233.

demagoguery, corruption, and lack of principle, Ishibashi believed that in time the people could be aroused to throw the rascals out under universal suffrage. Other specific reforms would encourage the parties to build mass bases; for example, Ishibashi opposed the Seiyūkai plan for smaller electoral districts in 1916 because he believed it would favor the continuing control of the local elite (*yūryokusha*); he preferred large districts, to benefit minority parties.[56] At this time Ishibashi preferred the European model of several ideological parties over the Anglo-American pattern of two large, composite parties that seemed to be emerging in Taishō Japan, although after World War II he would change his mind. Still, the structure of party politics was secondary to the fundamental principle of accountability to the electorate.

After a decade and a half of constantly criticizing governmental repression, Ishibashi regarded the Peace Preservation bill of 1926 as appalling but not surprising. The bill forbade organization or expression to bring about illegal change in the national polity, the governmental, military, and tax systems, and the security of private property. Ishibashi emphasized the bill's potential as a weapon against association and thought rather than action, adding that the term "illegal" was extremely vague in the context of existing laws regulating political activity such as labor unions and threats to peace, order, and public morals. When Home Minister Wakatsuki Reijirō and Legal Minister Ogawa Heikichi defended the bill in Diet debate on the grounds that it targeted revolutionaries, Ishibashi compared the ministers to Don Quixote tilting at windmills, for genuine revolutionaries were exceedingly few in number and unlikely to be dissuaded by the proposed law. He concluded that the real threats of force and violence against the constitutional order came from, first, the dominant class (*kenryoku kaikyū*), and second, the organs of repression established and authorized under laws like the Peace Preservation bill.[57]

56. *ITZ* 2:351–52; Kisaka, 232–33; Furuya, 328–37. For Ishibashi's harsher judgment of the prewar parties in his postwar memoirs see *ITZ* 15:109, 236. Tanaka also favored large electoral districts in "Genka ni okeru shinwaka no genryū o kyūmeisu," 42.

57. *ITZ* 5:49–52.

Much as Ishibashi disliked the Peace Preservation Law, he did not identify it as a turning point from the democratic tendencies of the 1920s to the authoritarian trends of the 1930s. In fact, he showed no serious alarm that Japan could be shifted from the path toward a fully representative and accountable parliamentary system until the February 26 incident of 1936. To some extent he was guilty of wishful thinking, consistently interpreting progressive victories as trends and new authoritarian institutions as aberrations. Nonetheless the 1920s did offer substantial evidence that his ideals were being realized. Universal manhood suffrage was passed in 1926. Party cabinets were inaugurated in 1919 and routinized in a "functioning two-party system" after 1924.[58] The vulnerability of the party cabinets in the global economic crisis after 1929 does not nullify the vigor of forces behind them during the earlier decades. Women's political participation advanced one step in 1922, and the Hamaguchi cabinet proposed a limited women's suffrage bill in 1931. The military role in the cabinet was slightly restrained by permitting retired as well as active officers to serve as heads of the military ministries between 1922 and 1936, and the House of Peers underwent a modest reform, to broaden its composition and weaken the influence of the nobility, in 1925. The second-to-the-last *genro*, Matsukata, died in 1924, and the surviving Saionji discretely accommodated his role to constitutional procedures. The only items in Ishibashi's reformist agenda that met no encouragement whatsoever were the restriction of the police's political role—which instead increased—and freedom of expression and association, which decreased.

The limited but promising achievements of Taishō democracy suggest several conclusions. First, contradictory trends could be interpreted in various ways, and certain avenues of development appeared open that history later slammed closed. Second, participation increased while freedom decreased, building a bridge to the mass mobilization policies of the thirties.[59] From this perspective, Ishibashi was mistaken in his be-

58. Imai Seiichi, "Seitō seiji to kokumin shisō," in Hashikawa and Matsumoto, eds., *Kindai Nihon seiji shisōshi*, vol. 2.

59. Watanuki, 44–48.

lief that universal manhood suffrage was inherently a means by which individuals could and would assert their interests, rather than a mechanism for their incorporation into prior state aims. On the other hand, his assertion that freedom of expression broadened the avenues of beneficial development would be proven correct in the contrapositive, as manipulated hysteria against dissent gradually narrowed policy options to certain disaster.

ORGANIZATION

The proliferation of voluntary associations during the Taishō era sustained Ishibashi's political optimism. Research societies among intellectuals and interest groups among workers, tenants, and women proliferated, publishing their views and establishing linkages with the political parties and the bureaucracy as well as with each other and the general public. Broad trends supported organizational proliferation. Occupational specialization and differentiation required new connections in both the private and public sectors, as well as between the two. Changes in class composition and relationships intensified the competition for political symbols. Since the organizations considered here were primarily organizations of opinion, they were supported by an expanding market of educated persons interested in public policy. Proliferating private associations were vulnerable to state incorporation or suppression, but they increased the difficulties of bureaucratic management and also survived in skeletal form to reassert claims on postwar politics and society.

Liberals such as Tanaka and Ishibashi, by temperament, upbringing, lifestyle, and belief, remained analysts more than activists, committed to the centrality of rational discourse in political and social processes. Indeed, their belief in impartiality often eclipsed what partisan activities they did undertake. Ishibashi published an account of the tenant movement in Kagaminakajō, in which he neglected to mention that he had served as an arbitrator on the tenants' side. None of the writers had any formal association with an interwar or wartime political party. Their preference for intellectual, rather than political, modes of activity and organization left diffuse and subtle traces instead of concrete institutional impact.

Despite limitations, academic and journalistic roles sustained various modes of organization that could be employed to support intellectual and political change. The organization was both formal—in journals and study groups (*kenkyūkai*), which ranged from the strictly private to the quasi-official—and informal, in support of one another by means of speeches, published writing, or personal gestures. Through such modes of organization Ishibashi joined movements to protect the Constitution in 1911–13 and 1924, protests against restrictions on expression under the Terauchi and Hara cabinets, and universal suffrage demonstrations in 1919. In addition to political movements, he maintained informal relations with labor, tenant, and social democratic (as well as feminist) organizations. Although few of the small intellectual organizations left internal records, even a sketchy examination of their structure, activities, and external relations is useful in locating Ishibashi's individual opinions within a broader context.[60]

Although formal organization inevitably encouraged elements of hierarchy and exclusivity, Ishibashi struggled to deemphasize the tendencies, and joined with others similarly inclined. No sentiment for his alma mater prevented sharp attacks on its founder, Ōkuma Shigenobu, for tolerating the censorship of *Seitō* and even Ōkuma's own journal *Shin Nihon*, and for upholding the absolute authority of the sovereign in a Diet speech during the period of his cabinet, as well as for interfering in Waseda personnel decisions "via the arbitrary control of private capital."[61] In his memoirs Ishibashi grumbled that as a recent Waseda graduate he had been expected to help decorate Ōkuma's home for New Year's festivities.[62] Such symbols of personal subservience as gifts to officers were taboo at *Shinpō* under Ishibashi's management, and the staff were expected to address supervisors by name ("Ishibashi-san") rather than the more conventional address by title ("*shachō*-san").[63]

60. For a useful typology of cultural organizations see Raymond Williams, 68.
61. *ITZ* 2:539; see also 1:41–44, 322, 366–67, 418.
62. *ITZ* 15:65.
63. Watanabe Tōru, "Sōron," 9.

Shinpō emphasized functional division of labor rather than a hierarchy of status or authority. Membership in groups such as the Liberal Lecture Society, the League for the Establishment of Universal Suffrage (Futsū Senkyo Kisei Dōmeikai), the Waseda/Tōyō Economic Society (Waseda, later Tōyō, Keizaikai), and the Pacific Research Society crossed occupational and institutional lines, including graduates and professors from more than one university, and reformist Diet members. The deemphasis of membership criteria expressed the groups' theoretical commitment to the concept of voluntary association, although there are counterexamples, such as the exclusion of Hasegawa Nyozekan from the Reimeikai at Tokyo University on the grounds that he was a journalist and not a scholar.[64] In general, voluntary associations, based on a common purpose or field of inquiry, were relatively open and egalitarian compared with the exclusive hierarchy prevailing within major institutions, and they developed as a counterforce to weaken pressures for conformity. Adherence to voluntary associations undergirded Ishibashi's willingness to challenge hierarchy and institutional cohesion.

Voluntary associations tended to increase in specialization over time. Whereas Tanaka and Shimamura had addressed the whole set of social and psychic cultural forces that sustained authority and constricted the self, Ishibashi moved gradually toward highly specialized political positions. His memberships in single-issue organizations would increase his influence, but diminish his opposition. Since the pragmatic practice of the Taishō state contrasted with its comprehensive ideology, reform of specific parts was more legitimate than abstract criticism of the whole. Here the primary emphasis is on a moderate level of protest that continued to assert comprehensive claims while functioning within legal limits.[65]

Ishibashi belonged to *kenkyūkai*, research groups that were of four types in terms of their politics and proximity to the centers of power. Academic groups such as the Liberal Lecture Society and the Waseda/Tōyō Economic Society confined their

64. On the Reimeikai see Peter Duus, *Party Rivalry and Political Change in Taishō Japan*. 114.

65. On specialization see Raymond Williams, 70.

activities to lecturing and publishing, encouraging comprehensive changes in public knowledge and consciousness but
denying their own political character, in a not always successful
attempt to avoid suppression. Activist groups such as the
League for the Establishment of Universal Suffrage organized
mass demonstrations and regional branches, while performing
the lecturing and publishing activities characteristic of academic groups. Lobbying organizations such as the Pacific Research Society also sustained academic functions, but in
addition they presented detailed policy proposals to the Diet;
the specificity of the proposals distinguished lobbying groups
from activist organizations, which petitioned the Diet in terms
of general principles. All the groups included both reformist
politicians and intellectuals, but the presence of bureaucrats
was rare and seems significant enough to merit a fourth category of organization, the quasi-official, represented by Ishibashi's participation in the Economic Study Association (Keizai
Kōkyūkai). Quasi-official groups were distinguished by temporal continuity, as well as a marked increase in the number
and specificity of policy proposals. A number of groups pro-
gressed through the four categories over time, with some economic study groups showing a similar progression without an
activist phase. Activism alone could seldom sustain a group
over the years against a low level of popular politicization and
a considerable amount of governmental harassment; the
League for the Establishment of Universal Suffrage dissolved
once the suffrage issue had been taken up by the major parties. Voluntary associations were plagued with the Hobson's
choice of incorporation into the political system or dissolution;
yet their form, cross-occupational groups for the deliberation
of public issues, originated outside the bureaucracy rather
than within it and changed the nature of the state even while
being incorporated within it. Moreover, academic, activist, lobbying, and quasi-official study groups were an important part
of social restructuring, and they accelerated the dissemination
of information that distinguished the Taishō era.

Leadership in the universal suffrage demonstration of
March 1, 1919, was the most dramatic instance of Ishibashi's
political activism. *Shinpō* affiliation with the suffrage move-

ment preceded Ishibashi's employment there, for the third editor, Uematsu, was a friend of socialist and labor reformer Katayama Sen and was deeply involved in the League for the Establishment of Universal Suffrage from its formation in 1900. The league had first petitioned the Diet for suffrage in 1900, collecting one thousand signatures, and it continued petitioning annually for a decade, winning the introduction of several universal manhood suffrage bills by league and House members such as Kōno Hironaka, and achieving the lower-house passage of one such measure in 1911. Forced to dissolve in the increased repression consequent on the Kōtoku trial, the league was reassembled in 1918 by Nakamura Tahachirō, Ōi Kentarō, and Katō Tokojirō; Ishibashi, Miura, and Sugiyama Yoshio of *Shinpō* joined its executive committee. Cresting in membership after the rice riots of 1918, the group formed regional organizations and sponsored lectures in 1919 and 1920. It orchestrated the most significant legal demonstration of the Taishō era but lapsed into inactivity after the forty-second Diet, when two parties, the Kenseikai and Rikken Kokumintō (People's Constitutional party), took up the cause of universal manhood suffrage in the lower house.[66]

The demonstration was large, legal, multi-class, and national in scope, and it claimed patriotic symbols such as the flag and the Charter Oath for the ends of democratization. Ishibashi read the Charter Oath aloud before a crowd estimated at ten thousand demonstrators and fifty thousand spectators. Although he had initially wondered whether an impartial journalist should join a mass demonstration, he described the demonstration as nonpartisan. The demonstrators, he observed, represented a cross section of society and different generations, including merchants, clerks, workers, and employees. Demonstrations occurred throughout the country and represented "the will of Tokyo and the nation."[67] Even the leaders were surprised by the turnout.

66. *ITZ* 3:531, 565; 15:98–99, 349–55; Hirano Yoshitarō, *Nakamura Tahachirō den*, 64–69; Matsuo Takayoshi, "Daiichiji taisen no futsū senkyo undō" and "Taishō demokurashii no ichi suimyaku," 1178. Shimura Hidetarō notes that Ishibashi was also associated with another suffrage organization, the Kensei Sakushinkai, in *Ishibashi Tanzan*, 129.

67. *ITZ* 3:27–28.

The mobilized people proved the paucity of governmental control mechanisms. The Ministry of Education was fairly successful in preventing student participation, which was illegal under the Public Peace Police Law of 1900. However, the police reluctantly approved the demonstration while attempting to impose some seventeen conditions to undermine its influence. They requested a change of date, since March 1 was a workers' holiday, and asked for a record of demonstrators' names and addresses. They banned red badges, singing with a band, bell and drum, fanfare of bugles, and banners; the national flag was permissible if not large in size. They barred the demonstrators from crowded areas such as the Ginza and required them to conclude by 2:00 P.M., under the pretext of avoiding disruption to traffic. Finally, to undermine the influence of the demonstration's intellectual and political leaders, the police required that no printed works be distributed or speeches given, and that no more than thirty Diet representatives lead the marchers. Ishibashi scornfully printed the police conditions in *Shinpō* and retorted that crowded conditions were the very point of a mass demonstration. The arbitrary and piecemeal restrictions proved futile. Demonstrators were too numerous to permit the recording of their names and addresses; the responsible police official thoughtfully fell ill at the last moment; and all conditions were dropped. Although universal manhood suffrage was not achieved until 1926, the demonstration prodded politicians, intellectuals, and bureaucrats to devise new channels of mass political participation.[68]

Formal and informal organization on behalf of dissenting views were both illustrated in the celebrated Morito Incident of 1920. Ishibashi supported Professor Morito Tatsuo of Tokyo University and editor Ōuchi Hyōe of *Keizaigaku kenkyū* (Economic studies), who were arrested and forced to resign their positions because of Morito's rather innocuous analysis of Petr Kropotkin's anarchism. The three doubtless were acquainted through economic circles, but the formal links between them were minimal. Ishibashi and Ōuchi both joined

68. Ibid.; Hirano, 66–67.

the Economic Study Association two years later. During the incident, informal and personal means of support predominated. First, Ishibashi published an article comparable to Morito's. Whether by design or accident, Ishibashi unveiled his own analysis of Kropotkin during the same month as Morito, predicting revolution ("a fundamental redistribution of wealth and power") in Japan in his own words and not as a translation:

> Why is global revolution occurring? . . . It will arise in any country to the extent that it adopts the capitalist organization of production. The capitalists' organization of industry results in their despotism, just as despotic politics treats the people as objects to be managed rather than informed. The rulers are content but the ruled are uneasy. Even if they are treated benevolently, they have no guarantee that benevolence will continue. And the natural tendency of humanity is for the rulers to exploit and subjugate the ruled to their own advantage. . . . It is patently obvious that Japan alone will not escape such a state of affairs.[69]

The content of the two articles does not explain why Morito went to jail whereas Ishibashi published with impunity. Rather, the small but independent structure of *Tōyō keizai shinpō*, with an influential business constituency, made it less susceptible to bureaucratic management. In contrast, at Tokyo University, the Ministry of Education was able to force Morito's and Ōuchi's resignation. Ministry of Education authority alone was insufficient to quell dissent, however; the Home Ministry entered to suppress publication of the offending issue while the Ministry of Justice prosecuted the two economists. Increasing administrative complexity in the government, and at Tokyo University, evidenced "the gradual breakdown of the Meiji system of bureaucratic management of intellectual life" and failed to stifle new voices.[70] The growing pluralism of institutions inside and outside the government complicated the task of ideological leadership, and simultaneous publication of similar or related views in a number of journals allowed journalists to test the limits of permissible discourse.

69. *ITZ* 3:368–69.
70. Byron Marshall, "Growth and Conflict in Japanese Higher Education, 1905–1930," in Najita and Koschmann, eds., *Conflict in Modern Japanese History*, 290–94.

A chorus of direct criticism of governmental action could be another means of informal alliance among dissenters. Ishibashi reiterated his support for freedom of thought and expression, coupled with a detailed summary of the Morito Incident, the following month. The *Ōsaka asahi*, Ōshima Shōtoku of Tokyo University, and Kimura Kyūichi of Waseda also defended Morito, whereas other journalists more cautiously criticized the Hara cabinet in general terms for exaggerating the dangers of new ideas and actually promoting social strife through repression. Although protest was cautious, Ishibashi believed that public opinion largely opposed the government's action. In addition to his direct and indirect support of Morito and Ōuchi in print, he visited the two men in prison to offer food and personal encouragement. Finally, he and other writers seized opportunities during the following months to launch harsher criticisms of administrative censorship in instances where the government had made a less serious commitment. For example, he compared the import ban on Norman Angell's *Why Freedom Matters* to the policies of the defunct czarist regime and cited journalist Ōba Kakō, who declared the ban illegal in *Nihon oyobi Nihonjin* (Japan and the Japanese). Ishibashi hoped to draw dissidents closer together in fact and in their public image, and to embarrass the government while alerting readers to the constant character of interference with opinion and the existence of those who opposed interference. Critical journalism cross-referenced individual views, and marked the emergence of an opinion media network with which both the government and interest groups had to deal.[71]

CONCLUSION

Tanaka, Yoshino, and Ishibashi shared a common intellectual and political context. Tanaka had endeavored to attack the state's holistic ideology by breaking down all customs and institutions into individual behavior. In doing so he had re-

71. *ITZ* 3:439–41; Shinobu, "Taishō seijishi no konpon mondai," 14–17; Ienaga Saburō, *Daigaku jiyū no rekishi*, 246; Kayahara Kazan, "Konjun yori konjun," in *Taishō dai zasshi*; Murobuse Kōshin, "Kageki shisō to Nihon," in *Taishō dai zasshi*, 38–39; Ōuchi Hyōe, "Ishibashi-san no koto," in Chō, ed., *Ishibashi Tanzan*, 8.

mained on a high level of abstraction, because to attack the state ideology directly was dangerous, and more importantly, because the fundamental character of state practice in fact accorded with his own philosophical stance. As Tetsuo Najita has observed,

> conceived in highly pragmatic and instrumentalist terms by Itō and his advisers, the Meiji Constitution was pinned to the assumption that rationally conceived laws could mediate between contending economic and political oligarchies in the modern developmental process. . . . It was this highly pragmatic conception of the legal order that the parties incorporated into their strategy of expanding their power. . . . Yet it was this very process developed within the confines of the Meiji Constitution that was tested by Yoshino and found woefully unsatisfactory.[72]

Alienation from state practices sustained Yoshino's idealist quest for an ethical framework to modify the "might of the sovereign political structure."[73] Thus, in his emphasis on the theory of sovereignty, Yoshino grasped the enduring power behind the temporal flexibility of state practices but downplayed countervailing organizations.

In contrast, Ishibashi, with classic liberal ambivalence, avoided conceptualizing the state at all. His political analysis was bifurcated between the real state and the possible state. The real state was a nasty amalgam of clique and factional interests, to be embarrassed or reformed when such moves were possible and avoided when they were not, rather like a moody but trainable bear. However, while concentrating on gradual reform Ishibashi retained a general vision of a possible state wholly subordinate to the popular will. That state could be a potent force for social progress but never a panacea, for the popular will would never be wholly coherent or free from conflict. The state itself could not mediate conflict, because it was granted no autonomous theoretical existence. However, the people could establish channels and procedures for mediating their own dissensions, and they could conceive of those channels and procedures as a democratic state. The

72. Najita, "Some Reflections," 63.
73. Ibid., 48.

absolute rejection of the autonomy of the state in theory encouraged mediation with its pragmatic practices.

In different ways Tanaka, Yoshino, and Ishibashi all experienced difficulty in linking the theoretical criticism of the state with practical politics. The state itself manifested extreme bifurcation between a totalitarian ideology and a web of flexible and pragmatic practices. The claims of the emperor-state, which were both transcendental and instrumentalist, became entangled in debate over these two philosophical positions, which Japanese intellectuals joined on the basis of their understanding of European and American idealism, pragmatism, and Marxism. The extremity of the polarization was paramount in the difficulties of reformers in linking critical thought and reformist action.

6

The Social Problem: Ishibashi on
Labor, Tenants, and Finance

Democracy was not a matter of political rights and freedom alone, but of fundamental structural change in the economy. Encompassing all of Ishibashi's specific goals was a concept of economic democracy, or "humanistic industrialization," which would result in a classless society with minimum standards of livelihood guaranteed for all. Economic goals could not be isolated from political reform. The means to humanistic industrialization ought to include unionization, strikes, and competitive interest politics as well as benevolent reform by the legislature and bureaucracy. Every Japanese should be guaranteed a decent standard of health and welfare; the full development of his or her individual potential, in institutions that all worked as educational processes; and a share in the participatory management of the government and the workplace. In the new society, "universal suffrage is the form, and the labor movement is foremost in the content."[1]

By recognizing the centrality of the social problem, Ishibashi left behind an older generation of Meiji liberals and literary intellectuals. He was determined to transcend the narrow political goals pursued by the mainstream Popular Rights movement leaders of the 1880s. In his early reviews of naturalist literature, he had criticized the naturalists for neglecting the concrete realities of economic life though he had welcomed their attempt to legitimize private experience as part of public

1. *ITZ* 3:391. Ishibashi first referred to a *jinteki sangyō kakumei* in 2:298–99; see also 4:188–200 and Watanabe Tōru, "Rōdō mondai—rōdō undō e no ronpyō," in Inoue and Watanabe, eds., *Taishōki no kyūshinteki jiyūshugi*, 500–01; Matsuo "Taishō demokurashii no ichi suimyaku," 1179.

discourse.[2] Neither movement had analyzed and criticized the state in fundamental terms, he concluded. State structure, procedure, and policy required reformulation, in order to encourage the people to achieve concrete measures of material comfort and personal growth in daily life. During the Taishō era the social problem and the labor problem moved to the forefront of the general-interest monthlies and their new, more leftist competitors, while wartime economic growth and uncertainty encouraged labor, tenants', and women's organizations. Most reformers agreed with Ishibashi that political rights were meaningless unless they could serve as the vehicle of economic reform on behalf of workers. Anezaki Masaharu (formerly of the Teiyū Ethical Society) demanded the "recognition of labor's essential humanity" in place of "paternalistic exploitation," recalling the society's opposition to paternalistic intellectual management.[3] Hoashi Riichirō, a student of John Dewey and Waseda professor, judged that the main force in Taishō protest was democratic socialism.[4]

Intellectuals' understanding of Western experience was central to their definition of the social problem. Apart from a few diehards who urged that unique Japanese characteristics would prevent a social problem from arising, the entire political spectrum focused on two global trends: state welfare provisions and labor militancy, particularly in the Soviet Union and Great Britain. The aroused and organized working classes of the two nations were studied as models to be emulated by the left, and specters to be vanquished by the right. Labor leaders scrutinized the programs of foreign unions and socialist parties, bureaucrats planned channels for activism and welfare legislation, while industrialists experimented with the Taylor system of management and combatted autonomous labor organization. Behind the distinct activities was a common perception that the day for social reconstruction had dawned

2. *ITZ* 1:62–63, 74–75; Matsuo, "Taishō demokurashii no ichi suimyaku," 1117–1118.

3. Anezaki, "Jinponshugi to jikkō." Anezaki campaigned for Ishibashi in the election of 1946; see *ITZ* 15:51.

4. Hoashi Riichirō, "Nihonjin wa kagekiteki kokumin ni arazu," in *Taishō dai zasshi.*

throughout the world; as Anezaki stated baldly, "The country that fails to undertake the task will fall behind."[5]

In Ishibashi's interpretation the world was in a period of fundamental upheaval, with revolutions in Russia, Germany, and Hungary, and labor protest in the United States and Great Britain as well as Japan. Strife arose because in those societies only capitalists had the opportunity to realize the self (*jiko o jitsugen suru*), and better education prompted workers to demand managerial responsibility as well as better wages and working conditions.[6] In the new society all would have equal responsibility and enthusiasm for production and social welfare. Concrete plans for the political participation of all men and women; the social organization of women, labor, and tenants, and a foundation of welfare guarantees would bring the children of workers to the starting gate if not the winners' circle. Beyond a conception of winners and losers, Ishibashi denied that any member of society ought to be barred from planning and policy making. Classes and poverty would disappear, but the division of labor and order would remain. Ishibashi's distinction between classes, on the one hand, and the division of labor, on the other, restated the Restoration ideal of meritocracy, which let individuals find their proper station in life but constrained them from bequeathing either success or failure to their children. Ishibashi's attempt to encourage individual specialization and competition, while abolishing hereditary status, was surely within the classic mold of modern Japanese political thought.

There was a strong socialist influence in Ishibashi's programs, but he distinguished himself from Marxists in several ways. In economics, he dismissed the labor theory of value as "quite outmoded," though less "perverse" than the anti-union ideology of capitalists.[7] Though capitalist hegemony was doomed, private capital would continue to play an important role in production under labor's electoral superiority and man-

5. Anezaki, "Jinponshugi to jikkō"; see also Najita, "Some Reflections on Idealism in the Political Thought of Yoshino Sakuzō," 50–51; and Silberman, "The Democracy Movement in Japan," 214–15.
6. *ITZ* 3:366–76.
7. *ITZ* 1:469–70.

agerial participation. In politics, Ishibashi did not reject violence unconditionally but believed that universal suffrage
would probably render it unnecessary; violence would arise
"only through the obstinacy of the privileged classes."[8] Revolution was unquestionably preferable to the continuation of
despotism, but it short-circuited the capacity of individuals and
societies for reflection and evolutionary growth. Thus Ishibashi clearly separated himself from orthodox Marxists, but
was very close to libertarian social democrats. Although he
sanctioned many social democratic policy positions, he termed
himself a liberal, as did John Dewey and John Maynard
Keynes, and that seems the most satisfactory term. Ishibashi,
like Dewey and Keynes, had learned from the socialists the
value of collective goals and organization, but still preserved
a more empirical, step-by-step, and experimental tendency in
formulating solutions. The liberals were disengaged from formal political organization; they cherished a vision of society in
permanent friction, yet amenable to rules rationally conceived.

LABOR

Liberals and social democrats were closely allied in the decade
following World War I, in their analyses, their goals, and their
perception of a broad alliance of democratic forces—"the people," poised against the ruling bureaucratic, military, financial,
and (in some accounts) academic cliques. In the case of *Shinpō*,
liberal-socialist connections were particularly strong and dated
back to the last decade of Meiji. *Shinpō*'s third editor, Uematsu
Hisaaki, had been a close friend of Katayama Sen, a Christian
socialist, and had joined Katayama's early attempts to organize
labor unions. In 1910 Katayama was hired, with Ishibashi, to
edit *Tōyō jiron*. By offering Katayama an extraordinary salary
of fifty yen a month, more than triple Ishibashi's pay, Miura
Tetsutarō supported Katayama, whose articles were banned
and organizations smashed.[9] Katayama, constantly harassed by
the police and arrested during the Tokyo streetcar strike of

8. *ITZ* 3:66–67.
9. Matsuo "Taishō demokurashii no ichi suimyaku," 1168; and idem, "Kyūshinteki
jiyūshugi no seiritsu katei," 55–57, 72.

1912, left for the United States in 1914, joined the Communist party, and never returned. Ishibashi remembered Katayama as "a warm person," of great intellectual vigor but less politically extreme than Ishibashi himself at the end of the Meiji period, and Ishibashi blamed Katayama's later turn to communism on the Japanese authorities.[10]

Katayama and other social democrats at Waseda deserve credit for *Shinpō*'s concrete information on factory conditions and workers' lives. Ishibashi's detailed knowledge of tuberculosis rates among female textile workers is one example. The topic was frequently discussed in the Waseda Economic Society (Waseda Keizaikai), which included early social democratic and labor organizers. The group moved to *Shinpō* offices in 1915, and renamed itself the Tōyō Keizaikai, inviting speakers such as Dr. Ishihara Osamu of the Home Ministry's investigative committee on factory conditions. Dr. Ishihara noted that the death rate among spinning girls was high, with tuberculosis accounting for death in 70 percent of the cases. The government had known about the health hazard since its first factory investigations in 1882; yet it had taken no action except to write spineless factory acts that were rarely enforced. In cooperation with labor and socialist activists and their sympathizers, such as Dr. Ishihara, *Shinpō* supported and publicized reformist research and organization, while labor and socialist activists lent concrete detail to *Shinpō*'s socio-economic theory.[11] Ishibashi's social democratic associations were to continue through the first world war as *Shinpō* hired one labor organizer, Akamatsu Katsumaro, and the son of another, Matsuoka Komakichi. In the thirties Ishibashi would meet with unionist Suzuki Bunji and *Kaizō* editor Yamamoto Sanehiko, and lecture on economics for the Social Democratic party (Shakai Minshūtō) and the Japan Federation of Labor (Nihon Rōdō Sōdōmei).[12]

Thus *Shinpō* from its origins had "no fear of the working class," as Matsuo Takayoshi has noted, but its specific policy recommendations changed over time as it grappled with var-

10. *ITZ* 15:87–90.
11. *ITZ* 3:310–12.
12. *ITZ* 3:561; 15:367–68, 372, 375, 380, 388.

ious aspects of the labor problem, and with changes in Western social and intellectual trends.[13] As early as the Russo-Japanese War, *Shinpō* editorials had cautioned that education was not a panacea for the labor problem and that changes in the tax and income distribution systems were essential. The journal began to consider the role of unions in 1910 under the impetus of strikes at Osaka munitions, Ashio copper mines, and Mitsubishi Nagasaki shipyards. At the time, *Shinpō* advocated freedom of association for unions but argued that Japanese-style personal relations would forestall severe labor strife. That suggestion was trounced by Miura as head editor, and by Ishibashi and Katayama at *Jiron*, from the outset of the Taishō period. Under Miura and Ishibashi, *Shinpō* gradually developed a vigorous critique of governmental economic policy since the Restoration, charging that the prosperity of merchants and industrialists had been bought at the expense of workers and peasants, in a policy of protection for the rich and laissez-faire for the poor. They demanded that expanded political participation be coupled with social and economic reform to enable and encourage all citizens to share in the making of national policies.[14]

Ishibashi addressed the social problem in terms of Tanaka's conception of nationality.

> Some say socialism will never come to Japan because Japanese are self-abnegating while Westerners are self-asserting. I disagree. Nationality is no more than the product of past politics, economics, and social organization. It must be suited to the environment, but the environment underwent a tremendous change in the Meiji Restoration. Statism and bureaucratism then took deep root in Japanese politics.[15]

Japan had no prophylactic against labor strife. Statism and bureaucratism, not national character, had sustained labor docility into the early Taishō years. As for the new industrial paternalism trotted out in the 1920s and eulogized as uniquely Japanese by Home Minister Tokonami Takejirō, Ishibashi noted

13. Matsuo, "Kyūshinteki jiyūshugi no seiritsu katei," 55–57.
14. Watanabe Tōru, "Rōdō mondai," 471–73, 484–85.
15. *ITZ* 2:176–79.

that Ford in the United States and Cadbury in Great Britain were trying similar systems.[16] Recent trends, however, could easily be challenged, and Ishibashi hoped that Japanese labor would soon defy statism and bureaucratism and reject employers' paternalism.

Shinpō was deeply influenced by changing labor movements in the West, especially Great Britain. In his maiden essay on the labor problem in 1912, Ishibashi quoted Labour party founder Keir Hardie in order to incite workers' political activism as well as economic goals: "Labor must become employers as well as employees, rulers as well as ruled. They must control the Diet, form a cabinet from their own class, and manage national affairs."[17] In 1918 *Shinpō* was one of the first journals to predict escalating Japanese labor strife.[18] The vigor of the British labor movement at the end of World War I seemed to be mirrored in Japanese strikes and rice riots, and Ishibashi and other members of the *Shinpō* staff relied on the British left to interpret Japanese trends and to advance pragmatic reforms. In Britain, labor's declining purchasing power, coupled with long-term social and intellectual change, had wrought a decisive change in the nature and goals of the labor movement. This change was analyzed in the 1918 Whitely report on coal nationalization, which stressed a managerial role for labor and urged the nationalization of heavy industry such as mines and railroads. The report was commended in *Shinpō*, then translated by Ishibashi and Akamatsu Katsumaro.[19] Thus, a variety of influences, from the Meiji socialist movement through instrumentalism to the British labor movement, coalesced in *Shinpō*'s social commentary to give it greater consistency than that of other contemporary liberal papers, such as the *Ōsaka asahi*.[20]

In addition to labor's political mobilization, Ishibashi called for a comprehensive program of livelihood protection. The young, pregnant, ill, and handicapped should be forbidden to

16. *ITZ* 3:323–25.
17. *ITZ* 1:469–70; see also 3:316.
18. Watanabe Tōru, "Rōdō mondai," 509.
19. Ibid., 498–99.
20. Ibid., 485; Iinuma Jirō, "Nōgyō mondai ron—toku ni *Ōsaka asahi shinbun* to taihi shite," in Inoue and Watanabe, eds., *Taishōki no kyūshinteki jiyūshugi*, 444.

work and granted public aid. A factory law truly guaranteeing
health and safety ought to replace the flimsy existing measures. A national employment registry should be established,
along with livelihood assistance for the jobless.[21] Public school
tuition should be abolished, and poor children should be
granted stipends for food and clothing.[22] Public hospitals
ought to be built for at least cholera and tuberculosis victims.
Ishibashi believed that the government could pay for social
insurance by reducing military expenditures (a daring suggestion in 1916, when Japan was at war). Committed to social
insurance since the 1910s, Ishibashi joined the Alliance for
National Health Care (Igyō Kokuei Kisei Dōmeikai) formed
by Suzuki Umeshirō of the Pacific Research Society in 1928.[23]

Unions were also an essential part of Ishibashi's plan for
social democratization. Japan's labor unions ought to be le-
galized by amendment to the Public Peace Police Law of 1900,
and unions ought to be organized industry-wide, to exclude
management, to have the right to strike, and to make political
as well as economic demands. Ishibashi supported the Yūaikai
demands for legalization of unions, a minimum wage, and an
eight-hour day, and even backed the union's challenge to the
government's selection of ILO delegates in 1919, a sensitive
issue for him, since Tanaka Takako was one of the choices. He
lambasted government harassment of the union movement,
which prevented unions from fulfilling a variety of essential
social purposes. Unions could be the most effective agency for
exposing and rectifying iniquities, such as the rate of tuberculosis among spinning girls, and inequities, such as dismal
wages. Unions could also serve to educate workers, administer
benefits, and eliminate fraud. Finally, unionization could increase productivity by forcing participatory management,
shorter hours, and better conditions, which would improve
workers' health and morale. Ishibashi believed that only vigorous, independent unions had the muscle to give labor a real
voice in management, and that cooperative management

21. *ITZ* 2:192–218; the city of Tokyo had already opened an employment agency
in 1911; see 1:165.
22. *ITZ* 2:302, 421–23.
23. *ITZ* 15:365.

would transform productivity increases from a capitalist windfall to a common goal.[24]

The reality of the Japanese labor movement was somewhat
different. Ishibashi's optimism seemed justified for a year or
two. The Home Ministry established a Social Bureau in 1922
to investigate the revision of the factory law and the legalization of unions, and granted administrative recognition to
unions in selecting ILO delegates. Five unionization bills were
introduced into the forty-fourth Diet, though in four respects
the government's bill fell far short of Ishibashi's proposals.
First, it proposed to treat unions as corporations, leaving open
the possibility of their liability for strike losses. Second, it sanctioned only craft, not general or industrial unions. Third, it
restricted union organization to the prefectural level and below. Fourth, it did not limit union membership to workers.
Ishibashi remarked that the bill had been drafted during the
preceding two years by the Ministry of Agriculture and Commerce and the Home Ministry, both characterized by "strongly
managerial attitudes."[25] Even this anemic bill failed to pass the
Diet, in part because advocates of stronger legislation proposed from the lower house refused to support it, and unions
remained formally illegal until the Allied Occupation.

Ishibashi's doubts concerning a swift victory for labor
deepened during the first half of 1922. Spring and summer
brought three great strikes: 4,197 workers at Yokohama shipyards for twenty-two days, 2,643 workers at the Sakurajima
factory of Osaka ironworks for thirty-nine days, and 3,700
workers at the Osaka and Amazaki plants of Sumitomo metals
for eleven days. The first two were dissolved with massive dismissals, eighty arrests, and no gains for the strikers. The Sumitomo strike ended with the firing of all activists, sixteen
arrests, and the collapse of the union.[26] In July Ishibashi
lamented:

> In Japan . . . the power of the capitalists is incomparably greater
> than that of the workers. The force with which the labor move-

24. *ITZ* 3:309–12, 316, 319–21, 329–36, 472.
25. *ITZ* 3:387–89.
26. Hayashi Hirofumi, "Sen-kyūhyaku-nijū nendai zenpan ni okeru rōdō seisaku
no tenkan," *Rekishigaku kenkyū*, no. 508 (1982): 52.

ment originally erupted now seems forgotten. And Japan is not yet sufficiently advanced to engender struggle between labor and capital. Rather, bureaucratism—a new form of despotism—collides with democracy. Although the cry for democracy is widely heard, in fact democracy is always trampled by bureaucracy. Yet it is vain to imagine that bureaucratism can crush democracy forever.[27]

The global forces of the people versus their erstwhile masters appeared neither as overwhelming nor as readily identifiable as they had in 1917; Ishibashi noted that even the Bolsheviks were being forced to compromise with capitalism in Lenin's New Economic Policy.[28]

Hereafter, Ishibashi's discussion of labor was more modest in scope, though he continued to urge labor's independent activism on its own behalf. Japan Federation of Labor president Suzuki Bunji was impressed by government aid for workers' housing after the Great Kantō Earthquake in 1923, and by the support of progressive bureaucrats in the Social Bureau. He led a more moderate turn in union policy in 1924, limiting labor goals to the legalization of unions and the recruitment of members. Ishibashi applauded Suzuki's realism but warned against labor's cooptation by government handouts. Subsequently, new control measures accompanying universal manhood suffrage were deployed against labor, while the Japan Industrial Club mounted an impassioned anti-union campaign. Ishibashi continued to chide capitalists for paranoia toward unions but found his attention preempted by fiscal and monetary policy in the wake of the earthquake, reconstruction capital demand, and the financial panic of 1927. For the editor of a business and financial journal, the daily reality of a traumatized and sullen economy in these years stunted visions of social transformation. Before considering his financial theory, however, it is first necessary to complete discussion of the social problem in which tenancy was a major issue.[29]

27. *ITZ* 4:221; 6:363.
28. "Shihonshugi imada shisezu," *TKS* 15 Mar. 1924.
29. Hayashi, 56–57, 60; Watanabe Tōru, "Rōdō mondai," 523–26.

TENANT FARMERS

Kagaminakajō, where Ishibashi had lived under the tutelage of Mochizuki Nikken at Jōonji between the Sino- and Russo-Japanese wars, afforded him an ideal opportunity to investigate tenant movements. In Yamanashi Prefecture, it was the center of the most severe disputes and had the highest percentage of unionized tenants in the nation; prefecture-wide unionization reached 41.6 percent by 1927. In Kagaminakajō, tenants had organized in December 1922, hoping to resolve long-standing grievances about rental rates and village land management. They affiliated with the Japan Farmers' Union (Nihon Nōgyō Kumiai) in February 1923 and invited officers of its Kantō branch, including President Suzuki Bunji, to join them in a march on the prefectural capital of Kōfu in April. Once assembled, some three hundred tenants began setting off firecrackers. The Kagaminakajō women's association and children greeted the protesters with shouts of *banzai*. The tenants held a lecture meeting at Jōonji before a crowd of twenty-five hundred, singing labor organizing songs and shouting invocations to the guardian deity of peasants before setting off toward Kōfu, carrying long pennants and straw banners. Picking up supporters from neighboring villages, the demonstrators numbered one thousand by the time they reached Kōfu, but their petition to the prefectural governor met no conclusive response. There was no violence save for some scuffling with hecklers from the National Essence Association (Kokusuikai).[30]

Ishibashi arrived in April and spent several days interviewing landlords and tenants at Jōonji and around the countryside.[31] He was asked to mediate on behalf of the Kagaminakajō union but was unable to achieve a breakthrough; the blame (according to union records) lay with the recalcitrance of the middle and rich farmers, who had now formed their own or-

---

30. Takegawa Yoshinori, *Yamanashi-ken nōmin undō shi*, 67–75; see also Ann Waswo, "In Search of Equity: Japanese Tenant Unions in the 1920s," in Najita and Koschmann, eds., *Conflict in Modern Japanese History*, 368.
31. *ITZ* 5:396–413.

ganization.[32] Upon returning to Tokyo, Ishibashi wrote a fairly
detailed account of his observations in *Shinpō*, omitting his own
role in the dispute and defining the locale more generally as
Nakakoma-gun to avoid identifying his informants. His observations offer a rare portrait of a Taishō intellectual returned to the countryside and the people he had grown up
with, and engaged in empirical observation, in sharp contrast
to the abstract and theoretical cast typifying writings from that
era.

During the three years before his visit, Ishibashi had advocated a tenant arbitration system, and in early 1920 he had
offered qualified support to a Ministry of Agriculture and
Commerce investigative committee report that proposed a tenancy arbitration system. However, the government's plan did
not require face-to-face negotiation between the two parties;
rather, it permitted them to accept or reject representatives
proposed by the local court. In Ishibashi's view an arbitration
system ought to encourage resolution at the hands of the
interested parties through their full engagement and argument with each other.[33] Personal appearance at arbitration
would be a disadvantage to landlords, who were accustomed
to relying on their lawyers.[34] Moreover, the government's plan
barred interested parties from publishing comments on the
rights and wrongs of the issue before and during arbitration.
Ishibashi, however, urged that the public had a right to hear
both sides and could play a role in showing both parties their
errors. The whole community's sense of equity would force a
resolution. While the government's plan prevented post-judg-
mental publication of the arbitration minutes except in special
cases, at the discretion of the local court, Ishibashi urged compulsory publication whether or not the arbitration process was
successful. Sunlight would serve the ends of justice in the present, and of historical documentation in the future. In short
Ishibashi urged that the Japanese people could resolve their
own conflicts, but resolution required open engagement rather
than nervous bureaucratic management.

32. Takegawa, 75.
33. *ITZ* 3:316–22; see also 4:413–18.
34. Waswo, 399.

Ishibashi's support for tenant unions preceded his visit to Kagaminakajō but became more vigorous thereafter. Whereas his earlier views were largely derived from his study of the labor problem, later editorials were more specific and clearly revealed the influence of his discussions with local union leaders. First, he urged the encouragement of cooperative farming, with a view to gradual amalgamation of landholdings to increase productive efficiency. Second, he revised his insistence that disputing parties must negotiate directly, conceding that tenants might prefer union officials to represent them. He criticized the tenant arbitration law that finally passed in 1924 for not acknowledging the important role of unions in organizing and articulating tenant grievances. Productive efficiency and union organization were greatly emphasized in the Kagaminakajō movement.[35]

Ishibashi eulogized the Kagaminakajō tenant movement for its emphasis on rational management. The tenants had a long-term plan of village improvement coupled with painstaking statistical and technological surveys of village problems. According to one union officer, "We are now demanding rent reduction, but that's not our central purpose. Our real purpose is the reform of agriculture and village government."[36] The union's bold demand for a permanent rent reduction of 40 percent was predicated on concepts of rational equity and future development. According to the union, village rents had long been high, averaging 51 percent on paddy fields and 73 percent on upland fields; moreover, they were extremely uneven because long-standing personal ties between landlord and tenant still impeded an open market. The detailed rent reduction plan called for equalization of rents between comparable holdings, as well as across-the-board reductions. More equitable rents would eliminate unproductive disputes, and the union would assume the responsibility for rent collection.[37] Savings on rent would be used in investment, with one-quarter going to the union for planning and technological improve-

35. "Chūmoku subeki kosakunin kumiai no sōka," *TKS*, 16 July 1921; Iinuma, 459–63.
36. Quoted in *ITZ* 5:405–06.
37. *ITZ* 25:408–09.

ment. Union officials and tenants explained in detail how cooperative management of seedling beds and mulberry trees,
along with improved drainage, would increase productivity
and eliminate waste; in the instance of the seedling beds, tenants had calculated the waste to amount to approximately one
hundred bags of unhulled rice a year. Ishibashi, after fifteen
years away from his home district, was profoundly impressed
by the tenants' recent educational attainments and initiative.[38]

In contrast, the landlords came across very poorly, and one
even dismissed the tenants' survey and planning with the jeer,
"Those guys are all talk."[39] The landlord, Ishibashi scoffed,
had done no research at all. Landlords had lost their original
economic and social functions and had evolved into a parasitic
class. Their original relationship to tenants as patrons to
clients, with reciprocal obligations, had eroded; "the authority
of village elders and the old social bonds are utterly gone."[40]
The commercialization of agriculture had alienated landlords
and tenants in three ways. First, landlords lived not from agriculture but from local industries such as sake brewing; thus,
they had become apathetic toward agricultural improvement.
Ishibashi observed that farming had undergone virtually no
change in his fifteen years' absence. Kagaminakajō tenants
had asked the village council collectively, and the landlords
individually, to capitalize technological improvements before
the tenants resorted to rent reduction demands, but their re-
quests had been refused. Landlords had more profitable investment opportunities in industry, which did give the tenants
some employment opportunities but did not compensate for
neglect of the land. Second, landlord-industrialists, as consumers of agricultural products, had a vested interest in low prices.
When tenant unions sought to raise prices through cooperative sale of cocoons, buyers, including landlords, simply went
outside the district to cut costs. That, of course, was capitalism,
but Ishibashi envisioned a capitalism mediated by a measure
of local control and local responsibility.[41]

38. Waswo has noted similar tenants' survey and planning activity in Shimane
Prefecture, 398–400.
39. *ITZ* 5:406.
40. *ITZ* 5:408.
41. *ITZ* 5:405–06, 399–400, 404.

Ishibashi believed that the issues were more complex than class struggle alone. There were cases where landlords had been benevolent, and tenants greedy. In one village the council, composed entirely of landlords, had voted an indemnity of over two hundred yen per *tan* (0.245 acre) in return for cultivators' rights lost in the expansion of the schoolhouse, rights ordinarily worth eighty to ninety yen per *tan*. Unfortunately the area in question included a field that one landlord cultivated himself, and this landlord had accepted his share of the munificent compensation. Subsequently the indignant tenants claimed that all cultivators' rights were worth two hundred yen per *tan*. In another instance the Kenseikai party had deliberately fomented a tenancy dispute in Seiyūkai party territory. Inflamed emotions resulted in stalemate and resort to the courts. The breakdown of traditional authority, Ishibashi believed, had to be followed by legitimate channels of broadly based participation in local affairs.[42]

Local self-government was possible because both sides to the dispute criticized themselves, revealing a common sense of equity. Many landlords blamed themselves for not fulfilling traditional social and economic obligations toward tenants. Tenants, on the other hand, acknowledged that they had driven rents up by trafficking in their cultivators' rights, and the union proposed to regulate this practice. Both sides, therefore, expressed a sense that the commercialization of agriculture had placed them in a position of violating moral norms, and those common moral norms might afford a basis for new, productive, and equitable local organization if permitted to work freely.[43]

Ishibashi believed that the solution was more industrialization, particularly in Yamanashi, which lagged behind more advanced regions of the country. Neither landlords nor tenants grasped broader national trends, and both groups were helpless before them. Yamanashi had, in the fifteen years Ishibashi had been away, stagnated into a quasi-colonial relationship with the great industrial and commercial cities, particularly Tokyo. The prefecture's famous quartz and leather products

42. *ITZ* 5:407–08.
43. *ITZ* 5:405–08; Takegawa, 70.

were now made with materials brought from outside, and silk-spinning and weaving had declined. Yamanashi now sent twenty thousand spinning girls to Matsumoto every year, a new and ominous development. "The export of labor, domestically or internationally, is a sure sign of poverty."[44] Labor export was more convenient since the Chūō national railroad line had been completed, but Yamanashi's own lagging industrial development drove its daughters away. Outside forces were overwhelming Yamanashi's economic and cultural life. The Kanegafuchi company had just purchased an old factory in Kōfu, and a Nagano industrialist had built a new factory. Tokyo dailies had overwhelmed the local newspapers, which lacked reporters with news-hound spirit and offered virtually no editorials. Residents had little opportunity to understand, let alone control, the conditions of their lives.

Ishibashi gradually approached his final judgment of blame for Yamanashi's economic stagnation. Development was not wholly lacking, and he enthused over Kōfu's visible changes with a hometown boy's pride. The small shops were more attractive; commerce had increased; and the main street that had once had houses along only one side had been transformed into a rectangular city. The city had built a hospital, city office, various banks and parks, and a zoo. Best of all, there was a train station, complete with platform, all in a mere fifteen years. Clearly Kōfu had benefited from the wartime boom. Yet the prosperity was due mainly to the train station and the army regiment quartered in the city, and not to a sound plan of regional development. And who was to blame for the deficiency?

> The governor is a bureaucrat from the central system. In today's system the position of governor is a stepping stone to greater heights; he has no interest in the advancement of the region, but prefers to sponsor the quick completion of impressive public works in the hope of a speedy ascension to success [*risshin shusse*] in the capital.[45]

44. *ITZ* 5:403; see also 401–04.
45. *ITZ* 5:404.

Yamanashi was being drained economically and culturally because it was politically subordinate to the central government. As merely one example of policy failure, subsidized rice was grown everywhere in Yamanashi even though the area was far better suited to grapes and other fruits. No research or experimentation in new crops was occurring because there was no planning agency rooted in the interests of local people.[46]

For Ishibashi landlord-tenant relations were a secondary theme within the broader issue of the whole people's relationship with their national government. Taishō tenants in advanced areas, he judged, had developed the initiative and entrepreneurship to outmaneuver their former masters, and tenants would assert their vastly superior numbers in local assemblies, and even the national legislature, once they achieved universal suffrage. The managerial expertise inherent in farming, and the strength of numbers, placed tenants in a far more advantageous position than Japan's still small minority of industrial laborers. Lingering landlord social authority could be surmounted by tenant participation in reformed national institutions.

Ishibashi underestimated the pull of traditional authority as well as the state's commitment to gutting local organization. However, he recognized a marked decline in landlords' economic and political power around the time of World War I. He was prepared to encourage their decline but believed that for two reasons formal landlord property rights ought to be preserved. First, redistribution would merely perpetuate small and inefficient holdings. Only greater productivity in both agriculture and industry could improve the lives of Japan's 5,455,000 agricultural households, whose numbers pressed on the arable land to the detriment of small landlords as well as tenants. Second, formal expropriation would discourage future savings. On the other hand, the oligopolistic character of landlords' property could be undermined by community organization in management and credit. On this basis Ishibashi approved Suzuki Bunji's plan for all-village unions, including

46. *ITZ* 5:398.

landlords, that would adjudge rent disputes, manage land, and encourage farming on a larger scale. The landlord class, already doomed by history, ought to be reabsorbed into a more broadly based community as individuals.[47]

FINANCIAL REFORM

Accounts of the Taishō democratic movement are seldom graced by reference to evolving financial theories. The topic has none of the pageantry of universal suffrage demonstrations, the elemental force of rice riots, or the philosophic and humanistic vision of literary and intellectual change. Yet Ishibashi's views on the gold standard and banking reform are essential to an understanding of the man and the era. They were democratic in the sense that they expressed the concepts of social equity and governmental accountability. By favoring stable domestic consumer purchasing power over stable exchange rates, his proposals aimed to rectify the drastic and unplanned redistribution of wealth that had attended Japan's wartime inflation and subsequent retrenchment. He suggested removing the Bank of Japan from the bureaucratic control of the Finance Ministry and subjecting it to public scrutiny and debate. He favored industrial expansion, and thus appealed to many businessmen and bureaucrats. Ishibashi's financial policies undergirded his entry into influential private economic study groups in the twenties, government consultations in the thirties, and national politics in the late forties. My present study, like other recent studies, stresses continuity in Japanese economic development and policy, but the continuity was a pluralistic interplay of opposing forces, and not a monolithic development of bureaucratic managerial tendencies.

The rice riots of August 1918 prompted Ishibashi to organize the Financial Systems Association (Kin'yū Seido Kenkyūkai, FSA) in order to study the relationship between prices, wages, governmental policy, and the international economy. The riots, beginning in a fishing village in Toyama Prefecture, rapidly spread to thirty-six cities, one hundred and twenty-

47. *ITZ* 5:410–13, 396–97. On governmental arrests of union leaders, coupled with protective measures for tenants, after 1927, see Waswo, 407–11.

nine towns and one hundred and forty-five villages, drawing some seven hundred thousand participants, defying police control, and forcing the government to call out the army in several locales. The scale of the riots bordered on national insurrection, and caused a crisis of governmental legitimacy. The imperial household, major zaibatsu, and representative wartime nouveaux riches each pledged hundreds of thousands of yen in relief; on the other hand, courts treated offenders severely. Immediate reporting of the details of the riots was banned, but gradually journalists and intellectuals seized the occasion to speculate in print on the capacity and willingness of their society to tolerate conflict or its suppression. Among these writers Ishibashi distinguished himself by offering analysis that was both short- and long-range, both economic and political.[48]

Ishibashi reasoned that the riots resulted from errors in wartime fiscal policy and gradual change in the structure of the Japanese economy, exacerbated by class conflict and political failure. War had brought inflation and an embargo on gold exports, permitting the value of the yen to fall and encouraging exports while cramping imports. The export of alternative cereal grains, a tax on colonial rice imports, and the dramatic expansion of the money supply had forced the price of rice to a level that *Shinpō* had described as famine during the previous March, when rising rates of suicide, child abandonment, and theft were reported. Particularly hard-pressed were those who faced rising consumer prices without countervailing increases in wages or the value of personal property: tenants, workers, teachers, low-grade officials, and corporate employees, including the lower ranks of the new middle class. The government had erred, Ishibashi complained, in failing to institute wartime bans on cereal exports and permitting duty-free imports of colonial rice. Palliatives, however, might have prevented the riots but failed to address more fundamental issues. First, industrialization made Japanese rice un-

48. *ITZ* 15:170, 359–60. The rice riots are succinctly analyzed in Oka Yoshitake, *Tenkanki no Taishō*, Nihon kindaishi taikei, vol. 5, 90–91; their significance to intellectuals has been examined by Peter Duus, "Liberal Intellectuals and Social Conflict in Taishō Japan," in Najita and Koschmann, eds., *Conflict in Modern Japanese History*, 424–46.

competitive in world markets, a concern Ishibashi had expressed half a dozen years earlier.[49] He suggested that the import duties on rice be eliminated in order to encourage Japan's
transition to a manufacturing economy, a point that enjoyed
considerable support among businessmen, since lower rice
prices permitted lower wages. Nonetheless, Ishibashi understood that the Japanese public was losing its tolerance for the
distinction between propertied classes, who could shield themselves from market fluctuations, and propertyless classes, who
could not. He acknowledged that social phenomena—hoard-
ing and speculation—not an insufficiency of production, were
the chief cause of the riots. The targets of the riots were, first,
suppliers of daily necessities beginning with rice, and second,
homes of wartime nouveaux riches and other symbols of conspicuous consumption. Although the rioters had not directly
attacked state authority, their punishment would have "fearful
consequences," for the real cause of the riots was a failure of
political "structure and personnel," which had neglected to in-
corporate public opinion and ensure stability of livelihood for
the ordinary family.[50]

While underlining the structural social and political causes
of the riots, Ishibashi sought amelioration through pragmatic
reform. Thus he stood apart from the moral evaluation of
rioters and government so popular among contemporary essayists. He rather enjoyed seeing the government embarrassed
for its exclusive structure, bureaucratic arrogance, and failures
of policy, but on the other hand he did not include street riots
among the most efficacious mechanisms of social progress. His
intense commitment to a high level of managerial rationality
insulated him from communitarian and symbolic modes of
protest. Yet he differed from more conservative analysts in
characterizing the rioters' grievances as wholly legitimate, and
blaming governmental structure and policy while only regret-
ting the people's behavior.

49. *ITZ* 1:471–77.
50. *ITZ* 2:74–78; see also 382–83; 3:204–05; Oka, *Tenkanki no Taishō*, 90–91.
Throughout the 1920s Ishibashi continued to fault the governmental policy of self-
sufficiency in rice, which he blamed on militarism, for example see *ITZ* 4:407–08.
Roger Bowen stresses market dependency as an influence on the Popular Rights
movement of the 1880s in *The Popular Rights Movement in Modern Japan*, 283.

Meanwhile, Ishibashi and Miura jettisoned laissez-faire in favor of progressive social and economic engineering. They supported wartime and postwar governmental regulation and planning of shipping, rice prices, fuels and essential raw materials, wages and working conditions, and municipal utilities, as well as a governmental role in education and research.[51] For *Shinpō* the issue of control versus laissez-faire belonged in the dustbin of history. The problem was the kind and degree of governmental planning, and the breadth of public access to its formative processes. On these points the *Shinpō* urged the enhancement of market trends, social equity, and local autonomy. As the government organized a monopoly system of rice support prices, Ishibashi presented an opinion to Takahashi Korekiyo of the Financial and Economic Investigative Committee (Zaisei Keizai Chōsakai), favoring low support prices with aid for producers' shifts to more competitive production.[52] He would never change his mind on this issue, and his intransigence on this point became a dire threat to his postwar cabinet, for gradually rice price supports acquired an ironclad constituency. In taxation *Shinpō* advocated the elimination of consumer excise taxes in favor of a graduated individual and corporate income tax, and a property tax contingent on thorough and equitable valuation. For local governments it recommended autonomous taxing powers over land sale profits.[53] On the problems of economic and financial policy, Ishibashi joined with influential policy study groups.

Through study groups Ishibashi influenced the reform of the Bank of Japan in 1927 and the restoration of the gold embargo prior to the expansive age of Takahashi finance after 1931. The gold embargo was closely related to banking reform and was one of the two most controversial issues in Japanese economic history, the other being the Matsukata deflation of the 1880s. In the changed context of Taishō politics, financial reform was widely debated in the Diet and the press. Ishibashi's influence radiated outward from individual editorials

51. Watanabe Tōru, "Keizai, zaisei seisaku ron," in Inoue and Watanabe, eds., *Taishōki no kyūshinteki jiyūshugi*, 417–19; on wages see *ITZ* 4:269–79.
52. *ITZ* 4:426–28; 5:305; and 14:78.
53. *ITZ* 5:375–95; Ishibashi, "Zeisei kaisei no yōmoku," *TKS*, 5 and 25 Jan., 5 Mar., and 4 Apr. 1918; and Watanabe Tōru, "Keizai, zaisei seisaku ron," 409.

through the small, academically oriented FSA, which he had organized in response to the rice riots, through the larger and more powerful Economic Study Association (Keizai Kōkyūkai, ESA), and finally to aspects of policy.[54]

Policy study groups, which proliferated during the 1920s, must be seen from a dual perspective. On the one hand they incorporated intellectuals into concerns posed by the state.[55] In this sense, intellectuals lost autonomy as they moved closer to public policy. Yet at the same time, such groups organized private opinion and consequently exposed policy making to a much wider range of social interests and professional perspectives. The proliferation of policy study groups reflected the growing importance of impartial expertise vis-à-vis either economic or bureaucratic sectional interests; it also represented an implicit governmental acknowledgment that the government could neither claim exclusive possession of expertise nor formulate and implement policy without substantial interpenetration with economic, academic, and media elites. In this sense the state, despite its continued advocacy of an exclusivistic ideology, must be seen as increasingly open to public scrutiny and pressure. The increase in both state incorporation of intellectuals and intellectual influence on policy marked a new stage in the ambivalent and interdependent relation between the state and the new urban professional and managerial middle class.

The FSA was organized in November 1922 with some thirty members drawn mainly from academia and financial journalism. Notable among them were professors Yahagi Eizō and Ōuchi Hyōe of the Tokyo University economics department; economic journalists Inoue Tatsukurō of *Chūgai shōgyō shinpō*; Miura and Ishizawa Kyūgorō with Ishibashi from *Shinpō*; and financiers Shimura Gentarō of Yokohama Specie Bank and

54. Mukai Toshio compares the gold embargo controversy with the Matsukata deflation in "Ōkurashō Yokinbu," in Katō Toshihiko, ed., *Nihon kin'yūron no shiteki kenkyū*, 340. Hugh T. Patrick offered an excellent summary of the economic context and results of the gold embargo in "The Economic Muddle of the 1920s," in James W. Morley, ed., *Dilemmas of Growth in Prewar Japan*.

55. H. D. Harootunian, "The Problem of Taishō," in Silberman and Harootunian, eds., *Japan in Crisis*; Marshall, "Growth and Conflict in Japanese Higher Education, 1905–1930."

Shitachi Tetsujirō of Japan Industrial Bank. Several aspects of the group merit its examination as an important force in financial policy. First, it continued into the post–World War II era, metamorphosed as the Economic Systems Association (Keizai Seido Kenkyūkai) in 1927, the Currency Systems Association (Tsūka Seido Kenkyūkai) in 1932, and the Financial Study Group (Kin'yū Gakkai) in 1943; here the designation Financial Systems Association (FSA) will be employed in all references to the prewar period. Second, it published a proposal for a central banking system in 1925 and two manifestos of long-term financial reform in 1927; for the latter two tracts, Ishibashi was the group's legal representative and principal author with Inoue and Yahagi.[56] Third, the group shared members with other important private think tanks. Ōuchi belonged to the Social Policy Association (Shakai Seisaku Gakkai) and had published a proposal for central bank reform with that group in 1919.[57] Ishibashi, Shimura, and Shitachi also belonged to the Economic Study Association described below. Since the FSA had a strongly academic character, its policy influence was subsumed within the slightly larger and much more powerful Economic Study Association.

The ESA was founded by Shitachi Tetsujirō in 1922, and Ishibashi joined the following year. Other bankers and banking officials in the group included Akashi Teruo of Daiichi Bank (Shibusawa Eiichi's son-in-law), Ikeda Seihin of Mitsui (who, like Ishibashi's wife, came from a samurai family in old Yonezawa *han*),[58] Yūki Toyotarō of the Bank of Japan; Diet representatives Ōguchi Tsurumu, Wakatsuki Reijirō, and Machida Chūji; economic analysts Katsuta Teiji, author of *Nihon no sangyō gōrika* (Industrial rationalization in Japan), Morita Hisashi of *Jiji shinpō*, Takahashi Kamekichi of *Shinpō*, Yamazaki Yasuzumi of *Yomiuri*, and Obama Toshie of *Chūgai shōgyō shinpō*, another Waseda graduate with a record of re-

56. Kin'yū Seido Kenkyūkai, "Chūō ginkō seido shian," *TKS*, 1 Feb. 1925; *ITZ* 15:360; Tsurumi Seiryō, "Ryōtaisen kanki no Nihon Ginkō," in Katō Toshihiko, ed., *Nihon kin'yūron no shiteki kenkyū*, 88; Asai Yoshio, "Nihon Kōgyō Ginkō," in ibid., 247.

57. On the Shakai Seisaku Gakkai see Kenneth Pyle, "The Advantages of Followership: German Economics and Japanese Bureaucrats, 1890–1925," *JJS* 1 (1974): 127–64; and Ōuchi, 9–10.

58. Imamura Takeo, *Ikeda Seihin den*, 16.

formism in the Tokyo streetcar strike and the Tuesday Society.[59] There were some two dozen other influential members, but those mentioned were to work with Ishibashi in other contexts. Katsuta, Takahashi, Yamazaki, Obama, Akashi, and Morita were to support Ishibashi's position on the gold standard. Katsuta, Takahashi, and Obama joined Ishibashi's Keynes Research Association. Machida Chūji, as minister of commerce and industry in 1935, was probably influential in placing Ishibashi on the Cabinet Research Bureau (Naikaku Chōsa Kyoku).

During the late thirties, Ishibashi's criticisms of armaments spending would reduce his policy influence to the mere analysis of mechanisms such as prices and savings rates, but amid the continuing controversy of the 1938 budget, ESA members Takahashi, Katsuta, and Obama served with him on the Finance Ministry's Central Committee on Commodity Prices (Chūō Bukka Iinkai); Takahashi, Ōguchi, Yamazaki, and Obama joined his Association for Contemporary Economic Studies (Jikoku Keizai Kenkyūkai) at the *Shinpō* offices the same year, while Takahashi, Obama and Ishibashi were consulted by Ikeda during his term as finance minister during 1938–39. Akashi joined the wartime and postwar Kin'yū Gakkai, heir of the FSA. Thus the ESA represented a long-term, multifaceted forum for the deliberation of economic policy issues.[60] Its influence was born with the financial problems that arose during the first world war.

World War I permitted a boom in Japanese exports to European and colonial markets. By 1919 the export value index was at 469.1 on a 1911 base, with imports at 423.0.[61] Heavy industrial development, induced by wartime shortages and long-term protective tariffs, markedly decreased import dependence; for example, Japan imported 51.4 percent of its steel and 79.9 percent of its machines during the 1910s, but only 40.3 percent and 17.8 percent respectively during the 1920s.[62] Yet even these striking figures fail to capture the sig-

59. *ITZ* 15:360.
60. Keizai Kōkyūkai, *Kin'yū seido kaizen'an.*
61. Kozo Yamamura, "The Japanese Economy, 1911–1931: Concentration, Conflicts, and Crises," in Silberman and Harootunian, eds., *Japan in Crisis*, 302.
62. Arisawa Hiromi, *Shōwa keizai shi*, 43.

nificance of the qualitative change in the Japanese and world economies:

> In the six years from the beginning of World War I in 1914 to the panic of March 1920, the economies of both Japan and the world were transformed. The war did not simply throw the global economy's interrelationships of production into temporary confusion. Rather, entire economic mechanisms, both domestic and international, of many nations went through a structural upheaval. . . . A further change, from Japan's perspective, was that the influence of world economic trends on the Japanese economy expanded considerably beyond their prewar levels.[63]

In 1917 the Finance Ministry embargoed gold exports and controlled foreign exchange through the Bank of Japan, exchange banks, and foreign deposits. Until 1924 there was general consensus that these measures would be temporary, pending a return to the gold standard and normalcy. The relative coherence of opinion reflected important aspects of Japan's international position. Since the nineteenth century the gold standard had been a hallmark of international respectability; as John Maynard Keynes described it, "as densely respectable as was ever met with, even in the realms of sex or religion."[64] Its orthodoxy was especially valuable to a racially and culturally distinct newcomer to the Western world order of industrial and imperial powers—to wit, Japan. Yet despite broad support for the gold standard, the cabinets of Hara Kei, Wakatsuki Reijirō, and Katō Tomosaburō did not realize their stated goal of a return to the gold standard at prewar parity, largely because Japanese prices were too high to support the prewar parity, and domestic interest groups lobbied against retrenchment.

The debate over financial reform involved issues of enormous stakes. These were, first, the availability and cost of industrial and commercial credit; second, Japan's relationship to the international economy; third, the institutional relationships between the Finance Ministry, the Bank of Japan, and

63. Takafusa Nakamura, *Economic Growth in Prewar Japan*, trans. Robert A. Feldman, 139; see also Hashimoto Jurō, "Senkanki Nihon shihonshugi bunseki no hōhō," *Rekishigaku kenkyū*, no. 507 (1982): 25–36.
64. John Maynard Keynes, *Essays in Persuasion*, 183.

various types of private banks, and, fourth, fiscal expenditure and its control by either central authorities or local governments, which were clamoring for revenue independence in order to meet rising educational costs and to provide public services for new workers in the boom areas. Politicians relied on ramshackle theories, which often led them to miscalculate the effects of the financial policies they advocated, and businessmen in comparable positions split according to their theoretical perspective.[65] When traditional theories were in tatters, and their applications subject to global reexamination, the debate rose to a high level of abstraction and made economists and journalists a significant force in providing arguments and predictions for the various interests involved. Journalists had more flexibility in crossing sectors than bureaucrats or businessmen enjoyed, and more time to read theoretical works; on the other hand, they reached a broader audience than most scholars.

Credit availability and interest rates for industrial expansion at home and abroad were the foremost financial issues for Taishō businessmen. Tight money and high interest rates in the twenties evidenced long-term and short-term problems. The wartime boom concentrated in the heavy and chemical industries, which required far more capital than the older light industries; moreover, the government did not sponsor the new industries as it had done for Meiji-period shipping and steel. The favored position of the old zaibatsu at the Bank of Japan, and the rise of new competitors, intensified the frictions of an outmoded system. Wartime demands for reform came most notably from Asian entrepreneur Nishihara Ryūsaṇ, infamous for serving as "the brains and the fixer" of the Terauchi cabinet and masterminding the high interest Nishihara loans to the tottering goverment of Republican China. In tandem with Finance Minister Shōda Kazue, Nishihara attacked the contractive policies of the Bank of Japan; the attack met with cries of jubilation from the new zaibatsu such as Suzuki, Kawasaki,

65. Miwa Ryōichi, "Kinkaikin seisaku kettei katei ni okeru rigai ishiki," *Aoyama keizai ronshū* 26, nos. 1, 2, and 3. For an interesting interpretation see Chō Yukio, "Nihon shihonshugi ni okeru riberarizumu no saihyōka: Ishibashi Tanzan ron," in Chō, ed., *Nihon keizai shisōshi kenkyū.*

and Kuhara, which had thrived on wartime inflation. The new zaibatsu wanted credit for further expansion but were shackled by postwar high interest rates and deflation, which increased the value of their massive debts. In addition, they leaned toward continental interests but found capital exports hampered by the existing fiscal structure. Finally, devaluation raised the cost of imports, benefiting producers of domestic substitutes. In contrast, many exporters of consumer goods, including Mutō Sanji of Kanegafuchi Spinning, believed that a rapid return to the gold standard at prewar par would enhance trade despite deflation. Although there may have been a general distinction in opinions between overseas investors and traders, Mutō's later shift to favor a lower valuation for the yen illustrates the confusion among contemporary businessmen in predicting the effects of alternative policies.[66]

A second issue was the institutional structure of the Bank of Japan and its relationship to member banks. The Nishihara-Shōda proposals, as elaborated in the Finance Ministry by Shōda and Mori Toshimurō, aimed to end the privileged relationship between the old zaibatsu and the Bank of Japan; however, they drew the Bank of Japan more closely under the administration of the Finance Ministry in a financial oligarchy. In contrast, Inoue Junnosuke and others in the Bank of Japan aimed at creating a "banker's bank" and using the bank's rediscounting policy to penetrate Asian markets. Consequently, new pressures arose to counter the influence of both the old zaibatsu and financial bureaucrats, and to make the Bank of Japan responsible to a newly broadened roster of member banks.[67]

The issues of financial policy and structure touched vital political and social concerns. During the early twenties the Seiyūkai party leadership, especially Takahashi Korekiyo, paid lip service to a return to the gold standard. In practice, however, the party moved to expand credit for Asian markets and continued its traditional pork barrel policies, tolerating a depre-

66. Tsurumi Seiryō, 60–63, 66, 71, 73; Mukai, 350. Shōda Kazue of the Finance Ministry is not related to Katsuta Teiji of the ESA though the two surnames are written with the same characters.
67. Tsurumi Seiryō, 61–63.

ciated yen in order to purchase local support by spending on armaments, schools, railroads, communication, and government buildings. The opposition Kenseikai party, and many financial and banking bureaucrats, favored retrenchment but differed on the details of tactics and timing. Deflation benefited industrial labor, especially in large-scale firms, by depressing prices faster than wages, but it increased unemployment and vitiated agriculture, where supply grew while deflation suppressed aggregate demand, and the absolute level of prices fell. *Shinpō* economist Takahashi Kamekichi described the social consequences of retrenchment as favoring rentiers over producers, for rentiers found the prewar values of paper assets restored as the yen rose. Yet another issue was the urgent need of local governments for revenue autonomy, for towns and villages could not cover the rising costs of education, and cities clamored for social welfare budgets in order to meet the needs of an influx of workers in heavy industry. Local government spokesmen and tax reformers supported the creation of a national reserve deposit system, with deposits that could be used for local, low-interest public capital expansion.[68]

During the early twenties most opinion leaders paid lip service to a return to the gold standard at prewar par, but the Great Kantō Earthquake of 1923 forced new perspectives. So severely did the earthquake skew the previously shaky financial structure that the value of ¥100 plummeted to $38.50 compared with its prewar standard of $50. By November of the following year Yokohama Specie Bank was issuing "gold dollar" notes for domestic consumer use at ¥5.02 and government-issued gold dollar demand notes rose to ¥6.50, creating a de facto dual value system, hitherto considered taboo. Although the government issued almost unlimited loans for reconstruction (including one for a new four-story concrete Shinpō office not completed until 1932), recovery was hampered by financial uncertainty, sluggish overall growth, and

68. Arisawa, 43–44; Tsurumi Seiryō, 66, 71; Mukai, 350. For two different views on wages during the 1920s see Yamamura, "The Japanese Economy," 307, and Ron Napier, "The Transformation of the Japanese Labor Market, 1894–1937," in Najita and Koschmann, eds., *Conflict in Modern Japanese History.*

problems of capital flow. The urgency of the situation precipitated a full-scale debate over financial reform and the gold
standard, not only in business journals but in other specialized
publications such as *Hōgaku kenkyū* (Legal studies) and *Teikoku
nōkai hō* (Imperial farm news), general-interest journals such
as *Nihon oyobi Nihonjin* and *Diamondo* (Diamond), and daily
newspapers such as the *Tōkyō asahi* and *Ōsaka mainichi*. A new
and broadly based economic sophistication emerged, with *Tōyō
keizai shinpō* as its most innovative theoretical and practical
voice.[69]

Debaters on finance now divided into four camps, three in
favor of returning to the gold standard (1) immediately and
without qualification, (2) after a period of preparation, especially by increasing reserves, and (3) at a lower valuation.
The fourth option was the abandonment of the gold standard
in favor of floating exchange rates, which were actually in effect but lacked theoretical sanction. *Shinpō* supported the third
alternative, and the paper led in theoretical sophistication, especially in integrating purchasing power and interest rates,
currency, and capital. Miura took an important step toward a
new *Shinpō* position by arguing the relationship of lower exchange rates to lower interest rates in the spring of 1924.
Miura was hardly first to express the idea, but he systemati-
cally linked it with institutional reform. In Miura's view, the
Bank of Japan had lost its flexibility by issuing bonds to guarantee and redeem the national debt, cramping funds available
to private firms and local governments. If the government
lowered the exhange rate, it in effect depreciated its debt and
encouraged cheaper credit. Miura's proposal struck at the
roots of the Bank of Japan credit system.[70]

Within months Takahashi went one step further by linking
credit availability and interest rates to capital demand. Capital
demand, he urged, was a function of production equipment
needs, consumption, and existing fixed and liquid capital. The
source of the first two was the people's savings and was
automatically regulated by an equilibrium of supply and de-

69. Tsurumi Seiryō, 82; Arisawa, 43; Mukai, 351.
70. Tsurumi Seiryō, 82; Miura Tetsutarō, "Waga kuni no kinri wa naniyue ni
takaki ka," *TKS*, 26 Jan.–22 Mar. 1924.

mand. Japan, however, was far from equilibrium in 1924 because of high interest rates due to past obligations. Therefore
liquid capital was restrained by lack of credit. Expansion of
the money supply would build confidence in industrial expansion; meanwhile, that portion of the money supply ex-
pended in the maintenance of the financial system, and
returns on capital, ought to be reduced. Takahashi's proposals
were particularly innovative in viewing capital as expanding
rather than fixed, treating it as almost identical with credit,
and grasping the relevance of capital reallocation to lower
interest rates. On the basis of Miura's and Takahashi's arguments, *Shinpō*, under Ishibashi as editor-in-chief, moved to advocate a return to the gold standard at a lower valuation
during the fall of 1924.[71]

Although *Shinpō* was far in advance of most contemporary
economic thinking, within its ranks Ishibashi was a follower
rather than a leader in 1924. The years between World War
I and the panic of 1927 comprised his self-education as an
economist. From the panic until the Manchurian Incident, he
would write almost exclusively of economic crisis and pragmatic response, but before that time approximately three-
quarters of his essays dealt with foreign policy, politics,
thought, and culture. Even in economic tracts his general education and synthetic outlook led him first to attempt to grasp
the whole process of Japanese industrialization in historical
and global perspective, and second to question its social consequences by addressing topics such as the interests of workers
and farmers. His emergence as editor-in-chief in 1924 doubtless sustained his sense of responsibility for integrating specialized insights and contributing to the general welfare. His
relentless reading program in British, American, German, and
Japanese tomes on finance, economics, and economic history
was impressive, especially considering the theoretical disarray
of the contemporary economic profession. Nonetheless, in the
financial theory of 1924 he trailed behind Miura, who had a
quarter-century of experience at the journal, and Takahashi,

71. Takahashi Kamekichi, "Kinri inkaron no konkyo," *TKS*, 5 and 24 May and 5
July 1924; Tsurumi Seiryō, 84–85; Watanabe Tōru, "Keizai, zaisei seisaku ron," 428–
29; Arisawa, 45.

who held a business degree from Waseda and had experience at Kuhara Copper as well.

Ishibashi was more influential in developing a volume theory of money and its application to the international balance of payments that gained influence among bankers during the late twenties and early thirties. His arguments gained credence after he and *Shinpō* predicted the disastrous consequences that were to ensue from Japan's return to the gold standard at prewar par, under Prime Minister Hamaguchi Osachi and his finance minister, Inoue Junnosuke, in January 1930. In March of the previous year, the journal had warned that the drift to a dual value system for domestic and international currency had confused interest rates, cramped borrowing, and generated excessive savings deposits of ¥200 million in the Bank of Japan. The excess currency, insofar as it was not absorbed in reduced purchasing power, would flee to high-interest foreign investment and low-cost foreign goods if the gold embargo were lifted at the old exchange rate. The outflow would be augmented by an estimated ¥300 million released by falling prices and financial contraction. "Could the financial world stand such a shock?" *Shinpō* concluded.[72]

"Could Inoue answer?" queried economic historian Tsurumi Seiryō, blaming the finance minister for a misguided policy predicated on a banker's view of capital as fixed in quantity and for failure to understand the role of capital allocation as a mechanism for setting interest rates.[73] Yet by 1929 Inoue believed that he had made ample allowance for timing and political strategy; in this, he was supported by Yūki of the ESA, Yamamuro Sōbun of Mitsubishi, and Kyoto University professor and Diet representative Ogawa Ryūtarō of the Minseitō (People's party). Throughout the decade, these moderates had been criticized for temporizing by advocates of an immediate return to the gold standard at prewar par: Yamamoto Tatsuo of the Bank of Japan, Shōda of the Finance Ministry, the Seiyūhontō, and economists Horie Kiichi and Toda Kaiichi. In addition the mainstream of financial bureaucrats

72. *TKS*, special issue on "Kin'yushutsu kaikin mondai," 15 Mar. 1929; see also *ITZ* 8:406–15.

73. Tsurumi Seiryō, 97, 70–74, 85.

and bankers favored using retrenchment, via a return to the gold standard, for the purpose of financial rationalization. Inoue's policy was supported by the Silk Growers' Association, the Tokyo and Osaka stock exchanges, the Tokyo and Kobe chambers of commerce, and the Japan Chamber of Commerce. Finally, the public in general was in awe of gold and fearful that the failure of retrenchment might invite horrifying consequences such as the French and German inflations, which were widely reported in Japanese newspapers.[74]

Although Ishibashi and *Shinpō* were short-term losers on the issue of the gold embargo, they had a host of influential supporters. Mutō Sanji had at first supported a rapid return to the gold standard at prewar par but drew closer to *Shinpō* as Kanegafuchi was badly hurt by contraction. Mutō consulted with Ishibashi periodically into the 1930s.[75] Ikeda Seihin is remembered as a supporter of lifting the gold embargo, but his biographer attributes that position to his friendship with Inoue dating back to their apprenticeship at the Osaka branch of Mitsui Bank, and records that after a sojourn in Europe and the United States Ikeda in fact warned Inoue about the effects of a sudden return to gold.[76] In a slightly different tone, Ikeda's own memoirs stressed his failure to grasp the full significance of his European experience and the general theoretical confusion of the issue; later as finance minister Ikeda would consult with former critics of the gold standard such as Ishibashi, Takahashi, Obama, and Yamazaki Yasuzumi.[77] These men strongly supported the *Shinpō* position along with Inoue Tatsukurō of the FSA; Katsuta, Akashi, and Morita of the ESA; Kagami Kenkichi of Mitsubishi; Nisshin Spinning president Miyajima Seijirō; Yano Tsuneta of Daiichi Life; Ambassador-at-Large Kasama Akio; Kiyosawa Kiyoshi of the *Asahi*; and the right wing of the labor and proletarian movements, including Suzuki Bunji and Akamatsu Katsumaro of the Shakai Minshūtō.[78]

74. Arisawa, 44–45.
75. Mutō Sanji, "Hamaguchi Shushō—Inoue Zōshō ni nozomu," in Nihon Ginkō Chōsakyoku, ed., *Nihon kin'yū shiryō, Shōwa hen*, vol. 22; see also Arisawa, 44.
76. Imamura, 189–91.
77. Ikeda Seihin, *Zaikai kaiko*, ed. Yanagisada Ken, 148; *ITZ* 15:153, 382.
78. Tanaka Ikuo, "Kinkaikin ronsō," in Chō Yukio and Sumiya Kazuhiko, *Kindai*

Meanwhile Takahashi Koreikiyo led the Seiyūkai toward positive management of an expansive domestic equilibrium with a floating exchange rate, low interest and foreign borrowing, and expansion of the reserves guaranteed by the Bank of Japan. He defined Japan as an underdeveloped country that required aggressive governmental management in order to enhance its international competitive edge. His views enjoyed some practical and theoretical support in the Finance Ministry, but they were opposed by the Bank of Japan on theoretical grounds and because the bank's structure could not transform itself into an organ for economic management. Still, the idea of a floating exchange rate gained support, notably from *Shinpō* in 1930 after evidence of the consequences of Inoue's return to gold. It was realized in the managed currency of Takahashi finance after 1931. Although no direct influence of *Shinpō* on Takahashi's views can be traced, *Shinpō* at the very least played an important role in preparing public opinion for new policies.[79]

The trend of opinion from the gold standard toward a managed currency raises the question of John Maynard Keynes's influence. Japanese economic theorists were working more from actual experience than from Keynes's theories; moreover, Keynes's definitive *General Theory of Employment, Interest, and Money* was not published until 1936 or translated until 1938. Nevertheless, Keynes was certainly known in Taishō Japan. Ishibashi introduced a synopsis of *The Economic Consequences of the Peace* to readers within three months of its publication in 1920; during the decade he also read *The End of Laissez-faire* and Keynes's essays in the *Manchester Guardian*. Miura translated Keynes's *A Treatise on Money* in 1924. Matsukata Kotarō, son of the architect of the great deflation of the 1880s, joined the ranks of translators of Keynes. Keynes's early works advocated a number of innovations for which a rudimentary institutional basis already existed in Japan: a floating currency to maintain stable domestic purchasing

Nihon keizai shisōshi, vol. 1, Kindai Nihon shisōshi taikei, vol. 5, 363; Sumiya Mikio, *Shōwa kyōkō: Sono rekishiteki igi to zentaizō*, 363; Tsurumi Seiryō, 88, 98–100; Chō, "Tanzan no keizai shisō," in Chō, ed., *Ishibashi Tanzan*, 165–66; *ITZ* 3:561.

79. Tsurumi Seiryō, 71, 86; *ITZ* 15:371.

power rather than fixed exchange rates; state management of currency and expertise, savings and investment, and population growth; and the consignment of many social functions to intermediate levels between state and individual, such as public corporations or socialized private firms in which management was divorced from capital. As a host of Japanese public figures developed one or another of these themes during the twenties and thirties, Keynes was seldom their first inspiration. He was, however, often an extraordinarily lucid and persuasive catalyst of strategies still in flux, and an eminent authority from a country deemed to be more advanced than Japan. In the 1930s, study of Keynes expanded through Shionoya Tsukumo's translation of the *General Theory*, and a proliferation of study groups, classes, synopses, and lecture series, including many programs at the *Shinpō* offices and national lecture tours by its staff.[80]

For Ishibashi, Keynes offered far more than a theory of managed currency. The two men shared a high respect for industrial efficiency and a sense of its sustained tension with nonmaterial human visions and values. As Keynes expressed it: "Modern capitalism is absolutely irreligious, without internal union, without much public spirit, often, though not always, a mere congeries of possessors and pursuers. Such a system has to be immensely, not merely moderately, successful to survive."[81] Ishibashi agreed, and he continued his quest for economic success with cultural and human meaning. The two shared negative reactions as well. Neither had much patience with politicians and their tendency to subordinate economic policy to short-sighted partisan gain, though both believed that economics ought to serve progressive political and social purposes. Both had a perchant for irony and satire. Keynes was a stimulus to Ishibashi as he was to many economists throughout the world who grappled with the shambles of prewar theories and systems.

80. Arisawa, 44–45; Tsurumi Sciryō, 75, 85; Shionoya Tsukumo, "Ishibashi-san to Keinzu," *Ishibashi Tanzan zenshū geppō*, no. 5 (Mar. 1971): 6–8; *ITZ* 3:144–72; Keynes, *Essays in Persuasion*, 313–19; Sumiya, 328; *ITZ* 15:357–82; Chō, "Tanzan no keizai shisō," 17; Takahashi Kamekichi, "Surudoi rojishan, sugureta jikkōka," in Chō, ed., *Ishibashi Tanzan*, 181.
81. Keynes, *Essays in Persuasion*, 306–07.

Meanwhile, the debate over the reform of financial policy also addressed questions of the structure of the Bank of Japan. Here the factions were different from those on the gold standard, and expansion versus contraction was far from the only issue. Antibureaucratic arguments were also prominent; for example, Mutō Sanji and Horie Kiichi of Tokyo University favored a return to the gold standard at prewar par along with banking reform at the end of World War I but complained that the Bank of Japan was an arm of the Finance Ministry and thus could not stop the expansion that they opposed. Nonetheless, expansionists seem to have been the stronger voice among bank reformers, as illustrated in Ishibashi's proposals, which were adopted by the FSA, modified by the ESA, and represented by ESA member Shimura Gentarō on the Investigative Committee on Financial Systems (Kin'yū Seido Chōsakai, ICFS) formed by the Finance Ministry under Inoue Junnosuke in 1926. Shimura, like Ishibashi, hailed from Yamanashi Prefecture; formerly president of the Kanagawa Agriculture and Construction Bank, he had arranged a low-interest loan of thirty-five thousand yen to a cooperative home reconstruction project that Ishibashi had organized in Kamakura after the earthquake.[82]

Reform proposals by Ishibashi, the FSA, and the ESA all stressed the supremacy of an independent central bank in financial policy and the priority of industrial and commercial expansion, though they differed on their finer points and especially on the degree and kind of public accountability that was desirable. The more academic FSA stressed a broader degree of participation noted in parentheses within the ESA proposal here:

1. Abolish direct government supervision of the central bank, whose president should have a business and academic background and be chosen from the Board of Directors (from the directors of member banks).
2. Make all banks members. (Limit stockholdings of directors and actively encourage participation of member banks.)[83]

82. Tsurumi Seiryō, 86–88; Shimura, 142.
83. See n. 56 above.

These proposals echoed several points of the wartime Nishi-hara-Shōda proposals, differing mainly in their antibureaucratic thrust. They would have ended the privileged relationship of the old zaibatsu with the Bank of Japan, but representatives of Mitsui, Mitsubishi, and Furukawa urged the benefits of overall financial reorganization for general economic expansion, and the zaibatsu had ample power to compete in liberalized capital markets. The proposals marked the high point of prewar financial reform. They would have created a national financial system operating on economic criteria, one more insulated from partisan politics, as well as facilitating credit expansion based on competitive industrial and commercial strength.

Powerful support for reform was undercut by the highly bureaucratic composition of the ICFS, which relied on a draft prepared by the Finance Ministry and retained ministerial control over the Bank of Japan. Shimura was thwarted in his attempts to introduce the FSA draft as a basis for legislation, and his more market-oriented approach was stymied by the panic of 1927. The resulting banking reform bill temporized by merely raising minimum capital requirements for banks and facilitating somewhat greater supervision by the government. Ironically, it worked to strengthen the role of the zaibatsu in investment banking by encouraging consolidation but failed to reform the whole structure of capital allocation. However, it prevented a recurrence of the 1927 panic.[84]

CONCLUSION

The 1920s debate over financial reform was largely ineffective in transforming financial policy due to structural limitations of the governmental and financial systems, competing political and economic interests that often reduced one another nearly to paralysis, fragmented theoretical conception and exogenous shocks such as the Great Kantō Earthquake and the collapse of the American stock market in 1929. Nevertheless, the effects of the debate were important, though largely outside ac-

84. Tsurumi Seiryō, 88–92; Mukai, 352; Patrick, "The Economic Muddle of the 1920s," 227; Yamamura, "The Japanese Economy," 316–23.

tual policy formation and institutional change. For Ishibashi as an individual, the debate meant the translation of his progressive political and social visions into highly technical financial and economic recommendations, and access to the centers of power. His membership in groups such as the FSA and the ESA, examined from a broader national perspective, represented the formation of a pluralistic elite of government officials, bankers, businessmen, professors, and economic journalists who continued to interact in the formation of economic policy through the 1950s. During the twenties the very tensions of the actors and their aims transformed economic theory, especially in the emergence of a dynamic conception of short- and long-term capital formation; similarly, the political competition surrounding the Taishō democratic movement prompted increasingly sophisticated theorizing about politics and society. Finally, reformers advanced the unprecedented conception that matters such as the exchange rates and credit mechanisms of the Bank of Japan, the selection of its president and determination of its policies, and its entire role in the economy, ought to be debated in the media and subject to public accountability.[85] Their frustrations were outweighed by their long-term contributions to a transformed debate about the nature of governmental institutions.

On the one hand, financial reform was part of Ishibashi's broader commitment to governmental accountability and social equity. Believing parliamentary democracy to be the best governmental system yet devised, Ishibashi also never doubted its relation to social reform. Political reform could not substitute for social reform, for reorganization of factories, villages, and neighborhoods for greater participation and autonomy was a separate task. However, the greatest barriers to grassroots activity were a stifling central bureaucracy and police repression. Political freedom and parliamentary processes could smash legal barriers to change. Popular government could also increase social welfare by enacting measures for livelihood protection. Increased social well-being, on the other hand, would enhance the possibility and efficacy of political

85. Tsurumi Seiryō, 86, 89.

reform, for Ishibashi somewhat naively believed that local politics at least would emerge as a major preoccupation of a people educated and freed from the threats of repression and impoverishment. Although he did not imagine that one or another of his proposed reforms could succeed in isolation, he did concentrate on specific measures according to the conditions of the moment.

On the other hand, Ishibashi's specialization in financial theory, under the wrenching demands of the interwar years, sapped the vigor and flexibility of his social vision. As the 1920s drew to a close Ishibashi, now in his mid-forties, had come a long way from his precipitate enthusiasm for Lenin a decade earlier. In 1927 he chided labor for refusing to understand that it risked massive unemployment in a return to the gold standard at prewar par, and he labeled those workers and their leaders who supported the gold standard, or were apathetic toward it, as ignorant and undiscerning (*muchi muken*).[86] The world's leading economists were also confused by the death throes of the gold standard, and several labor leaders had supported Ishibashi's position that traditionalism invited economic catastrophe, but Ishibashi's patience was exhausted. He was discouraged by the fragility of popular movements in the face of governmental suppression and paternalism. He was also losing confidence that the people could design policies appropriate to an advanced industrial society. Although he never acquiesced in stifling popular participation, and never recommended leaving national policy in the hands of experts, he tacitly acknowledged that universal manhood suffrage after 1927 had not brought the nation closer to those policies that he considered appropriate. He blamed the level of popular consciousness as well as the remaining undemocratic features in the institutional structure. Social policy was no longer in the forefront of his attention, as he grew increasingly preoccupied with technical analysis, in cooperation with the elite, in the hope of influencing economic policy. Nevertheless, the Manchurian Incident and the Pacific War era

86. *ITZ* 6:363–64.

prompted his renewal of arguments for parliamentary politics, freedom of expression, reformist social engineering, and a conciliatory foreign policy that he had developed during the Taishō years.

7

The Pacific War: Ishibashi and the *Tōyō keizai shinpō*, 1931–1945

The Manchurian Incident of 1931 divided epochs in modern Japanese history. Marking the army's preference for unilateral action over negotiation abroad and democracy at home, the incident also displayed the diminishing numbers and disarray of liberals. Intellectuals and politicians took up the cry to transcend the Constitution and capitalism in an ill-defined "new structure," a "Shōwa Restoration." On his deathbed in 1932, Tanaka Ōdō sensed the unpopularity of his optimistic gradualism amid the economic, international, and domestic crises of the 1930s, declining an offer to reprint his books with the bitter comment, "In today's Japan no one would want to read them."[1] Escalating censorship stifled the pundits, forcing the resignation of the entire editorial staff of *Chūō kōron* in 1942 and closing the journal completely in 1944.[2] Under these conditions, Ishibashi Tanzan's position as editor-in-chief of a major economic and financial newspaper, *Tōyō keizai shinpō*, afforded a unique opportunity to preserve aspects of his liberal legacy.

Throughout the Pacific War Ishibashi was faithful to his earlier beliefs. Between 1931 and 1945 he consistently defended parliamentary institutions, a reformed but fundamentally capitalist economy, accommodation with revolutionary nationalism in China, and conciliatory negotiation with the United States and Great Britain. On the opposite side of the ledger, he never embraced either the symbols or the substance

1. Quoted in *ITZ* 15:48. Ishibashi was still editing Tanaka Ōdō's complete works in 1939, and resumed immediately after the end of the war.
2. Ben-Ami Shillony, *Politics and Culture in Wartime Japan*, 126.

of wartime ideology: Japan's unique virtues, a pan-Asian mission, imperial divinity, spiritual mobilization, or glorification of the military. True, he made tactical concessions by increasing his subtlety of rhetoric, abandoning causes already lost, and narrowing his focus to current issues. Despite his growing caution half a dozen *Shinpō* articles were banned in their entirety after the Manchurian Incident. Many more provoked police visits, and a three-quarter cut in *Shinpō*'s paper allocation after Pearl Harbor served as a measure of punishment as well as conservation.[3]

Ishibashi was not a heroic resister, but a savvy journalist determined to remain in touch with his readers and out of jail. Nevertheless, his warnings of impending disaster were unmistakable. He survived to become finance minister in the first cabinet of Yoshida Shigeru in 1946, foremost architect of postwar economic reconstruction policies as minister of international trade and industry under three Hatoyama cabinets, and prime minister in 1956. By doing so he enjoyed vindication of his prewar views and proved that liberalism continued within the pluralistic elite of twentieth-century Japan.

Ishibashi's sterling establishment credentials were invaluable because he represented the views of an embattled minority. A financial journal may thrive on depression and uncertainty. *Shinpō* sales increased by an average of fifty copies per week at each of its small distributors and newsstands during the fifteen months after the gold embargo was reimposed in December 1931. The estimated circulation had grown from five thousand at the time of the Russo-Japanese War to thirty thousand in the mid-1930s, while the staff had swollen from twenty-five to seventy-five in 1932 and over two hundred by 1942. Ishibashi worried about his employees while steering a course between capitulation to censorship and dissent so bold as to close the operation entirely. Naturally, the large staff also indicated the journals' vigor and influence. *Tōyō keizai shinpō* was no *samizdat*. A new four-story concrete building, completed in 1931, housed a Japan Economic Club (Nihon Keizai Kurabu), where some of the nation's leading businessmen and

3. On the censorship of *Shinpō* during the Pacific War era see Ishibashi, "Henshūshitsu yori," *TKS*, 19 Mar. 1932; *ITZ* 12:142–47, 13:227–28, and 15:370–90.

intellectuals congregated. An English-language bimonthly, the *Oriental Economist,* was launched in 1934. The Japan Economic Club expanded to branches in twenty-nine cities by 1942. Ishibashi and leading staff analysts journeyed about the country every few months lecturing at club branches as well as business and community organizations and public schools. Success rewarded a reliable record of economic reporting, forecasting, and theorizing from a spectrum of viewpoints.[4]

Advertisers in both the Japanese and English periodicals constituted a veritable directory of Japan, Incorporated: the old zaibatsu and major banks, new zaibatsu and Asian imperial ventures such as the Manchurian Development Corporation and the Taiwan and Greater Japan Sugar companies, and light industry such as textiles. A 1931 *Shinpō* survey of readers showed most of the respondents to be employed in modern, large-scale enterprises, especially finance, with a strong stake in the international economy and finance capitalism. In addition, Ishibashi's frequent public lectures to community, labor, and consumer organizations, and his articles for the *Yomiuri* newspaper, *Chūgai shōgyō shinpō, Jiji shinpō, Fujin no tomo,* and *Kaizō* gave him access to a major portion of the literate public.[5]

Advertising policy may have evaded risk by straddling an editorial spectrum (as corporate political contributions were diversified from extreme right to extreme left), or it may have been a purely marketing strategy. Readers may have utilized the *Shinpō's* reporting and ignored its editorials. Nonetheless, Ishibashi's sustained control of so major a business journal suggests at the very least a broader basis of tolerance than is often assumed, and a challenge that critics answer his policy proposals. Moreover, several liberal positions were attractive to

    4. Watanabe Tōru, "Sōron," 26–30, and Eguchi Keiichi, "Santō shuppei—Manshū jihen o megutte," in Inoue and Watanabe, eds., *Taishōki no kyūshinteki jiyūshugi,* 392; *ITZ* 9:391–92, 15:139; Oka Yoshitake, "Kunizukuri ni chi no shio," in Chō, ed., *Ishibashi Tanzan,* 4; Miyazawa Masanori, "Gaikō hyōronka no teikō," in Dōshisha Daigaku Jinbun Kagaku Kenkyūjo, *Senjika teikō no kenkyū,* vol. 1, 27–30; Shimura, 193–95; Ishibashi Tanzan, "Twenty Years with the *Oriental Economist,*" *OE* 21 (June 1954): 292–93.
    5. Watanabe Tōru, "Sōron," 30; Y. Takenobu, *The Japan Yearbook, 1930.*

segments of the business and financial community. Although few shared Ishibashi's theoretical defense of parliamentary politics, business had made practical accommodations with the parliamentary parties that were fairly reliable bulwarks against either popular agitation or governmental economic management. Ishibashi's support of Finance Minister Takahashi Korekiyo's economic policies favored Japanese exports and the concentration of capital under private rather than state or military auspices. His conciliatory foreign policy promised uninterrupted trade with the West. Ishibashi's liberalism supported both the status quo and its gradual reform, as it had in earlier decades, but in the more violent context of 1930s politics his commitments to the Constitution and capitalism emerged more clearly. Those Taishō conservatives and liberals who clung to their previous positions found themselves drawn together in the face of physical, ideological, and institutional assaults from the radical right and segments of the military.[6]

Powerful connections protected most of Ishibashi's editorials from censorship, but he belonged to no clearly discernible faction. Behind-the-scenes support for his Japan Economic Club came from Baron Makino Nobuaki, a constitutional monarchist who served as Lord Privy Seal until 1936 and was the father-in-law of Yoshida Shigeru. Ishibashi and Yoshida met only once during the 1930s, but Makino is said to have sheltered Ishibashi from General Tōjō's anger in 1944. Makino shared neither Ishibashi's detachment from the emperor-state nor his respect for Chinese sovereignty, but he was generally inclined to amicable relations with the West and constitutional procedures. Rumors circulated that Ishibashi had support from moderates in the Foreign Ministry as well, notably Shidehara Kijūrō (whose elder brother had been Ishibashi's middle school principal in Yamanashi) and Shigemitsu Mamoru, who would later consult with Ishibashi on the restoration of relations with the Soviet Union under the Hatoyama cabinet. According to his son Ishibashi Tan'ichi, Ishibashi drew close

6. Arthur E. Tiedemann, "Big Business and Politics in Prewar Japan," in James W. Morley, ed., *Dilemmas of Growth in Prewar Japan*; "Takeiei wa naritatanai," *Shūkan Tōyō keizai* 53 (22 July 1978): 52–58.

to Makino and Shidehara only after the outbreak of war with China.[7]

Corporate supporters included Dan Takuma, director of Mitsui holding company before his assassination by ultrarightists in 1932, and Ikeda Seihin, who succeeded Dan before becoming president of the Bank in Japan in 1937, and replaced Kaya Okinori as finance minister in the first Konoe cabinet in May 1938. Ikeda continued to seek Ishibashi's counsel on economic and financial questions. Kanegafuchi's Mutō Sanji, a leading proponent of corporate paternalism who had served as a management delegate to the 1919 ILO Conference with Tanaka Takako, was a charter member of the Japan Economic Club. Of course Mitsui and Kanegafuchi were heavily dependent on international trade. Makino, Dan, Ikeda, and Mutō all had studied in the United States and evidenced the sophisticated cosmopolitanism typical of returned students, a chameleon-like mixture of selective admiration for Western ideas and institutions and morbid sensitivity to American nativism.[8]

Some political party leaders as well valued Ishibashi's economic expertise, internationalism, and public defense of their role in the government. Machida Chūji, founder of *Tōyō keizai shinpō*, president of the Minseitō, and minister of commerce and industry under the Okada cabinet in 1935, invited Ishibashi to join the Cabinet Research Bureau (Naikaku Chōsa Kyoku), though his membership ended when that body was reorganized as the Cabinet Planning Board (Naikaku Kikaku Chō), with a stronger commitment to economic mobilization, in 1937. Seiyūkai president Hatoyama Ichirō was certainly Ishibashi's mentor in 1950s politics, but Ishibashi's diary recorded only one meeting with him between 1931 and 1945. Ishibashi harshly criticized Hatoyama's ideological nationalism as education minister in the early thirties; he reserved his highest political praise for Minseitō dissident Saitō Takao.

7. Shillony, *Politics and Culture in Wartime Japan*, 103; Miyazawa, 27–30; *ITZ* 15:370–390; interview, Ishibashi Tan'ichi, 26 Dec. 1983.

8. Hiroshi Mannari found that as of 1920 almost one-quarter of the highest business leaders had studied abroad, most often in Europe or the United States; *The Japanese Business Leaders*, 174–75. Marshall, *Capitalism and Nationalism in Prewar Japan*, 66, 86–88, 102.

Thus broad affinities outweighed narrow partisan or factional alignments. The political motives of Ishibashi's illustrious associates were neither simple nor lucid, but some of the most powerful men in Japan either welcomed his liberal views or tolerated them in a spirit of continued elite pluralism and solidarity.[9]

In addition to powerful connections, *Shinpō*'s financial independence sustained its trenchant analysis. The company's stock was held in common by the employees, with 1,386 of the 1,400 shares in the name of Ishibashi as editor-in-chief. An aggressive expert staff earned *Shinpō* the metaphor of a Zen monastery in its mountain fastness in the popular appellation "Tōyō-san Keizai-ji" (Mount Oriental Economic Temple). Such independence was rare among newspapers and journals, which ordinarily depended on major stockholders or lenders outside the editorial staff.[10]

Shinpō claimed authority through its forty-year history of expert and accurate economic prediction. The *Oriental Economist* trumpeted its "staff of seasoned investigators," "unique mass of data," and editor-in-chief whose past decade of Keynesian recommendations on the gold standard has been "approved by events."[11] Global economic uncertainty increased the demand for expertise and the opportunity for intellectuals to influence public policy. Thus *Shinpō* became a small but significant contender in the plurality of elite institutions that were definitive of prewar Japanese politics, and the journal shared in the defense of those institutions as they were attacked during the 1930s by a different claim to authority, the virulent iconoclasm justified in terms of the imperial will.

Ishibashi united with segments of the business, political, and intellectual elite in favor of maintaining the political order, preserving and expanding capital, and trading with the West. He accepted the Meiji Constitution, attributing its inequities and inefficiencies to the remnants of feudal despotism rather than to fundamental structural flaws in the modern state and

9. *ITZ* 8:540; 9:41; 15:373–80.
10. Watanabe Tōru, "Sōron," 9–10.
11. "Forward," *OE* 1 (May 1934); Takahashi, "Surudoi rojishan, sugureta jikkōka," and Kōno Tetsurō, "Furii shinkingu no tenkai," both in Chō, ed., *Ishibashi Tanzan.*

believing that its difficulties could be overcome through gradual reform and education. His fundamental acceptance of the
status quo (at least in preference to the radical right) and his
realistic proposals of concrete and practical answers to national
problems fitted perfectly within the framework of elite discourse established during the preceding decades. The framework was skewed but not obliterated during the Pacific War
era. The establishment character of Ishibashi's liberalism is
clearly evident in his positions on parliamentary politics, capitalism, and foreign policy.

PARLIAMENTARY POLITICS

For Ishibashi the central political issues of the 1930s were the
relationship of the cabinet to other institutions and freedom
of expression. The first issue was relevant to all the political
maneuvers of the decade. After the Manchurian Incident, cabinet formation was removed from the public forum of the legislature to informal consultation among the powerful. The
army and navy grew bolder, exploiting international tensions
and their constitutional independence. The army and navy
ministers were drawn from the services, thus placing the survival of the cabinet at the mercy of the general staffs. All ministers also enjoyed the constitutional privilege of direct access
to the emperor, a considerable advantage in the maneuvering
before Imperial Conferences, where fundamental policy decisions were ratified. Floating amid other independent power
centers, the cabinets of the 1930s became unstable and ineffective. Consequently, various supraministerial or supracabinet
agencies were proposed, but these too failed because of the
entrenched resistance of established institutions. Thus all political forces were drawn into the problem of cabinet formation
and cabinet prerogatives. Ishibashi was almost alone in his consistent advocacy of freedom of expression but regarded this
freedom as the only cure for an increasingly unaccountable
and secretive government.

The first major shift in the cabinet's position was the divorce of the position of prime minister from the legislative
majority. Whereas during the 1920s party cabinets had ap-

peared to be an effective vehicle by which to achieve consensus among multiple, autonomous government agencies and private interests, global crisis during the 1930s strengthened the claims of expertise by career military, economic, and foreign policy officials. Moreover, the parties were closely associated with liberal policies now viewed as outmoded: cooperation with the West, arms limitation, and competitive interest politics. Their traditional dependence on local elites and their sluggishness in cultivating a mass base and ideological appeal, even after the inauguration of universal manhood suffrage in 1926, made them vulnerable to caricature as the venal vehicles of selfish special interests. Ironically, escalating attacks on the parties, in principle and in terrorist practice, probably increased their dependency on traditional supporters and frustrated the development of new mass strategies. Simultaneously their decreasing power in the central government hampered their accustomed pork barrel tactics. After 1932 elder statesmen, bureaucrats, and military men as well as many party politicians favored nonpartisan or whole-nation cabinets, selected by negotiation among themselves.[12]

The leaders were well aware of their own disunity, which defied the transcendent or whole-nation principle. Behind the ideology two fundamental alternatives to party cabinets emerged. One was an insistence on bureaucratic managerial expertise as the only authoritative determination of the national interest, a classic theme of the Meiji settlement, which, however, had been obscured by the growing complexity and pluralism of the Taishō era. The other option was some new relationship of elite and masses, in either a totalitarian mass party or a misty unity of emperor and subject in direct imperial rule. Army factions in particular encouraged the latter alternative as they contested the civil bureaucracy for control of policy. Yet neither bureaucratic expertise nor mass mobilization resolved the fundamental structural problem of competing institutions, each legally responsible to the emperor alone. The political parties, while acquiescing in nonpartisan cabinets, continued to play a critical role as mediators, brokers,

12. Gordon Berger, *Parties Out of Power in Japan, 1931–1941*, 45–79; David Titus, *Palace and Politics in Prewar Japan*, 311–33.

and ratifiers in the quest for authoritative national policies. Conflict became privatized and increasingly obscure.

Ishibashi's judgment was the dismal one that the parties had not governed especially well, and the new alternatives were even worse. He had always rejected bureaucrats' claims that they spoke for the national interest, arguing that bureaucrats served clique interests and that expertise was widely diffused in academia, business, and the media. The proposals for a mass party or direct imperial rule he deemed both arcane and repressive. He clung to the principle that party cabinets were essential to democracy and the pragmatic argument that, under so-called nonpartisan cabinets, national policy was steadily deteriorating.

After Japan's defeat he would say that *Shinpō* should have suspended operations during the Manchurian Incident, but at that time his editorials differed little from those of earlier decades. He felt rising concern over army machinations in North China in 1935, alarm after the February 26 Incident of 1936, and desperation over the escalating war with China and suppression of dissent in 1938. In 1932, in contrast, *Shinpō* acquiesced in the creation of a Japanese puppet state in Manchuria. Confident that the foreign policy issues surrounding the incident could be resolved and that the economy would recover from depression after Japan had abandoned the gold standard, Ishibashi considered the suspension of party cabinets to be temporary and reversible. He called for a return to party cabinets each time he criticized the political fragility and indecision of the nonpartisan Inukai, Saitō, and Okada cabinets (1931–36) and blamed their flaws on the lack of a majority in the lower house. He took issue with members of the diplomatic corps such as Yoshida, who sought a nonpartisan and professional foreign policy, by attesting that foreign policy had been more stable in the era of party cabinets. Still, he expressed confidence in the Japanese government against both Anglo-American criticism and fascist ideology, and did not anticipate either a global war or a domestic transformation.[13]

13. *ITZ* 8:63, 82; 9:25–27, 36, 88, 92; 11:20.

Ishibashi did not see the limited freedom of Japanese subjects growing narrower during the early 1930s. He defended
freedom of speech for Japanese Communists even in *Shinpō*,
where a 1932 essay by Kawakami Hajime proclaimed: "I caution that the bourgeoisie, however cornered, will not be driven
to the wall by natural causes. . . . That which can drive them
to the wall is *none other than the Communist party*. The day-by-
day rise of fascism in the capitalist countries, which demands
the suppression of *this Communist party*, is the militarism that
heralds the demands of the bourgeoisie [emphasis added]."[14]
Kawakami's essay was published with only the italicized passages deleted, a feat that would have been impossible in any
other journal in 1932, when the left confronted full-scale police assault. Ishibashi did not demand freedom of speech and
association for ultranationalists until a case of parliamentary
procedure involving the expulsion of veteran labor activist Nishio Suehiro from the Diet in 1938.[15] He wrote a fond obituary
for his former *Shinpō* colleague Katayama Sen, who died in
Moscow in 1933. He even reminded his readers of Taishō cultural trends: the theater founded by Shimamura Hōgetsu and
Matsui Sumako, whom Katayama had admired; Tanaka's interpretation of Fukuzawa Yukichi as a pioneer in the legitimation of individual desire; and the spirit of the independent
scholar-critic in the media.[16]

The Minobe Affair of 1934–35 revealed that Ishibashi had
overestimated liberal strength. Since 1903 Minobe Tatsukichi,
a professor of constitutional law at Tokyo Imperial University,
had taught the orthodox legitimation of elite pluralism. His
theory of the emperor as an organ of the state, rooted in imperial German jurisprudence, separated legal constitutional
procedures, which constituted the substance of government,
from the mythology of imperial divinity, which expressed the
historic and cultural unity of the Japanese people. Minobe denied the rightist constitutional interpretation that organs of

14. Kawakami Hajime, "Kachi hōsoku kara mita kinhon'isei hakai no igi," *TKS*, 13
Feb. 1932.
15. Watanabe Tōru, "Sōron," 9–10.
16. Ishibashi defended the freedom of speech of Japanese Communists in *ITZ*
9:492–96, 507–08, 529–30; 11:56. On his relationship with Katayama Sen see 15:87–
89.

the government could be altered according to the imperial will; instead he emphasized the autonomy of the legislature and the legitimacy of party cabinets and popular representation. Although his insistence on state sovereignty was philosophically distinct from Ishibashi's instrumentalist vision of the state as an artifact for the realization of popular needs, both men upheld the enhanced role of political parties during the 1920s. Minobe's theory also served as the leading justification of bureaucratic legitimacy, for it was only by disallowing the personal will of the divine emperor that bureaucrats could claim authority in rational management and structured expertise. Simultaneously supporting both the parties and the bureaucracy, Minobe's theory gave theoretical expression to the interpenetration of the two during the early twentieth century.[17]

The fragility of elite coalition and the impetus of an altered international context were evident as Minobe abandoned the parties, and the parties abandoned Minobe. By 1932 Minobe preferred nonpartisan over party cabinets, dismissing the parties as too contentious and venal to manage the national economy in an age of crisis. Thus he intensified his long-term identification with the established centers of bureaucratic power; in turn, a strident mélange of rightist journalists, scholars, military men, and politicians denounced his organ theory as treason against the divine imperial will. Revelation of the content of the imperial will could, of course, occur to anyone and thus constituted the ultimate ideological ploy of contenders for power from outside and within the establishment. During the spring of 1934 the majority Seiyūkai took up the anti-Minobe cause in the Diet in order to embarrass the nonpartisan Okada cabinet, thus illustrating Ishibashi's contention that prime ministers who lacked a lower-house majority were most vulnerable. Minobe was stripped of all honors and awards; his textbooks were banned; and he retired from public life until the Occupation, when he was consulted about the drafting of a new constitution.[18]

17. Miller, 27, 63–66.
18. Ibid., 176–219; Berger, 60–63.

Ishibashi continued to defend the principles rather than the realities of parliamentary politics, upholding Minobe's freedom of expression and chastising the Seiyūkai. He was forced to choose between the bureaucratic establishment that Minobe represented and the radical right. Still, the issue of freedom of expression was alive. Many journalists criticized Minobe's attackers, but academic dissent was largely stilled by increased police and administrative supervision and temporary suspension of a score of prominent constitutional scholars from public and private institutions.[19]

Despite the furor of the Minobe affair, the election of February 1936 reaffirmed the predominance of both major parties against contenders from right and left. No mandate for further renovation of the political order was forthcoming. The election was quickly followed by an abortive army coup on February 26. A clique of army officers and troops seized the War Ministry and attempted (with three successes) to assassinate senior statesmen, financiers, and military officers who, the rebels believed, still defended liberal international capitalism. Finance Minister Takahashi was one victim, and retired Lord Privy Seal Makino a target. The rebel ideology of a Shōwa Restoration required the overthrow of privileged classes in terms of imported Marxist definitions of exploitation, and offered nativist denunciations of the elite as a barricade obstructing the spiritual unity of the emperor with his people. The army quashed the rebellion and punished its instigators, but it blamed liberal politicians and maneuvered to exclude them from the subsequent government of Hirota Kōki, strengthening military influence over the cabinet. Meanwhile, a chorus of influential officials spoke out in favor of the anticapitalist and antiliberal aims of the rebels, demanding economic centralization, the nationalization of major industries, and chauvinistic national unity under the throne.[20]

The February 26 Incident alarmed Ishibashi, who threw his editorial support to the brash Minseitō representative Saitō

19. Miller, 227, 249, 253; *ITZ* 9:520, 10:5.
20. Ben-Ami Shillony, *Revolt in Japan: The Young Officers and the Feb. 16, 1936 Incident*, 56–71; James B. Crowley, "A New Deal for Japan and Asia: One Road to Pearl Harbor," in Crowley, ed., *Modern East Asia: Essays in Interpretation*, 249–51; Berger, 76–79.

Takao. Saitō, the most articulate party politician to challenge the military during the 1930s, had graduated from Waseda University some years ahead of Ishibashi. There is no record of a prewar acquaintance between the two, though Saitō as home minister would join Ishibashi in Yoshida Shigeru's first cabinet in 1946. Saitō had earned a law degree from Yale University, won thirteen elections, and served on the cabinet staffs of Prime Ministers Hamaguchi and Saitō. His Diet speeches against militarism and for parliamentary procedure in 1936, 1938, and 1940 tested the outer limits of dissent from within the centers of power. In his "Speech on the Army Purge," Saitō attacked the military influence in politics and cogently rebutted the rebels' ideas.[21]

Ishibashi applauded Saitō's speech: "The Imperial Diet has revealed its existence to the Japanese people."[22] The speech had won support from the public and the press, who thereby had shown "almost as much courage as Saitō."[23] Ishibashi expediently discouraged emotional attacks on the army, "which belongs to the throne and the whole people," but reiterated the core issue: the military ought not to intervene in politics.[24] He deplored the army's visions of radical social and political transformation and blamed the execution of eighteen officers and four civilian rebels on fanaticism: "What *is* a Shōwa Restoration? It should be cursed for requiring a sacrifice like this!"[25]

Ishibashi sympathized with the depression-era rural misery that had shaped the social views of many young officers, but he urged a gradual solution within the capitalist framework by means of parliamentary processes. Rebel initiative and its manipulation by senior officers were a mortal threat to the constitutional system. Constitutional government had proven itself superior to the old Tokugawa system in rectifying social injustice but required patience: "The procedures and time alone have the effect of preventing social and class friction,

21. Saitō Takao, *Saitō Takao seiji ronshū*, 270–93.
22. *ITZ* 10:43.
23. *ITZ* 10:19, 21.
24. *ITZ* 10:44.
25. *ITZ* 10:48–49.

which arises from rapid change."[26] The new defensive caution against social and class friction little resembled Ishibashi's exultation in the workers', tenants', and women's movements of the Taishō era. Protest had taken a violent and utopian form he could not sanction. He edged closer to defenders of the political and social status quo but continued to demand freedom of expression and party cabinets.

After the February 26 incident, the armed services heightened their political impact by turning to supporters in the bureaucracy and Diet in an attempt to create a national defense state capable of mobilization for total war. During the fall of 1936 Army Minister Terauchi Hisaichi and Navy Minister Nagano Osamichi proposed a comprehensive plan to strengthen cabinet authority over the government by creating supraministerial agencies and realigning existing agencies; tightening state control over trade, fuel and power, and transportation and communication; and enhancing cabinet independence from the Diet and the political parties. Chief among the plan's supporters were the reformist bureaucrats, a younger generation strongly committed to state centralization and economic management, expanded national power, and an independent and pan-Asianist foreign policy. The reformist bureaucrats were joined by like-minded intellectuals in the Shōwa Research Association (Shōwa Kenkyūkai). Certain new zaibatsu saw magnificent opportunities in continental expansion and government armaments contracts, although much of the older leadership of both large and small concerns balked at state economic management. The most articulate and public opposition came from the leadership of the major parties.[27]

Ishibashi, rejecting the reformist rhetoric decorating the military's proposals, judged the proposals unconstitutional. The Constitution might require amendment from time to time, but the real problem was the threat of war, an issue he raised in earnest for the first time in November 1936. The military and the reformist bureaucrats themselves urged a cau-

26. *ITZ* 10:47.
27. Bernard Silberman, "The Bureaucracy as a Political Force, 1920–1945," in James W. Morley, ed., *Dilemmas of Growth in Prewar Japan*, 60–67, 73; Berger, 93–99; Miles Fletcher, *The Search for a New Order: Intellectuals and Fascism in Prewar Japan*, 99–105.

tious China policy and negotiation with the West in order to allow further time for military and economic mobilization. In Ishibashi's view, however, the problem was not whether army leaders were currently adventuristic or restrained, but whether they shaped national policy at all. Moreover, military mobilization was more likely to cause than to prevent war. Military influence had risen due to the termination of party cabinets: "What passes for national policy is now determined irresponsibly."[28] Legislative politics ought to serve as a microcosm for the resolution of debate and conflict in society at large but had been circumvented: "Rightists and fascists charge their enemies with being anti-Japanese, antipatriotic. Legislative politics is precisely the opposite. Ism's and policies must be drawn into the free market."[29] The Diet fulfilled Ishibashi's hopes, thwarting all proposed reforms save the enlargement of the Cabinet Research Bureau into a planning board, at which point Ishibashi resigned from the body.

The first cabinet of Prince Konoe Fumimaro, formed in June 1937, realized Ishibashi's worst fears. Escalating a minor skirmish in China into a holy crusade, Konoe proposed to create a New Asian Order requiring the overthrow of Chiang Kai-shek and his replacement by a new government more amenable to Japanese hegemony. To enlist the Japanese economy in this effort, the government in February 1938 introduced a National Mobilization Bill aiming at comprehensive economic planning and centralization. Ishibashi and major party leaders opposed the bill, but their tortuous arguments, and the Diet's ultimate capitulation to a compromise version, revealed the collapse of public liberal defense of the status quo.[30]

Immediately prior to the introduction of Konoe's National Mobilization Bill, Ishibashi advanced an unprecedented analysis of Japan's unique national polity (*kokutai*). The Japanese Constitution, he pleaded, was an imperial gift and thus utterly different from systems founded on popular sovereignty. Was he experiencing a change of heart? On the contrary. He urged that the emperor had bestowed a Constitution that prohibited

28. *ITZ* 10:58–59
29. Ibid.
30. Berger, 149–61.

despotism and required liberalism (*jiyūshugi*), as evidenced in the use of the term freedom (*jiyū*) in the Constitution and in Itō Hirobumi's quasi-official commentaries.[31] The strained line of reasoning concluded that the Constitution, and hence liberalism, could be abrogated only by imperial command. Never before had Ishibashi described the Constitution as liberal; as recently as 1936, he had defended democracy solely on the basis of the Charter Oath and pragmatic reasoning. Never before had he suggested that the emperor could alter the Constitution, although that line of argument was harmless in practice as a new roster of imperial household officials maneuvered desperately to sustain the emperor's detachment from politics. With his back to the wall, Ishibashi finally joined conservatives such as Makino in orthodoxy, using the imperial will to defend liberalism against the mobilization bill. Still, the globalism of Ishibashi's perspective was more striking than the nationalism, for he noted grimly that Germany and Italy had recently violated their constitutions, and even the United States appeared vulnerable after Roosevelt's attempt to pack the Supreme Court.

Ishibashi anticipated the arguments of Diet opponents of the bill, led by Saitō Takao, who declaimed that the legislature had no authority to consider the measure. The mobilization bill would alter the rights and duties of subjects set forth in the Constitution; thus it could be enacted only by the emperor himself. Popular representatives defended themselves by renouncing the authority to consider their own emasculation, and imperial ideology compounded the political confusion of 1930s Japan. Konoe passed the bill by a combination of threats and promises. Public defense of the political and economic status quo was drawing to a close, though a degree of institutional independence for the parties and business would continue throughout the war.[32]

Meanwhile, Ishibashi lambasted the Konoe cabinet's use of sloganeering and panic mongering to rouse mass enthusiasm for war with China. In a slam at Konoe's brain trust, the Shōwa Research Association, Ishibashi urged that the nation required

31. *ITZ* 11:36–39; see also Titus, *Palace and Politics in Prewar Japan*, 326–31.
32. Berger, 149–61; Saitō Takao, 2–42.

a people's brain trust. Slogans such as "one hundred million hearts beating as one" were no substitute for debate and criticism; "the government is not a temple or a school, and the people expect more than moral lectures."[33] Military preparations such as air raid drills and resource conservation measures merely spawned confusion and alarm, and censorship failed to win cooperation. The problems arose, Ishibashi believed, because the China War represented no genuine national aspiration. In contrast, if the Konoe cabinet wished to observe authentic national unity, it ought to visit Chiang Kai-shek's wartime capital of Chungking. Ishibashi believed that the Japanese people "despised" the war and were unimpressed by the stream of pronouncements from the cabinet, Foreign Ministry, and military, which were mutually contradictory and "reeking of propaganda."[34] In retaliation, the Cabinet Information Bureau, formed in 1937 to organize media support for the war, singled out *Tōyō keizai shinpō* and *Chūō kōron* for refusal to cooperate and began to maneuver against them.[35]

The final Diet challenge to the China War, by Saitō in 1940, provoked Ishibashi's most vitriolic (and perhaps belated) attack on governmental policy making. Saitō's blast against the hypocrisy of army propaganda was stricken from the Diet record; thus it was off limits for Ishibashi's editorial, though its content was doubtless well known to him. Strategically avoiding direct comment on the China War, Ishibashi launched a critique of the structure of Japanese decision making. The factionalized military role in politics had brought untold confusion, since it was impossible to determine who spoke for the services. More pessimistic than Yoshida and Makino, who saw a Manichean struggle between liberal civilians and aggressive officers, Ishibashi chastised the civil government for capitulating to the army: "The master in his own house is neither duped by his apprentice, nor sat upon by his wife's buttocks."[36]

33. *ITZ* 10:444.
34. *ITZ* 11:67–70.
35. Hatanaka, 34.
36. *ITZ* 11:137; see also Shillony, *Politics and Culture in Wartime Japan*, 27. Hatoyama's faction, known as the Dōkōkai and including Ishibashi's old friends Uehara, Tagawa, Suzuki Bunji, and Ozaki, also opposed Saitō's expulsion; Itō Takashi, " 'Jiyūshugisha' Hatoyama Ichirō—sono senzen, senchū, sengo," in Kindai Nihon Ken-

The civil government was weak because it had failed to win the confidence of the people. When the Minseitō and Diet leadership determined to expel Saitō from both the party and the House, Ishibashi accused the Diet of lacking wisdom and guts (*kenshiki mo naku, koshi mo nai*), adding that the people considered the legislature a contemptible dupe of the military. Ishibashi's essay was somewhat procedural, defending normal constitutional government without directly supporting Saitō's denunciation of the China War. Had Saitō or Ishibashi realized by 1940 that neither moralism nor proceduralism would halt the momentum of the Japanese empire? Neither had much influence, save to implant memories among their countrymen that would serve to win Saitō reelection as an independent in 1942 and elevate both men to cabinet positions in 1946.

Even after Saitō's expulsion from the Diet, Ishibashi occasionally reminded his readers of the merits of party cabinets and parliamentary politics. Editorials questioning the reasons for the resignation of the third Konoe cabinet in July 1941, and for a governmental plan to advance the graduation dates of middle and high school students in September 1941, were deleted in their entirety by the censors.[37] Ishibashi was able to publish criticism of the formal dissolution of the parties in 1940, comparing Konoe's "new political structure" to Tokugawa despotism.[38] Pearl Harbor brought stringent paper rationing and new censorship laws that forbade the press to weaken the people's martial spirit. For the first time, readers were at risk as the government demanded the subscribers' lists of *Kaizō*, *Chūō kōron*, and other banned journals.[39] Ishibashi's liberal arguments were reduced to the merest hints, and his paper allocation was cut to one-quarter of its prewar total. In contrast the *Economist* was more compliant and retained its paper allocation, serving governmental policies and perhaps

---

kyūkai, ed., *Taiheiyō sensō: Kaisen kara kōwa made*, Kindai Nihon kenkyū, vol. 4, 59–60.

37. *ITZ* 12:651–52; for an excellent account of governmental pressure and internal staff divisions at *Shinpō* during these years see Matsuo Takayoshi, "Jūgonen sensōka no Ishibashi Tanzan," in Nihon Seiji Gakkai, ed., *Kindai Nihon no kokkazō*.

38. *ITZ* 11:145–48.

39. Hashikawa Bunsō, "Tanzan to Kiyoshi," in Chō, ed., *Ishibashi Tanzan*, 46–47; Hatanaka, 36.

giving English-language readers a lopsided impression of
Ishibashi's editorial stance.[40] As a majority of his staff urged
greater compliance with government propaganda, Ishibashi
held modest goals: to preserve *Shinpō's* existence as an economic research center, to employ fellow liberals who were
driven out of other publications, and perhaps to offer the
slightest assurance to like-minded readers that they were not
alone.[41] He confided to Kiyosawa Kiyoshi that most of his en-
ergy was spent "trying to keep my wife from going mad."[42] His
son Kazuhiko was presumed dead on Kwajalein in February
1944.[43]

Still Ishibashi spoke out. When the Tōjō cabinet resigned
in July 1944 with the conventional wish that its successor bring
unity to the people and enlist talent in the service of the nation, Ishibashi's lead editorial sneered that the Tōjō cabinet
had conceded its errors in bringing mourning to the people
and commanding no talent. The outgoing cabinet had to
shoulder the blame for the crises facing the nation. The people felt no sense of responsibility toward the war; their initiative was crushed, their outlook grim. Food shortages were
desperate. War production figures were wildly in error, and
the cabinet could not manage sectional struggle among "so-
called production managers" and businessmen. Only free
expression would end military intimidation of civilian leaders.[44] The article was cut by the censors, but it indicates his
views at the time, which were certainly known at least among
the political and business elite. Ishibashi was only one of many
prominent men of widely disparate political orientations, including Yoshida and Hatoyama, who seized the moment to
maneuver against Tōjō; in Ishibashi's case, however, the opportunism of his timing was meliorated by the consistency of
his principles.[45]

40. Ishibashi noted the distinction between the Japanese and English journals in
"Twenty Years with the *Oriental Economist*," 292–93. The more propagandistic tone of
the English-language journal is evident in a comparison of "The 1938 Outlook" (Jan.),
14–16, with *ITZ* 11:6–23.
41. *ITZ* 15:172–74; Miki Yōnosuke, "Jaanarisuto Sōri," in Tanzankai, ed., *Meihō
Tanzan: Ishibashi Tanzan shokan no atogaki*, 148, 151.
42. Kiyosawa Kiyoshi, *Ankoku nikki*, vol. 2, 35.
43. *ITZ* 15:390.
44. *ITZ* 12:142–47.
45. Miyazawa, 29–37; on the anti-Tōjō maneuvers see Itō, " 'Jiyūshugisha' Hato-

Readers encouraged his editorial independence by letter, phone call, and word of mouth.[46] The German defeat served as another occasion for Ishibashi to resume his support of democracy by blaming the catastrophe first on the Nazi leaders, and second on "the German people, who failed to use their Constitution and Diet."[47] Publication continued to the end, despite a move to Yokote in Akita Prefecture when the Tokyo office building burned and most of Ishibashi's papers, including Tanaka Ōdō's manuscripts and students' lecture notes, were destroyed in an attempted evacuation.[48] Luckily Ishibashi had thoughtfully purchased a printing shop in Yokote some years earlier. The day after Japan's surrender Ishibashi's headline proclaimed: "The Gate to Japan's Rebirth—The Road Ahead Is Bright."[49]

CAPITALISM

The economy changed less abruptly than politics between 1931 and 1945. From the twenties through the fifties Ishibashi observed the historic dynamism of Japanese capitalism, damaged only by unsound governmental policies. During the twenties he had judged the economy vigorous enough to admit the participatory management of women, workers, and tenant farmers and still compete in international markets. In the early thirties he proposed ambitious educational reform and agrarian relief. Since he believed in Japan's competitive strength in global markets, he rejected the concept of a regional yen bloc. In an ironic paradox the nationalists who rhapsodized about Japan's unique cultural virtues deemed its economy too fragile to cope without an empire, whereas the skeptical Ishibashi understood that the economy, for all its injustices and travails, possessed an immense momentum and adaptability. He was

---

yama Ichirō," 59–60; John Dower, *Empire and Aftermath: Yoshida Shigeru and the Japanese Experience, 1878–1954*. Makino is said to have protected Ishibashi and *Shinpō*, but Machimura Kingo, who was head of the Home Ministry Police Bureau at the time, confirms Tōjō's desire for vengeance but insists that his agency's motive in resisting Tōjō's will was merely a jurisdictional dispute; interview, 29 Dec. 1983.

46. Hatanaka, 36.
47. *ITZ* 12:187.
48. Hattori et al., 15–16; Shimura, 199.
49. *ITZ* 13:1.

the only member of the Finance Ministry's Special Investigative Committee on Wartime Economics (Senji Keizai Tokubetsu Chōsa Iinkai) who scoffed at the economic consequences of losing the empire, insisting that Japan proper would not only survive but become one of the four great economic powers of the world.[50]

As an economist Ishibashi had two objections to militarism. The Japanese economy could grow more rapidly by exporting to wealthy markets in the industrial nations and using the exports to purchase raw materials from all over the world. The most appropriate policy even in an age of global protectionism was to make unilateral concessions leading toward global free trade. In addition, Japan lacked the requisite industrial and resource strength to defeat the United States, Great Britain, and the Soviet Union, even with the added raw materials of the yen bloc. The yen bloc was not sufficiently developed to absorb Japan's industrial exports, and the extraction of colonial resources could be bought only in political and military terms, the terms of empire that Ishibashi had long considered too costly.

Convinced that trade and military expansion were contradictory, Ishibashi grappled with Japan's image problem, for in Western public opinion, aggressive export promotion and the conquest of Manchuria tended to fuse into a single danger signal. The *Oriental Economist* proposed to win foreign understanding that Japanese hegemony in Manchuria and export expansion were no less legitimate than European or American empires and trade. Since the unequal treaties, Japan had been determined to participate in international politics and economics on the same terms as the great Western powers. The bloc economy theorists also cited Western precedents and demanded an Asian Monroe Doctrine. Both sides acquiesced in a world order defined by the advanced capitalist countries, the difference being whether that order was defined as global or regional.[51]

50. Nakayama Ichirō, "Takken," in Chō, ed., *Ishibashi Tanzan*, 156; *ITZ* 12:255–58; 13:48–54. Kimura Kowashi also remembers Ishibashi as one of the few people who were optimistic about Japan's economic recovery without the empire; see *Gendai hyōron shū*, Gendai Nihon bungaku taikei, vol. 97, 376.

51. Akira Iriye, *Power and Culture: The Japanese-American War.*

Ishibashi's economic analysis, like his political commentary, changed in 1936. He generally supported governmental policy except for military spending until 1936, and opposed military mobilization thereafter. Distanced from the centers of power after 1938, he returned to economic planning for defeat in 1943 and held a number of consultive posts after the formation of the peace-seeking Suzuki cabinet in April 1945. Throughout the Pacific War era he located the constraints on Japanese growth not within the economy itself, but in social unrest and international politics. His confidence was bolstered by the effects of fiscal and monetary policies he had espoused prior to their adoption by Finance Minister Takahashi Korekiyo.

Takahashi reversed the disastrous economic policies of the previous Hamaguchi cabinet. Hamaguchi had returned to the gold standard at pre–World War I par with an uncanny sense of mistiming, three months after the collapse of the American stock market in October 1929. The rollback of domestic inflation to achieve a sound currency failed to keep pace with plummeting international markets, especially the decline in American silk imports. Meanwhile, the government bit the bullet of budgetary retrenchment, compounding the effects of balance of payments deficits, rampant speculation against the yen, massive outflows of short- and long-term capital, idle industrial capacity, unemployment, and a precipitous drop in the living standards of the rural majority of Japanese. By May 1930 Ishibashi was ready to jettison the gold standard in favor of an administered currency, anticipating Takahashi's move.[52] The gold standard, Ishibashi argued, was a "superstition" to which the welfare of the people and the health of national finance should not be sacrificed.[53] The currency ought to be based on the state of the economy and to aim at constant consumer purchasing power. Immediate depreciation of the currency by abandoning the gold standard was essential. The Hamaguchi cabinet's retrenchment, which he dubbed "the policy of depression," had appreciated the currency and thus

---

52. *ITZ* 15:201–03; Nakamura Takafusa quoted in "Takeiei wa naritatanai," 53; Tanaka Ikuo, "Kinkaikin ronsō," 363.
53. *ITZ* 7:212–19.

forced down wages and salaries, credit and debt, and savings in an arbitrary redistribution of wealth and income.[54] His alternative proposal was to abandon the gold standard for a floating exchange rate, which could enhance the competitive potential of Japanese exports, and to increase public spending through deficit financing. Both measures would encourage a rise in commodity prices to the benefit of farmers.

While acknowledging Keynes's inspiration, Ishibashi claimed domestic precedents for an administered currency. Japanese use of the gold standard since 1897 had been exclusively for international trade and had been subject to governmental management in three ways. First, gold had never circulated widely within Japan. Second, a large part of Japan's reserves had been held in convertible paper in London, constituting a gold-exchange standard rather than strict correlation of the currency with gold. Finally, the Japanese government had circumvented legal restrictions on foreign borrowing, practicing unrestricted bond issue, which was adopted by the other advanced countries after World War II. From these precedents Ishibashi hoped that Japan could lead the world toward an administered currency system.[55] The time lag characterizing the introduction of Western thought had been overcome; in economic policies, Japan was ahead of the other advanced industrial countries, though a second time lag would ensue from Japan's economic and cultural autarky during World War II. Ishibashi publicly anticipated Takahashi's pioneer program and facilitated "one of the most successful combinations of fiscal, monetary and foreign exchange rate policies, in an adverse international environment, that the world has ever seen."[56]

Takahashi took Japan off the gold standard in December 1931 and increased government expenditures by 26 percent in two years, with three-quarters of the increase deficit-financed. While taxes and interest rates were held down, the net domestic product grew at a comparable rate in a "textbook

54. Ibid., 314–72; Watanabe Tōru, "Keizai, zaisei seisaku ron," 435–41.
55. Ishibashi cited historical precedent for a managed currency in *ITZ* 9:249–51; cf. Hugh T. Patrick, "External Equilibrium and Internal Convertibility in Financial Policy in Meiji Japan," *Journal of Economic History* 25 (1965): 208–20.
56. Patrick, "The Economic Muddle of the 1920s," 265.

case of demand expansion."[57] Although 62 percent of the budget increase was for military expansion stimulated by the Manchurian crisis, military spending remained at a flat 6.8 percent of the gross national product until 1936. Recovery was far more complex than an armaments race, for the multiplier effect assured boosts in all industries. The heavy and chemical enterprises, aimed in the direction of long-term structural predominance since the end of World War I, benefited from a variety of nonmilitary factors: revival of demand suppressed by the depression since the late 1920s; new technology facilitating import substitution in large-scale electrical equipment, spinning and weaving machinery, machine tools, and industrial machinery; and new products such as aluminum, magnesium, synthetic fiber, and automobiles. Industrial output rose by 81.5 percent between 1931 and 1934.[58]

The boom in Japanese exports brought foreign charges of dumping and retaliation through discriminatory tariffs. Ishibashi stressed Japan's sacrifices in the export drive, and the lack of alternatives. First, Japan's terms of trade had dramatically deteriorated. Between 1932 and 1936 real exports increased by 270 percent (with most of the increase occurring after the abandonment of the gold standard), but real imports rose by only 48 percent; in other words, Japan maintained its balance of payments by accepting a declining quantity of goods in exchange. Second, a trade surplus within the yen bloc was counterbalanced by deficits outside it. The only alternative would have been to reduce imports still further, but essential industrial raw materials purchased mainly from Western countries constituted nearly all of Japan's import bill.[59] The system of exchange controls with which Takahashi had replaced the gold standard was later adopted by the United States, Great Britain, and Germany, and incorporated into the international economy at Bretton Woods in 1944, making Takahashi "a pioneer in international economic policy."[60]

57. Nakamura, *Economic Growth in Prewar Japan*, 236.
58. Patrick, "The Economic Muddle of the 1920s," 257; Alan S. Milward, *War, Economy and Society, 1939–1945*, 30.
59. *ITZ* 9:404.
60. Nakamura, *Economic Growth in Prewar Japan*, 232–33.

The period of Takahashi finance (1931–36) was analytically distinct from subsequent wartime controls. First, governmental policy, while unblushingly committed to economic management, relied primarily on fiscal and monetary mechanisms rather than direct regulation of labor, raw materials, and industrial organization. The policy was startlingly successful, with several implications for postwar continuity. The concentration of capital that had followed World War I accelerated as the growth of heavy industry outpaced agriculture, light industry and services. The concentration of capital, however, did not result in monopoly under either state or private auspices. The zaibatsu were badly damaged by the about-faces in monetary policy between 1929 and 1931 and further handicapped since the subsequent boom centered in areas of zaibatsu weakness. Those heavy industrial companies that the zaibatsu did control increased their managerial independence, while new zaibatsu arose in the growth sectors. Although the gap between modern and traditional economies widened, within the modern sector major conglomerates increased in number and oligarchic competition. Among major industrial nations Japan, most vulnerable to the collapse of world markets in the depression, was the first to recover, approaching capacity operation in 1936.[61]

"It was too late," judged Ishibashi in his postwar memoirs.[62] The army had exploited the depression to create state monopoly capitalism in Manchuria and had ambitions of extending that system to Japan proper in a regional bloc. The army exploited rural discontent through its monopoly on mass organization in the reserve, youth, and women's units.[63] Yet Ishibashi's designation of the Manchurian Incident as a turning point in economic relations, as in politics, came from hindsight. During the early 1930s he urged that Japanese and foreign capital be permitted to compete freely in Manchuria. He also criticized the portion of Takahashi's budget devoted to armaments, preferring rural relief and educational reform, but showed little fear of regional or global conflagration.[64]

61. Ibid., 252.
62. *ITZ* 15:203.
63. Patrick, "The Economic Muddle of the 1920s," 259; *ITZ* 8:517–19.
64. *ITZ* 9:16–19.

Ishibashi's proposals for social reform stressed expansionary government spending, in contrast to his 1920s emphasis on the legal and political rights of workers, tenants, and women and their associations. He urged the construction of public works, rural relief through nationalization of health care, temporary support prices for Japanese rice, and governmental encouragement of crop diversification. In 1936 he advanced a sweeping proposal to reduce the number of agricultural households by two-thirds, with government-sponsored retraining and reemployment in rural industry, which would profit from new demand for agricultural machinery and other goods by the more prosperous remaining farmers. He also suggested upgrading rural education and modifying the tortuous tracking and examination requirements that barred most farm children from higher education. The strength of Japan's economy depended on the talents of its people, not the size of its empire or the power of its armed forces. Rural welfare required cutting military expenditures, especially as full-capacity production signaled the advisability of fiscal restraint by 1936. Criticism of the armaments industry brought a police investigation to *Shinpō* in 1933. By late 1934 Takahashi began to question the military increases he had earlier sanctioned, and his doubts led to his assassination in the February 26 Incident.[65]

Takahashi's assassination marked the replacement of economic by military criteria in budget design. As early as 1935, Ishibashi predicted the approaching necessity of tax increases. However, the new finance minister, Baba Eiichi, introduced a 1937 budget of three billion yen, nearly half for army and navy appropriations, to be financed by large individual and corporate tax hikes and a ¥1,980 million bond issue, up 20 percent over the previous year's deficit. During 1936 and 1937 the Diet resisted large-scale budgetary expansion as it contended against efforts at administrative reorganization and comprehensive economic regulation. However, public dissent

65. *ITZ* 9:295, 331–36, 395; 10:494–504; Nakamura, *Economic Growth in Prewar Japan*, 238. The Shōwa Research Association was also strongly interested in rural relief, and Ishibashi joined one of the group's early discussion sessions in 1934. He disassociated himself thereafter, however, though he continued a number of panel and speaking arrangements with Rōyama Masamichi. Sakai Saburō, *Shōwa Kenkyūkai: Aru chishikijin dantai no kiseki*, 17.

was muted after the outbreak of the China War; in fact, Ishibashi even accused the government of manipulating the China
War in order to pass its budgets for long-range military expansion.[66]

Ishibashi urged the least possible economic control through
the regulation of investment alone, not consumption or trade.
He was unwilling to trust the bureaucracy or anyone else
with the kind of comprehensive economic management proposed in 1936–37. Overinvestment in arms production was
devastating the balance of payments, creating bottlenecks and
inefficiency, and generating rampant inflation. If more armaments were truly essential, he urged they be produced by
multiple shifts rather than new investment, or be acquired by
purchase in international markets using gold exports (though
the latter policy would have posed a serious constraint to confrontation with the Anglo-American navies). If government
spending could not be reduced, it ought to be covered by
tax increases rather than public debt or complex administrative regulation. Tax increases would automatically reduce consumption and imports and increase surplus labor. More
fundamentally, he viewed arms spending as inherently unproductive and likely to escalate international tensions.[67]

As the budgetary expansion of 1936–37 evoked widespread
dismay among businessmen and party politicians, Ishibashi
met three times with Baba in attempts at compromise. These
years were the peak of a minor but fairly regular pattern of
government consultation since 1931. He was called to testify
before Takahashi and Baba in the Finance Ministry, the Cabinet Research Bureau, and the Ministry of Commerce and Industry, where he met future finance minister Ishiwata Sōtarō.
Subsequently his policy consultations declined, save on technical matters such as commodity prices, until Ishiwata named
him to the Special Investigative Committee on Wartime Economics, a top-secret group constituted in October 1944 with

66. *ITZ* 11:8; Nakamura, *Economic Growth in Prewar Japan*, 263–67; Berger, 112–
41.
67. *ITZ* 10:141–46, 157, 165, 464, 480–81; widespread resistance to wartime economic controls and heavy taxes, the neglect of peacetime production, and labor shortages among the silk and rayon manufacturers of Fukui Prefecture have been noted
by Kurosaki Seisuke, "Senjika no chūshō kinu-jinken kigyōsha ishiki," *Shakai keizai
shigaku* 45 (1979): 58–80.

the dangerous assignment of planning for the inevitable defeat. After the formation of the peace-seeking Suzuki cabinet in April 1945, Ishibashi was suddenly appointed to committees on economic planning under the Diet, the Finance Ministry, and three cabinet agencies. But between 1938 and 1943 his counsel was rarely sought by official bodies.[68]

As the China War escalated in the spring of 1938, Ishibashi reached for visions beyond his own time and place. He added Tanizaki Jun'ichirō's modern Japanese translation of the *Genji monogatari* and Albert Einstein's *The Evolution of Physics* to his usual reading program in political economy. More remarkably, he resumed the study of his father's faith, the Buddhism of Nichiren, which he had neglected since his youth. He quotes Nichiren eight times in his relatively brief wartime writings, in contrast with four references during the preceding twenty-five years. What drew Ishibashi to this medieval monk, most noted in all Japanese history for intolerance and nationalism? Ishibashi admired Nichiren's detestation of cant and his unswerving devotion to principle, though Ishibashi's principles were different.[69]

Ishibashi quoted Nichiren's diatribes against medieval political leadership while condemning the Konoe cabinet's expansion of war with China. He approvingly described Chinese resistance against Japan, in which all classes and occupations cooperated, as the fulfillment of Nichiren's demand that the Lotus Sutra be read with one's whole body as well as one's mouth and mind. The situation in Japan, he added laconically, was entirely different. He recalled Nichiren's warnings that Japan's evil rulers would bring about its destruction at the hands of the invading Mongols when he denounced Germany's unreliability as an ally after the conclusion of the Nazi-Soviet nonaggression pact.[70] Japan's national symbols, its religious and imperial traditions, were complex and multivocal.

---

68. *ITZ* 15:369–88. Ishibashi's role in planning for defeat is discussed in 13:632–33 and 15:651–52; Kiyosawa 1:137 and 2:210; Miyazawa, 229–37. Ishibashi's wartime economic consulting was important in protecting his remaining freedom of expression; interview, Ishibashi Tan'ichi, 26 Dec. 1983.

69. *ITZ* 15:384. See 15:370–90 for a chronology of Ishibashi's visits to Nichiren temples. Nichiren's writings are translated in Laurel Rasplica Rodd, *Nichiren: Selected Writings*, see esp. 96 and 107.

70. *ITZ* 11:55, 59, 527, 559; 12:562, 569.

Ishibashi, who had avoided them when confident of the success of pragmatic reasoning, now turned to them in desperation that verged on despair.

During the same period Ishibashi resumed his editing of Tanaka Ōdō's work, and he began to write of economics and war in a more philosophical vein, recalling the role of the Taishō scholar-critic. Early 1938 marked the "most perilous point in our country's history," but not for reasons of national finance.[71] Governmental budgets had been viable but material goods insufficient during World War I in Britain, France, and the United States as well as Germany. The consequences of war were unpredictable to either side, and the role of chance and accident increased as war was prolonged. World War I had brought Russian communism, German inflation, and chaos in the world economic and financial system. Japan's economic recovery since 1931 had also been the work of chance: "There was no leadership or principle, and the people were blind."[72] In economics Ishibashi noted the same fundamental problem as in politics, the drift and instability of nonpartisan cabinets that lacked a popular mandate. By January 1941 Ishibashi predicted that the Japanese economy would collapse if the China War were prolonged.[73]

When the freezing of Japanese assets in the United States prompted the Japanese government to make yet another effort to achieve comprehensive control over raw materials, production, consumption, and distribution, Ishibashi propounded his first full-blown defense of capitalism. National military mobilization was antithetical to capitalism. Capitalism would last another century until its ultimate replacement by a global planned economy. Conceding that the failures of capitalism and parliamentary politics after World War I had given rise to communism and fascism, he faulted the newer systems for a lack of "technological advance and persons able to use it."[74] Japan had the same problems as communist and fascist countries insofar as "the economy today is stimulated not by in-

71. *ITZ* 11:52–56.
72. Ibid.
73. *ITZ* 11:23; 12:45, 5.
74. *ITZ* 12:54; cf. 9:351. On governmental economic controls see Nakamura, *Economic Growth in Prewar Japan*, 293–94.

creased productivity but by war demands," which benefited no
one except "bureaucrats."[75] Bureaucrats answered to no one,
in contrast with political parties, who were accountable at least
to capitalists, and capitalists, who could fail. For all its flaws,
capitalism was the best system Japan could sustain in the foreseeable future.

Ishibashi issued a final warning that not only the economic
system but the nation itself risked destruction in April 1942.
To lull the censors, he began with references to the Sino- and
Russo-Japanese wars, both victories.[76] However, he reminded
his readers that during the Russo-Japanese War *Shinpō* had
been alone among Japanese newspapers in predicting that Japan would not win an indemnity. *Shinpō* had not joined in "the
government and people's trumpeting of martial virtues."[77] The
high costs of the war had been unexpected to all save the
Shinpō staff. "No one begins a war expecting to lose."[78] The
present war would be entirely different from past wars in
scope and cost and would be decided by the relative industrial
and resource strength of the combatants.[79] Few of his long-
time readers were likely to have missed the point that victory
would not be Japan's.

Although Ishibashi acutely noted Japan's wartime weakness
and its peacetime strength, his fears that the state would absorb or destroy capitalism were exaggerated. The enhancement of state controls, though remarkable from a Japanese
domestic vantage, was weak and belated compared with the
structural change in the Soviet Union, Germany, and even the
Allies. The ambitious plans for full and united governmental
economic management were never realized, largely because
the government was divided and businessmen were able to retain some independence of operation while benefiting from
war contracts. The Japanese state had neither the repressive
capacity of the Nazis, nor the mass support that enabled Brit-

75. *ITZ* 12:56.
76. *ITZ* 12:106.
77. *ITZ* 12:108.
78. *ITZ* 12:109.
79. Ibid., 117. See Milward, 36, for a comparison of Japan's industrial capacity
with that of other major combatants; for example, in 1937 Japan produced 3.5 percent of the world's capital goods, compared with the United States' 41.5 percent.

ain and the United States to effect substantial wartime modification of economic relationships. Economic continuity with powerful business support surely explains Ishibashi's preeminent role in the cabinets of the 1950s.[80]

FOREIGN POLICY

China was the most intractable problem facing Japanese officials and diplomats during the thirties, and the one on which Ishibashi had least to say. He found no easy answers to the clash of Chinese nationalism with long-standing Japanese interests and treaty rights, a confrontation complicated by foreign manipulation and Chinese civil war. After the Manchurian Incident he abandoned *Shinpō*'s historic opposition to empire and excused the army role in Manchuria as a defense of concessions won in the Russo-Japanese War. However, his acquiescence in the detachment of Manchuria did not imply the abrogation of Chinese sovereignty in China proper, which he emphatically opposed. His central concern was the long-term emergence of a viable national government in China. His historical paradigm was Japan's own pre-Meiji period, in which antiforeign agitation had served as a weapon to overthrow the ancient regime. After the Restoration Japan had opened itself to foreign culture and trade, and so would China.

Shinpō's acquiescence in the Manchurian Incident came slowly, nearly a year after the army's initial move, in an editorial in January 1932 that demanded the protection of Japan's treaty rights and interests but rejected the creation of a new state. A more belligerent manifesto the following month justified Japan's intervention on the grounds that China could not keep peace and order in Manchuria. After the creation of the puppet state of Manchukuo in March, Ishibashi never again took up the question of Chinese sovereignty there. He later apologized for the silence, but never explained it. Repression was not the reason, for that failed to stifle him during the

80. Milward, 31, 117–18; Dower, 287–91. Richard Rice, "Economic Mobilization in Wartime Japan: Business, Bureaucracy and Military in Conflict," *JAS* 38 (1979): 689–706.

Siberian Intervention or during the far more dangerous context of later war with China and the United States. Public opinion overwhelmingly supported the army, leaving other problems more amenable to discussion. Ishibashi may have been reluctant to embarrass the new cabinet of Inukai Ki, for, though Inukai lacked a parliamentary majority, he was a party politician chosen to restore civil command over the military. Certainly the rising violence of the Japanese expulsion movement in China was relevant, for Ishibashi contemptuously dubbed the Chinese government a spoiled child that demanded abrogation of extraterritoriality while failing to preserve foreign lives and property. Still, he renounced the army's vision of an exclusive sphere of planned economy in Manchuria, advocating international investment through an Open Door.[81]

Even hindsight fails to clarify the wisdom of Ishibashi's decision to accept Japan's position in Manchuria. The refusal of China, the League of Nations, the United States, and Great Britain to recognize Manchukuo relegated Japan to a diplomatic twilight zone. In addition, the army's success in Manchuria invigorated the promilitary, anticapitalist, and pan-Asian forces that Ishibashi opposed in the home islands. On the other hand, neither the West nor China was in any sense prepared for confrontation over Manchuria. Many prominent diplomats and officials such as Yoshida and Makino believed that the West would ultimately acquiesce in the Japanese status quo in Manchuria; until 1938, Britain inclined in that direction in the hope of protecting its other Far Eastern interests, and the United States set a precedent for abrogating its nonrecognition policy in the case of the Soviet Union in 1933. Ishibashi was not wholly unrealistic in arguing that Anglo-American recognition could be gained by encouraging free trade in the area, compromising on armaments control, and avoiding unilateral Japanese action in the future. However, his old argu-

81. *ITZ* 8:20–21, 52–59; 9:92; James B. Crowley, *Japan's Quest for Autonomy and Security*, 149–56; Eguchi, 384–86; an army attempt to persuade Ishibashi to acknowledge the Manchurian puppet state is described in Ōhara Manpei, "Nitchū fukkō ni okeru Ishibashi-san no yume," *JS*, no. 16 (Aug. 1980): 35–45.

ment that the empire was not worth its cost would have served him better when the forces of Chinese revolution arrived in Manchuria.[82]

Barring reckless Japanese intervention, Ishibashi argued, China proper could become a fertile field for Japanese and Western investment, negotiated through the Chinese government in good faith and without coercion. China needed to reduce commodity and consumer imports, raise agricultural production and develop transportation such as railroads. Demand would increase, and Japan alone would not be able to meet China's need for foreign capital; therefore it was counterproductive to antagonize the West by a unilateral policy of hegemony. Ishibashi acknowledged that international trade and investment benefited the developed countries more than the undeveloped (and he differed from ideologues of the co-prosperity sphere and the Axis in firmly insisting that Japan was in the camp of the "haves" rather than the "have-nots"). Nevertheless, he was convinced that China could benefit from the international economy, and mitigate its negative effects, if firmly united under an effective central government.[83]

By the summer of 1935 Ishibashi had shifted emphasis from Chinese ineptitude to Japanese terrorism and folly. A sound China policy was unattainable under the constant threat of independent army action. China's resilient culture and social solidarity made the continent a peculiarly inappropriate arena for rash military action. Referring to a precedent most readers would remember, the revolution of 1911, Ishibashi cautioned: "In the ebb and flow of Chinese history, too much emphasis has been placed on force and violence, as it was by the Manchu dynasty. A famous Chinese proverb says, 'Good swimmers drown.' "[84] He insisted on conciliatory diplomacy even after the outbreak of war. While Prime Minister Konoe and Foreign Minister Hirota quickly exploited the hostilities to demand a fundamental solution to Sino-Japanese tensions, Ishibashi urged the government to "avoid posing problems in exces-

82. Dower, 97, 209–22; *ITZ* 10:466–67.
83. *ITZ* 9:91–92, 523–24; 10:477–80.
84. *ITZ* 9:87

sively fundamental terms, which merely invites stalemate" and "not ask the politically impossible of Peking."[85]

Although Ishibashi had once professed to scorn idealistic pacifism, his arguments during the first six months of the China War were as much a plea for decency as a case for the national interest in peace. He portrayed the Western historical record in the Far East, beginning with the efforts of American consul Townsend Harris to win Japanese trust during the expulsion movement of the 1850s, as relatively benign compared with Japanese adventurism. Whereas America and Europe had sent honorable persons to teach in Japan, Japan had sent its dregs to China; Chinese graduates of Japanese schools were ashamed to admit the fact, and Chinese students in Japan were exploited in lodging and universities. Pan-Asianists glorified a cultural affinity that entitled Japan to lead Asia, but Ishibashi retorted that any such affinity had been destroyed by the Twenty-One Demands of 1915. His reflection on Japan's transgressions weighed more heavily than his fear of damage to his country; he had little fear of Chinese resistance, though he admitted the possibility of something like the Spanish Civil War.[86] In January 1938 Prime Minister Konoe's stated intention of overthrowing Chiang Kai-shek triggered a sharp rise in Ishibashi's concern. Konoe's advisers in the Shōwa Research Association, especially the leftists among them, acknowledged Chinese nationalism as an inevitable uprising against Western semicolonial exploitation, but they dismissed anti-Japanese nationalism as mere political manipulation. In their analysis the sinister machinations of Chiang, the Shanghai capitalists, and the British were steadily drawing China into the Western capitalist bloc, and thwarting the achievement of authentic national unification and development. Suffering China could be freed from its travails only by the deus ex machina of Japanese management, smashing Western imperialism and its Chinese puppets by military force.[87]

85. *ITZ* 10:115; Crowley, *Japan's Quest for Autonomy and Security*, 340.
86. *ITZ* 10:465–73; 11:520–22.
87. James B. Crowley, "Intellectuals as Visionaries of the New Asian Order," in James W. Morley, ed., *Dilemmas of Growth in Prewar Japan*; and Fletcher, 106–16.

Many leftists were beguiled by the internationalist and anticapitalist themes in wartime ideology. For example, Asian scholar Takeuchi Yoshimi recalled that his youthful Comintern bias blinded him to the volcanic force of Chinese nationalism. Until the postwar era he had not read Ishibashi's writings. Until he read Ishibashi's wartime writings, he had not believed that any Japanese, particularly a bourgeois liberal, could understand Chinese nationalism. Takeuchi praised Ishibashi for his wartime disdain for the Coprosperity Sphere and his sympathy with Chinese nation-building. The foundation of Ishibashi's progressive views, Takeuchi concluded, was Ishibashi's own benign nationalism. Takeuchi correctly identified the antinational overtones of intellectual support for war, and he distinguished them from Ishibashi's vision of a plurality of autonomous nations and national cultures existing in cooperative interdependence.[88]

Ishibashi accused Konoe of increasing the danger of foreign aid to China from the League of Nations, the Nine-Power Treaty Conference and the Soviet Union. Fear of confrontation with the West was the wellspring of journalistic criticism of the China War during 1939, but the general-interest journals also published essays by Chou En-lai, Mao Tse-tung, and Chiang Kai-shek. Ishibashi too began to stress the vigor and autonomy of Chinese resistance. In January 1941 he wrote that "the formation of Wang Ching-wei's [collaborationist] government has not ended opposition to Japan. British and American aid to Chungking is much smaller than Japan's expenditures, and not the reason for Chinese resistance."[89] Thereafter, his attention was absorbed primarily by Japan's rapidly deteriorating relationship with Britain and the United States.

The Western inspirations of Ishibashi's thinking are obvious: Tanaka's American instrumentalism, the Open Door and Wilsonian diplomacy, and Keynesian economics. The most significant lessons that he drew from his own history

88. Takeuchi Yoshimi, "Waga Ishibashi hakken," in Chō, ed., *Ishibashi Tanzan*, 28–31.

89. *ITZ* 12:3–8; see also Matsuo Takayoshi, "Miura Tetsutarō cho 'Shina jihen shori no hōshin' ni tsuite," *Ishibashi Tanzan zenshū geppō*, no. 15 (Sept. 1972): 13–16.

were the beneficial effect of cultural borrowing and the baneful pressures of foreign coercion on Japan in the mid-nineteenth century. His interpretation of modern Japanese history sensitized him to the futility of intervention in the Russian and Chinese revolutions and armed him with a commitment to racial, cultural, and national pluralism rare in the contemporary West (or in Japan). But, like Tanaka and Shimamura, he distinguished Western liberal and humanitarian ideals from Western realities, and condemned Western racism and imperialism. He reserved the right to judge American thought and action in terms of its intrinsic validity for Americans and for the world. Committed to Anglo-American ideals, which he had made his own, Ishibashi grew increasingly critical of American foreign and economic policy. He was internationalist but not pro-American.

In 1936 he had denounced the hypocrisy of the United States in constructing international policies—the Open Door and the League of Nations—which it subsequently refused to support. The Open Door applied only to China, and not to the American or European empires. Rebutting remarks by Senate Foreign Relations Committee chairman Key Pittman that Japanese expansion narrowed American markets, he retorted that Japan's territory and population were much smaller than those of the American and British empires, which contracted Japanese markets and furthermore had been "snatched from other races, and not long ago."[90] Still, Ishibashi disdained to carry the argument one step further and justify Japanese aggression. Rather, he renounced Pittman's zero-sum view of world trade, in which one country's gains were another's loss; the expansion of the world economy would benefit both Japan and the United States.

Support for global free trade from President Roosevelt and Secretary of State Cordell Hull delighted Ishibashi, but he confessed to an "empty feeling" that the ideals would be asserted only on behalf of American self-interest: "It is certainly convenient for the United States, which has a huge territory and does not need more, to take the position that other parts of

90. *ITZ* 10:83–85.

the world should not fall under the control of other powers, leaving scope for the chaos of free economic competition."[91] The remark must have lifted the spirits of the bloc economy theorists, but Ishibashi went on to disappoint them, grappling with the political impossibility of global free trade in the contemporary international environment. As interim compromise measures he suggested that Japan unilaterally introduce free trade in its colonies, terminating preferential treatment for Japanese products, and that the United States reduce its sizable trade surplus with Japan by modifying restrictions on Japanese imports.

Ishibashi realized that war with China increased the chances of Japanese confrontation with the West, and he saw Japan's foreign policy drifting like its faction-ridden politics and its lopsided armaments economy: "Withdrawal from the League of Nations and the Naval Conference were momentous events, but not decided or resolute measures of our government and people. We were drawn by the various internal and external trends like sleepwalkers. The great powers, economically and politically weak, were unwilling to intervene in the Far East at that time."[92] The era of American isolation was drawing to a close as Japan continued military expansion. The signing of the Tripartite Pact with Germany and Italy in September 1940 was a crisis in Anglo-American aid to China and resistance against Japan. Ishibashi's warning against reliance on Germany, which had signed a nonaggression treaty with the Soviet Union, had been censored in its entirety a year earlier. Despite the increasing caution with which he now constructed editorials to appease the censors, his dismay was evident:

> Not one soul in the country doubts that we should take the Tripartite Pact as our standard; the question is how. The United States may choose to increase aid to Britain, or pressure our country diplomatically and economically. The alliance will limit American intervention and thus is a great victory for our country. Yet no one can know what happenstance, what great changes will occur. The first benefits will accrue to Germany and Italy in Europe. England and the United States will fail to grasp Japan's

91. *ITZ* 10:94; see also 11:77, 221–30; Matsuo, "Miura Tetsutarō," 16.
92. *ITZ* 11:52–56.

peaceful intentions. If the new structure is realized we can succeed. The economic problem is not so easy.[93]

Since Ishibashi had previously condemned the new structure, his doubts were profound. The Tripartite Pact merely increased Japan's problems by linking it with the number one Anglo-American enemy. Germany could not invade America, but if Germany fell, Japan would be invaded. Ishibashi's opposition to the pact was shared by textile manufacturers and other business leaders who aimed at Western markets. They were supported by Rikkyō University economics professor Itabashi Kikumatsu in *Shintaku to shōken* (Trusts and securities), whereas army officer Mitsui Sakichi attacked business for sympathy toward England. Opposition, however, was overwhelmed by Japanese invasion of French Indochina and the American resistance.[94]

Ishibashi abandoned his pleas for Japanese-American conciliation after the Hull note of November 26, 1941. The Hull note was highly provocative in demanding that Japan withdraw its forces not only from Indochina but also from China (in which the United States of course included Manchuria), and return to the status quo ante of 1931. The note was not amenable even to discussion in the current Japanese political climate. Ishibashi published a translation and resignedly echoed the official policy that "Japan should prepare for both war and peace." Although some historians hold that the Hull note had little influence on the Pearl Harbor attack, planned weeks before, the despair of so inveterate a compromiser as Ishibashi suggests that, at the very least, the Hull note was important in uniting Japanese public opinion around an image of American intransigence.[95]

CONCLUSION

The financial crisis of 1929–31 deepened Ishibashi's relationships with business leaders and economic specialists in the gov-

93. *ITZ* 11:157–59.
94. The covert opposition of some textile manufacturers is recorded in "Takeiei wa naritatanai," 53, and of other business spokesmen in Matsuo, "Miura Tetsutarō," 16.
95. *ITZ* 12:72–74.

ernment, bringing him into formal advisory positions rather
than detached opinion leadership. *Shinpō* also thrived on economic uncertainty and grew in size and influence. The depression engendered crises of authority and legitimation, requiring
new visions as well as technical expertise. Ishibashi's reputation
was enhanced by his accurate prediction that recovery could
be stimulated if the gold standard were abandoned and government spending increased. The success of Takahashi finance buoyed his confidence in the steady growth of Japanese
industry and exports. Growth, he believed, could support the
reform of rural education, health care, and means of livelihood. The new contours of social unrest turned his emphasis
from popular movements to social engineering. In other ways
too he drew closer to segments of the bureaucracy, defending
the constitutionalist Minobe Tatsukichi and urging the authority of the Foreign Ministry over the army. Acquiescence
in the Japanese presence in Manchuria may have been the
price Ishibashi paid for continuing influence.

Fundamental intellectual commonalities underlay Ishibashi's
cooperation with disparate political and business leaders. He
defined the problems facing the nation in tandem with leaders
of domestic renovation and foreign expansion such as the
Shōwa Research Association. It was his solutions that differed.
He conceded that the political parties were corrupt and self-
serving but demanded more reliance on parliamentary processes, rather than less. He charged Japanese capitalism with
spawning massive social inequity but identified militarism and
its coddling of heavy industry as the culprit; he defended a
reformist capitalism and denied the army's pretensions as the
vanguard of spiritual and moral purification. He was dis-
turbed by civil war and violent anti-Japanese outbursts in
China but blamed Japanese adventurism rather than Chinese
perversity or Western and Soviet manipulation. He denounced
the hypocrisy of Great Britain and the United States as those
countries proclaimed free trade while practicing protectionism, decried Japanese expansion while retaining their own empires, and discriminated against the Japanese race. Still, he
urged that Japan should take the lead in offering concessions
toward free international trade since that system so well served

Japan's interests. He shifted, during the 1930's, from applauding the Russian Revolution to identifying it with German and Italian "absolutism," but scoffed at anticommunist and anti-Semitic crusaders. His treatment of the critical issues from a pragmatic rather than moral perspective appealed to establishment circles as the radical right swelled with the winds of spiritual passion.

Within the parameters of enhanced relations with the established centers of power, Ishibashi was able to preserve something of the spirit of Taishō liberalism. Especially before 1936 he continued to remind his readers of the value of individual freedom and initiative, and the pluralistic vitality of Taishō culture. He also preserved the tradition of journalistic independence. Feminism, perhaps the weakest of Taishō reform movements, vanished from his writings during this era, but he worked with Ichikawa Fusae on economic education for housewives at the Japan Economic Club, and he had determined to found a women's economic journal (*Fujin keizai zasshi*) in July 1941. Finally, his unshakable commitment to parliamentary politics and party cabinets throughout the war was one of the most remarkable legacies of the Taishō era.[96]

Ishibashi's solidarity with established institutions was shattered by the February 26 Incident of 1936 and the outbreak of the China War in 1937, for he had failed to grasp the magnitude of the threat posed by military self-aggrandizement and civil fragmentation. Between the escalation of the China War in 1938 and the signing of the Tripartite Pact in 1939, he realized that his political influence was minimal, that governmental control over both expression and the economy was increasing, that global war was very likely, and that there were no hopeful omens for the reformist designs that he had pursued over the last three decades. If any alternative course of action crossed his mind at this time, he did not confide it to his closest friends. In his postwar memoirs he would write that *Shinpō* should have ceased publication after the Manchurian Incident, since any public role short of martyrdom inevitably lent support, however grudgingly given, to the war effort. The

96. *ITZ* 15:388.

question of whether he might have done more, or less, was very much on his mind at his son's memorial service when he declared, "I am a liberal but not a traitor."[97]

Ienaga Saburō and Hashikawa Bunsō have classified Ishibashi as an active, legal resister.[98] There was no organized, active illegal resistance. Nor did Japanese intellectuals alienate themselves from their people, language, and culture in exile, apart from a few such as Nosaka Sanzō who joined the Chinese Communists. The other choices were prison, and perhaps death, or passive resistance exemplified by a few writers who chose "absolute silence" and lived by manual labor. The exile, martyrdom, or silence of a handful of celebrated intellectuals is remembered in Japan as a significant expression of uncompromising ideals, a powerful cultural symbol. Yet Ishibashi showed a different kind of courage by upholding his long-standing belief in compromise, gradualism, and persuasion amid moral ambiguity and personal danger.

By maintaining his public forum through compromise, he helped to sustain a subdued and outnumbered constituency for parliamentary politics, minimal government economic control, and amicable relations with the West, positions he shared with sectors of business, the parties, and the bureaucracy. The political parties and Japanese capitalism survived, but foreign policy foundered over the dual demands for Asian empire and Anglo-American conciliation. Ishibashi was one of the few who, as early as 1936, grasped the contradictory nature of these ends, and opted for the more beneficial relationship with the West.

97. *ITZ* 13:228.
98. Saburō Ienaga, *The Pacific War, 1931–1945*, 19; Bunsō Hashikawa, "The 'Civil Society' Ideal and Wartime Resistance," in Koschmann, ed., *Authority and the Individual in Japan*, 131.

8

History as Postwar Politics:
Ishibashi, the Allied Occupation,
and the Liberal Democratic Party

During the Pacific War era most Japanese intellectuals and
politicians ignored or even attacked the Taishō democratic
movement. They vilified its leading ideas such as liberalism as
alien and outdated, and smeared its leading interest groups
such as political parties and unions with charges of divisive
self-interest. Under the Allied Occupation, however, the problem of democracy once again moved to center stage. Ishibashi
argued that Taishō Japan had already assimilated the rudi-
ments of democratic institutions, ideas, and behavior. He supported Occupation political reforms but questioned the
radicalism of Occupation social and economic engineering.

The Occupation responded with bafflement, then suspicion,
and finally rancor, for its dominant faction held a different
view of modern Japanese history, a liberal interpretation of
fascism in which class polarization and renitent feudal ideology
had engendered Japanese militarism. Occupation reforms
were designed to redress the balance of Japan's politics by
transforming its social structure. Ishibashi's criticisms of the
Occupation and his financial policy became linked to questions
of class interest and thus to the sources of Japanese militarism.
Once again, as in the Taishō era, history became the subject
of acute political competition, but this time Ishibashi spoke
from the center of power as finance minister rather than from
his editorial office, and his interpretations of Japanese society,
culture and history were enmeshed in the complex realities of
actual economic policy in a devastated land.

In Ishibashi's view, prewar Japan had been authoritarian but not fascist, and had been moving gradually toward parliamentary democracy until deflected by the strains wrought by global economic nationalism and domestic rural poverty on a fragile political system. Hence, he downplayed class polarization and other aspects of the social system as causes of Japanese militarism, clinging to his Taishō thesis of a more fundamental polarization between the bureaucracy and the people. A more glaring deficiency that he saw in SCAP (Supreme Command of the Allied Powers) historiography was the distance that it placed between Japan and the United States. American democracy was marred by racial and class divisions at home and economic nationalism abroad. Hence Ishibashi locked horns with those SCAP officials who held dual assumptions about exceptional American righteousness and exceptional Japanese iniquity. During the course of the Occupation, in fact, his praise of American ideals was largely displaced by anger toward American arrogance. The Government Section of the Occupation disappointed him not only by belittling his cause, the Taishō democratic movement, but also by assaulting his political integrity and purging him from public office. There were still greater issues behind his change of heart, for he was witnessing a transformed global context in which the United States emerged as a Cold War superpower. In this context he formulated his goals for postwar Japan. Parliamentary politics was first, as it had been for decades. Now, however, national economic recovery and independence were a close second. SCAP economic policy was deemed detrimental to the second goal.

National survival and recovery preempted Ishibashi's attention as minister of finance, displacing the broader vision he had been able to express as an essayist. He would make some extraordinary compromises with the conservative party leadership and stress economic growth as a panacea for Japan's postwar ills. Acutely aware of the role that rural poverty had played in supporting rightist ideology during the thirties, he believed that only expanded national wealth would dissolve the collectivism that had made the village vulnerable to authoritarian manipulation from the centers of power. Yet his shifts of emphasis were within the framework of his prewar discourse, which had stressed pragmatic gradualism above all. He did not wait a day after Japan's surrender to reiterate his Taishō reform program. He edited the republication of Tanaka's study of Ninomiya Sontoku in 1948 with a eulogy to Tanaka's "support and perfection of Japanism in its true meaning."[1] All in all his principles and approach were remarkably consistent.

FROM JOURNALISM TO POLITICS

It was as a journalist that Ishibashi first responded to Japan's defeat and occupation, for he did not decide to participate in politics until 1946. During that time his editorials revealed an ambivalence toward authority that would distinguish his relationships with the Occupation and with mainstream politicians during his terms as finance minister in 1946–47, minister of international trade and industry in 1954–56, and prime minister in 1956. In Yokote in Akita Prefecture, where *Shinpō* printed its last wartime issues, Japan's surrender brought panic. Local officials lacked the most basic plans but fanned hysteria by urging household heads to bury their valuables and to send their wives and children to the countryside. Rumor was rife: The Americans planned to turn Japan into an agricultural country; Occupation troops would consume all the housing and food; they would include Chinese thirsting for revenge and unshackled by any restraint; they would overturn village government councils. To dispel panic Ishibashi addressed *Shinpō* employees on the day of the surrender, lectured in Yokote City Hall the following day, and published articles in Akita prefectural papers and in *Shinpō*. He spread reassurance about the equitable intentions of the Allies and the bright hopes for Japan's future. He praised Occupation planning to the point of factual error, stating that the suggestions of turning Japan into an agricultural country were nothing more than the Japanese government's wartime propaganda. The Atlantic

1. Ishibashi Tanzan, preface to Tanaka Ōdō, *Hyuumanisuto Ninomiya Sontoku*, Ōdō senshū, vol. 3; on the role of rural poverty in spawning militarism see *ITZ* 8:517–19; 13:408.

Charter and the Potsdam Declaration, he insisted, promised policies for the benefit of the Japanese people.[2]

Ishibashi's potential utility to the Occupation impressed the first head of the Economic and Scientific Section (ESS), Colonel R. C. Kramer. A businessman who had long admired the *Oriental Economist* for its internationalism and objectivity, Kramer met with Ishibashi on September 30 to request cooperation, and the following day ordered the Japanese government to assist the journal in resuming publication in Tokyo.[3] Even before Kramer left his post in December, however, Ishibashi's relations with SCAP had begun to deteriorate. His editorials on compliance and reconstruction continued regularly from August 15 to November 29, when he castigated instances of American crimes in Japan and Soviet looting, arson, murder, and abuse of Japanese prisoners in Manchuria. This editorial was partially deleted by Occupation censors. Even so, he had conceded that the violence was unexpected, that the Allies came not in war but in peace, and that atrocities were not the policy of the high command. His stated intentions in criticizing the Allies were to inform his readers and to discourage new atrocities.[4]

Current events were not the only subject of Occupation censorship, which extended to theoretical and historical works including such favorites of Ishibashi as Fukuzawa Yukichi's *Autobiography* and Karl Bebel's *Women under Socialism*.[5] Ishibashi began to complain privately to John T. Simonelli and C. Abernethy of the Economic Research Division. He did not mention Occupation censorship in his published editorials.[6]

2. *ITZ* 13:8–10, 24–28, 37–41. On Japanese interpretation of the Potsdam Declaration see Ray Moore, "Reflections on the Occupation of Japan," *JAS* 38 (1979): 725–29, 733. Marlene Mayo discusses American proposals to convert Japan to an agricultural country in "American Economic Planning for Occupied Japan: The Issue of *Zaibatsu* Dissolution, 1942–45," in Lawrence H. Redford. ed., *The Occupation of Japan: Economic Policy and Reform*, 208, 216.

3. Memorandum to the Central Liaison Office, Tokyo, 1 Oct. 1945, Ishibashi Tanzan file, Box no. 2275e, Government Section, SCAP Collection, National Archives; *ITZ* 13:224–25.

4. *ITZ* 13:42–43, 591.

5. Hatanaka, 143–47. See also William J. Coughlin, *Conquered Press: The MacArthur Era in Japanese Journalism*, 46–58.

6. Ishibashi Tanzan, *Tanzan nikki*, 134, 252. The diary lists titles of editorials that were never published due to Occupation censorship or editorial discretion.

He had been more aggressive in pressuring the Japanese government to abolish wartime controls over opinion, complaining on August 28 that Prince Higashikuni's promise to return to prewar freedoms did not go nearly far enough.[7] He took full advantage of burgeoning political controversy, consulting with Communists who had returned from jail and exile, and denouncing the retention of former special higher police officials in governmental office.[8] Thus his criticisms of Occupation censorship were only one aspect of a broad exploration of political pluralism, though they have received considerable attention since few Japanese went public with their grievances.

Ishibashi assessed Japan's misdoings far more critically than America's. He warned his readers that Americans felt intense antagonism toward Japan because of war atrocities, which were the responsibility of all the Japanese people. But first of all he repudiated Japan's prewar leadership, particularly the political parties, which had begun by trying to use the military as a pawn in their own power struggles, and ended by cravenly serving it. Ishibashi blamed the parties more than the Meiji Constitution, which, he admitted, placed the parties in an intrinsically weak position; nonetheless, the parties had come close to commanding the military and bureaucracy during the 1920s in spite of constitutional barriers. On the grounds that a legal and political basis for civilian control had existed, Ishibashi repudiated an unusually broad spectrum of prewar political leaders, including men widely identified as liberals. He wrote a public letter to Prince Konoe Fumimaro demanding that Konoe answer to the Japanese people for the China Incident and the Axis Alliance. By assigning particular responsibility to civilians, especially Konoe, Ishibashi distanced himself from conservatives such as Yoshida Shigeru who sought to pinpoint blame on the military. Secondarily he charged that all Japanese in positions of influence, and last of all the whole people, shared in responsibility for the war. Only after prolonged and pointed criticism of Japanese behavior did Ishibashi conclude that historians would probably regard

7. Ishibashi, "Enter Prince Higashikuni's Cabinet," *OE* 12 (1945): 234.
8. *ITZ* 13:153.

economic nationalism, in which the Allies had participated, as
the most fundamental cause of the war.[9]

Ishibashi also renounced the emperor cult as it was expressed in certain rituals and in daily life. In an unusually
strident editorial he demanded the abolition of Yasukuni
Shrine, which honored the war dead. The shrine linked family
bonds and religious feeling to the military; its name meant
peace but its reality meant war. The issue was an important
one, for in the following decades ministers of the ruling Liberal Democratic party (Jiyū Minshutō, LDP) visited Yasukuni
first as individuals and then in their official capacity with increasing frequency. In judging that this national symbol could
not be salvaged, Ishibashi departed from the mainstream leadership. He also urged that the Western system of dating, not
the imperial reign-year, be used in the calendar.[10]

In the Occupation as in the Taishō era the meaning and
validity of national symbols were once again contested, and
Ishibashi seized every possible occasion to manipulate the past
in accord with his own vision of democracy. Civil liberties had
precedents in the demands of the Popular Rights movement,
and even earlier in ancient freedom to lampoon the imperial
household, from the *Kojiki* and *Nihon shoki* to Rai Sanyō.[11] The
Meiji Charter Oath, a staple of Taishō liberal discourse, was
resurrected by Prince Higashikuni and even by the emperor
in his surrender speech.[12] The orientation toward indigenous
precedents was particularly evident in Ishibashi's analysis, published in March 1946, of the new Constitution. He was certainly aware of SCAP control over its content, for he had met
often with his old friend Uehara Etsujirō, who served on the
drafting committee. He praised the Constitution for "using
Japanese tradition in a healthy and fruitful way" although it
was far more radical than expected.[13] The framers might have
gone even further, for the monarchy was neither "rational nor

9. *ITZ* 13:44–45, 56–57; 14:11; 15:109–10, 236. On Konoe and Yoshida see
Dower, 294–303.
10. *ITZ* 13:54–56, 161–62.
11. Ishibashi, "The Higashikuni Cabinet Resigns," *OE* 12 (1945): 276–79.
12. Ishibashi, "Enter Prince Higashikuni's Cabinet," 238; 13:14–15, 31–33.
13. *ITZ* 13:84–87.

necessary" in contemporary society.[14] Nonetheless, the imperial house had played a great role in legitimizing change in
the Restoration and might serve as a "symbol of impartiality"
under democracy.[15] In Ishibashi's view preservation of the
monarchy was the right of the culturally distinctive Japanese
people and could play a utilitarian role in sanctioning rationally conceived policies.

Assertions of indigenous precedents for Occupation reforms were double-edged. At times Ishibashi and other intellectuals displayed emotional and conceptual discomfort with
the degree of change brought by the Occupation, but they also
grappled to attach historical legitimacy and national consciousness to the new institutions. Whereas conservatives eulogized
the prewar state and society, and SCAP saw little merit in any
aspect of Japanese history, Ishibashi selected elements of
change and flexibility, and looked to popular movements, to
support a positive evaluation of the national past. From this
perspective Ishibashi eulogized what liberal precedents he
could find, rejected Yasukuni Shrine as hopelessly enmired in
the authoritarian and militaristic past, and pronounced the imperial institution to be politically neutral.[16]

Ishibashi's trenchantly independent journalism was important to the whole process by which national politics were recast
and national symbols were reinterpreted, under the Occupation. His truly liberal and distinctive positions were his enthusiasm for civil liberties, his willingness to work with the left,
including Communists, his broad indictment of prewar leadership, and his rejection of symbols such as Yasukuni Shrine.
These positions placed him closer to the left than to prewar
officials such as Yoshida and Hatoyama Ichirō. However, his
differences with prewar political leaders, even their "liberal"
wing, were offset by commonalities that enabled old and new
leaders to coalesce at the centers of power.

Despite his intellectual independence Ishibashi was drawing
closer to the political mainstream. He garnered political sup-

14. Ibid.
15. Ibid.
16. Yoshida's use of Japanese precedent was quite different; see Dower, 320–29.

port by preserving a critical stance toward SCAP. He believed
that criticism was part and parcel of the democratic intentions
of SCAP, that SCAP officers often underestimated the complexity of reforms that they proposed (especially in economics), and that certain SCAP reforms such as the renunciation
of war in the Constitution were "extremist and unrealistic," and
unparalleled in any country in the world.[17] These dissatisfac-
tions formed a common ground between Ishibashi and those
whose unease with the Occupation was more firmly rooted in
attachment to the old order.

Finally, Ishibashi was actually growing more conservative. In several instances he retreated from his Taishō positions, notably in labeling women's suffrage "premature."[18] The
change is perplexing. He was older; he was disillusioned with
the results of popular activism in both the twenties and the
thirties; he was near desperation about the state of the Japanese economy; and he was, by the spring of 1946, seeking
election as a member of the conservative Liberal party (Jiyūtō).
His eclectic and empirical tendencies emerged more strongly
than ever, creating a crazy quilt of policy recommendations
from right to left, and obfuscating his placement in the political spectrum.[19] He gained his support from single-issue alliances across the political spectrum, from the moderate left on
civil liberties and power-sharing, and from conservatives and
businessmen who recalled his acute analyses of the gold embargo, Takahashi finance, and wartime controls.

Ishibashi's entry into politics was also contingent on a politically mobile Hatoyama faction operating in a structure of
power inherited from the Pacific War era. The wartime established parties had begun to seek Ishibashi's counsel as soon
as defeat was certain. In March 1945 he had met with a Diet
group that aimed at reorganizing wartime representatives into
new postwar political parties, the Shin Seiji Kessha Junbi Sewa
Iinkai (later the Dai Nippon Seiji Kai). The personnel and internal relationships of the group perpetuated the structure
that the political parties had assumed under the Imperial Rule

17. *ITZ* 13:87.
18. *ITZ* 13:61–62.
19. See, for example, *ITZ* 13:176–77.

Assistance Association. The Dai Nippon Seiji Kai, largest element in the Diet at the end of the war, held 349 seats and was
composed of a majority of old Seiyūkai and Minseitō members; it was loyal to the government and the army. Hatoyama
and his followers (the wartime Dōkōkai, including Saitō Takao)
were a renegade faction, distinguished by antibureaucratic attitudes and passive resistance rather than opposition to military mobilization; they were virtually powerless. The first
problem of the Liberal party was to avoid the taint of col-
laboration.[20]

Hatoyama hoped to recruit prewar socialists as well as new
faces drawn from local politics, the bureaucracy, academia,
and journalism. Shimanaka Yūsaku of *Fujin kōron* and *Chūō
kōron* was enlisted as an adviser, along with Minobe Tatsukichi.
By November 9 Ishibashi had become a consultant to the Liberals. The new party included forty-three Diet members at its
founding, with great gains expected in the upcoming election.
Thirty of the forty-three were subsequently purged, but the
leadership, except for Hatoyama, was untouched, and the
party held 143 seats after the election. Meanwhile, Yoshida
Shigeru replaced the purged Hatoyama as president of the
Liberals. A significant emerging power bloc in search of a
fresh image made Ishibashi the finance minister in the first
Yoshida cabinet in May 1946.[21] The relationship between Yoshida and Ishibashi was strained, for Yoshida was a former
Foreign Ministry bureaucrat who opposed repeal of the Peace
Preservation Law and legalization of the Communist party, rejected coalition with right-wing socialists, despised liberal men
of culture, and envisioned a polity in which "the strong state
would take precedence over the autonomous and liberated individual."[22] It was rumored that Yoshida did not want Ishibashi
in his cabinet but was pressured by industrial and financial
circles.

Organizational continuity was even more pronounced in
economics than in politics. Ishibashi's governmental consul-

20. *ITZ* 15:391, 393, Itō Takashi, *Shōwaki no seiji*, 219–21.
21. Itō, *Shōwaki no seiji*, 231–32, 268.
22. Dower, 370; also Shimura, 227; Ishibashi Tan'ichi interview, 26 Dec. 1983; *ITZ* 15:395.

tancies, which had revived during the last months of the war, expanded after Japan's surrender. He was appointed to the Finance Ministry's Committee on Postwar Currency Policy (Sengo Tsūka Taisaku Iinkai) in August, and its Investigative Committee on the Financial System (Kin'yū Seido Chōsakai) in December, to the Ministry of Commerce and Industry's advisory roster in November, to the Cabinet Committee on Economic Reconstruction (Chūō Keizai Saiken Iinkai) in February 1946, and to the Finance and Foreign Ministries' Committee for Conservators of Closed Institutions (Heisa Kikan Hoei Iinkai) as well as the Central Liaison Office's advisory roster in April. Economic policymakers continued their prewar and ·wartime associations while tapping nongovernmental expertise on domestic and foreign, especially Allied, economic systems and affairs. New policy input from private business and the media was essential in order to cope with new conditions and to replace those officials who were purged. In addition to his public record in *Shinpō*, Ishibashi had close ties with leading businessmen from the Japan Economic Club and his lecture tours. The confidence of the financial world was crucial to his rise to prominence.[23]

By his own account Ishibashi had no desire to enter politics before 1946, although his friends Matsuoka Komakichi (Socialist) and Uehara Etsujirō (Liberal) had urged him to join them in party activity immediately after Japan's surrender. However, he gradually determined that his experience in the debate over the gold embargo was relevant to reconstruction, and that the Taishō democratic movement had proven the limits of liberal journalism. The death of his son in battle had shattered his optimism about the power of public opinion to change state policy.[24] Once he had determined to enter politics he still hesitated over the choice of a party affiliation. He particularly lacked personal connections among the Liberals though their president, Hatoyama, was an old acquaintance. The Liberals, however, evidenced a diversity of opinion that

23. *TN*, 68–69, 73–74, 77, 80; *ITZ* 15:393–95.
24. *ITZ* 13:175–79; 14:496–97; Ishibashi, "Zōshō jidai o furikaette (1)," *JS* 18 (Feb. 1981): 26–27; interviews with Tani Kazushi, 19 Dec. 1983, and Ishibashi Tan'ichi, 26 Dec. 1983.

he found conspicuously lacking among the Socialists (Sha-kaitō). He was also detached from the Progressive party (Shin-potō), which was coalescing under *Shinpō* founder Machida Chūji, which "advocated a strange form of controlled economy, and was considered far right by the Communists, but at least had freedom of thought."[25] The ideologically anemic Liberals afforded minimum pressure toward conformity and maximum opportunity to inject his firmly defined opinions into public policy.

Ishibashi's initial electoral support was outside the mainstream of the old established parties. Speakers in his first election campaign of April 1946, in the second district of Tokyo, included Tokyo University professor of religion Anezaki Masaharu, veteran of the prewar democracy movement; journalist Hani Motoko of the women's magazine *Fujin no tomo*; Yamada Saburō, a scholar of international law at Tokyo University; and Ozaki Yukio—all distinguished for their progressive views. Ishibashi even spoke at a meeting in support of Communist Nosaka Sanzō's united popular front. He lost the election. His second campaign, after he had served a year as finance minister, was waged in the second distrt of Shizuoka, a center of strong Nichiren belief where his father had served as abbot. Ishibashi won a resounding victory against a nationwide Socialist tide just before his purge in May 1947.[26]

FROM POLITICS TO PURGE: MINISTER OF FINANCE

Immediate postwar economic policy confronted massive destruction and critical shortages of all the basic elements of livelihood. The loss in national wealth has been estimated at one-quarter of the total, comparable to that of the Soviet Union but far greater than that of Western Europe. Capital stock and national income were at the levels of the mid-1930s, with a population grown by one-quarter. The demobilization of soldiers, shutdown of military production, and repatriation of Japanese nationals from the empire brought the number of unemployed to 13.1 million. The first two postwar harvests

25. *ITZ* 15:198–99.
26. *ITZ* 15:51; 395; *TN*, 102, 111; Itō, *Shōwaki no seiji*, 263; Shimura, 226.

were at 60 percent of previous levels, because wartime necessity had both drained the best labor and machinery for military use and disrupted the supply of chemical fertilizer. Coal,
steel, electricity, housing, and food were insufficient. Shortages and governmental payment of wartime obligations
spawned dizzying inflation, with the index price level of 100
in August 1945 rising to 346.8 by September, and 1,184.5 by
the following March. The legalization of unions and the diffusion of democratic ideology encouraged labor strikes and
near insurrection. The difficulty of formulating a minimally
adequate economic policy was further complicated by the persistence of old jurisdictional squabbles, and the addition of an
entirely new element: the Allied Occupation.[27]

The postwar Japanese government inherited a vastly expanded repertoire of economic control mechanisms. In finance, planning had replaced the market in the allocation of
real resources and liquid capital, especially since the formation
of the Nationwide Financial Control Association in 1942. The
Ministry of Commerce and Industry (MCI) had gained a planning capability when the Cabinet Planning Board was merged
with it into the Ministry of Munitions, and had gained further
powers through its Enterprises Bureau. Postwar foreign trade
was organized by the Board of Trade on a government-to-
government basis after February 1947, and its authority passed
to the new Ministry of International Trade and Industry
(MITI) in 1949. Heavy industry and particularly financial institutions had also consolidated, simplifying bureaucratic management. Postwar crisis predisposed governmental and private
leaders to retain these powerful institutions.[28]

The Allies were sanguine about Japanese bureaucratic concentration and hostile to Japanese corporate power; Ishibashi
felt quite the opposite. Liquidation of the zaibatsu was a central plank in the SCAP program, for the family-owned con-

27. Milward, 322–23; Kozo Yamamura, *Economic Policy in Postwar Japan: Growth
Versus Economic Democracy*, 21; Takafusa Nakamura, *The Postwar Japanese Economy: Its
Development and Structure*, trans. Jacqueline Kaminski, 14, 21–22; Dower, 293; Chalmers Johnson, *MITI and the Japanese Miracle: The Growth of Industrial Policy, 1925–
1975*, 177–78.
28. Nakamura, *The Postwar Japanese Economy*, 18; Johnson, 319–20; Leon Hollerman, "International Economic Controls in Occupied Japan," *JAS* 38 (1979): 714–15.

glomerates were blamed for the undemocratic concentration of power and wealth that had, in the SCAP thesis, led to military expansion. From the autumn of 1945 through his tenure as finance minister, Ishibashi pleaded the utility of the zaibatsu in economic recovery. Their dissolution would decrease productive efficiency by encouraging competition among too many small enterprises, reducing national income, and making poverty universal. Dissolution would also disrupt capital markets and impede the recovery of foreign trade, in which the zaibatsu organized the exports of small firms.

The destruction of militarism would be worth any sacrifice, Ishibashi argued, but the combines were the result rather than the cause of state supremacy, and they were considerably smaller than American corporate empires. Thus Ishibashi contested the sine qua non of SCAP historiography, that Japanese society constituted a wholly different type from that of the United States. The two capitalist countries differed in emphasis and degree rather than in kind. The concentrated economic power of the zaibatsu was a social and political problem that ought to be postponed until the urgent issues of livelihood and recovery were resolved. Ishibashi's 1946 financial policy in fact favored heavy industry and mining, which were dominated by zaibatsu firms.[29]

Ishibashi is most famous, or notorious, for expansionary theories that were tarnished by the brutal inflationary realities of occupied Japan. As a journalist and as finance minister he urged deficit spending to break the bottlenecks of production. According to his analysis, inflation was a secondary problem; the primary problems were absolute shortages of goods and services, unused industrial capacity, and unemployed labor. The immediate postwar inflation was not true inflation attending an overheated economy at capacity production; rather, it was the inevitable result of collapsing confidence in the credit system, obligatory government payments to individuals and corporations, Occupation expenses, and the diminished

29. On the punitive character of Occupation economic policy in contrast to its beneficent political reform see Mayo, 221–22; on interpretations of Japanese history in the American government see Dower, 301, and Moore, 730–31; on the zaibatsu see *ITZ* 13:68–70; 15:195-98; *TN*, 63–64; on the actual effects of zaibatsu dissolution, Yamamura, *Economic Policy in Postwar Japan*, 34–35.

power of the state to commandeer savings and discourage
pent-up consumption. Even at a deficit the state ought to provide reconstruction capital for heavy industry, and ought to
manage consequent inflation via currency conversion and livelihood stipends to consumers. Ishibashi believed that the people would benefit from the revival of production more than
they would lose to inflation.[30]

By the spring of 1946, as finance minister, Ishibashi renounced deficits and advocated balancing the general account; the problem was how. He was still convinced that public
funds were needed to revive the production of essential commodities such as coal, food, fertilizer, steel, and cement until
full employment was achieved. He played a critical role in securing a cabinet commitment to these policies over Yoshida's
fear of inflation. In addition, he proposed to adjust tax ex-
emptions for inflation, rationalize scales, and improve collection. A more comprehensive national health insurance plan
was an urgent necessity under postwar hardships. Minimal dis-
cretionary spending for recovery and welfare broke the back
of a budget already overburdened with inescapable postwar
expenses.[31]

The 1946 budget was out of control, totaling ¥119 billion,
of which 40 percent was deficit financed. Ishibashi's supplement projected a deficit of ¥30 billion with new appropriations of 7.7 billion for the repatriation of Japanese nationals,
4.3 billion for production subsidies (primarily rice), 14.7 billion
for Occupation expenditures in Japan and 1.2 billion in Korea,
22.2 billion for unemployment compensation (bringing the
year's total to one-third of general revenue), and 3 billion for
welfare payments.

Ishibashi's major proposals for government savings were,
first, to postpone or reduce payment for Occupation expenses,
wartime guarantee obligations, and interest on the national
debt, and, second, to auction selected public properties, while
improving the return on the remainder. Each of these sug-

30. *ITZ* 13:369–70; 15:98; a similar explanation of postwar inflation is advanced
by Nakamura, *The Postwar Japanese Economy*, 22, 32.
31. *ITZ* 13:93–94, 134–43, 183; on criticisms of SCAP tax policy see Yamamura,
Economic Policy in Postwar Japan, 23–24. On Ishibashi's influence over Yoshida's economic policy see Ishibashi, "Zōshō jidai o furikaette (1), 27.

gestions had powerful enemies. Occupation construction consumed nearly all the cement and glass produced in 1946 as well as a good share of the Japanese budget. By the end of the year, first Ishibashi and then Yoshida implored General MacArthur to reduce costs, especially in construction, and they won guidelines for spending by American forces in 1947. Corporations and rentiers demanded wartime guarantee payments and interest on the national debt, although SCAP and the Socialists urged that these payments be canceled. Special accounts for national enterprises such as railroads continued massive deficits into 1947 while the general account moved closer to balance under Ishibashi's administration, projecting a reduced deficit of ¥11 billion for 1947.[32]

Inflation continued unchecked under the subsequent Katayama cabinet, with prices multiplied by one hundred over their prewar level, and wages by fifty-seven, in June of 1948.[33] Nevertheless in 1947 signs of recovery were evident, especially in coal production. Recovery was stimulated first by circumventing the Occupation's plans to nullify wartime guarantee payments; second, by the priority production system implemented through the Reconstruction Finance Bank and the Economic Stabilization Board; and third, by restrictions on labor.

Wartime guarantee payments were the first and most tortuous issue that Ishibashi faced in the Yoshida cabinet. The Japanese government owed money for wartime contracts, compensation for requisitioned shipping, guarantees on loans from banks to munitions companies, indemnities to companies against losses in relocation and enemy action, and other wartime insurance. The guarantees totaled some ¥95 billion, of which 53 billion was owed to munitions firms, 21 billion to zaibatsu firms, and 21 billion to other companies and individuals. At the war's end the Japanese government moved rapidly to pay these obligations, disbursing ¥26.6 billion in the first

32. *ITZ* 13:186–208; Ishibashi, "Zōshō jidai o furikaette (1)," 38; Endō Shōkichi, Katō Toshihiko, and Takahashi Makoto, *Nihon no Ōkura Daijin*, 231–33; on the issue of Occupation expenses see "Zōshō jidai o furikaette (1)," 30, 43, 45.

33. *ITZ* 13:134–43. On the consumer price index, which, with the black market included, was rising 40 percent per month in 1947, see Nakamura, *The Postwar Japanese Economy*, 33–35.

three months after the surrender, and budgeting about 20 percent of the 1946 general account for this purpose. The payments, however, were suspended by SCAP order in the spring
of 1946.[34]

There were two sides to the guarantee issue. The case
against the payments was the simpler of the two. The sums
required did not exist. Economist Ōuchi Hyōe of Tokyo University argued that the government could not raise more than
half the amount by special taxes, nor could it afford to incur
still more debts and pay the interest thereon. Even if the payments were fiscally possible, they would perpetuate inequali-
ties of wealth by means of windfalls for the military-industrial
complex. The case for continuing partial payment rested on
economic recovery and the legitimacy of the government. Ongoing firms could use the guarantee payments to liquidate
bonds, and companies in dissolution could return the sums to
stockholders. Either possibility would generate desperately
needed capital for conversion to peacetime production and
reconstruction. On the other hand default would bankrupt not
only munitions firms, which were scheduled for dismantling
in any case, but banks, insurance, and shipping companies,
which were essential to recovery. Without elaborate counter-
measures, default would mire surviving financial and real assets, organizations and workers in a quicksand of accounting,
legal, and tax problems that would take years to solve. Moreover, delay over the issue slowed the shift of demand from
military to industrial goods, whereas abrogation would violate
civil law and erode the remaining legitimacy of an already be-
labored government. Thus the need for compromise was perceived beyond the zaibatsu and munitions firms throughout
business, finance, and the Japanese government; and Colonel
R. C. Kramer, first head of ESS, lent support to this view
before his demobilization in December of 1945.[35]

It was unthinkable for the government to renege on its
debts, Ishibashi declared in December 1945. Instead, he supported a proposal of the Greater Japan Tax Association (Dai

34. Arisawa, 277–78; Johnson, 177–78, 184; Nakamura, *The Postwar Japanese
Economy*, 31; Watanabe Takeshi, *Senryōka no Nihon zaisei oboegaki*, 31–32.
    35. *ITZ* 13:94, 97, 141.

Nippon Zeimu Kyōkai) to pay the guarantees, institute a special property tax in order to siphon off windfall profits, and legislate procedures for the receiver-end management of bankrupt firms. He continued to defend this basic policy as finance minister despite the decision of ESS, announced by General William M. Marquat on May 31, that the government should recoup its wartime guarantee disbursements via a 100 percent tax. Throughout the ensuing four months of negotiations, the Japanese government struggled to modify the SCAP plan, to buy time to work out technical accounting and bankruptcy procedures, and to persuade ESS that a panel of American financial experts ought to be invited and consulted.[36]

Tensions rose over the wartime guarantee issue because SCAP was unwilling to execute its will by fiat. It attempted to strengthen the authority of the democratically elected Japanese government after April 1946 by avoiding formal intervention. It also circumvented the four-power Allied Council, formed the same month, which had the authority to refer SCAP directives to the eleven-member Far Eastern Commission for reevaluation. Marquat warned the Finance Ministry's liaison that since the involvement of the Allied Council might not be to Japan's advantage, the 100 percent tax plan must be presented to the Diet as an initiative of the Japanese government.[37]

The cabinet resisted, agreeing on a counterproposal by June 13. It resolved to terminate guarantee payments to munitions companies as demanded by the General Headquarters (GHQ); to insulate bank deposits below ¥10,000 from the resulting losses; to tax away half the other guarantee payments; to pay the balance in government bonds at 20 percent interest; and to raise requisite government revenues by inaugurating a property tax, securing a reduction in Occupation expenditures, and importing food on credit. Ishibashi drafted the government's position and presented it to Walter LeCount in

36. *ITZ* 13:107–09; *TN*, 123; Ishibashi, "Zōshō jidai o furikaette (1)," 31–32; "Removal from Office of Finance Minister Tanzan Ishibashi," 1 May 1947, Ishibashi Tanzan file, Box no. 2275e, Government Section, SCAP Collection, National Archives.

37. W. MacMahon Ball, *Japan: Enemy or Ally?*, 29; Ishibashi, "Zōshō jidai o furikaette (1)," 33; Watanabe Takeshi, 32.

Marquat's absence on June 17. The GHQ disapproved the plan on June 20. On June 26 Ishibashi rejected an ESS counterproposal that proposed a 71 percent tax on interest payments on the national debt and vetoed even partial payments to any corporation. Simultaneously he persuaded Yoshida to petition MacArthur for an economic mission of experts comparable to the recently arrived educational mission, since the expertise of leading ESS officials was widely questioned by Japanese financial, economic, and business leaders. The following day the Government Section, with input from ESS, prepared a memo resolving that SCAP would purge Ishibashi from public office if the Japanese government refused to do so. That decision would require eleven months in its implementation because of SCAP's recent resolve to avoid direct orders.[38]

Meanwhile, Ishibashi's intransigence stirred wholesale Japanese stonewalling on the guarantee payments issue. On July 10, Yoshida asked MacArthur for a formal order on behalf of ESS policies. Ishibashi, unwilling to implement ESS policies as the intent of the Japanese government, offered his resignation, but Yoshida refused it. On July 22 MacArthur replied that the 71 percent tax on interest on the national debt could be scrapped, but that otherwise the ESS counterproposal was to be implemented as the policy of the Japanese government. Ishibashi held out for a formal order until August 2, and Yoshida wrote yet another letter to MacArthur.[39] Meanwhile the Finance Ministry began drafting the relevant legislation in a sustained spirit of evasion, according to ESS. The ministry's purpose, in ESS eyes, was class interest: "It was another attempt to shift the burden of war losses from the industrial and financial owners to the Japanese people—by the simple expedient of maximizing government compensations."[40] The immediate effect of wartime guarantee payments was in fact to burden taxpayers in order to avoid corporate bankruptcies,

38. See n. 37 above; interview with Kiuchi Naotane, 31 Oct. 1983.
39. Watanabe Takeshi, 35–37; Ōkurashō Zaiseishishitsu, ed., *Tai-senryōgun kōshō hiroku: Watanabe Takeshi nikki*, 18–21.
40. "Removal from Office of Finance Minister Tanzan Ishibashi," 1 May 1947.

but ESS's single-minded insistence on class polarization made it oblivious to elements of economic and financial reason in the Japanese plan.

SCAP initiative on the wartime guarantee payments accomplished little. Legislation enabled bankrupt companies and financial institutions to dissolve and reform, and the wartime alignments of financiers and producers (*keiretsu*) resurrected themselves. Conflict between the Finance Ministry and SCAP continued under the ensuing Katayama and Ashida cabinets until a Government Section plan to remove the ministry's authority over budgeting and currency was vetoed by the U.S. National Security Council. Wartime and postwar financial policy could not easily be shifted in its course, because it encompassed a broad network of institutions and pressures.[41]

The abrogation of wartime guarantee payments led directly to a different system of providing capital for priority production under the Reconstruction Finance Bank (RFB), conceived by a planning committee formed on June 25 with Ishibashi as chairman, and the Economic Stabilization Board (ESB), which he chaired from January 28, 1947. The bank opened in January 1947 to reorganize financial organs and to provide capital for priority industries; it furnished three-quarters of all investment capital until its activities were suspended by the Dodge Plan in 1949. In founding the bank, the cabinet resolved on an expansionary fiscal policy at Ishibashi's urging.[42] While the bank was a Japanese government initiative, it operated under the comprehensive planning and coordination of the Economic Stabilization Board, which had been established in May under aggressive SCAP urging. Ishibashi disliked the ESB's charter of integrated planning and control in production, distribution, finance, prices, and transport. The ESB drew its personnel largely from the Ministry of Com-

41. Nakamura, *The Postwar Japanese Economy*, 17, 31–32, and idem, "SCAP to Nihon: Senryōki no keizai seisaku keisei," in Nakamura, ed., *Senryōki no keizai to seiji*, 13–14.

42. Ishibashi, "Zōshō jidai o furikaette (1)," 39; *TN*, 142, 163; Keizai Kikaku Chō, ed., *Gendai Nihon keizai tenkai: Keizai Kikaku Chō sanjūnen shi*, 28; Johnson, 179; Arisawa, 288; Dower, 342; Watanabe Takeshi, 33; Yamamura, *Economic Policy in Postwar Japan*, 27.

merce and Industry, with authorization and experience from
wartime economic controls.[43] Thus it practiced direct economic
management quite distinct from the cabinet's fiscal engineering. The distinction paralleled that between the expansionary
Takahashi finance of the early thirties on the one hand, and
the attempts at direct control during the late thirties on the
other.[44]

Ishibashi criticized the economic bureacrats, headed by
Hoshijima Nirō at MCI, for the slow revival of production,
and he believed that Yoshida felt the same.[45] On January 28,
1947, Yoshida appointed Ishibashi to succeed Zen Keinosuke
as chairman of the board when Zen resigned because Ishibashi
had objected to the sweeping character of proposed controls.
ESS sided firmly with the economic bureaucrats. MacArthur
wrote to Yoshida on March 22 demanding "the integrated series of economic and financial controls which the current situation demands."[46] ESS blamed Ishibashi for contriving "to
control the Japanese Economic Stabilization Board to prevent
that Board from becoming an effective organization."[47]

The affinities between SCAP New Dealers and MCI economic bureaucrats during the late forties suggest parallels between Japanese and American experience in the thirties and
the war. However, ESS, in tandem with the Japanese Communist party, yearned for price stability with an ardor unex-
celled by the staunchest of fiscal conservatives. ESS was
morally committed to Japanese workers, who lost purchasing
power under inflation, and against capitalists, who were able
to depreciate their debts while profiteering from shortages
and speculation.[48] Since SCAP's interpretation of the causes of
the war emphasized class polarization, the linkage of inflation
to the interests of the elite and price stability to the needs of

43. Keizai Kikaku Chō, 24; Johnson, 33, 179–83.
44. Ishibashi, "Ways for Japan's Economic Survival (3)," *OE* 18 (1951): 648–50.
45. *TN*, 138, 179; Ishibashi, "Zōshō jidai o furikaette (1)," 29; Matsubayashi Matsuo, ed., *Kaikoroku: Sengo Tsūsan seisaku shi*, 38; *ITZ* 13:148–49.
46. Quoted in Ball, 61–62; see also Keizai Kikaku Chō, 28–29.
47. "Removal from Office of Finance Minister Tanzan Ishibashi," 1 May 1947.
48. *ITZ* 14:3–4. Union official Haraguchi Yukitaka believed that "Ishibashi finance" enriched capitalists and killed workers, but Haraguchi changed his mind later
on the basis of Ishibashi's policies as minister of international trade and industry; see
his "Mazu hataraku mono no seikatsu kōjō," in Tanzankai, ed., *Meihō Tanzan*, 134.

the masses placed Ishibashi squarely in the militarist camp and enlisted the erstwhile proponents of national mobilization as allies in creating a new structure for Japanese society. An *Oriental Economist* editorial urging that economic controls be limited to rice, coal, and foreign exchange was rebutted by General Courtney Whitney, under MacArthur's byline, with accusations of militarism, imperialism, and totalitarianism.[49]

The affinities between SCAP and economic bureaucrats were blurred by SCAP ideology, which exaggerated the gulf between Japanese and American capitalism at the same time that it ignored distinctions within the former. Ishibashi distinguished Takahashi finance from wartime economic controls in testimony at the Tokyo war crimes trials, endeavoring to date war planning from after 1937, but in the prosecution's thesis Japanese policies after the Manchurian Incident were all of a piece.[50] To complete Ishibashi's more nuanced array of prewar paradigms, Nakamura Takafusa recently compared the Dodge Plan, which terminated expansionary postwar finance, to Inoue Junnosuke's return to the gold standard in 1930.[51] Whereas prewar distinctions were blurred through the SCAP looking glass, postwar antagonisms between fiscal management and direct control were probably exaggerated. Ishibashi too was now prepared to tolerate the wartime governmental economic controls for the time being, but Japanese bureaucrats manipulated SCAP for new powers. Their quarrels were refracted in the United States when *Newsweek* and *Fortune* staged Ishibashi's debut as a free enterpriser crucified on a cross of economic control. Even while attacking SCAP, the conservative journals accepted the conceptual paradigm that located Japan and the United States in different categories of historical experience; thus, they cast a moderate critic of Jap-

49. Douglas MacArthur, "Japan: An Economy of Survival," *Fortune* 39 (June 1949): 95. General Whitney's authorship of the piece is attributed in Justin Williams, *Japan's Political Revolution under MacArthur: A Participant's Account*, 87–88.

50. *Kyokutō Kokusai Gunji Saiban Kiroku: Eibun sokkiroku*, vol. 72: 25, 413–25, 424 (7–11 Aug. 1947); *TN*, 86.

51. Nakamura, *The Postwar Japanese Economy*, 39; see also his "SCAP to Nihon," 10–11. John Dower noted a more liberal fiscal policy in subsequent Yoshida Cabinets than in SCAP's Dodge line, but that distinction emerged early in the Occupation and was largely the work of Ishibashi, who stood apart from the social and ideological reaction of Yoshida's group; see Dower, 274.

anese society as a rightist and visionaries of American exceptionalism as leftists. However, laissez-faire had no defenders
in occupied Japan, and Ishibashi was closer to ESS and the
New Deal than to the American right.[52]

Despite real differences, the RFB and the ESB cooperated
in instituting a priority production system, especially in coal.
After December 1946, Ishibashi himself recognized the need
for a stronger coal authority in the ESB in order to raise production to thirty million tons in 1947. Coal came first in plans
for priority production to stoke the steel and fertilizer industries, increase food production, and revive transportation.
Consumption of the 1946 coal output, a mere 21 million tons,
by the Occupation and railroads left virtually none for industrial use.[53] Wartime annual output of 40 million tons had
collapsed after the repatriation of conscripted Korean and
Chinese miners and the dissolution of the zaibatsu, which had
been major mine owners. The RFB targeted one-third of its
loans to the coal industry. Meanwhile Ishibashi authored a
plan for national mine management that was adopted under
the subsequent Socialist Katayama cabinet, and coal production benefited from bipartisan cooperation through the next
decade. Despite embittered labor relations the goal of 30 million tons of coal output was achieved in 1947.[54]

On food production Ishibashi saw no reason to alter his
Taishō position and spoke on the radio to urge cooperative
farming in order to increase efficiency and prevent a disastrous shortfall in the 1947 harvest. He held no brief for landlords but criticized the Occupation for drafting strict laws
against accumulation; the new laws would perpetuate small,
inefficient holdings. He chafed at governmental subsidies for
rice production and urged that the buying price gradually be
adjusted in order to encourage cooperative management, a

52. For example Ishibashi strongly opposed the premature lifting of wartime controls in *ITZ* 13:119–20.
53. Ishibashi, "Zōshō jidai o furikaette (1)," 29; Keizai Kikaku Chō, 27; Nakamura,
The Postwar Japanese Economy, 33; Johnson, 179–83.
54. *ITZ* 14:17; Ishibashi, "Ways for Japan's Economic Survival (2)," *OE* 18 (1951):
633; idem, "Zōshō jidai o furikaette (1)," 30–31. On the coal nationalization plan see
also Wada Hiroo, "Kanōsei o himeta Sōsai," in Tanzankai, ed., *Meihō Tanzan*, 69. Takahashi Toshirō described coal production as an area of bipartisan cooperation in an
interview, 7 Jan. 1984.

decrease in the number of farm households, and greater efficiency. Import competition would also force greater efficiency in Japanese agriculture; he had been offering this argument for the last three decades, and would offer it for another, to little avail.[55]

In labor policy Ishibashi renewed his encouragement of conciliation with capital and questioned the Occupation's trade union law, which assumed a conflict of interest between the two parties. The collapsed economy of 1946, Ishibashi believed, was the best possible argument for cooperation. He favored councils of management and labor at the plant or company level; there were prototypes for these in the wartime Patriotic Industrial Associations (Sangyō Hōkoku Kai). Over these bodies were to be enterprise wage committees, structured by geographic area and composed of labor, management, and a third party. Better organization of job seekers and a minimum wage were Ishibashi's only concessions in this singularly standpat program.[56]

Labor unrest reached a peak in plans for a general strike on February 1, 1947 (Ni-ichi Zenesuto). The anticipated strike, squelched by General MacArthur at the eleventh hour, was the most momentous crisis of the Occupation, raising the menacing possibility that SCAP would use force to supply itself with transport, communication, and utilities. The strike's failure isolated the Communist leaders, who had been prepared to defy MacArthur. In the government the threat of a general strike triggered far-reaching waves of panic, which were evident in a ban on strikes by public employees enacted under the subsequent Katayama cabinet, and in the conservatives' commitment to increasing police powers over the following decade.[57]

Ishibashi, rather than the labor minister, presided over negotiations with the unions because the government rested its case on the state of the exchequer. The government offered raises ranging from 32.5 to 100 percent, averaging 42 percent

55. *ITZ* 13:76–77, 216ff.; 14:71–80; 15:214–215; Ishibashi, "Three Vital Bills before the Diet," *OE* 12 (1945): 362.

56. Ishibashi, "Industrial Democratization (3)," *OE* 13 (1946): 121; *ITZ* 13:110–11, 141–43. On wartime unions see Nakamura, *The Postwar Japanese Economy*, 18.

57. Nakamura, *The Postwar Japanese Economy*, 29.

overall; however, the unions demanded 100 to 1,000 percent
in accord with the consumer price index. Ishibashi typically
refused to commit himself to either extreme, offering an eclectic set of pragmatic compromises that encouraged the split of
moderate from radical labor.[58] His calm conciliation was significant during a month of angry meetings marred by tirades,
walkouts, and no-shows on both sides. He sanctioned Mac-
Arthur's order halting the strike. At the same time, he differed
from conservatives in declaring Japan to be in no danger of
revolution and persistently questioned expanded police powers.[59] The incident actually enhanced Ishibashi's political relationships with the Socialist and Progressive parties, who now
disassociated themselves from the Communists. In February
Ishibashi, Nishio Suehiro, and Kawai Yoshinari constructed a
program for a three-party coalition. The achievement was remarkable since Ishibashi's resignation from the Finance Ministry had long been on the Socialist platform. The agreement,
however, was quickly rendered moot by the Liberals' defeat in
the April election.[60]

Ishibashi's financial policies, though bitterly controversial,
were firmly grounded in his experience of the gold embargo,
Takahashi finance, and wartime controls. The sincerity and
coherent theoretical basis of his policies were acknowledged by
contemporaries across the political spectrum. Socialist Wada
Hiroo, who succeeded Ishibashi as head of the ESB, praised
his concessions to reasonable union demands and his populist
(*minkan*) orientation. Tokyo University economist Ōuchi Hyōe,
who roundly opposed the wartime guarantee payments, identified Ishibashi as the only person on the other side who
understood economic theory. Ōuchi's colleague Nakayama
Ichirō, and economic journalist Obama Toshie, praised Ishibashi's tolerance for inflation as a means of breaking bottlenecks in production.[61] Obama and Ōuchi were from the

58. Nishio Suehiro, "Yo no 'santō renritsu' to Ishibashi-san," in Chō, ed., *Ishibashi
Tanzan*, 68; Shimura, 220–22; Ishibashi, "Zōshō jidai o furikaette (2)," 37; *ITZ* 13:203;
TN, 181–83.
59. Ishibashi, "Zōshō jidai o furikaette (2)," 36; *ITZ* 13: 202–05; 14:281–84,
15:19–21.
60. Nishio, 68–69; Ishibashi, "Zōshō jidai o furikaette (1)," 42.
61. Wada, 69; Ōuchi, 10; Nakayama Ichirō, "Taikei naki taikei, Ishibashi keizai-

prewar Financial Systems Association; Nakayama had chaired the Special Investigative Committee on Wartime Economics; and Wada served with Ishibashi in the Yoshida cabinet. They represented an important segment of economic policy thinking across academic, journalistic, and political lines. Ishibashi's policies, however, were abhorrent to the Occupation.

THE POLITICS OF PURGING

Public office purges were only one arm of Occupation policies aimed at exorcising Japanese militarism and nurturing democratic tendencies. Conceptions of the meaning of the purge inevitably varied according to the particular officials concerned and according to the issues of the moment. "Quite early in the Occupation, the purge program became associated with the democratization effort (albeit in a negative manner) so that it became a vehicle for removing from office any person deemed inimical to the growth of democracy in Japan."[62] Arbitrary application was restrained, however, by detailed purge criteria, which made nearly all purges automatic, based on the purgees' having held positions in organizations, and by the formation of Japanese government screening and appeal committees, which were generally sensitive to the financial and emotional hardships visited upon purgees. Nevertheless, a small fraction of purge cases lacked these safeguards. Media purges ("category G") were based on textual analysis as much as on formal position. Memoranda purges of about one hundred persons were ordered by SCAP over a contrary judgment by the Japanese screening committee. From these two types of purges were to arise the most bitterly controversial instances, including Ishibashi's case, which was both a category G and a memoranda purge.

Category G was part of the basic purge order SCAPIN-550 (Japanese government Imperial Ordinance No. 1 of January 1947), which ordered the removal from government office

gaku," in Chō ed., *Ishibashi Tanzan*, 265; Obama Toshie, "Kakudai kinkō ōi ni yare," in Tanzankai, ed., *Meihō Tanzan*, 94.
    62. Hans Baerwald, *The Purge of Japanese Leaders under the Occupation*, 2.

(defined as all ranks of *chokunin* and above plus equivalent positions in public corporations) and the exclusion from future entry into public service (defined as all positions in central and local government and other agencies) of various groups of officials, politicians, military officers, and ideologues.[63] Purgees were also barred from holding positions in the information media, publishing political analysis, and consulting with government officials.[64] Although there were loopholes in the restrictions on purgees (such as the right to engage in academic publishing) and violations were routine, a purge was still a weighty set of constraints that in many cases barred middle-aged individuals from the only type of work that they were qualified to perform. Moreover, violators of purge restrictions were investigated through surveillance, phone tapping, and mail censorship, and subject to fines and imprisonment. Purgees had no legal protection, since a purge and its appeal were administrative rather than criminal proceedings.

Category G was the vaguest of the purge criteria, the only one that was not automatic according to an individual's position in an organization.[65] Included in Category G was "any person who has played an active and predominant governmental part in the Japanese program of aggression or who by speech, writing or action has shown himself to be an active exponent of militant nationalism and aggression."[66] It was sparingly applied to the information media, resulting in only 1,328 purges, mainly in government organs; only 710 individuals were purged in the private information media. Unlike military officers, police, or party politicians, journalists in general were not tarred with primary war guilt or targeted for removal in the transfer of power. Nonetheless, the Government Section's interpretation of the causes of the war blamed the media for drowning popular protest under a flood of propaganda.[67]

    63. Ibid., 62–63.
    64. Ōta Takeshi, "Kōshoku tsuihō," in *Kataritsugu Shōwashi*, Gekidō no hanseiki, vol. 5, 255–56. Ōta was the chief secretary of the Central Screening Committee on Fitness for Public Office. See also Baerwald, 70.
    65. Ōta, "Kōshoku tsuihō," 254–55.
    66. Government Section, Supreme Command of the Allied Powers, *Political Reorientation of Japan, Sept. 1945 to Sept. 1948*, vol. 1, 22; Baerwald, 20–21; *ITZ* 13:605.
    67. Ōta, "Kōshoku tsuihō," 261; Baerwald, 95.

The Government Section was concerned with Ishibashi's purge from the first year of the Occupation until the peace treaty was signed six years later. It shared responsibility with several other institutions, interacting by largely informal channels. Before January 1947 the Government Section had conducted purge screening in concert, though not always in cooperation, with military intelligence and the Japanese government's Central Liaison Office. Ishibashi, like all Diet candidates in the election of April 1946, had been screened and passed by the Japanese government and the Counter-Intelligence Section.[68] However, his post in the Yoshida cabinet triggered a more thorough scrutiny, and from June 17 the Government Section collected detailed information, beginning with a note that Ishibashi's wartime economic consultancies were minor and not subject to the purge.[69]

On June 26, at the height of contention about the guarantee payments, a secret memo from Courtney Whitney, Charles Kades, and Frank Rizzo declared that SCAP would order Ishibashi's purge if the Japanese government refused to do it independently. The memo asserted that Ishibashi did fall within the purge criteria as president and chief editor of Tōyō Keizai Shinpō corporation, which had "consistently supported the policies and activities of the ultra-nationalist and militarist groups."[70] It was documented by some twenty-seven paragraph-length quotations from editorials by Ishibashi and staffers that had appeared in the English-language *Oriental Economist* during the five years preceding Pearl Harbor. The quotations praised Japan's role in China, the Axis Alliance, and the Tōjō cabinet while criticizing American policy toward Japan. The *Economist* had been somewhat more propagandistic than *Shinpō*, but prewar journalism was not the Government Section's main interest in Ishibashi's case. As Ishibashi's defenders retaliated, SCAP's documentation gradually expanded

68. Ōta, "Kōshoku tsuihō to shikaku shinsa," in Andō Yoshio, ed., *Shōwa seiji keizai shi e no shōgen*, vol. 2, 54; Baerwald, 90.
69. Colonel Bratton from Lieutenant Colonel T. P. Davis, 17 June 1946, Ishibashi Tanzan file, Box no. 2275e, Government Section, SCAP Collection, National Archives. SCAP records cited below are from this file unless otherwise noted.
70. "Removal and Exclusion of Cabinet Minister—Tanzan Ishibashi," 26 June 1946.

to include the Japanese-language journal and books published by the corporation, but these were an afterthought to the political motives specified with startling frankness in the initial memo.

The Government Section's decision that Ishibashi would be purged stressed his policies as finance minister, arguing that; "Ishibashi, in his first few weeks in office, has displayed an underlying lack of harmony with known policies of the Supreme Commander on financial and economic problems and has been reluctant to implement the program for the settlement of Claims for War Materials, War Insurance and War Damages. . . ."[71] The Government Section quoted from ESS files to support this charge. The GS memo conceded that Prime Minister Yoshida had vigorously protested that the purge of any one of his ministers would "jeopardize the accomplishment of vital governmental measures to promote national recuperation."[72] However, Whitney, Kades, and Rizzo coolly rejected Yoshida's dire forecast: "On the contrary, the removal of this Minister would offer the Prime Minister an opportunity to replace him with one less vulnerable to political attack and in whom the Supreme Commander, the Diet, and the Japanese people could repose greater confidence."[73] Ishibashi's political vulnerability was a peculiar issue for the Government Section to raise after the 1946 elections, a time when SCAP was shunning direct orders in order to enhance the legitimacy of the new parliamentary politics. Possibly Yoshida, and certainly the Socialists, wanted Ishibashi's resignation, but that issue might have been left to the Japanese. In fact, the problem of wartime guarantee payments was paramount. Virtually the entire Japanese government opposed the cancellation of the payments, but Ishibashi was a particularly effective and aggressive spokesman. His departure would facilitate SCAP financial policy.

Postwar policy differences, of course, were not included among the purge criteria, except in cases of opposition to fundamental Occupation objectives. On the other hand, in bor-

71. Ibid., 2.
72. Ibid., 7.
73. Ibid., 14.

derline cases of wartime behavior, postwar politics was sometimes considered in order to recommend an expedient le-
niency. For example another journalist, Ashida Hitoshi, had
been exempted from the purge at the Occupation's request
since his role in the Progressive party was deemed constructive. Although a certain flexibility was appropriate to the Occupation's aim of facilitating a new and democratic Japanese
leadership, the admission of postwar political criteria to even
a marginal role inevitably meant that standards of judgment
for wartime behavior differed from one individual to the next.
In Ashida's case the small circulation of the *Japan Times*, which
he had edited, was cited to illustrate the unimportance of its
propaganda, but *Tōyō kezai shinpō's* comparable circulation was
credited with "power to shape an important sector of public
opinion."[74]

In September Ishibashi heard from Asakai Kōichirō of the
Liaison Office that the Economic and Scientific Section was
angered at his handling of the wartime guarantee payments,
and he discussed the problem at a cabinet meeting. The issue
was forwarded to the Japanese government's newly constituted
Central Screening Committee on Fitness for Public Office
(Chūō Kōshoku Tekihi Shinsa Iinkai). Chaired by Matsushima
Shikao, the committee had Ōta Takeshi as its secretary, and
included Kimura Kozaemon, Miko Jirō, Hara Yasusaburō,
Ōkōchi Kazuo, Shōno Riichi, Unno Shinkichi, and, repre-
senting the media, Iwabuchi Tatsuo and Katō Masuo. Katō has
recorded that the Government Section immediately began
pressing for quick decision about *Shinpō*. Since Katō and Tanaka Mitsuo, second in command of the Political Bureau at
the Liaison Office, believed that preparations for media
purges were yet incomplete, they personally examined issues
of *Shinpō* and the *Economist* from the 1937–41 period.[75]

Katō and Tanaka reported on March 25 that *Shinpō's* liberal
criticism of governmental policy had been outstanding in the
wartime context: "If this magazine company, hence, is to fall
under the purge order, all other publishing firms, newspapers

74. Baerwald, 95–96.
75. *TN*, 147–48, 201; Ōta, "Kōshoku tsuihō," 245; Katō Masuo, "*GHQ* to Ishibashi tsuihō," *Ishibashi Tanzan zenshū geppō*, no. 13 (Oct. 1970): 7–9.

and magazine companies then existed [*sic*] in Japan should receive similar treatment without a single exception."[76] Their report noted that the views expressed in *Shinpō* and *Economist* editorials had been diverse, and that thirty-nine articles in 230 issues of the former, and nine in fifty-five issues of the latter, had violated the purge criteria. However, they also cited thirty-eight *Shinpō* editorials from the same period that "advocated liberalism, world peace and internationalism" and "actually refuted the ideology which is considered a violation" of the purge criteria.[77] Katō and Tanaka denied Ishibashi's individual responsibility for all views expressed in corporate publications, not only because the journal had been divided in its internal politics and under external pressure, but also because pluralistic debate was central to the value system that Ishibashi had been defending. Since Ishibashi had often summarized governmental policy before criticizing it, they demanded interpretation of "viewpoint, content, and spirit . . . in their entirety,"[78] and rejected the Government Section's method of brief quotation out of context. On this basis they vigorously denied that Ishibashi fit within the purge criteria. After their investigation Yoshida attempted to dispel rumors with the announcement that Ishibashi's screening had been completed.[79]

The Government Section was not satisfied. At its insistence, the Central Screening Committee appointed a new six-member media subcommittee, which immediately took up Ishibashi's case on April 25. The subcommittee revised the fine points of the Katō and Tanaka report to find even fewer violations of the purge directive. Eleven editorials previously counted as violations were now deemed innocuous on the grounds that the authors had employed prevailing rhetoric in order to criticize it. On the other hand, four signed articles by outside writers were newly cited as violations, bringing the total number of violations to thirty-two from

76. From Katō and Tanaka 1745, 25 Mar. 1947, 7.
77. Ibid., 3, 1.
78. Ibid., 1.
79. *ITZ* 15:400; *TN*, 205.

a five-year period. In contrast to Katō and Tanaka, the new subcommittee cautiously withheld interpretation of its findings, merely presenting its statistics to the full committee.[80]

On May 2 the Central Screening Committee unanimously voted to pass Ishibashi. Although few of their individual opinions are available, Iwabuchi Tatsuo, who had twice been arrested for wartime criticism, had published articles in *Shinpō* during the period in question. Secretary Ōta and member Katō both later described Ishibashi's purge as one of the half-dozen egregious injustices among some two hundred thousand purges. Ōta further noted that SCAP had previously overruled the committee, or requested reconsideration, in deeply divided decisions, but had never before overruled the unanimous committee. When it did so, committee members felt that their credibility had been impeached, and that their persistence in purging thousands of powerful and influential persons had gone unremarked.[81]

While the Central Screening Committee was deliberating, the Government Section continued to gather material on Ishibashi's political influence, including a March 7 *Asahi* article that stated that he had "aspirations of becoming either Prime Minister or President of the Liberal Party."[82] That month the Ashida Liberals formed the Democratic party (Minshutō) with Progressive party defectors and independents, aiming at coalition with the right-wing socialists in an anti-Yoshida conservative unity. At this convenient juncture Nosaka Sanzō of the Japan Communist party submitted information to the Government Section that *Shinpō* had helped the army to station spies in wartime China in the guise of reporters. Although Nosaka's accusation has been supported by recent scholarship, such practices were too widespread in wartime journalism to

80. "Investigation of the Publications of *Tokyo* [sic] *keizai shinpō*," 30 Apr. 1947; "Chōsa no kekka," n.d.; "Members of the Proposed Public Information Media Sub-Committee," 25 Apr. 1947; see also DRF Information Note no. 195, Diplomatic Records Section, State Department Decimal Files 894.00, 16 Aug. 1948.

81. Katō Masuo, 7–9; Ōta, "Kōshoku tsuihō," 274, and idem, "Kōshoku tsuihō to shikaku shinsa," 54–55.

82. "Diet Press Gallery," 7 Mar. 1947.

merit purging; moreover, Nosaka was doubtless smarting from the Communists' debacle in the abortive general strike of February 1947.[83]

Ishibashi's policies as finance minister had raised legitimate and fundamental questions about the direction of postwar Japanese society. The wartime guarantee payments had resulted in windfalls to the old holders of wealth and power. Rapid inflation had created other pernicious consequences. As one examiner for the SCAP Civil Censorship Detachment noted, "his policies earned the then Jiyūtō (Liberal party) the solid backing of the *shin-yen* (new yen) class of postwar profiteers— blackmarketeers, contractors, and miscellaneous racketeers."[84] The GS assiduously sought evidence that Ishibashi consorted with blackmarketeers and accepted payoffs, a charge that was never proven despite phone taps, surveillance, and correspondence intercepts by the Civil Intelligence Division and the Japanese Attorney General's Office.

By April 30, research analyst Guy Wiggins had prepared the Government Section's definitive memorandum in support of Ishibashi's purge. He cited reports from Japanese investigative committees, as well as Ishibashi's wartime writings, with barbed selectivity, describing the discovery of thirty-two offending articles in five years as a "powerful indictment" and arguing that the mixed editorial content of the journal evidenced a Machiavellian design to lull skeptical businessmen into supporting imperialism.[85] Wiggins concluded that as a writer, editor, and publisher Ishibashi had "supported military and economic imperialism in Asia, advocated Japan's adherence to the Axis, fostered belief in the inevitability of war with the Western Powers, and urged the imposition of totalitarian controls over the Japanese people."[86] This passage, quoted by Whitney to Yoshida and thence to the Japanese press, would be Ishibashi's only explanation for his purge until October, when he procured a copy of Wiggins's entire memorandum. So remote was it from Japanese readers' perceptions of the

83. Nosaka Sanzō to Marcum, 1 Apr. 1947; Itō, *Shōwaki no seiji*, 273–74; Matsuo, "Jūgonen sensōka no Ishibashi Tanzan," 231–32.
84. Civil Censorship Detachment, 9 Oct. 1948.
85. "Memorandum for the Record," 30 Apr. 1947, 2, 1.
86. Ibid., 20.

wartime *Shinpō* content that its publication, even without comment, cast substantial doubt on the qualifications of GS officials to translate and interpret Japanese editorials.

Yoshida strove vainly to assert the supremacy of his duly elected government. ESS rallied round the Government Section with a lengthy complaint about Ishibashi's financial policies and announced its intention "to assist the Government Section in the event that an appeal is made by the Japanese Government on behalf of Mr. Ishibashi."[87] On May 7 Courtney Whitney issued a memorandum ordering Ishibashi's purge.[88] On May 15 Yoshida complied in a cabinet order, but he pointedly requested that "in the screening of information media, special consideration be given to all the factors calculated to determine their character, as it is a matter likely to have far-reaching effect on the Japanese people."[89] He also published Wiggins's charge of imperialism and totalitarianism, a move interpreted as a subtle denial of his own responsibility in the matter. Ishibashi himself may well have encouraged Yoshida's strategy of seeking to publicize Occupation responsibility for unpopular decisions, for Ishibashi's use of the press to call the power holders to account dated back to the Taishō era. Readers were expected to see between the lines. On June 27 the subsequent Katayama cabinet sustained Yoshida's concern about information media purges by changing the standards, limiting purging to periodicals that had published more than ten offending articles annually.[90] The new criteria excluded *Shinpō* and set the stage for an appeal.

Purgees could ask for reconsideration by the Central Screening Committee, by a higher Japanese government appeal committee, and by the Prime Minister; however, to lift memoranda purges required GS approval. In memoranda cases both the Japanese government and SCAP disclaimed responsibility; the purgee had the right to appeal to agencies that lacked the authority to restore his or her rights, but not to those that had such authority. Ishibashi was unable to get

87. "Removal from Office of Finance Minister Tanzan Ishibashi," 1 May 1947.
88. Memorandum for Central Liaison Office, Tokyo, 7 May 1947.
89. Letter from Kiyoshi Yamagata, 17 May 1947; "Ishibashi Tanzan, Finance Minister," 16 May 1947.
90. "Purging in Japanese Journalism," *OE* 14 (1947): 549.

an appointment with General Whitney during the following year. The confusion of formal and informal authority made personal mediation systemic; the GS received a copy of Ishibashi's appeal and prepared rebuttals with ESS cooperation, and Ishibashi obtained Wiggins's original indictment. The adversaries, however, could not engage directly.[91]

The confusion of authority, and the techniques that Japanese used to manipulate it, are strikingly reminiscent of prewar politics. Ishibashi's defenders cherished two preeminent Taishō ideals: first, expertise, the legitimation of decision makers by their qualifications rather than their class, clique, or geographical origins. It became an issue in regard to both Ishibashi's financial policies and the GS's interpretation of wartime thought and behavior. The second was accountability, the right of the public to know who made governmental policy, and to criticize it. Insofar as these ideals were not fulfilled under the Occupation, Japanese strategies were equally familiar: informal mediation, publication to the limits of governmental toleration, and gradual reform of specific measures (such as the information media purge criteria). Although the Occupation was aware of Japanese maneuvering, it was oblivious to the long-term value orientations and behavioral patterns in political resistance. For example MacArthur saw no opposition to the Occupation save from the extremes of right and left,[92] and even so distinguished a scholar as Sir George Sansom described Ishibashi as a "fundamentally anti-white" proponent of the old order.[93] Their judgments overlooked a subdued but substantial intellectual disaffection from the Occupation, which arose not because the Occupation overturned the old order but because it was neither expert nor accountable. Ishibashi criticized the Occupation for ruling from behind the throne and for permitting Japanese politicians and bureaucrats to abuse the names of MacArthur and SCAP as they had once abused the name of the emperor.[94] The Oc-

91. From Mr. Hara, 26 May 1947; *ITZ* 13:224; Baerwald, 54, 58, 60.
92. MacArthur, 74.
93. In Katharine Sansom, *Sir George Sansom and Japan: A Memoir*, 152. See also *TN*, 93.
94. *ITZ* 14:270–71; Ishibashi, "What I Expect from 1952," *OE* 19 (1952): 10; and idem, "On Anti-Americanism in Japan," *OE* 20 (1953): 613–16.

cupation's insensitivity to central themes in indigenous democratization has continued to draw complaints in recent
histories.[95]

Ishibashi's purge was one of the scattered but significant
episodes in which the Japanese people learned that their con-
querors exercised enormous power with little accountability
and less information. Yet Japanese criticism has been tempered by the realization that, in occupied Japan, American
power was exercised fairly well if judged by the standards of
actual historical occupations and other contemporary governments. Perhaps it is most appropriate to let Ishibashi conclude
in his own words: "Luckily I was purged by SCAP and not by
Stalin."[96]

Ishibashi's powerful supporters inside and outside the Liberal party raised an immediate outcry. Even before Yoshida's
formal purge order, MacArthur was petitioned by prominent
journalists Baba Tsunego, Itō Masanori, Suzuki Bunshirō,
Obama Toshie, Itakura Takuzō, Furugaki Tetsurō, Shirayanagi
Shūko, Hasegawa Nyozekan, and Hani Motoko; political leaders from the bureaucracy and parties, conservative to socialist,
including Matsuoka Komakichi, Ashida Hitoshi, Yamasaki Takeshi, Uehara Etsujirō, Nishio Suehiro, Miki Takeo, Hoshijima
Nirō, Ikeda Hayato, and Ichikawa Fusae; educators Ayusawa
Iwao, Suehiro Izutarō, Ōuchi Hyōe, and Abe Yoshishige;
bankers and businessmen Kurusu Takeo, Ichimada Hisato,
and Toda Toyotarō. Their prestige and diversity are impressive. The petitioners insisted that Ishibashi and *Shinpō* had
"persistently advocated opinion directly opposed" to imperialism and totalitarianism and that Ishibashi's purge would inspire "deep misgivings for the future of democracy in Japan."[97]

While supporters petitioned on Ishibashi's behalf, his domestic political enemies worked against him from behind the
scenes. Although the Liberal party had suffered a setback in

95. Ikuhiko Hata, "Japan under the Occupation," in Lawrence H. Redford, ed.,
21.
96. *ITZ* 14:309–10.
97. Letter to General MacArthur, 12 May 1947; see also Matsuoka Komakichi,
"Sonkei dekiru Ishibashi-san," in Tanzankai, ed., *Meihō Tanzan*, 137; Hani Keiko,
"Omoide," in Chō, ed., *Ishibashi Tanzan*, 208; and Ichikawa Fusae, "Fujin Keizaikai no
omoide," in ibid., 257.

the April 26 elections and the Yoshida cabinet resigned on May
20, Ishibashi had won a Diet seat against a national Socialist
tide, and he promised to be a strong voice in economic policy
in the foreseeable future. Policy opponents and political rivals
were legion and perhaps included Yoshida himself. Yoshida
counseled Ishibashi to "just imagine that he had been bitten
by a mad dog," an expression of passivity that Ishibashi and
others found surprising.[98] Chief Cabinet Secretary Hayashi
Jōji and Vice Liaison Officer Yamagata Kiyoshi asked Ishibashi "how in good conscience the prime minister can allow
the assertion that *Tōyō keizai shinpō* supported militarism to be
published as the view of the Japanese government."[99] Later
American documents would report Yoshida's maneuvering
against the lifting of Hatoyama Ichirō's purge.[100] Other rivals
in the Liberal party and the Finance Ministry sought information to support Ishibashi's purge.[101]

On October 27, Ishibashi submitted his appeal to the Central Screening and Appeal committees. A week later, with the
same panache he had shown against Terauchi and Tōjō, he
called a press conference to distribute copies of the appeal and
explain his side of the story. The conference angered the Government Section, but he was in no way punished. He had an
effective right to speak in his own defense, though not to appeal directly to those who had judged him. His appeal to the
Central Screening and Appeal committees was a cogent interpretation of his wartime essays in terms of context and rhetorical strategy, but it was beside the point if his policies as
finance minister were the true cause of his purge.[102]

Textual interpretation no longer interested the GS, if indeed it ever had; even the issues of financial policy were lost
in the mists of personal animosity through which glimmered

98. Dower, 332; see also Harry Emerson Wildes, *Typhoon in Tokyo: The Occupation
and Its Aftermath*, 138.

99. *TN*, 199–200.

100. From W. J. Sebald to the Secretary of State, 24 July 1948, Diplomatic Records
Section, State Department Decimal Files 894.00; "View of Reformists in Political Circles on Hatoyama Ichirō," 30 May 1951, Hatoyama Ichirō file, Box no. 2275b, Government Section, SCAP Collection, National Archives.

101. Suzuki Mosaburō, "Retsuretsutaru heiwa e no netsui," in Chō, ed., *Ishibashi
Tanzan*, 61–62.

102. *TN*, 205, 231–38.

the light of the Allies. Major Jack Napier's draft rebuttal accused Ishibashi of "confusion," "damaging admissions," "befuddlement," "delusions," and a "cunning campaign to obscure the real nature" of his wartime journalism.[103] Napier was career army and did not like to be crossed. He greeted Ishibashi's loss of employment in both government and journalism with malicious relish, "inasmuch as the personnel of this Headquarters do not have the leisure so abundantly enjoyed yet so unprofitably employed by the former Finance Minister."[104] Napier was particularly offended by Ishibashi's failure to condemn Japanese policy in moral terms. He supplied what Ishibashi lacked, and devoted the last four pages of his rebuttal to an indictment of the Axis cause. General Whitney also joined the moral crusade by writing to Ambassador George Atcheson that failure to hold Ishibashi responsible for his misdoings would be "a travesty on right and justice, and a mockery of the memory of those dead whose blood was the price exacted so that arrogance and irresponsibility might not rule over the lives of men and the destinies of nations."[105] The cultural roots of the GS's moral fervor were as deep as those of Ishibashi's conviction that he had employed appropriate means to admonish an abitrary and authoritarian government. Moral judgment was also predicated on an interpretation of modern Japanese history entirely incompatible with Ishibashi's pragmatic meliorism.

The structural flaws of Japanese society and history were a fundamental premise of SCAP reforms. The survival of wartime liberals in positions of influence challenged a major Occupation thesis that Japan had no indigenous basis for democracy, no usable past. As General MacArthur put it: "Tucked away there in the North Pacific, the Japanese had no realization of how the rest of the world lived. They had evolved a feudalistic system of totalitarianism which had produced results which were almost like reading the pages of mythology."[106] Below MacArthur a powerful segment of GS and

103. "Draft: Ishibashi Report," 24 Nov. 1947.
104. Ibid.
105. "Memorandum for the Record," 1 Dec. 1947; General Whitney to Ambassador Atcheson, 15 July 1947.
106. Quoted in Dower, 278.

ESS officers propounded an interpretation of the military-industrial complex predicated on the gap between privileged and exploited classes. The interpretation could not encompass an articulate Japanese Keynesian who stepped forth from business and financial circles to question Occupation economic policy and to denounce other major American policies (such as prewar tariffs and Occupation censorship) as profoundly illiberal. The Occupation had been prepared for any form of resistance except liberal criticism. Ishibashi's real challenge to the GS worldview was that, as a trenchant critic of the establishment from within its ranks, he existed at all.

Ishibashi's appeal was not answered until May 10, 1948. The date coincided with the end of the purges and the beginning of reinstatement to full public rights for most purgees. On that day, 1,119 of the media purges were lifted; soon another 209 were ended through appeal. Purges continued to be lifted until by the time of the peace treaty negotiations there were only 8,710 persons still under the purge. They were "ultra-rightists, selected military men, terrorists, and opponents of SCAP policy" such as Ishibashi, the strange bedfellows of Occupation politics. Some twenty of the protracted purges were memoranda cases, including Ishibashi and Hatoyama Ichirō. Ishibashi's appeal was denied—the last word on the subject until his purge was lifted three years later. The appeal committee had voted unanimously in Ishibashi's favor, but appeals of memoranda purges required SCAP approval and the GHQ was adamantly against him.[107]

Under the purge Ishibashi returned to journalism, writing "academic" articles on economic theory and history for *Tōyō keizai shinpō*, meeting with former associates including both purgees and office-holders, and forming a Liberal Thinkers Society (Jiyū Shisō Kyōkai) in deliberate reference to Tanaka's Taishō Liberal Lecture Society. He served as chairman of the board of Dengen Industries and its subsidiary, International Electric, and also joined important private economic policy

107. Ōta, "Kōshoku tsuihō," 261–65; Watanabe Tadao, "Ishibashi Daijin," in Chō, ed., *Ishibashi Tanzan*, 211–13; see also Shigeru Yoshida, *The Yoshida Memoirs*, trans. Kenichi Yoshida, 164–65; *ITZ* 15:402; *TN*, 218.

study and lobbying organizations such as the Japan Economic Rehabilitation Association (Nihon Keizai Saiken Kyōkai),
which was drawn mainly from business and academia but also
included the former heads of quasi-official wartime trade associations. Gradually Ishibashi and other purgees moved from
discretion to purge violations so blatant that the Finance Ministry invited Ishibashi to lecture during the final weeks of his
purge. Suspected of purge violations, especially stirring up opposition to the Dodge line economic stabilization program,
Ishibashi was under surveillance by the attorney general's office with reports to Major Napier from June 1949 until his
purge was lifted.[108]

During his purge Ishibashi attempted to rally foreign support. He enjoyed a considerable Anglo-American acquaintance, dating from his founding of the *Oriental Economist* in
1932, that included George C. Allen and Elizabeth Schum-
peter. Some of his foreign admirers were within SCAP itself,
for Ishibashi heard from Charles Kades via intermediaries that
his appeal had triggered a fierce dispute there. Kades complained to Whitney that "an official holding a high responsible
position at SCAP" had said, "You may not like Ishibashi but
he was the smartest man in the Japanese government."[109] Ishibashi also enjoyed support from reporters including Burton
Crane of the *New York Times*, Roger Baldwin of *Reader's Digest*,
and Karl Bachmeyer of *Newsweek*. They served as one conduit
of information to and from Ishibashi, the Government Section, and the Japanese government. The *Newsweek* connection
was particularly important, as its foreign editor, Harry F. Kern,
organized the American Council on Japan to attack SCAP policies of industrial deconcentration and economic purges. On
May 26, 1947, *Newsweek* accused SCAP of purging economic
leaders essential to Japan's reconstruction.[110]

108. "Ishibashi Tanzan," 30 July 1951; from Nihon Keizai Saiken Kyōkai to Ishibashi Tanzan, 20 Aug. 1947; Major Jack P. Napier from Director Mitsusada Yoshi-
kawa, 13 July and 9 Sept. 1949; 12 July and 1 Nov. 1950; Ishibashi, "Zōshō jidai o
furikaette (1)," 25; see also *TN*, 200–46; *ITZ* 13:402, 664.
109. Charles Kades, "Memorandum for General Whitney," 25 Oct. 1947.
110. Ishibashi, "Refutation of the Memorandum Believed to Have Served as the
Basis for my Removal from Public Office," 22 Oct. 1947; *ITZ* 15:398–402; *TN*, 201–

Kern attempted to exploit State Department doubts about SCAP by submitting Ishibashi's account of his purge to Assistant Secretary of State Charles E. Saltzman. The State Department confirmed Ishibashi's story, and worried about unilateral SCAP action, especially since State had been uninformed both about the prominent Japanese who had petitioned MacArthur on Ishibashi's behalf, and about Whitney's refusal to make an appointment with Ishibashi. Consequently, Saltzman advised General G. L. Eberle, acting chair of the Army's Civil Affairs Division, that "further information and comment from SCAP may be required."[111] No reply is at hand, but by February 1951, Ishibashi was sufficiently in the good graces of the American government to meet with John Foster Dulles, special envoy charged with negotiating a peace treaty. The reversal depended on his developing relationship with Hatoyama Ichirō.

FROM PURGE BACK TO POLITICS

Ishibashi and Hatoyama were very different, but their common purge experience and the prospect of power drew them together. Hatoyama was a career party politician with an unusual commitment to the parliamentary system; for that reason he was more congenial to Ishibashi than Yoshida, who was a career bureaucrat. Of Seiyūkai lineage, Hatoyama also was sympathetic to Ishibashi's expansionary finance. Yoshida opposed rearmament, mainly for budgetary reasons, but Hatoyama strongly favored it, and Ishibashi cautiously sanctioned it as a prerequisite of full sovereignty, and an alternative to reliance on the United States. On other issues Hatoyama and Ishibashi were still further apart. In particular, Hatoyama was

---

04, 228–33; "Memorandum for General Whitney," 25 Oct. 1947; G. C. Allen, *Appointment in Japan: Memories of Sixty Years*, 130; Howard Schonberger, "The Japan Lobby in American Diplomacy, 1947–1952," *Pacific Historical Review* 46 (1977): 327–59.

111. Charles Saltzman to G. L. Eberle, 3 Sept. 1948; see also Harry F. Kern to Charles Eskridge Saltzman, 6 Aug. 1948; Franklin Ray from Charles C. Stelle, 16 Aug. 1948; J. M. Allison from J. F. Ray, 16 Sept. 1948; all in Diplomatic Records Section, State Department Decimal Files 894.00, National Archives; on Ishibashi's meeting with Dulles see *ITZ* 15:405.

a vitriolic anticommunist who had suppressed dissidents, and Ishibashi had accused him of fascism in editorials during the early 1930s.

Hatoyama's purge was a borderline case, ordered by SCAP memorandum over a narrow screening committee majority in Hatoyama's favor.[112] His purge also differed from Ishibashi's in that it was based on political behavior and organizational membership, as well as written opinions. His purge, however, even more than Ishibashi's, had a political motive: "His removal from the succession to the premiership would have a salutary effect upon Japanese politics in forcing a more realistic realignment of political parties, for the breakup of the Jiyūtō (Liberal party) would almost inevitably follow, with an alignment of liberal elements of that party with the Shakaitō (Social Democratic party) and the most conservative elements with the Shimpotō."[113] On this basis the Government Section had purged Hatoyama just as he prepared to form a cabinet in May 1946, and his successor Yoshida had chosen Ishibashi as finance minister. Subsequently the Government Section's best-laid plans went far agley. Far from splitting, the Liberals survived a troubled Socialist interregnum to dominate the 1950s, and Hatoyama in exile led the Japan Democratic party (Nihon Minshutō) toward an anti-Yoshida conservative unity.

It was after his purge, rather than before it, that Ishibashi became identified as a member of Hatoyama's faction. There is no hint that his link with Hatoyama might have been a factor in his purge. As a member of Yoshida's cabinet, he had not met often with Hatoyama or his followers, who were intensely suspicious of Yoshida. In fact, Ishibashi had been publicly discussed as an independent rival to both Hatoyama and Yoshida. The purge drew the two closer together. They complemented each other's political assets. Ishibashi fulfilled Hatoyama's rather desperate need for an untainted postwar liberal image and enhanced his pose as the hapless victim of arbitrary Oc-

112. Ōta, "Kōshoku tsuihō," 249; and idem, "Kōshoku tsuihō to shikaku shinsa," 55. For Ishibashi's criticisms of Hatoyama see *ITZ* 8:539–40 and 14:496–97.

113. "Applicability of 4 J. 1946 Directive (SCAPIN 550) 'Removal of Undesirable Personnel from Public Office' with respect to Hatoyama Ichirō," 13 Mar. 1946, Hatoyama Ichirō File, Box no. 2275b, Government Section, SCAP Collection, National Archives.

cupation machinations. Ishibashi also brought the respect of economic and financial circles, which Hatoyama lacked. Ishibashi was chagrined that Yoshida had not opposed his purge more vigorously, and he was drawn to Hatoyama's broad and deeply rooted network of followers. After the formation of the Japan Democratic party in 1949, Ishibashi met occasionally with Hatoyama and followers such as Nomura Kichisaburō, Ashida Hitoshi, Kamina Kazuo, Kōno Ichirō, and Asakawa Eijirō.[114] By 1949 the Hatoyama and Ishibashi purges were discussed as one. After Hatoyama and Ishibashi met with Dulles, SCAP was amenable to restoring their public rights, but Yoshida stalled. Ishibashi's purge was lifted on June 26, 1951, and Hatoyama's on August 6, less than a month before the San Francisco peace talks opened.

Unease with both American and Soviet power led to Ishibashi's interest in rearmament. He shared neither Hatoyama's enthusiasm nor the left's unconditional opposition to the prospect. Japan could not enjoy full sovereignty without armed forces, and could not depend on the United States indefinitely. On the other hand Ishibashi echoed Yoshida's view that a military could be maintained and supplied only at the expense of economic development. Still, his rapprochement with the Democrats offended the dominant liberals, and he bolted from the Liberal party three times before his return to the cabinet under Democrat Hatoyama in 1954. His qualified support for rearmament was in part a concession to Hatoyama, and a clever one, for it greatly enhanced his appeal in the Liberal Democratic party (Jiyū Minshutō, or LDP, formed when the Liberals merged with the Democrats in 1955), but cost him little in support from liberal intellectuals and journalists, who still preferred him over the majority party's mainstream.[115]

Freed from his purge, Ishibashi lifted his inkbrush to detail his pent-up dislike of the deflationary Dodge Plan. He returned with relish to the issues of Takahashi and Ishibashi expansion versus Inoue and Dodge contraction, appealing to

114. *ITZ* 15:403–06.
115. *ITZ* 14:42–43, 52, 156, 312–15; Shimanaka Hōji, "Yajin saishō hōdan," in Tanzankai, ed., *Meihō Tanzan*, 35–36. On Ishibashi's departures from the Liberal party, see "Haran ni tonda isshō: Nitchū, Nisso dakai ni sokuseki," *Asahi shinbun*, 25 Apr. 1983, evening edition.

the people's desire for a higher living standard and castigating economic bureaucrats. Although Ishibashi admired Takahashi finance, he believed that, in the fifties, expansion should be stimulated by means of domestic consumption rather than government spending. He began with the argument that high productivity rather than low cost was the key to export performance, and he criticized the Dodge line for a quick fix of cheap exports achieved by forcing prices down at the expense of future development. To lower prices, the Ministry of International Trade and Industry discouraged consumption. Consumption, Ishibashi demurred, was the point; what else is an industrial policy for?[116] Domestic demand was the basis of all production, and it ought to be expanded rather than denounced in moral terms. Since consumption and investment ordinarily rose and fell together, what the bureaucrats defined as "excessive investment" might in fact be a shortage of demand.[117] In Japan consumption and investment were historically unbalanced, because an insufficiency of private savings since the Meiji period had been supplemented by public debt. Now, however, Ishibashi wanted to reduce public expenditure, increase consumption, and benefit export industries by effecting economies of scale. Prices would rise, but inflation could be offset by improved equipment, lower interest rates, and rationalized organization, especially in small and medium enterprise and in agriculture.[118] Ishibashi "combined export promotion and high-speed growth into a coherent theory," according to his first vice-minister, Hirai Tomisaburō, and, as minister of international trade and industry after December 1954, Ishibashi laid the groundwork for the successive booms of the late 1950s and 1960s.[119]

Ishibashi's positive policy penetrated the Ministry of International Trade and Industry at an extraordinarily auspicious moment in Japanese economic history. Productive efficiency

116. Ishibashi continued to draw parallels between Takahashi finance and his expansionary proposals for the 1950s in *ITZ* 14:63–66 and Ishibashi, "Ways for Japan's Economic Survival (3)," *OE* 18 (1951): 648–50.
117. *ITZ* 14:177; Ishibashi, "The World and Japanese Economy in 1954," *OE* 21 (1954): 136–42.
118. *ITZ* 14:243.
119. Quoted in Johnson, 229; interview with Hirai, 12 Jan. 1984.

had been increased by the post-Korean War retrenchment during 1953–54. With heavy industry consolidated, the time was ripe for an improvement in consumer demand, particularly in the face of a global economic upswing.[120] Ishibashi believed that the key to future growth was to encourage consumption, light industry, and small firms. He continued the care and feeding of selected cartels, selling off old military fuel facilities to new petrochemical companies.[121] His affection for market mechanisms was not sufficiently dogmatic to set him against economic bureaucrats in MITI, according to his second vice-minister, Ishihara Takeo.[122] However, he also took the initiative in encouraging the production of consumer goods, for the threefold purpose of increasing exports, living standards, and jobs. Six hundred thousand Japanese were still unemployed, a fraction of the immediate postwar millions, but still a source of acute concern when coupled with underemployment in agriculture and small business.[123] Ishibashi's most dramatic proposal was a tax cut of ¥100 billion. It was implemented by Ikeda Hayato after the Ishibashi cabinet and led directly to the boom of 1958–61.[124]

Small and medium enterprises employed a majority of Japanese workers and suffered from instability; from low wages, benefits, and profit rates; and from poor working conditions. The differential in wage rates between large and small business, which was the greatest obstacle to Ishibashi's long-sought minimum wage law, had widened during the Korean War. A pay scale high enough to be meaningful in large firms would bankrupt hordes of small businesses. Ishibashi coupled minimum wages and labor standards with assistance to small business in credit, managerial rationalization, technological improvement, cooperative organization, and export promotion. President Haraguchi Yukitaka of the Sōhyō federation of

120. *ITZ* 14:86–87, 139; Ishihara in Matsubayashi, 54; Ishibashi, "Plan for a Self-supporting Economy," *OE* 21 (1954): 347–54; Nakamura, *The Postwar Japanese Economy*, 47–48; Hirai Tomisaburō in Matsubayashi, 43; and Ishihara Takeo in ibid., 53.
121. Johnson, 236.
122. Ishihara in Matsubayashi, 53, and in interview, 8 Dec. 1983.
123. *ITZ* 14:215.
124. *ITZ* 14:337, 341, 348; Nakamura, *The Postwar Japanese Economy*, 131; Johnson, 16.

unions supported him. Aid to small industry culminated in 1957 in large-scale public loans to these firms and revision of the Credit Insurance Associations Law and the Special Machine Industry Encouragement Measures Law. Ishibashi's attempts to bring agriculture under MITI, however, met adamant resistance from Kōno Ichirō, minister of agriculture.[125]

Exports doubled between 1953 and 1956.[126] Ishibashi remembered only too well the foreign resistance to Japanese exports, and the accusations of dumping, of the early 1930s; the economic nationalism of both Japan and its trading partners had been one of the principal causes of the second world war.[127] Export promotion by means of productivity and economies of scale, rather than low prices and cheap labor, would alleviate foreign resentment of Japanese competition. Foreign protectionism could be avoided only if Japan increased imports along with exports, and Ishibashi followed his man-in-the-street economics to the conclusion that imported goods and services were the purpose of exports, just as consumption was the purpose of production. He threatened to nationalize Japanese exporters who refused to act with reciprocity in international trade; there were definite limits to his preference for market mechanisms. Finally, he proposed the revival of trade and cultural exchange with the People's Republic of China.[128]

Ishibashi's well-regarded tenure as minister of international trade and industry under Hatoyama in 1954–56 made him a serious candidate for prime minister, but tensions within the LDP over foreign policy, agricultural subsidies, and personalities were also important. Hatoyama was forced to retire after his diplomatic initiative toward the Soviet Union failed to resolve territorial and trade disputes; however, the move had been so popular among the people that open opposition to relations with communist countries was politically impossible. After Hatoyama's retirement Kishi Nobusuke lost the presi-

125. Ishihara in Matsubayashi, 51–54; Haraguchi, 134; Matsubayashi, 65.
126. Satō Eisaburō, "Ishibashi Sensei to Jinmu keiki," in Tanzankai, ed., *Meihō Tanzan*, 262.
127. Hirai in Matsubayashi, 117.
128. *ITZ* 14:249–51, 257–59.

dency of the Liberal Democratic party by only seven votes. Kōno Ichirō, Ishibashi's leading antagonist over the problem of rice subsidies, deserted Hatoyama's heirs to support Kishi. On the other hand Yoshida, who had remained aloof from the LDP under Hatoyama, now favored anyone but Kishi. Reformers such as Miki Takeo and Ishida Hirohide, who had supported Ishibashi since the spring of 1956, united with followers of Ishii Mitsujirō to defeat Kishi on the second ballot, and the victory was a watershed in Miki's and Ishida's careers. At the pinnacle of public office Ishibashi lasted only two months, from December 23 through February 25, 1957, when he tendered his resignation because he was hospitalized with pneumonia and required a lengthy convalescence. Neither he nor his associates ever volunteered any other explanation for his resignation; if there was one, it must be inferred from the dreams and realities that surrounded his short-lived cabinet.[129]

The short-lived Ishibashi cabinet, like all lost causes, has been pursued by the specters of unfulfilled hopes. Ishibashi's prewar record as an out-of-power Taishō liberal contrasted sharply with that of his successor Kishi, member of the Chōshū clique, defender of the reactionary scholar Uesugi Shinkichi versus Yoshino Sakuzō, leading reformist bureaucrat, and indicted war criminal. In contrast Shimanaka Hōji, son of Shimanaka Yūsaku, described Ishibashi as the first "pure opinion leader" to become prime minister. Liberal journalists had not been fully satisfied with Ishibashi's performances in cabinet ministries, nor with his qualified support of rearmament. Even so, Ishibashi was identified as a man of the people (*minkan no hito*). Supporters expected him to shift the balance of power away from bureaucrats and bureaucrats-turned-politician, to inject a reformist spirit deemphasizing money politics and factional alignments, and to encourage rational policy debate while improving relations with the opposition. Finally, not only supporters but also the general public expected Ishibashi to normalize relations with China as Hatoyama had done with the Soviet Union.[130]

129. Gotō Fumio, Uchida Kenzō, and Ishikawa Masumi, "Sengo hoshu seiji no tesseki, 5: Ishibashi seiken kara Kishi seiken e," *Sekai*, no. 417 (Aug. 1980): 246–51; Shimura, 240–41; interview with Ishida, 6 Jan. 1984.
130. Shimanaka, 49; Gotō et al., 256–57; Kawasaki Hideji, *Yūki aru seijikatachi*,

Ishibashi's own career and opinions, as well as the structure of Japanese politics in the fifties, cast doubt on these extravagant expectations. Ishibashi had vision but also political savvy, and he consistently distinguished his individual opinions from his cooperation with broad coalitions, with a keen eye to ultimate goals in the former and immediate possibility in the latter. The popular image of Ishibashi as less corrupt and more rationally oriented to policy issues is not a false one, but it must be seen within the context of postwar politics and not as a deus ex machina outside it. His election as president of the LDP had been decided by money politics and factional loyalties; although it is the loser, Kishi, and not Ishibashi who has been most criticized on these points, the Ishibashi campaign was accused of promising offices in return for contributions because it particularly lacked funds.[131] The new cabinet had the support of only 40 percent of the electorate, and even supporters expected it to face a general election soon because of Ishibashi's long-standing hostility to the rice price supports. Ishibashi's faction resembled an intellectual salon and was one of the loosest in the LDP. It was ill-prepared for contention with the tighter Kishi and Satō groups, whose consolidation proceeded apace. The appointment of Kishi, who was anathema to Peking, as Ishibashi's foreign minister was the best evidence against the possibility of a breakthrough with China, and Ishibashi himself stated that he would encourage trade but not open diplomatic relations with the People's Republic.[132] Ishibashi's cabinet passed intact to Kishi.[133]

Negative expectations of the Ishibashi cabinet were also exaggerated, especially in the United States. Gotō Fumio, who worked in the Washington *Asahi* office at the time, recalls that the State Department was utterly confounded and requested background from the Japanese press. (State's apparent failure to locate Ishibashi's exhaustive purge files in the SCAP records

357–60; and Abe Shinnosuke quoted in ibid., 369–70. For Ishibashi's criticisms of factional and money politics see *ITZ* 14:332.

131. Gotō et al., 247–53; Arisawa, 362. Gotō estimates Kishi's expenditures at ¥100 million and Ishibashi's at 60 million, whereas Jon Halliday gives figures nearly double those amounts in *A Political History of Japanese Capitalism*, 267.

132. Gotō et al., 253–60; Shimanaka, 41; *ITZ* 14:330, 350–51.

133. Gotō et al., 250.

will surprise no experienced researcher.) The American press
too was surprised and portrayed Ishibashi as violently anti-
American. Yet by all accounts Ishibashi was both unwilling,
and politically unable, to abrogate the U.S.–Japan Security
Treaty, though he consistently urged that the relationship
should evolve toward more equal terms.[134]

Exaggerated expectations hid kernels of truth. The Socialist
party discerned the possibility of consultation on the budget
and foreign policy, leading toward a two-party alternation in
power.[135] Wada Hiroo characterized the election of Ishibashi
as the LDP president, the first such contest in which vote
counts were made public, as a turning point that evidenced
the majority party's internal diversity; Asanuma Inejirō was
highly cooperative in initial budget planning.[136] They welcomed Ishibashi's tested commitment to political pluralism.
His sudden resignation won widespread admiration and surprise; a prime minister was not expected to yield the reins so
gracefully.

Ishibashi could neither reverse the forces of history nor lose
himself within the mainstream. His foreign policy would have
differed from Kishi's, perhaps not so drastically as by opening
relations with China, but by being less centered on Taiwan and
more sensitive to pluralistic cooperation among communist
and noncommunist Asian states, and more independent of the
United States. As elder statesman and Diet member until 1963,
he demanded that the United States change its judgment of
China as an aggressor, and he proposed to expand trade with
China and the Soviet Union, especially by reexamining the list
of embargoed exports. He is said to have opposed the succession of Kishi, and he and his supporters played a meaningful
role as opposition to Kishi, defending civil liberties and castigating a subordinate role vis-à-vis the United States. When
Kishi suddenly moved to increase police powers and to subject
public university professors to an efficiency rating system,

134. Ibid.; Katagiri Yoshio, "Nichi-Bei ryōkoku no sonshitsu," in Tanzankai, ed.,
Meihō Tanzan, 258.
135. *ITZ* 14:336; Ishibashi and Suzuki Mosaburō, "Jimin, shakai ryōtōshu taidan,"
in Tanzankai, ed., *Meihō Tanzan*, 48; Gotō et al., 255–57.
136. Wada, 67–68; Asanuma Inejirō, "Rekidai Shushōchū no ishoku," in Tanzankai, ed., *Meihō Tanzan*, 272; Miki Takeo, "Hoshu seitō no dappi e," in ibid., 52–53.

Ishibashi and rival conservatives including Yoshida, Ashida, and Hatoyama joined in the criticism of Kishi.[137]

After Hatoyama's death in 1959, Ishibashi gave free rein to his dislike of armaments, while continuing to deplore the Cold War and American hegemony. He declared that the U.S.–Japan Security Treaty violated the Constitution, a rather opportunistic position in light of his original opposition to the antiwar clause.[138] He made two trips to Peking in 1959 and 1964, which were landmarks in opening political, cultural, and economic relations.

After Ishibashi's first visit to China in 1959, he criticized the security treaty more sharply and nearly broke with the mainstream LDP. He called the treaty the chief obstacle to normalization between the two leading nations of East Asia, and urged that it might be subject to more frequent revision or even abrogation but could not be maintained as it stood. Still, after that visit, he urged no sudden change in relations with the United States or the Soviet Union.[139] Despite his moderation, he signed a joint communique with the Chinese Communists declaring politics and economics to be inseparable, thus stirring up a hornet's nest in the LDP, which considered expelling him. Matsumura Kenzō and Takasaki Tatsunosuke supported him and followed with their own visits to China, opening possibilities that had been closed since the Korean War.[140] During the security treaty crisis of 1960 Ishibashi sided with Ikeda, Matsumura Kenzō, Miki, and Ishii against Kishi, Satō, Ōno Banboku, and Kōno Ichirō; however, he demurred at the Socialist party's refusal to recognize the treaty.[141] At the same time he demanded the immediate opening of diplomatic relations with China and indicted the United States as the main obstacle to a peaceful solution of the Taiwan problem.[142]

By the mid-1960s the octogenarian Ishibashi pronounced that Japan could not defend itself by means of arms but should strive to strengthen the United Nations, a full circle back to

137. Gotō et al., 249, 263–64; *ITZ* 14:386.
138. Gotō et al., 249; *ITZ* 14:387–90.
139. *ITZ* 14:424–25, 437.
140. Ōhara, "Nitchū fukkō ni okeru Ishibashi-san no yume," 44.
141. George R. Packard, *Protest in Tokyo: The Security Treaty Crisis of 1960*, 70.
142. *ITZ* 14:392–98.

his call for abandonment of the empire and support for the
League of Nations in 1921. He further predicted that the
American forces in Vietnam could neither win nor extricate
themselves; the United States faced the same dilemma that
General Ugaki Issei had encountered in China during the
1930s.[143] The comparison was published in English in the *Oriental Economist*, perhaps for the edification of any former
SCAP officials who could be persuaded to reconsider their
sociology of militarism. Yet despite a mild relish for American
embarrassment, Ishibashi analyzed foreign affairs in a spirit
of reason and hope.

CONCLUSION

Ishibashi's postwar career continued the eclectic rationality
and pragmatic gradualism that had typified his prewar journalism. Fantasy was always near at hand in the conglomeration
of unlike elements, such as Socialist Eda Saburō's call for a
British-style parliament, a Soviet welfare system, an American
standard of consumption, and the Japanese Constitution's
peace clause. Ishibashi liked Eda's idea.[144] Yet his analysis is
still relevant to an ongoing debate about the purposes of the
Japanese nation. In the debate Kenneth Pyle has identified
four viewpoints—progressive, liberal, mercantile, and nationalistic.[145] Ishibashi straddled the progressive view, which identifies Japan with the developing countries, demands pacifism,
and offers a fundamental critique of Japanese society, and the
liberal view, which identifies Japan with the Western democracies and is optimistic about Japanese society but hostile to
Japanese and American exceptionalism. If Ishibashi's eclecticism ensured that no one agreed with him across the board,
his open-minded pragmatism won him a host of allies on particular issues and general respect for his fairness. Remarkably,
the outlines of most of his positions had been sketched during
the Taishō era.

143. *ITZ* 14:419–21; Ishibashi, "A Proposal for the China Problem," *OE* 33 (1965):
140.
144. *ITZ* 14:465.
145. Kenneth Pyle, "The Future of Japanese Nationality: An Essay in Contemporary History," *JJS* 8 (1982): 244–49.

Although the details of policy and politics during the fifties were tortuous, certain themes are clear. Ishibashi continued to hold a high regard for the progressive potential of the Taishō era. This view caused great tension with the Occupation, which saw little or no indigenous democratic potential in Japan. SCAP reforms and purges initially favored Ishibashi's entry into politics by demanding new policies and displacing the old guard, but the Cold War fostered SCAP's alliance with wartime economic bureaucrats, and a McCarthyist approach to critics. Meanwhile, Ishibashi had lost much of his confidence in the power of journalism and public opinion, a change that propelled him into politics despite doubts about the parties. Practical politics and the devastated postwar economy contravened his liberal ideals; most notably, he now favored big business and growth at any price, particularly during his tenure as finance minister. In contrast, his policies at MITI rested on a consolidated heavy industrial base and aimed at improved conditions for small and medium enterprise, labor, and consumers along with equity for Japan and its partners in foreign trade. Meanwhile, his purge had drawn him close to the political faction of Hatoyama Ichirō in a curious blend of "rightist" support for Japanese rearmament and "leftist" relations with the Soviet Union and the People's Republic of China, in independence from American Cold War policy. His Taishō legacy was most evident in his final rejection of the U.S.–Japan Security Treaty in favor of a "Little Japan" engaged in multilateral world trade, and in his continued opposition to restraints on civil liberties by either the Occupation or the postwar Japanese government.

No significant historical movement leaves a pure or simple legacy. The Taishō democratic movement furnished the experience without which the Occupation might well have ended in disaster. Watanuki Jōji has judged that "the tradition and accumulated potential of Japanese liberalism, as evidenced by what is called Taishō democracy and enlightened bureaucrats, provided the background and the tools for reform under the Occupation."[146] However, renitent tensions between the men of

146. Watanuki, 44.

letters in journalism and the media and even the most enlightened of bureaucrats expanded the roster of conceptual
and policy options in politics, just as the balance between fiscal
management and direct control, and expansion and price stability, revitalized economic policy. Though legal change
heightened the pluralistic contention of agencies and interest
groups beyond its prewar limits, politics settled into an unprecedented consensus for growth and stability. In that sense
Taishō democracy was absorbed, and dissolved, into the dominant institutions. Or was it? During the fifties and sixties Ishibashi periodically renewed the complaint that Japan had the
form but not the spirit of democracy.[147] His old friends would
have been pleased.

147. *ITZ* 14:294; 15:185–87; "What I Expect from 1952," *OE* 19 (1952): 10.

Conclusion: The Legacy
and Limits of Taishō Liberalism

The Taishō period opened possibilities that history later closed. The age, like the years preceding the Meiji Restoration, was fraught with discord and vision. Unlike the Restoration, the Taishō era did not coalesce in a new institutional order. Yet just as Meiji images and symbols could not be confined within the new institutions, Taishō values outlasted the Meiji order. Taishō liberals anticipated a new society combining merit, freedom, participation, and productivity, to emancipate the whole range of human creativity. They did not anticipate the destruction of the Pacific War—in Ishibashi's case, not until the late 1930s. They were perhaps naive, yet if we fail to recapture the historical context of that naiveté, the contradictions of opportunity and oppression that they discerned in their society, then their words have no meaning.

Tanaka, Shimamura, and Ishibashi have been almost wholly overlooked in studies of the Taishō democratic movement. Since Ishibashi was the first and most liberal Taishō journalist to become a postwar prime minister, some explanation for the oversight seems required. Japanese scholars have shown an enduring predilection, in thought, for transcendent ideals like those that Tanaka called the "goose that laid the golden egg of absolutism." In institutions, Japanese scholars have emphasized the imperial universities, and in class, either the crème de la crème or the workers and peasants. Until quite recently a vast middle ground—pragmatic compromise, private institutions, and the middle class—has been left untouched. The very diversity of Taishō opinion is interesting, but it is less significant than the questions of what conditions stimulated the writers' originality, sustained their independence, and linked them to the larger whole.

Political and conceptual ambivalence sustained the intellectual pluralism of the Taishō era in several ways. The leaders of the Meiji Restoration had been as ambivalent as the liberalism that would challenge their achievements. On the one hand, they demanded submission from the people by perpetuating the rule of local cliques from the samurai class and by constructing a transcendent ideology of imperial divinity to make political obedience a religious duty. On the other hand, they demanded new activity and initiative from Japanese subjects. They institutionalized the slogan of rule by men of talent, the ideal of meritocracy based on competition. They inaugurated new modes of mass participation in education and established a conscript army, initiating the whole male population in the rudimentary means with which to compete for wealth and power. They encouraged or at least tolerated private business, education, and journalism in limited autonomy. The pragmatic reforms accorded with a tradition in which authority and its symbols could be manipulated and reinterpreted in adaptation to changing circumstances. In the early twentieth century, conservatives had growing doubts about the social and intellectual change that the Restoration had unleashed. Their frantic attempts to revive the ethos of submission, were, as Ishibashi expressed it, like rushing to the side of a dying man with a glass of water. The Taishō democratic movement was part of the whole elite's effort to find new social values and patterns of organization.

The most articulate members of the new urban professional and managerial middle class, journalists and intellectuals, were ambivalent in their relationship to the state. They were the creation of the state, not its creator, and they tended to welcome state power in order to advance industrialization and to protect Japan's national independence from the West. Detached from their provincial origins, they were generally blasé about the new state's assault on local autonomy and popular culture, at least until the tenant movements of the 1920s placed the issue in a new political perspective. Intellectuals of the new middle class led the parliamentary and social reform movements of the 1920s, but few resisted militarism and repression during the 1930s. Nevertheless, more fundamental commitments to a new kind of society—pluralistic, meritocratic, reformist, and capitalist—survived the Pacific War era, obstructing the ambitions of fascist ideologues and defining postwar Japanese society. Thus the Occupation, which ruled through a structurally intact Japanese administration and failed to decentralize big business, effected less significant change than did the emergence of the urban new middle class at the turn of the century.

Members of the urban new middle class experienced constant governmental interference in their publications and classrooms, their businesses, their shrines and temples and neighborhood organizations, their exercise of professional expertise and their family relations, morals, and choice of entertainment. An educated and upwardly mobile elite, they were quick to resent the state's narrow base of power and broad moral claims. The liberals in this study, I think, represented the most avant-garde voice of the urban new middle class and anticipated later national trends. A relatively independent institutional base at Waseda University and in journalism encouraged their quest for a rational political and social order. The achievement of a certain status as intellectuals and critics sustained their commitment to values widely held in their society—meritocracy, mass participation, and pragmatic adaptation—while their impotence before the pinnacles of wealth and power goaded their counterattack by means of critical reason. Their sensitivity to collective needs was not an attenuation of their democratic theory but its basis, for in their judgment, it was only national policy—the broadening of opportunity beyond hereditary status lines and the increase of production—that made individual choice and free public participation more than an enticing fantasy. They drew from an extraordinary range of foreign opinion to analyze the broad patterns of modernity, linking philosophy and literature, society, history, politics, and finance in their individual essays and in their interactions with one another.

The relationship between Western-derived institutions (the constitutional order and industrial capitalism) and Japanese society was another area of ambivalence that liberal thought addressed. Tanaka, Shimamura, and Ishibashi all insisted on freedom of expression and the equality of women, positions for which they found precious little precedent in their own society. They welcomed the adoption of Western institutions, especially a parliament and the franchise that they believed had already established a nucleus of democratic government under the Constitution of 1890. The legislature was weak within the government and initially represented only 3 percent of the population based on a property tax of fifteen yen a year; the writers themselves lacked the franchise before the Russo-Japanese War since they earned only three to twenty yen a month. They also lacked legitimacy as independent intellectuals and a loyal opposition. Finally, they were beset by sweeping censorship laws forbidding the disturbance of public order and morals. Under these conditions they encouraged a mass change in values, a surge of popular demand, which they believed could broaden the franchise and bring the legislature to the center of governmental power. Tanaka expressed the priority of public enlightenment by distinguishing the form of democratic institutions, which Japan had imported from the West, from the spirit of democratic institutions, which still was lacking. The spirit of democracy could be annoyingly vague in Taishō writings, but the theoretical question that it addressed, the relationship of institutions to culture, was a central one in the modern world, especially for non-Western nations attempting to borrow Western industrial or political forms.

Tanaka's and Ishibashi's critique of the empire lent a new dimension to the theme of form and spirit. They determined that Western liberal ideals had reached Japan in tandem with Western imperialism and military pressure; international competition and fear of colonization had strengthened military and authoritarian elements in Japan while thwarting progress toward a more just political and social order. Nearly all Japanese criticized Western imperialism, but Tanaka and Ishibashi achieved a rare theoretical consistency by arguing that Japanese militarism and imperialism would have the same distorting effect on Korean, Chinese, and Russian state formation.

Thus their theory of international relations balanced political idealism with cultural relativism. Democracy was an ideal form of government, but the reality of Western imperialism had distorted that ideal in the West and in its victims throughout the world. Japanese imperialism was replicating these pernicious effects. Each nation could achieve democracy only if left free to develop autonomously, on the basis of its own culture.

It was the cultural question, the sense of need for a new ethics, literature, and national value system, that united the diverse insights of reformist intellectuals. Although by hindsight Ishibashi's explicit political and social programs seem most coherent, Shimamura may well have had a broader audience for his tortuous inquiries into the nature of selfhood, artistic expression, and the new woman. His penchant for human contradiction, even eccentricity, encouraged an open-minded curiosity in Ishibashi and others among his students. It was Tanaka who daringly defied Japanese philosophy to reason from actual situations to principles rather than the reverse; who conceived of institutions as instruments to meet individual needs; and who developed an interpretation of Meiji history compounded of beneficent Western democracy and distorting Western imperialism. His ideas would lend conceptual unity to Ishibashi's interest in nearly every political issue through the Taishō and early Shōwa years. Tanaka Takako is easily trivialized in two of her many roles, as the upper-class young lady traumatized by workers' sufferings and as the self-abnegating wife of the scholar; yet it was she who played a definitive role in family counseling and other welfare efforts on behalf of women and children, efforts that continued to grow during the war years while the movement for political rights withered. The unity of protest against the suppression of selfhood by any means, familial or artistic, political or economic, attested to the comprehensive claims of the state in attempting to direct all aspects of national life.

As for the limits of prewar liberalism, the writers themselves offered a number of cogent explanations. Tanaka Ōdō chastised Japanese intellectuals for transcendent abstraction and mysticism to the neglect of public policy. Shimamura demonstrated the precarious social and political niche of the creative artist, and the painful doubt that private experience could or even should impinge on public values. Tanaka Takako attested to the burdens that an ideology of feminine submission and an economy of subordination placed on women. Tanaka Ōdō and Ishibashi traced bureaucratism and militarism to Japan's confrontation with Western power in the Meiji Restoration, and Ishibashi grasped the threat that the Japanese empire posed to Taishō democracy. They also commented at length on the vulgar self-interest of the ruling bureaucratic, military, and financial cliques, who conspired to propagate an ethos of altruism among the common people and to ensure that the self-interest of labor, tenant, and women's organizations lacked legitimacy. All three writers denounced censorship and the suppression of opinion, warning of the ways in which obscurantism cramped growth and choice; all criticized the outmoded ethos of hierarchy and submission even as it continued to be propagated in public schools and in the media.

Ishibashi articulated a detailed agenda for universal suffrage and the reform of the House of Peers, the military, the police, and local government. He also perpetuated the Taishō legacy by analyzing the instability of unrepresentative government and the international economy, and by denouncing a reckless foreign policy, throughout the Pacific War. These were persuasive points about the forces against prewar liberalism. The only major omission in the writers' critiques was the rural majority of the population, and the growth of army reserve and patriotic organization in the countryside; even here, however, Ishibashi would have insisted that the real problem was the usual target of his fusillades, an arrogant, arbitrary, and stifling central bureaucracy, and not the level of popular consciousness. The writers' awareness of the opposing forces suggests that the limits of liberalism were in the conditions that surrounded it, and not in liberal confusion and error. I am less inclined to chastise their weakness, which has loomed so large in many accounts of Taishō democracy, and more inclined to admire their dedication to the public interest, their vision of broader human possibilities, and their courage against censorship by the state and censorship by public opinion.

The forces arrayed against liberalism meant that its influence would leave diffuse traces in thought and culture that were more enduring than institutional achievements. Of course all men won the franchise, and women gained the right to attend political meetings. A variety of social legislation was passed, including the administrative recognition of labor unions during the 1920s. These measures could be turned to the purposes of strengthening and consolidating the state. The deeper element of social change lay in the creation of a sizable public who had become accustomed to a steady diet of vigorous debate over culture and philosophy, the arts and letters, the woman question, the historical evolution and value of their institutions, and the policies appropriate to their polity, society, economy and finance, and foreign relations. The complexity of the issues and their broadening constituency had encouraged a proliferation of private organizations for research and publicity, activism, lobbying, and policy formulation. During the Pacific War, liberalism and voluntary associations were suppressed, but they survived to become forces in postwar politics.

Another kind of argument for the power of the Taishō democratic movement lies in the forces required to quell it. The death throes of the gold standard, the Great Kantō Earthquake of 1923, and the financial panic of 1927 were of the utmost importance in constricting Ishibashi's earlier visions of political and social transformation. The effects of financial panic and natural disaster on the parties and labor, tenant, and women's organizations have yet to be analyzed. However, these travails, particularly the earthquake, were windfalls for the state in the sense that it could extend benevolence and at the same time direct panic against dangerous thought and undesirable persons. Popular movements were less resilient. The onslaught of the Great Depression upset legal procedures and institutions, increased governmental controls, and undercut individual independence in all advanced industrial nations, as Ishibashi warned when he cited Franklin D. Roosevelt's attempt to pack the Supreme Court. However, Japan alone of the colonial powers faced a full-blown revolution threatening its overseas territories and creating a crisis atmosphere. As this series of disasters fell upon Japan's young and shallow parliamentary tradition, the persistence of some values and a few voices is more remarkable than the default of much of the Taishō program. Those who were not silenced were remembered in 1945 along with the broader sphere of debate and action to which they had once belonged.

Even more remarkable was the state's shift of tactics prompted by popular movements. Shibamura Atsuki has described a broad reorientation of social policy, from suppression and rules to education and organization, during the 1920s.[1] The crises of the thirties sparked a renewal of repressive tactics along with an unprecedented flood of propaganda and a maze of new patriotic organizations. Escalating repression was a clearcut liberal defeat. Other 1930s initiatives were rebuttals to liberal philosophy and politics, contingent on the prior existence of the ideology that they rejected. For example, Arakawa Ikuo has castigated Shōwa intellectuals for placing pragmatism before principle, supporting domestic regimentation and foreign expansion.[2] The pragmatism was not Tanaka's or Ishibashi's, despite efforts by some commentators such as Seki Eikichi to enlist Tanaka in the national cause after his death in 1932.[3] Nevertheless, liberals' enthusiasm for pragmatic institutional restructuring lent legitimacy and sophistication to different movements for new structures after 1931. In that sense Tanaka's instrumentalism infused a new theoretical complexity into Ogyū Sorai's conviction that institutions were no more than the artifacts of changing social needs. Liberals' quest for selfhood was vilified, but reformist bureaucrats retained other Taishō questions at the center of public discourse: What were the contours of a new relationship between elite and masses? By what means might the plurality of independent governmental institutions be integrated, and their legitimacy and authority enhanced? How could the empire be reconciled with rising Asian nationalism? How could capitalist corporations be constrained by broader concerns of the national interest? What was the answer to rural poverty? And

1. Shibamura, 65.
2. Arakawa Ikuo, *Sen-kyūhyaku-sanjū nendai: Shōwa shisōshi,* 20–21, 24–41, 168–80.
3. Seki Eikichi, "Bunka shakai no dōki," in *Shakaigaku kenkyū,* 250ff.

how could the talents of women be utilized? The institution-
alization of some progressive social ideals, such as family counseling, preserved a liberal legacy while discouraging unqualified opposition.

To a surprising extent, Taishō reformers anticipated the direction of postwar society. Artistic autonomy is fully developed,
reflecting credit on Shimamura and other founders of a new
national culture. Their demands for freedom of expression
and a full-fledged parliamentary system have been realized, at
least in the legal sense. They anticipated a more open competition for wealth and power and protection for the disadvantaged within a social division of labor, and this design too
was extraordinarily prescient. Yet another instance of foresight
is Ishibashi's insistence since 1921 that a little Japan without
an empire would be more prosperous; he developed theories
of multilateral global trade and cultural exchange decades before these policies became Japan's leading options. He used
Keynesian finance in his postwar cabinet positions.

The legitimation of individual self-interest, key to the Ta-
naka/Ishibashi agenda, seems as remote as ever, or at least it
has been transmuted into Shimamura's blend of subjectivity,
aesthetic appreciation, and consumption rather than asserted
in claims on the state and society. Protest groups, including
environmental and citizens' movements, must still defend
themselves against accusations of selfishness, and their explanation of enlightened self-interest sounds a great deal like Tanaka's philosophy.[4] The concept of legitimate self-interest is
weakest among women, and here too Shimamura proved to
be the more accurate observer. Although Tanaka and Ishibashi
insisted on functional equality with men in the public sphere,
they ignored the future of the home and children. Shimamura's commitment to the legal and moral equality of the
sexes, with extreme functional segregation, was far closer to
the attitudes of most of the Japanese urban middle class today.

Ishibashi's postwar career adds a paradoxical twist to this
account of a vigorously pluralistic Taishō democratic movement. Once again interpretations of Japan's past history were

4. Margaret McKean, *Environmental Protest and Citizen Politics in Japan,* 29.

hotly contested to justify or oppose present policies, especially SCAP's radical social engineering during 1945–47. The Government Section's thesis of Japan's class polarization and fascism offered no independent niche for Ishibashi's Keynesian finance nor for his assumption of his right to criticize Occupation policy. SCAP identified the Taishō liberal with the Axis, while cooperating more amicably with economic bureaucrats who actually had managed Japan's war effort. Ishibashi's criticism of SCAP, including his growing distrust of the global employment of American power, was well within his Taishō heritage, and his attempted resistance by appeal to public opinion was also well-practiced. His disaffection from the Occupation, and his rapprochement with the Hatoyama faction and big business, however, were decidedly more conservative. He acquiesced in a new trend toward stability and consumption, narrower and more cautious in its parameters than the Taishō critical spirit. Yet he never ceased defending civil liberties, and he finally rediscovered his pacifism. He ended his political career as a statesman, and, in a phrase used by journalists and bureaucrats alike, a man of the people, calling the government to account in the prophetic tones of a Nichiren priest.

New political and social critics, and new theories of the nature of repression, of course passed Ishibashi by in the Shōwa era. Nevertheless, the rise of liberalism between 1905 and 1931 was part of an age of vigor, life, and vitality. The old rules of authority and status were tottering, while unmanageable bureaucracies and conglomerates were not yet secure in their place; neither had a truly mass culture emerged to screen individuals and movements from effective expression and action. The brief hiatus between old and new controls nourished an extraordinary spirit of experiment and possibility.

Bibliography

ARCHIVES

Carbondale, Illinois. Morris Library. The John Dewey Papers and the Archives of the Open Court Publishing Company.

Chicago, Illinois. University of Chicago. Register, Instructor's Reports, Convocation Programs.

Lexington, Kentucky. Lexington Theological Seminary. Snodgrass Papers, Annual Report of the Treasurer of the Kentucky Christian Education Association.

Palo Alto, California. Stanford University Archives.

Tokyo. Kokuritsu Kokkai Toshokan. Kensei Shiryōshitsu.

Tokyo. Kokuritsu Komonjokan.

Tokyo. Ōkurasho Zaiseishishitsu.

Tokyo. Private Collection of Professor Hanzawa Hiroshi, Tokyo Kōgyō University. Handwritten copies of letters from Tanaka Ōdō to his family from Tsuruoka, Lexington, and Chicago, 1889–96 (originals lost).

Tokyo. Tōyō Keizai Shinpō Archives. Originals of *Ishibashi Tanzan nikki*.

Tokyo. Waseda University Daigakushi Henshūjo. Tanaka Ōdō, "Rirekisho."

Washington, D. C. National Archives. SCAP Collection and State Department Decimal Files.

INTERVIEWS

Hirai Tomisaburō, former vice-minister of international trade and industry.

Ishibashi Tan'ichi, son of Ishibashi Tanzan.

Ishida Hirohide, former journalist at *Nihon keizai shinpō*, Diet representative and labor minister.

Ishihara Takeo, former vice-minister of international trade and industry.

Kimura Ki, Waseda University graduate and journalist.

Kiuchi Naotane, former head of the Board of Trade.

Machimura Kingo, former head of the Home Ministry Police Bureau.

Miyakawa Saburō, former head of the Nihon Keizai Kurabu.
Ōhara Manpei, formerly Ishibashi Tanzan's personal secretary.
Grace Snodgrass, daughter of Eugene Snodgrass.
Takahashi Toshirō, formerly of the Ministry of International Trade
   and Industry.
Tanaka Miki, daughter of Tanaka Ōdō.

WORKS IN JAPANESE

All Japanese-language books are published in Tokyo unless
otherwise noted.

Andō Minoru. "Ishibashi Tanzan no gunjihi ron ni tsuite: 1920–
   1930 nendai no ronsetsu." In Tanaka Hiroshi, ed., *Kindai Nihon
   ni okeru jaanarizumu no seijiteki kinō*. Ochanomizu, 1982.
Anezaki Masaharu. "Jinponshugi to jikkō." In Ōta Masao, ed., *Shiryō:
   Taishō demokurashii ronshō shi*, vol. 1. Shinsen, 1971.
———. "Kaikai no shi." *Rinri kōenshū*, no. 1 (1900): 2–3.
Arakawa Ikuo. *Sen-kyūhyaku-sanjū nendai: Shōwa shisōshi*. Aoki, 1971.
Arase Yutaka. "Taishū kankaku to shuppan jōtai: Senkanki Nihon
   ni okeru." *Shisō*, no. 689 (Nov. 1981): 192–200.
Arisawa Hiromi. *Shōwa keizai shi*. Nihon Keizai Shinbun, 1976.
Asai Yoshio. "Nihon Kōgyō Ginkō." In Katō Toshihiko, ed., *Nihon
   kin'yūron no shiteki kenkyū*. Tokyo University Press, 1983.
Asanuma Inejirō. "Rekidai Shushōchū no ishoku." In Tanzankai, ed.,
   Meihō Tanzan: Ishibashi Tanzan shokan no atogaki. Hifumi, 1957.
Asukai Masamichi. "Roshia kakumei to Nikō jiken." In Inoue Kiyoshi
   and Watanabe Tōru, eds., *Taishōki no kyūshinteki jiyūshugi: 'Tōyō kei-
   zai shinpō' o chūshin toshite*. Tōyō Keizai Shinpō, 1972.
Baba Keinosuke. "Sōda Hakushi no tetsugaku shisō." In Sōda Haku-
   shi Gojūnenki Kinenkai, comp., *Sōda tetsugaku e no kaisō*. Sōbun,
   1975.
Chō Yukio, ed. *Ishibashi Tanzan: Hito to shisō*. Tōyō Keizai Shinpō,
   1974.
———. "Nihon shihonshugi ni okeru riberarizumu no saihyōka:
   Ishibashi Tanzan ron." In Chō, ed., *Nihon keizai shisōshi kenkyū*.
   Mirai, 1963.
———. "Tanzan no keizai shisō." In Chō, ed., *Ishibashi Tanzan: Hito
   to shisō*. Tōyō Keizai Shinpō, 1974.
Chūō Kōron, ed. *Chūō kōron nanajūnen shi*. Chūō Kōron, 1965.

Eguchi Keiichi. "Santō shuppei—Manshū jihen o megutte." In Inoue Kiyoshi and Watanabe Tōru, eds., *Taishōki no kyūshinteki jiyūshugi: 'Tōyō keizai shinpō' o chūshin toshite.* Tōyō Keizai Shinpō, 1972.

Endō Shōkichi, Katō Toshihiko, and Takahashi Makoto. *Nihon no Ōkura Daijin.* Nihon Hyōron, 1964.

Fujo shinbun.

Fukuda Tokuzō. "Tadashii rikai o yōsu." In *Taishō dai zasshi.* Ryūdō, 1978.

Fukushima Shirō. *Fujin sanjūgonen.* Fujo Shinbun, 1935.

Furuya Tetsuo. "Fuashizumu zenya no seijiron." In Inoue Kiyoshi and Watanabe Tōru, eds., *Taishōki no kyūshinteki jiyūshugi: 'Tōyō keizai shinpō' o chūshin toshite.* Tōyō Keizai Shinpō, 1972.

Gendai hyōron shū. Gendai Nihon bungaku taikei, vol. 97. Chikuma, 1973.

Gotō Fumio, Uchida Kenzō, and Ishikawa Masumi. "Sengo hoshu seiji no tesseki, 5: Ishibashi seiken kara Kishi seiken e." *Sekai,* no. 417 (Aug. 1980): 246–68.

Gotō Yasushi. "Kindai tennōsei ron." In Rekishigaku Kenkyūkai, Nihonshi Kenkyūkai, ed., *Kōza Nihonshi,* vol. 9. Tokyo University Press, 1970.

Haga Noboru. *Kindai Nihon shigaku shisōshi.* Kashiwa, 1974.

Hani Gorō. "Taikeiteki tetsugakusha *Systematiker* toshite no Fukuzawa Sensei." In Ichimura Hiromasa, ed., *Ronshū: Fukuzawa Yukichi e no shiten.* Risei, 1973.

Hani Keiko. "Omoide." In Chō Yukio, ed., *Ishibashi Tanzan: Hito to shisō.* Tōyō Keizai Shinpō, 1974.

Haraguchi Yukitaka. "Mazu hataraku mono no seikatsu kōjō." In Tanzankai, ed., *Meihō Tanzan: Ishibashi Tanzan shokan no atogaki.* Hifumi, 1957.

"Haran ni tonda isshō: Nitchū, Nisso dakai ni sokuseki." *Asahi,* April 25, 1983, evening edition.

Haruhara Akihiko. *Nihon shinbun tsūshi.* Gendai Jaanarizumu, 1969.

Hasegawa Tenkei. "Shizenha ni taisuru gokai." In *Meiji bungaku zenshū,* vol. 43. Chikuma, 1967.

Hashikawa Bunsō. "Tanzan to Kiyoshi." In Chō Yukio, ed., *Ishibashi Tanzan: Hito to shisō.* Tōyō Keizai Shinpō, 1974.

Hashimoto Jurō. "Senkanki Nihon shihonshugi bunseki no hōhō. *Rekishigaku kenkyū,* no. 507 (1982): 25–36.

Hatanaka Shigeo. *Shōwa shuppan dan'atsu shi.* Tosho Shinbun, 1977.

Hattori Bennosuke et al. "Tanaka Ōdō no hito to shisō o kataru." *Jiyū shisō,* no. 7 (Nov. 1977): 1–27.

———. "Jiyū shisōka Ninomiya Sontoku to Ishibashi Tanzan." *Jiyū shisō*, no. 5 (Apr. 1977): 34–40.

Hayashi Hirofumi. "Sen-kyūhyaku-nijū nendai zenpan ni okeru rōdō seisaku no tenkan." *Rekishigaku kenkyū*, no. 508 (1982): 49–64.

Hirano Yoshitarō. *Nakamura Tahachirō den*. Nikkō, 1938.

Hiratsuka Raichō. *Genshi, josei wa taiyō de atta*. 4 vols. Ōtsuki, 1975.

———. "Nora-san ni." *Seitō* 2 (Jan. 1912): 133–41.

———. "Yonda *Maguda*." *Seitō* 2 (June 1912): 6–13.

Hoashi Riichirō. "Nihonjin wa kagekiteki kokumin ni arazu." In *Taishō dai zasshi*. Ryūdō, 1978.

"Honshi sōkan no shimei to kongo." *Tōyō keizai shinpō*, 14 Nov. 1925.

Ichikawa Fusae. "Fujin Keizaikai no omoide." In Chō Yukio, ed., *Ishibashi Tanzan: Hito to shisō*. Tōyō Keizai Shinpō, 1974.

———. *Watakushi no fujin undō*. Shugen, 1972.

Ichimura Hiromasa, ed. *Ronshū: Fukuzawa Yukichi e no shiten*. Risei, 1973.

Ichiyama Morio. *Noda no rekishi*. Ron, 1979.

Ide Fumiko. *Seitō*. Kōbundō, 1961.

———. *Seitō no onnatachi*. Kaien, 1975.

Ide Fumiko and Esashi Akiko. *Taishō demokurashii to josei*. Gōdō, 1977.

Ienaga Saburō. *Daigaku jiyū no rekishi*. Hanawa, 1962.

———. "Keimō shigaku." In *Meiji shiron shū*, vol. 1. Meiji bungaku zenshū, vol. 77. Chikuma, 1974.

Iida Taizō. "Taishō chishikijin no seiritsu to seiji shisō: Bunmei hihyōka o chūshin ni." Ph.D. diss., Tokyo University, 1973.

———. "Taishōki bunmei hihyōka chosaku ichiran." *Hōgaku shirin* (Hōsei University) 80 (1982): 130–244.

Iinuma Jirō. "Nōgyō mondai ron—toku ni *Ōsaka asahi shinbun* to taihi shite." In Inoue Kiyoshi and Watanabe Tōru, eds., *Taishōki no kyūshinteki jiyūshugi: 'Tōyō keizai shinpō' o chūshin toshite*. Tōyō Keizai Shinpō, 1972.

Ikeda Seihin. *Zaikai kaiko*, ed. Yanagisada Ken. Sekai no Nihon, 1949.

Ikimatsu Keizō. *Taishōki no shisō to bunka*. Aoki, 1971.

Imai Seiichi. "Seitō seiji to kokumin shisō." In Hashikawa Bunsō and Matsumoto Sannosuke, eds., *Kindai Nihon seiji shisōshi*, vol. 2. Kindai Nihon shisōshi taikei, vol. 4. Yūhikaku, 1973.

———. "Taishō demokurashii." In *Nihon no rekishi*, vol. 23. Chūō Kōron, 1966.

Imamura Takeo. *Ikeda Seihin den*. Keiō Tsūshin, 1962.

Inoue Kiyoshi. *Nihon joseishi*. Seishindō, 1954.

————. "Nihon teikokushugi hihan." In Inoue and Watanabe Tōru, eds., *Taishōki no kyūshinteki jiyūshugi: 'Tōyō keizai shinpō' o chūshin toshite*. Tōyō Keizai Shinpō, 1972.

Inoue Kiyoshi, ed. *Taishō no seiji to shakai*. Iwanami, 1969.

Inoue Kiyoshi and Watanabe Tōru, eds. *Taishōki no kyūshinteki jiyūshugi: 'Tōyō keizai shinpō' o chūshin toshite*. Tōyō Keizai Shinpō, 1972.

Inoue Tetsujirō. "Kokumin shisō no mujun." In Ōta Masao, ed., *Shiryō: Taishō demokurashii ronsō shi*, vol 1. Shinsen, 1971.

Ishibashi Tan'ichi. "Katei de no chichi no danmen." In Chō Yukio, ed., *Ishibashi Tanzan: Hito to shisō*. Tōyō Keizai Shinpō, 1974.

Ishibashi Tanzan. "Chūmoku subeki kosakunin kumiai no sōka." *Tōyō keizai shinpō*, 6 July 1921.

————. "Henshūshitsu yori." *Tōyō keizai shinpō*, 19 Mar. 1932.

————. *Ishibashi Tanzan zenshū*. 15 vols. Tōyō Keizai Shinpō, 1970–72.

————. "Shihonshugi imada shisezu." *Tōyō keizai shinpō*, 15 Mar. 1924.

————. *Tanzan nikki*. Tōyō Keizai Shinpō, 1974.

————. "Zeisei kaisei no yōmoku." *Tōyō keizai shinpō*, 5 and 25 Jan., 5 Mar., and 4 Apr. 1918.

————. "Zōshō jidai o furikaette (1 and 2)." *Jiyū shisō*, nos. 18 and 19 (Feb. and May 1981): 25–45 and 35–57.

Ishibashi Tanzan and Suzuki Mosaburō. "Jimin, shakai ryōtōshu taidan." In Tanzankai, ed., *Meihō Tanzan: Ishibashi Tanzan shokan no atogaki*. Hifumi, 1957.

Ishibashi Umeko. "Omoide no ki." *Ishibashi Tanzan zenshū geppō*, no. 15 (1972): 4–11.

Ishida Takeshi, ed. *Fukuzawa Yukichi shū*. Kindai Nihon shisō taikei, vol. 2. Chikuma, 1975.

Ishikawa Takuboku. "Jidai heisoku no genjō." In *Gendai Nihon bungaku zenshū*, vol. 32. Chikuma, 1975.

————. "Seikyū na shisō." In *Gendai Nihon bungaku zenshū*, vol. 32. Chikuma: 1975.

————. *Takuboku zenshū*. Kaizō, 1929.

Ishizuki Shizue. "Fujin undō no tenkai." In Koyama Hitoshi, ed., *Taishōki no kenryoku to minshū*. Hōritsu Bunka, 1980.

Isomura Eiichi, ed. *Gyōsei saishin mondai jiten*. Teikoku Chihō Gyōsei Gakkai, 1972.

Itō Takashi. " 'Jiyūshugisha' Hatoyama Ichirō—sono senzen, senchū, sengo." In Kindai Nihon Kenkyūkai, ed., *Taiheiyō sensō: Kaisen kara kōwa made*. Nenpyō: Kindai Nihon kenkyū, no. 4. Yamakawa, 1982.

_____ . *Shōwaki no seiji*. Yamakawa, 1983.

Iwano Hōmei. *Hōmei zenshū*. 18 vols. Kokumin Tosho, 1922.

_____ . "Wakamiya, Tanaka hikaku ron." *Chūō kōron* 32, no. 12 (Dec. 1917): 70–74.

Jiyū shisō, no. 33, Sept. 1984.

Jō Ichirō. *Hakkinbon hyakunen*. Tōgen, 1969.

Kamitsukasa Shōken. "Shimamura Hōgetsu ron: Bundan no gaimu daijin." *Chūō kōron* 26, no. 7 (July 1911): 100–02.

Kano Masanao. "Atarashii kokuminzō no keisei." In Hashikawa Bunsō and Matsumoto Sannosuke, eds., *Kindai Nihon seiji shisōshi*, vol. 1. Kindai Nihon shisōshi taikei, vol. 3. (Yūhikaku, 1974).

_____ . *Taishō demokurashii*. Nihon no rekishi, vol. 27. Shōgakkan, 1976.

Katagiri Yoshio. "Nichi-Bei ryōkoku no sonshitsu." In Tanzankai, ed., *Meihō Tanzan: Ishibashi Tanzan shokan no atogaki*. Hifumi, 1957.

Katano Masako. "Ryōsai kenboshugi no genryū." In Kindai Joseishi Kenkyūkai, ed., *Onnatachi no kindai*. Kashiwa, 1978.

Katō Masuo. "GHQ to Ishibashi tsuihō." *Ishibashi Tanzan zenshū geppō*, no. 13 (Oct. 1970): 7–9.

Katō Toshihiko, ed. *Nihon kin'yūron no shiteki kenkyū*. Tokyo University Press, 1983.

Kawakami Hajime. "Kachi hōsoku kara mita kinhon'isei hakai no igi." *Tōyō keizai shinpō*, 13 Feb. 1932.

Kawamura Kōshō. *Meiji Taishō Nichiren monka Bukka jinmei jiten*. Kokusho Kankōkai, 1978.

Kawasaki Hideji. *Yūki aru seijikatachi*. Senseki, 1971.

Kawata Shirō. "Minponshugi ni kansuru ichi kōsatsu." In Ōta Masao, ed., *Shiryō: Taishō demokurashii ronsō shi*, vol. 1. Shinsen, 1971.

Kayahara Kazan. "Konjun yori konjun." In *Taishō dai zasshi*. Ryūdō, 1978.

Keizai Kikaku Chō, ed. *Gendai Nihon keizai tenkai: Keizai Kikaku Chō sanjūnen shi*. Ōkurashō, 1976.

Keizai Kōkyūkai. *Kin'yū seido kaizen'an*. Keizai Kōkyūkai, 1927.

_____ . "Nihon Ginkō kaizen'an." In *Kin'yū seido kaizen'an*. Keizai Kōkyūkai, 1927.

Kikuchi Masanori. *Roshia kakumei to Nihonjin*. Chikuma, 1973.

Kimura Kyūichi. "Demokurashii no shinri." In Ōta Masao, ed., *Shiryō: Taishō demokurashii ronsō shi*, vol. 1. Shinsen, 1971.

Kindai Joseishi Kenkyūkai, ed. *Onnatachi no kindai*. Kashiwa, 1978.

Kin'yū Seido Kenkyūkai. "Chūō ginkō seido shian." *Tōyō keizai shinpō*, 21 Feb. 1925.

Kisaka Jun'ichirō. "Taishōki no naisei kaikaku ron." In Inoue Kiyoshi and Watanabe Tōru, eds., *Taishōki no kyūshinteki jiyūshugi: 'Tōyō keizai shinpō' o chūshin toshite*. Tōyō Keizai Shinpō, 1972.

Kisaki Masaru. *Kisaki nikki*. Tosho Shinbun, 1965.

Kiyosawa Kiyoshi. *Ankoku nikki*. 3 vols. Hyōron, 1970–72.

Kodama Katsuko. *Fujin sanseiken undō shōshi*. Domesu, 1981.

Kōno Tetsurō. "Furii shinkingu no tenkai." In Chō Yukio, ed., *Ishibashi Tanzan: Hito to shisō*. Tōyō Keizai Shinpō, 1974.

Koyama Hitoshi, ed. *Taishōki no kenryoku to minshū*. Hōritsu Bunka, 1980.

Kuno Osamu and Tsurumi Shunsuke. *Gendai Nihon no shisō*. Iwanami, 1956.

Kurosaki Seisuke. "Senjika no chūshō kinu-jinken kigyōsha ishiki." *Keizai shigaku* 45 (1979): 58–80.

Kuwabara Takeo et al. "Jaanarizumu no shisōteki yakuwari." In Kuno Osamu and Sumiya Mikio, eds., *Shidōsha to taishū*. Kindai Nihon shisōshi kōza, vol. 5. Chikuma, 1960.

Kuwaki Genyoku et al. "Matsui Sumako no shi ni tsuite." *Waseda bungaku*, ser. 2, no. 159 (Feb. 1919): 27–34.

Kyokutō Kokusai Gunji Saiban Kiroku: Eibun sokkiroku, vol. 72: 25, 413–24 (7–11 Aug. 1947).

"Kyōman o imashimeru." *Yomiuri shinbun*, 5 May 1915.

Maruyama Masao. "Fukuzawa Yukichi no tetsugaku." In *Gendai Nihon shisō taikei*, vol. 34. Chikuma, 1963.

Masamune Hakuchō. "Shimamura Hōgetsu ron." *Chūō kōron* 26, no. 7 (July 1911): 94–97.

Masuda Hiroshi. "Ishibashi Tanzan no Manshū hōki ron." *Kokusai seiji*, no. 71 (Aug. 1982): 72–92.

―――. "Ishibashi Tanzan no Roshia kakumeikan: Yoshino Sakuzō to no hikaku kōsatsu." *Jiyū shisō*, no. 14 (Feb. 1980): 15–36.

―――. "Ishibashi Tanzan no tai-Bei imin fuyō ron." *Jiyū shisō*, no. 21 (Nov. 1981): 28–49.

Masuda Hiroshi, ed. *Shō Nihonshugi: Ishibashi Tanzan gaikō ronshū, 1913–1967*. Sōshisha, 1984.

Matsubayashi Matsuo, ed. *Kaikoroku: Sengo Tsūsan seisaku shi*. Seisaku Jihō, 1973.

Matsui Sumako. "Nora to Maguda ni tsuite." *Chūō kōron* 28 (special issue on "Fujin mondai," July 1913): 90–106

Matsumoto Kappei. *Nihon shingeki shi*. Chikuma, 1966.

Matsumoto Sannosuke. "Seiji to chishikijin." In Hashikawa Bunsō and Matsumoto, eds., *Kindai Nihon seiji shisōshi*, vol. 2. Kindai Nihon shisōshi taikei, vol. 4. Yūhikaku, 1973.

Matsuo Takayoshi. "Daiichiji taisen no futsū senkyo undō." In Inoue Kiyoshi, ed., *Taishōki no seiji to shakai*. Iwanami, 1969.

———. "Jūgonen sensōka no Ishibashi Tanzan." In Nihon Seiji Gakkai, ed., *Kindai Nihon no kokkazō*. Nenpyō seijigaku, 1982. Iwanami, 1982.

———. "Kokumin shuken ronsha Ishibashi Tanzan." *Ishibashi Tanzan zenshū geppō*, no. 5 (Mar. 1971): 4–6.

———. "Kyūshinteki jiyūshugi no seiritsu katei." In Inoue Kiyoshi and Watanabe Tōru, eds., *Taishōki no kyūshinteki jiyūshugi: 'Tōyō keizai shinpō' o chūshin toshite*. Tōyō Keizai Shinpō, 1972.

———. "Miura Tetsutarō cho 'Shina jihen shori no hōshin' ni tsuite." *Ishibashi Tanzan zenshū geppō*, no. 15 (Sept. 1972): 13–16.

———. *Taishō demokurashii*. Iwanami, 1975.

———. "Taishō demokurashii no ichi suimyaku: Ishibashi Tanzan to sono senkōshatachi." In Akamatsu Toshihide Kyōju Taikan Kinen Jigyōkai, ed., *Akamatsu Toshihide Kyōju taikan kinen: Kokushi ronshū*. Bunkō, 1972.

Matsuoka Komakichi. "Sonkei dekiru Ishibashi-san." In Tanzankai, ed., *Meihō Tanzan: Ishibashi Tanzan shokan no atogaki*. Hifumi, 1957.

Miki Takeo. "Hoshu seitō no dappi e." In Tanzankai, ed., *Meihō Tanzan: Ishibashi Tanzan shokan no atogaki*. Hifumi, 1957.

Minami Hiroshi. *Taishō bunka*. Keisō, 1965.

Mitani Taiichirō. *Taishō demokurashii ron*. Chūō Kōron, 1974.

———. "Taishō demokurashii to Amerika." In Saitō Makoto et al., eds., *Nihon to Amerika: Hikaku bunka ron*. Nan'undō, 1973.

Mitsui Kōshi. "Kuwaki Hakushi to Tanaka Ōdō Shi no sansō o shitekisu." *Shin Nihon*, May 1918, 7–9.

Miura Tetsutarō. "Manshū hōki ka gunbi kakuchō ka." *Tōyō keizai shinpō*, 5 Jan.–5 March 1913.

———. "Saikin seiken no shinsō." *Tōyō keizai shinpō*, 5 July 1914.

———. "Sangyōjō no daini ishin." *Tōyō keizai shinpō*, 25 Aug. 1912.

———. "Waga kuni no kinri wa naniyue ni takaki ka." *Tōyō keizai shinpō*, 26 Jan.–22 Mar. 1924.

Miwa Ryōichi. "Kinkaikin seisaku kettei katei ni okeru rigai ishiki." *Aoyama keizai ronshū 26, nos. 1, 2, and 3 (1974)*.

Miyazawa Masanori. "Gaikō hyōronka no teikō." In Dōshisha Daigaku Jinbun Kagaku Kenkyūjo, *Senjika teikō no kenkyū*, vol. 1. Misuzu, 1969.

Mukai Toshio. "Ōkurashō Yokinbu." In Katō Toshihiko, ed., *Nihon kin'yūron no shiteki kenkyū*. Tokyo University Press, 1982.

Murakami Nobuhiko. "Fujin mondai to fujin kaihō undō." In Iwanami Kōza, *Nihon rekishi*, vol. 18. Iwanami, 1975.

Murobuse Kōshin. "Kageki shisō to Nihon." In *Taishō dai zasshi.* Ryūdō, 1978.

Mutō Sanji. "Hamaguchi Shushō—Inoue Zōshō ni nozomu." In Nihon Ginkō Chōsakyoku, ed., *Nihon kin'yū shiryō, Shōwa-hen.* Ōkurashō, 1968.

Nakajima Kotō. "Bungei Iin toshite tekitō na hito." *Chūō kōron* 26, no. 7 (July 1911): 104.

Nakamura Kichizō et al. "Matsui Sumako to Shibata Kan." *Chūō kōron* 27, no. 7 (July 1912): 125–47.

Nakamura Kōichi. "Tairiku mondai no imeeji to jittai." In Hashikawa Bunsō and Matsumoto Sannosuke, eds., *Kindai Nihon seiji shisōshi,* vol. 2. Kindai Nihon shisōshi taikei, vol. 4. Yūhikaku, 1973.

Nakamura Takafusa. "SCAP to Nihon: Senryōki no keizai seisaku keisei." In Nakamura Takafusa, ed., *Senryōki no keizai to seiji.* Tokyo University Press, 1979.

Nakanishi Keijirō. *Waseda Daigaku hachijūnen shi.* Waseda University Press, 1962.

Nakauchi Toshio. *Kindai Nihon kyōiku shisōshi.* Kokudo, 1973.

Nakayama Ichirō. "Taikei naki taikei, Ishibashi keizaigaku." In Chō Yukio, ed., *Ishibashi Tanzan: Hito to shisō.* Tōyō Keizai Shinpō, 1974.

————. "Takken." In Chō Yukio, ed., *Ishibashi Tanzan: Hito to shisō.* Tōyō Keizai Shinpō, 1974.

Nakayama Shinpei, Nakamura Kichizō, and Ihara Seiseien. "Hōgetsu—Sumako gōshi no ki." *Chūō kōron* 34, no. 2 (Feb. 1919): 41–72.

Nishida Kitarō. *Jikaku ni okeru chokkan to hansei.* Iwanami, 1924.

Nishio Suehiro. "Yo no 'santō renritsu' to Ishibashi-san." In Chō Yukio, ed., *Ishibashi Tanzan: Hito to shisō.* Tōyō Keizai Shinpō, 1974.

Obama Toshie. "Kakudai kinkō ōi ni yare." In Tanzankai, ed., *Meihō Tanzan: Ishibashi Tanzan shokan no atogaki.* Hifumi, 1957.

Oda Yorozu. "Kokutai to minsei." In Ōta Masao, ed., *Shiryō: Taishō demokurashii ronsō shi,* vol. 1. Shinsen, 1971.

Ogura Masatarō, comp. *'Tōyō keizai shinpō' genron rokujūnen.'* Tōyō Keizai Shinpō, 1955.

Ōhara Manpei. "Nitchū fukkō ni okeru Ishibashi-san no yume." *Jiyū shisō,* no. 16 (Aug. 1980): 35–45.

Oka Yoshitake. "Kunizukuri ni chi no shio." In Chō Yukio, ed., *Ishibashi Tanzan: Hito to shisō.* Tōyō Keizai Shinpō, 1974.

————. *Tenkanki no Taishō.* Nihon kindaishi taikei, vol. 5. Tokyo University Press, 1969.

Ōkurashō Zaiseishishitsu, ed. *Tai-senryōgun kōshō hiroku: Watanabe Takeshi nikki.* Tōyō Keizai Shinpō, 1983.

Ōnishi Hajime. "Kyōiku chokugo to rinri." In *Ōnishi Hajime zenshū*. 6 vols. Keihō, 1906.

Ono Hideo. *Nihon shinbun hattatsu shi*. Gogatsu, 1982.

Ōta Masao, ed. *Shiryō: Taishō demokurashii ronsō shi*. 2 vols. Shinsen, 1971.

Ōta Takeshi. "Kōshoku tsuihō." In *Kataritsugu Shōwashi*. Gekidō no hanseiki, vol. 5. Asahi Shinbun, 1977.

―――. "Kōshoku tsuihō to shikaku shinsa." In Andō Yoshio, ed., *Shōwa seiji keizai shi e no shōgen*, vol. 2. Mainichi Shinbun, 1972.

Ōtsuki Ken. *Gakkō to minshū no rekishi*. Shin Nihon, 1980.

Ōuchi Hyōe. "Ishibashi-san no koto." In Chō Yukio, ed., *Ishibashi Tanzan: Hito to shisō*. Tōyō Keizai Shinpō, 1974.

Ōyama Ikuo. "Gaitō no gunshū." In *Taishō dai zasshi*. Ryūdō, 1978.

Ozaki Hirotsugu. *Shimamura Hōgetsu*. Nihon kindaigeki no sōshi-shatachi, vol. 1. Mirai, 1965.

Ozaki Moriteru. *Nihon shūshoku shi*. Bungei Shunjū, 1967.

Ozaki Shirō. *Waseda Daigaku*. Bungei Shunjū, 1953.

Saitō Michiko. "Hani Motoko no shisō." In Kindai Joseishi Ken-kyūkai, ed., *Onnatachi no kindai*. Kashiwa, 1978.

Saitō Takao. *Saitō Takao seiji ronshū*. Izushi-machi, Izushi-gun, Hyōgo-ken: Saitō Takao Sensei Kenshōkai, 1961.

Sakai Saburō. *Shōwa Kenkyūkai: Aru chishikijin dantai no kiseki*. Tii Bii Esu Buritanika, 1979.

Satō Eisaburō. "Ishibashi Sensei to Jinmu keiki." In Tanzankai, ed., *Meihō Tanzan: Ishibashi Tanzan shokan no atogaki*. Hifumi, 1957.

Satogami Ryūhei. "Taishō demokurashii to Kizokuin." In Inoue Ki-yoshi, ed., *Taishōki no seiji to shakai*. Iwanami, 1969.

Seki Eikichi. "Bunka shakai no dōki." In *Shakaigaku kenkyū*. Keimei, 1932.

Senzenki Kanryōsei Kenkyūkai, ed. *Senzenki Nihon kanryōsei no seido, soshiki, jinji*. Tokyo University Press, 1981.

Shibamura Atsuki. "Dai toshi ni okeru kenryoku to minshū no kōdō." In Koyama Hitoshi, ed., *Taishōki no kenryoku to minshū*. Hōritsu Bunka, 1980.

Shimamura Hōgetsu. *Kindai bungei no kenkyū*. Hakubunkan, 1909.

―――. "Kindai bungei to fujin mondai." *Chūō kōron* 28 (special issue on "Fujin mondai," July 1913): 2–23.

―――. "Kindai fujin no jikaku no naiyō." In *Taishō dai zasshi*. Ryūdo, 1978.

―――. "*Ningyō no ie* to Ipusen no sakugeki jutsu." *Chūō kōron* 28 (Spring supplement, Apr. 1913): 123–33.

Shimamura Hōgetsu, trans. *Ningyō no ie. Waseda bungaku*, ser. 2, no. 50 (January 1910): 1–139.

Shimanaka Hōji. "Yajin saishō hōdan." In Tanzankai, ed., *Meihō Tanzan: Ishibashi Tanzan shokan no atogaki*. Hifumi, 1957.

Shimura Hidetarō. *Ishibashi Tanzan*. Tōmei, 1966.

"Shina osorubeshi." *Tōyō keizai shinpō*, 5 Apr. 1910.

Shinobu Seizaburō. *Taishō seiji shi*. Keisō, 1968.

————. "Taishō seijishi no konpon mondai." In Rekishi Kagaku Kyōgikai, ed., *Minshushugi undō shi*, vol. 2. Azekura, 1977.

Shionoya Tsukumo. "Ishibashi-san to Keinzu." *Ishibashi Tanzan zenshū geppō*, no. 5 (Mar. 1971): 6–8.

Shirayanagi Shūko. "Eiyūsen kara minshūsen e." *Chūō kōron* 33, no. 10 (Oct. 1918): 33–50.

Sōda Kiichirō. *Bunka kachi to kyokugen gainen*. Iwanami, 1972.

Sotani Hiromi. "*Fujin kōron* no shisō." In Kindai Joseishi Kenkyūkai, ed., *Onnatachi no kindai*. Kashiwa, 1978.

Suehiro Shigeo. "Shin Nichiro kyōyaku ni tsukite." *Gaikō jihō*, no. 189 (15 Sept. 1912): 11–20.

Sugimori Hisahide. *Takida Chōin: Aru henshūsha no shōgai*. Chūkō Shinsho, 1966.

Sumiya Mikio. *Shōwa kyōkō: Sono rekishiteki igi to zentaizō*. Yūhikaku, 1975.

Suzuki Mosaburō. "Retsuretsutaru heiwa e no netsui." In Chō Yukio, ed., *Ishibashi Tanzan: Hito to shisō*. Tōyō Keizai Shinpō, 1974.

Tagawa Daikichirō. "Shina manyū shokan." *Tōyō keizai shinpō*, 15 and 25 July 1915.

"Tai-Shi mondai wa haruka ni kyoku o musubu no yūdan o nozomu." *Yomiuri shinbun*, 4 May 1915.

Taishō dai zasshi. Ryūdō, 1978.

Takahashi Kamekichi. "Kinri inkaron no konkyo." *Tōyō keizai shinpō*, 5 and 24 May, and 5 July 1921.

————. "Surudoi rojishan, sugureta jikkōka." In Chō Yukio, ed., *Ishibashi Tanzan: Hito to shisō*. Tōyō Keizai Shinpō, 1974.

Takayama Chogyū. "Bunmei hihyōka toshite no bungakusha." In *Gendai Nihon bungaku zenshū*, vol. 59. Chikuma, 1958.

Takegawa Yoshinori. *Yamanashi-ken nōmin undō shi*. Kōfu: Yamanashi Rōshi Shinbun, 1934.

"Takeiei wa naritatanai." *Shūkan Tōyō keizai* 53 (22 July 1978): 52–58.

Takeuchi Yoshimi. "Waga Ishibashi hakken." In Chō Yukio, ed., *Ishibashi Tanzan: Hito to shisō*. Tōyō Keizai Shinpō, 1974.

Tanaka Ikuo. "Kinkaikin ronsō." In Chō Yukio and Sumiya Kazuhiko, eds., *Kindai Nihon keizai shisōshi*, vol. 1. Kindai Nihon shisōshi taikei, vol. 5. Yūhikaku, 1971.

Tanaka Ōdō (Kiichi). "Ayamaretaru Ninomiya Sontoku." *Tōyō jiron* 2, no. 7 (Aug. 1911): 91–94.

———. "Bungei hogo mondai." *Chūō kōron* 25, no. 4 (Apr. 1910): 140–42.

———. "Bungei no shōka." *Tōyō jiron* 2 (July 1911): 974–81.

———. *Fukuzawa Yukichi*. Jitsugyō no Sekai, 1915.

———. *Fukuzawa Yukichi*, ed. Sugimori Kōjirō. Ōdō senshū, vol 2. Seki, 1948.

———. "Gakumon no dokuritsu no igi to han'i to junjo to o ronzu." *Chūō kōron* 33, no. 1 (Jan. 1918): 64–92.

———. "Genka ni okeru shinwaka no genryū o kyūmeisu." In *Sukui wa hansei yori*. Jitsugyō no Sekai, 1923.

———. "Hiratsuka Raichō Shi ni ataete Shi no fujinkan o ronzu." *Chūō kōron* 30 (special issue on "Taishō shin kiun," July 1915): 104–27.

———. "Hyōronka toshite no Tokutomi Sohō." *Shin Nihon* 7, no. 5 (1917): 89–105.

———. *Hyuumanisuto Ninomiya Sontoku*, ed. Ishibashi Tanzan. Ōdō Senshū, vol. 3. Seki, 1948.

———. "Ichi no rikai to shiryoku o kakeru Nihon." *Chūgai* 2, no. 1 (Jan. 1918): 38–50.

———. "Iwano Hōmei Shi no geijutsukan to jinseikan to o ronzu." *Chūō kōron* 24 (Sept. 1909): 19–71.

———. "Jinsei hyōron no igi to jinsei hyōronka no shikaku." *Chūō kōron* 25, no. 7 (July 1910): 30–42.

———. "Jiyū shisōka no rinrikan." In *Shosai yori gaitō ni*. Kōbundō, 1911.

———. "Jon Juui [*sic*] no tetsugaku." In *Sōzō to kyōraku*. Ten'yū, 1921.

———. "Joshi kyōiku zakkan." *Rinri kōenshū*, no. 90 (Feb. 1910): 50–61.

———. "Kaihōsha Uiriamu Jiemusu [*sic*]." *Waseda bungaku*, ser. 2, no. 118 (Sept. 1915): 2–16.

———. "Kinsei bundan ni okeru hyōron no kachi." In *Shosai yori gaitō ni*. Kōbundō: 1911.

———. "Ko Kyōju Uiriamu Jiemusu [*sic*] o tsuiokusu." In *Tetsujinshugi*, vol. 1. Kōbundō, 1912.

———. *Ninomiya Sontoku*. Kōbundō, 1911.

———. "Nishida Hakushi no tetsugaku shisaku no tokuchō to kachi to o ronzu." *Waseda Daigaku shi* 2, no. 3 (Mar. 1969): 47–89.

————. "Rinri shisō kaihō no yōkyū." *Tōyō jiron* 3, no. 7 (1912): 935–44.

————. "Sekai heiwa no risō ni chinamite shoka no bunkashugi o kentōsu (1 and 2)." *Chūō Kōron* 37, special issue on "Sekai heiwa to jinruiai" (July 1922): 4–48, and no. 8 (Aug. 1922): 4–72.

————. "Shōdō to shisō." In *Gendai bunka no honshitsu*. Tōyō Keizai Shinpō, 1929.

————. *Shosai yori gaitō ni*. Kōbundō, 1911.

————. *Sōzō to kyōraku*. Ten'yū, 1921.

————. *Sukui wa hansei yori*. Jitsugyō no Sekai, 1923.

————. *Tettei kojinshugi*. Ten'yū, 1918.

————. "Tettei kojinshugi." In *Tettei kojinshugi*. Ten'yū, 1918.

————. *Tettei kojinshugi*, ed. Hasegawa Nyozekan. Ōdō senshū, vol. 1. Seki, 1948.

————. "Tettei kojinshugisha no ren'aikan, kekkonkan." In *Sukui wa hansei yori*. Jitsugyō no Sekai, 1923.

————. "Tōzai bunmei yūgō no igi oyobi keika o ronzu." In *Shosai yori gaitō ni*. Kōbundō, 1911.

————. "Waga kuni ni okeru shizenshugi o ronzu." *Myōjō* (Aug. 1908): 1–113.

————. "Wakaki josei no tame ni gakusei no igi o kōzu." In *Ōdō joseikan*. Bungei tetsugaku kōza, no. 5. Ōnishi, 1921.

————. "Yo ga kokuminshugi no shuchō." *Chūō kōron* 30, no. 6 (June 1915): 18–37.

————. "Yokubō no risōka, hōritsuka." In *Tettei kojinshugi*. Ten'yū, 1918.

Tanaka Sumiko, ed. *Josei kaihō no shisō to kōdō*. Vol. 1, *Senzen hen*. Jiji Tsūshin, 1979.

Tanaka Takako. "Fujin no shakai jigyō." *Katei shūhō*, no. 520 (13 June 1919): 3.

————. "Ko Tanaka Ōdō no zōsho ni tsuite." *Shobutsu tenbō* (Dec. 1932): 54–56.

————. *Tōyō*. Yōa, 1943.

Tanzankai, ed. *Meihō Tanzan: Ishibashi Tanzan shokan no atogaki*. Hifumi, 1957.

Teiyū Rinrikai. "Teiyū Konwakai setsuritsu no shui." *Rinri kōenshū*, no. 1 (1900):1.

Tokoro Shigemoto. *Kindai shakai to Nichirenshugi*. Nihonjin no kōdō to shisō, vol. 18. Hyōron, 1972.

Tōyama Sentarō. "Raidō o imashime." In *Taishō dai zasshi*. Ryūdō, 1978.

Tōyō keizai shinpō. Special issue on "Kin'yushutsu kaikin mondai." 16 March 1929.

Tsurumi Seiryō. "Ryōtaisen kanki no Nihon Ginkō." In Katō Toshihiko, ed., *Nihon kin'yūron no shiteki kenkyū*. Tokyo University Press, 1983.

Tsurumi Shunsuke. "*Chūō kōron* no rekishi." *Shisō*, no. 476 (Feb. 1964): 121–29.

Tsutoi Kiyotada. "Nihon ni okeru taishū shakai to hyōjunka." *Shisō*, no. 688 (Oct. 1981): 178–200.

Uchikawa Yoshimi. "Shinbun dokusha no hensen." *Shinbun kenkyū*, no. 120 (July 1960): 19.

Ueda Kimiko. "*Ningyō no ie* o yomu." *Seitō* 2 (Jan. 1912): 126–32.

Uehara Etsujirō. *Hachijūji no omoide*. Uehara Etsujirō Kaikoroku Kankōkai, 1963.

———. "Nihon minken hattatsu shi daiikkan (shohan, 1916)." In Uehara Etsujirō Jūsankai Kikinen Shuppan Kankōkai, ed., *Uehara Etsujirō to Nihonkoku Kenpō*. Uehara Etsujirō Jūsankai Kikinen Shuppan Kankōkai, 1974.

———. "Yoshino Hakushi no kenpōron o hyōsu." In Uehara Etsujirō Jūsankai Kikinen Shuppan Kankōkai, ed., *Uehara Etsujirō to Nihonkoku kenpō*. Uehara Etsujirō Jūsankai Kikinen Shuppan Kankōkai, 1974.

———. "Yoshino Hakushi no kenpōron to minponshugi." In Uehara Etsujirō Jūsankai Kikinen Shuppan Kankōkai, ed., *Uehara Etsujirō to Nihonkoku kenpō*. Uehara Etsujirō Jūsankai Kikinen Shuppan Kankōkai, 1974.

Uematsu Hisaaki. "Futsū senkyoan no shōsoku ika." *Tōyō keizai shinpō*, 25 Feb. 1911.

———. "Giin kaikaku." *Tōyō keizai shinpō*, 5 Apr. 1907.

Ueno Yōko. "*Ningyō no ie* yori josei mondai e." *Seitō* 2 (Jan. 1912): 62–111.

Uesugi Mitsuhiko. "Taishōki jiyūshugisha no taigaikan: Ishibashi Tanzan o rei toshite." *Takachiho ronsō* (Apr. 1980): 73–100.

Uesugi Shinkichi. "Minponshugi to minshushugi." In Ōta Masao, ed., *Shiryō: Taishō demokurashii ronsō shi*, vol. 1. Shinsen, 1971.

Wada Hiroo. "Kanōsei o himeta Sōsai." In Tanzankai, ed., *Meihō Tanzan: Ishibashi Tanzan shokan no atogaki*. Hifumi, 1957.

Wakamori Tarō and Yamamoto Fujie. *Nihon no joseishi*. 6 vols. Shūei, 1971.

Watanabe Tadao. "Ishibashi Daijin." In Chō Yukio, ed., *Ishibashi Tanzan: Hito to shisō*. Tōyō Keizai Shinpō, 1974.

Watanabe Takeshi. *Senryōka no Nihon zaisei oboegaki.* Nihon Keizai Shinbun, 1966.

Watanabe Tōru. "Keizai, zaisei seisaku ron." In Inoue Kiyoshi and Watanabe, eds., *Taishōki no kyūshinteki jiyūshugi: 'Tōyō keizai shinpō' o chūshin toshite.* Tōyō Keizai Shinpō, 1972.

———. "Rōdō mondai—rōdō undō e no ronpyō." In Inoue Kiyoshi and Watanabe Tōru, eds., *Taishōki no kyūshinteki jiyūshugi: 'Tōyō keizai shinpō' o chūshin toshite.* Tōyō Keizai Shinpō, 1972.

———. "Sōron." In Inoue Kiyoshi and Watanabe, eds., *Taishōki no kyūshinteki jiyūshugi: 'Tōyō keizai shinpō' o chūshin toshite.* Tōyō Keizai Shinpō, 1972.

Yamamoto Fumio et al., eds. *Nihon masu komyunikeeshon shi.* Tokyo University Press, 1970.

Yamamoto Shirō. "Chūgoku mondai ron." In Inoue Kiyoshi and Watanabe Tōru, eds., *Taishōki no kyūshinteki jiyūshugi: 'Tōyō keizai shinpō' o chūshin toshite.* Tōyō Keizai Shinpō, 1972.

———. *Taishō seihen no kisoteki kenkyū.* Ochanomizu, 1970.

Yamamoto Taketoshi. *Shinbun to minshū.* Kinokuniya, 1982.

Yamanouchi Mina. *Yamanouchi Mina jiden.* Shinjuku, 1975.

Yoshida Seiichi. *Kindai bungei hyōron shi.* 2 vols. Shibundō, 1975.

———. *Shizenshugi no kenkyū.* 2 vols. Tōkyōdō, 1965.

Yoshino Sakuzō (Furukawa Gakujin). "Roshia no kakumei." *Chūō kōron* 32, no. 4 (Apr. 1917): 121ff.

Yoshino Sakuzō. "Iwayuru shuppei ron ni nan no gōriteki konkyo ariya." *Chūō kōron* 33, no. 4 (Apr. 1918): 1–30.

———. "Kensei no hongi o toite sono yūshū no bi o nasu no michi o ronzu." In Ōta Masao, ed., *Shiryō: Taishō demokurashii ronsō shi,* vol. 1. Shinsen, 1971.

———. *Nisshi kōshō ron.* Keihō, 1915.

———. "Shina ni taisuru nijūichi kajō." In Matsuo Takayoshi, ed., *Yoshino Sakuzō: Chūgoku Chōsen ron.* Tōyō Bunko, 1970.

———. "Tandoku wagi no kaishi ni yotte Rokoku wa nanimono o eran to suru." *Chūō kōron* 33, no. 1 (Jan. 1918): 95–105.

WORKS IN ENGLISH

Adachi, Yasushi. "Aspects of Pragmatism in Japan." M.A. thesis, University of Texas, 1969.

Akita, George. *The Foundations of Constitutional Government in Modern Japan.* Cambridge: Harvard University Press, 1970.

Allen, G. C. *Appointment in Japan: Memories of Sixty Years.* London: Athlone Press, 1983.

Andrews, Nancy. "The Seitōsha: An Early Japanese Women's Organization, 1911–1916." *Papers on Japan*, no. 6. Cambridge: Harvard East Asia Research Center, 1972.

Arima, Tatsuo. *The Failure of Freedom: A Portrait of Modern Japanese Intellectuals*. Cambridge: Harvard University Press, 1969.

Ayusawa, Iwao F. *A History of Labor in Modern Japan*. Honolulu: East-West Center Press, 1966.

Baerwald, Hans. *The Purge of Japanese Leaders under the Occupation*. University of California Publications in Political Science, vol. 8. Berkeley and Los Angeles: University of California Press, 1959.

Ball, W. MacMahon. *Japan: Enemy or Ally?* New York: John Day, 1949.

Bamba, Nobuya and John F. Howes, eds. *Pacifism in Japan: The Christian and Socialist Tradition*. Kyoto: Minerva, 1978.

Bartholomew, James. "Japanese Modernization and the Imperial Universities, 1876–1920." *Journal of Asian Studies* 37 (1978): 251–72.

Beard, Charles A. *The Administration and Politics of Tokyo—A Survey and Opinions*. New York: Macmillan, 1923.

Bellah, Robert. *Tokugawa Religion: The Values of Preindustrial Japan*. New York: Free Press, 1957.

Berger, Gordon. *Parties out of Power in Japan, 1931–1941*. Princeton: Princeton University Press, 1977.

Bourne, Randolph. "Twilight of the Idols." *Journal of the Seven Arts* 2 (1917): 688–702.

Bowen, Roger. *The Popular Rights Movement in Modern Japan*. Berkeley and Los Angeles: University of California Press, 1980.

Chambliss, William. *Chiraijima Village*. Tucson: University of Arizona Press, 1965.

The Civil Code of Japan, trans. W. J. Sebald. Toronto: Butterworth, 1934.

Cole, Robert E., and Ken'ichi Tominaga. "Japan's Changing Occupational Structure and Its Significance." In Hugh T. Patrick, ed., *Japanese Industrialization and Its Social Consequences*. Berkeley and Los Angeles: University of California Press, 1976.

Conte, James T. "Overseas Study in the Meiji Period: Japanese Students in America, 1867–1902." Ph.D. diss., Princeton, 1977.

Cooley, Charles. H. *Social Organization*. New York: Charles Scribner's Sons, 1929.

Coughlin, William J. *Conquered Press: The MacArthur Era in Japanese Journalism*. Palo Alto, California: Pacific Books, 1952.

Coyne, Fumiko H. "Censorship of Publishing in Japan, 1868–1945." M.A. thesis, University of Chicago, 1967.

Crowley, James B. "Intellectuals as Visionaries of the New Asian Order." In James W. Morley, ed., *Dilemmas of Growth in Prewar Japan.* Princeton: Princeton University Press, 1971.

————. *Japan's Quest for Autonomy and Security.* Princeton: Princeton University Press, 1966.

————. "A New Deal for Japan and Asia: One Road to Pearl Harbor." In Crowley, ed., *Modern East Asia: Essays in Interpretation.* New York: Harcourt, Brace, and World, 1971.

Dazai, Osamu. *The Setting Sun,* trans. Donald Keene. London: Peter Owen, 1958.

Dewey, John. *The Early Works of John Dewey,* ed. Jo Ann Boydston. 6 vols. Carbondale: University of Southern Illinois Press, 1971–72.

————. *Essays in Experimental Logic.* New York: Dover, 1916.

————. *Individualism Old and New.* New York: Minton Balch, 1930.

————. "Japan Revisited: Two Years Later." In Joseph Ratner, ed., *Characters and Events.* New York: Octagon, 1970.

————. "Liberalism in Japan." In Joseph Ratner, ed., *Characters and Events.* New York: Octagon, 1970.

————. Review of Lester Ward, *The Psychic Factors of Civilization.* In *The Early Works of John Dewey,* vol. 4. Carbondale: University of Southern Illinois Press, 1971.

Dilatush, Lois. "Women in the Professions." In Joyce Lebra et al., eds., *Women in Changing Japan.* Boulder: Westview, 1976.

Dower, John W. *Empire and Aftermath: Yoshida Shigeru and the Japanese Experience, 1878–1954.* Cambridge: Harvard University Press, 1979.

Duus, Peter. "Liberal Intellectuals and Social Conflict in Taishō Japan." In Tetsuo Najita and J. Victor Koschmann, eds., *Conflict in Modern Japanese History: The Neglected Tradition.* Princeton: Princeton University Press, 1982.

————. *Party Rivalry and Political Change in Taishō Japan.* Cambridge: Harvard University Press, 1968.

————. "Whig History, Japanese Style: The Minyūsha Historians and the Meiji Restoration." *Journal of Asian Studies* 33 (1974): 415–36.

————. "Yoshino Sakuzō: The Christian as Political Critic." *Journal of Japanese Studies* 4 (1978): 301–25.

Dykhuizen, George. *The Life and Mind of John Dewey.* Carbondale: Southern Illinois University Press, 1973.

Etō, Jun. "Modern Japanese Literary Criticism." *Japan Quarterly* 12 (1965): 177–86.

Fjelde, Rolf, trans. *Ibsen: The Complete Major Prose Plays*. New York: Farrar, Strauss, and Giroux, 1978.

Fletcher, Miles. *The Search for a New Order: Intellectuals and Fascism in Prewar Japan*. Chapel Hill: University of North Carolina Press, 1982.

Gluck, Carol N. "Japan's Modern Myth: Ideology in the Late Meiji Period." Ph.D. diss., Columbia University, 1977.

Government Section, Supreme Command for the Allied Powers. *The Political Reorientation of Japan, September 1945 to September 1948*. 2 vols. Washington, D.C.: U.S. Government Printing Office, 1949.

Griffin, Edward G. "The Universal Suffrage Issue in Japanese Politics, 1918–1925." *Journal of Asian Studies* 31 (1972): 275–90.

Halliday, Jon. *A Political History of Japanese Capitalism*. New York: Monthly Review, 1975.

Hane, Mikiso. *Peasants, Rebels, and Outcastes: The Underside of Modern Japan*. New York: Pantheon, 1982.

Hanley, Susan B., and Kozo Yamamura. *Economic and Demographic Change in Preindustrial Japan, 1600–1868*. Princeton: Princeton University Press, 1977.

Harootunian, H. D. "Between Politics and Culture: Authority and the Ambiguities of Intellectual Choice in Imperial Japan." In Bernard S. Silberman and H. D. Harootunian, eds., *Japan in Crisis: Essays on Taishō Democracy*. Princeton: Princeton University Press, 1974.

————. "Ideology as Conflict." In Tetsuo Najita and J. Victor Koschmann, eds., *Conflict in Modern Japanese History: The Neglected Tradition*. Princeton: Princeton University Press, 1982.

————. "The Problem of Taishō." In Bernard S. Silberman and H. D. Harootunian, eds., *Japan in Crisis: Essays in Taishō Democracy*. Princeton: Princeton University Press, 1974.

Hasegawa, Nyozekan. *The Educational and Cultural Background of the Japanese People*. Tokyo: Kokusai Bunka Shinkōkai, 1937.

————. *Japanese Character and Culture*, trans. John Bester. Palo Alto, California: Kodansha, 1965.

Hashikawa, Bunsō. "The 'Civil Society' Ideal and Wartime Resistance." In J. Victor Koschmann, ed., *Authority and the Individual in Japan*. Tokyo: Tokyo University Press, 1978.

Hata, Ikuhiko. "Japan under the Occupation." In Lawrence H. Redford, ed., *The Occupation of Japan: Economic Policy and Reform*. The Proceedings of a Symposium Sponsored by the MacArthur Memorial, 13–15 Apr. 1978. Norfolk, Virginia: The MacArthur Memorial, 1980.

Haugen, Einar. *Ibsen's Drama: Author to Audience.* Minneapolis: University of Minnesota Press, 1979.

Hollerman, Leon. "International Economic Controls in Occupied Japan." *Journal of Asian Studies* 38 (1979): 707–19.

Huber, Thomas M. *The Revolutionary Origins of Modern Japan.* Stanford: Stanford University Press, 1981.

Huffman, James L. *Politics of the Meiji Press: The Life of Fukuchi Gen'ichirō.* Honolulu: University of Hawaii Press, 1980.

Ienaga, Saburō. *The Pacific War, 1931–1945*, trans. Frank Baldwin. New York: Pantheon, 1978.

Iriye, Akira. *Power and Culture: The Japanese-American War.* Cambridge: Harvard University Press, 1981.

Ishibashi, Tanzan. "Enter Prince Higashikuni's Cabinet." *Oriental Economist* 12 (1945): 233–38.

_____. "The Higashikuni Cabinet Resigns." *Oriental Economist* 12 (1945): 276–79.

_____. "Industrial Democratization (1, 2, and 3)." *Oriental Economist* 13 (16 and 23 Feb. and 2 Mar. 1946).

_____. "The 1938 Outlook." *Oriental Economist* 5 (1938): 14–16.

_____. "On Anti-Americanism in Japan." *Oriental Economist* 20 (1953): 613–16.

_____. "Plan for a Self-supporting Economy." *Oriental Economist* 21 (1954): 347–54.

_____. "A Proposal for the China Problem." *Oriental Economist* 33 (1965): 137–42.

_____. "Three Vital Bills before the Diet." *Oriental Economist* 12 (1945): 360–63.

_____. "Twenty Years with the *Oriental Economist.*" *Oriental Economist* 21 (1954): 292–93.

_____. "Ways for Japan's Economic Survival (1, 2, 3, and 4)." *Oriental Economist* 18 (4, 11, 18, and 25 Aug. 1951).

_____. "What I Expect from 1952." *Oriental Economist* 19 (1952): 10–12.

_____. "The World and Japanese Economy in 1954." *Oriental Economist* 21 (1954): 47–51.

James, William. *The Letters of William James*, ed. Henry James. 2 vols. Boston: Atlantic Monthly Press, 1920.

Japanese Women (Tokyo, ed. Ichikawa Fusae).

Johnson, Chalmers. *MITI and the Japanese Miracle: The Growth of Industrial Policy, 1925–1975.* Stanford: Stanford University Press, 1982.

Kaibara, Ekken. *The Way of Contentment and the Greater Learning for Women*, trans. Ken Hoshino. London: John Murray, 1913.

Katō, Shūichi. "The Mass Media, Japan." In Robert E. Ward and Dankwart A. Rustow, eds., *Political Modernization in Japan and Turkey*. Princeton: Princeton University Press, 1964.

Kawabata, Yasunari. *The Existence and Discovery of Beauty*, trans. H. Viglielmo. Tokyo: Mainichi Shinbun, 1969.

Kawai, Kazuo. *Japan's American Interlude*. Chicago: University of Chicago Press, 1980.

Keynes, John Maynard. *The Economic Consequences of the Peace*. New York: Harcourt, Brace and Rowe, 1920.

———. *Essays in Persuasion*. London: Rupert Hart-Davis, 1952.

Kidd, Yasue Aoki. "Women Workers in the Japanese Cotton Mills, 1880–1920." *Cornell University East Asia Papers*, no. 20, 1978.

Kim, Young C. *Japanese Journalists and Their World*. Charlottesville: University of Virginia Press, 1981.

Kinmonth, Earl M. "Fukuzawa Reconsidered: *Gakumon no susume* and Its Audience." *Journal of Asian Studies* 37 (1978): 677–98.

———. *The Self-Made Man in Meiji Japanese Thought*. Berkeley and Los Angeles: University of California Press, 1981.

Koschmann, J. Victor. *Authority and the Individual in Japan: Citizen Protest in Historical Perspective*. Tokyo: Tokyo University Press, 1978.

Koyama, Takashi. *The Changing Social Position of Women in Japan*. Geneva: United Nations Press, 1961.

Kuno, Osamu. "The Meiji State, Minponshugi, and Ultra-Nationalism." In J. Victor Koschmann, ed., *Authority and the Individual in Japan: Citizen Protest in Historical Perspective*. Tokyo: Tokyo University Press, 1978.

Large, Stephen. "Buddhism and Political Renovation in Prewar Japan: The Case of Akamatsu Katsumaro." *Journal of Japanese Studies* 9 (1983): 33–66.

Lebra, Joyce, et al., eds. *Women in Changing Japan*. Boulder, Colorado: Westview, 1976.

Lebra, Takie Sugiyama. "Japanese Women in Male Dominant Careers: Cultural Barriers and Accommodations for Sex-Role Transcendence." *Ethnology* 20 (1981): 291–306.

Lifton, Robert J., et al. *Six Lives, Six Deaths: Portraits from Modern Japan*. New Haven: Yale University Press, 1979.

Lu, David J. *Sources of Japanese History*, vol. 2. New York: McGraw-Hill, 1974.

MacArthur, Douglas. "Japan: An Economy of Survival." *Fortune* 39 (June 1949): 74ff.

McKean, Margaret. *Environmental Protest and Citizen Politics in Japan.* Berkeley and Los Angeles: University of California Press, 1981.

Mannari, Hiroshi. *The Japanese Business Leaders.* Tokyo: Tokyo University Press, 1974.

Marshall, Byron K. *Capitalism and Nationalism in Prewar Japan.* Stanford: Stanford University Press, 1967.

_____ . "Growth and Conflict in Japanese Higher Education, 1905–1930." In Tetsuo Najita and J. Victor Koschmann, eds., *Conflict in Modern Japanese History: The Neglected Tradition.* Princeton: Princeton University Press, 1982.

_____ . "Professors and Politics: The Meiji Academic Elite." *Journal of Japanese Studies* 3 (1977): 71–98.

Maruyama, Masao. *Studies in the Intellectual History of Tokugawa Japan,* trans. Mikiso Hane. Tokyo: Tokyo University Press, 1974.

Matsumoto, Sannosuke. "The Roots of Political Disillusionment: 'Public' and 'Private' in Japan." In J. Victor Koschmann, ed., *Authority and the Individual in Japan: Citizen Protest in Historical Perspective.* Tokyo: Tokyo University Press, 1978.

Matsumoto, Sheila. "Women in Factories," in Joyce Lebra et al., eds., *Women in Changing Japan.* Boulder: Westview, 1977.

Matsuo, Takayoshi. "Profile of an Asian Minded Man, 8: Sakuzō Yoshino." *The Developing Economies* 4 (1966): 388–403.

Matsushita, Kiichi. "Citizen Participation in Historical Perspective." In J. Victor Koschmann, ed., *Authority and the Individual in Japan: Citizen Protest in Historical Perspective.* Tokyo: Tokyo University Press, 1978.

Matthewson, Rufus W. *The Positive Hero in Russian Literature.* Stanford: Stanford University Press, 1975.

Mayo, Marlene. "American Economic Planning for Occupied Japan: The Issue of *Zaibatsu* Dissolution, 1942–1945." In Lawrence H. Redford, ed., *The Occupation of Japan: Economic Policy and Reform.* The Proceedings of a Symposium Sponsored by the MacArthur Memorial, 13–15 Apr. 1978. Norfolk, Virginia: The MacArthur Memorial, 1980.

Mead, George H. *Movements of Thought in the Nineteenth Century,* ed. Merritt H. Moore. Chicago: University of Chicago Press, 1936.

Miller, Frank O. *Minobe Tatsukichi: Interpreter of Constitutionalism in Japan.* Berkeley and Los Angeles: University of California Press, 1965.

Mills, C. Wright. *Sociology and Pragmatism.* New York: Galaxy, 1966.

Milward, Alan S. *War, Economy and Society, 1939–1945*. Berkeley and Los Angeles: University of California Press, 1977.

Minear, Richard. *Japanese Tradition and Western Law: Emperor, State, and Law in the Thought of Hozumi Yatsuka*. Cambridge: Harvard University Press, 1970.

────── . *Victor's Justice: The Tokyo War Crimes Trial*. Princeton: Princeton University Press, 1972.

Minichiello, Sharon. *Retreat from Reform: Patterns of Political Behavior in Interwar Japan*. Honolulu: University of Hawaii Press, 1984.

Mitchell, Richard H. *Censorship in Imperial Japan*. Princeton: Princeton University Press, 1983.

Miyamoto, Ken. "Itō Noe and the Bluestockings." *Japan Interpreter* 10 (1975): 190–204.

Molony, Kathleen. "One Woman Who Dared: Ichikawa Fusae and the Japanese Women's Suffrage Movement. Ph.D. diss., University of Michigan, 1980.

Moore, Ray A. "Reflections on the Occupation of Japan." *Journal of Asian Studies* 38 (1979): 721–34.

Morley, James W. *The Japanese Thrust into Siberia, 1918*. New York: Columbia University Press, 1957.

Morris, Ivan. *The Nobility of Failure: Tragic Heroes in the History of Japan*. New York: New American Library, 1975.

Mosk, Carl. *Patriarchy and Fertility: Japan and Sweden, 1880–1960*. New York: Academic Press, 1983.

Mouer, Elizabeth Knipe. "Women in Teaching." In Joyce Lebra et al., eds., *Women in Changing Japan*. Boulder: Westview, 1977.

Murakami, Yasuke. "The Age of New Middle-Mass Politics: The Case of Japan." *Journal of Japanese Studies* 8 (1982): 29–72.

Najita, Tetsuo. *Hara Kei in the Politics of Compromise*. Cambridge: Harvard University Press, 1967.

────── . *The Intellectual Foundations of Modern Japan*. Englewood Cliffs, N.J.: Prentice-Hall, 1974.

────── . "Some Reflections on Idealism in the Political Thought of Yoshino Sakuzō." In Bernard Silberman and H. D. Harootunian, eds., *Japan in Crisis: Essays on Taishō Democracy*. Princeton: Princeton University Press, 1974.

Najita, Tetsuo, and J. Victor Koschmann, eds. *Conflict in Modern Japanese History: The Neglected Tradition*. Princeton: Princeton University Press, 1982.

Najita, Tetsuo, and Irwin Scheiner, eds. *Japanese Thought in the Tokugawa Period, 1600–1868*. Chicago: University of Chicago Press, 1978.

Nakamura, Mitsuo. *Modern Japanese Fiction, 1868–1926.* Tokyo: Kokusai Bunka Shinkōkai, 1968.

Nakamura, Takafusa. *Economic Growth in Prewar Japan,* trans. Robert A. Feldman. New Haven: Yale University Press, 1983.

———. *The Postwar Japanese Economy: Its Development and Structure,* trans. Jacqueline Kaminski. Tokyo: Tokyo University Press, 1980.

Napier, Ron. "The Transformation of the Japanese Labor Market, 1894–1937." In Tetsuo Najita and J. Victor Koschmann, eds., *Conflict in Modern Japanese History: The Neglected Tradition.* Princeton: Princeton University Press, 1982.

Noguchi, Takehiko. "Love and Death in the Early Modern Novel." In Albert M. Craig, ed., *Japan: A Comparative View.* Princeton: Princeton University Press, 1979.

Nolte, Sharon. "Democracy and Debate in Taishō Japan: Tanaka Ōdō, 1867–1932." Ph.D. diss., Yale University, 1979.

———. "Individualism in Taishō Japan." *Journal of Asian Studies* 43 (1984): 667–83.

———. "Industrial Democracy for Japan? Tanaka Ōdō and John Dewey." *Journal of the History of Ideas* 45 (1984): 277–94.

———. "National Morality and Universal Ethics: Ōnishi Hajime and the Imperial Rescript on Education." *Monumenta Nipponica* 38 (1983): 283–94.

Oka, Yoshitake. "Generational Conflict after the Russo-Japanese War." In Tetsuo Najita and J. Victor Koschmann, eds., *Conflict in Modern Japanese History: The Neglected Tradition.* Princeton: Princeton University Press. 1982.

———. *Konoe Fumimaro: A Political Biography,* trans. Shumpei Okamoto. Tokyo: Tokyo University Press, 1983

Okamoto, Shumpei. "The Emperor and the Crowd: The Historical Significance of the Hibiya Riot." In Tetsuo Najita and J. Victor Koschmann, eds., *Conflict in Modern Japanese History: The Neglected Tradition.* Princeton: Princeton University Press, 1982.

———. "Ishibashi Tanzan and the Twenty-one Demands." In Akira Iriye, ed., *The Chinese and the Japanese: Essays in Political and Cultural Interaction.* Princeton: Princeton University Press, 1980.

———. *The Japanese Oligarchy and the Russo-Japanese War.* New York: Columbia University Press, 1970.

Okazaki, Yoshie. *Japanese Literature in the Meiji Era,* trans. H. Viglielmo. Tokyo: Ōbun, 1955.

Packard, George. *Protest in Tokyo: The Treaty Crisis of 1960.* Westport, Conn.: Greenwood, 1978.

Patrick, Hugh T. "The Economic Muddle of the 1920s." In James W. Morley, ed., *Dilemmas of Growth in Prewar Japan*. Princeton: Princeton University Press, 1971.

————. "External Equilibrium and Internal Convertibility in Financial Policy in Meiji Japan." *Journal of Economic History* 25 (1965): 189–213.

Patrick, Hugh T., ed. *Japanese Industrialization and Its Social Consequences*. Berkeley and Los Angeles: University of California Press, 1976.

Pierson, John D. *Tokutomi Sohō, 1863–1957: A Journalist for Modern Japan*. Princeton: Princeton University Press, 1980.

Powell, Brian. "Matsui Sumako: Actress and Woman." In W. G. Beasley, ed., *Modern Japan: Aspects of History, Society, and Literature*. Berkeley and Los Angeles: University of California Press, 1975.

Powles, Cyril F. "Abe Isoo." In Nobuya Bamba and John F. Howes, eds., *Pacifism in Japan: The Christian and Socialist Tradition*. Kyoto: Minerva, 1978.

"Purging in Japanese Journalism." *Oriental Economist* 14 (1947): 549.

Pyle, Kenneth B. "Advantages of Followership: German Economics and Japanese Bureaucrats, 1890–1925." *Journal of Japanese Studies* 1 (1974): 127–64.

————. "The Future of Japanese Nationality: An Essay in Contemporary History." *Journal of Japanese Studies* 8 (1982): 223–64.

————. *The New Generation in Meiji Japan*. Stanford: Stanford University Press, 1969.

Randall, John H. "Dewey's Interpretation of the History of Philosophy." In Paul A. Schilpp., ed., *The Philosophy of John Dewey*. Evanston, Illinois: Northwestern University Press, 1939.

Rapp, William V. "Firm Size and Japan's Export Structure: A Microview of Japan's Export Competitiveness since Meiji." In Hugh T. Patrick, ed., *Japanese Industrialization and Its Social Consequences*. Berkeley and Los Angeles: University of California Press, 1976.

Redford, Lawrence H., ed. *The Occupation of Japan: Economic Policy and Reform*. The Proceedings of a Symposium Sponsored by the MacArthur Memorial, 13–15 Apr. 1978. Norfolk, Virginia: The MacArthur Memorial, 1980.

Reich, Pauline C., et al. "Japan's Literary Feminists: The *Seitō* Group." *Signs* 2 (1976): 280–91.

Rice, Richard. "Economic Mobilization in Wartime Japan: Business, Bureaucracy, and Military in Conflict." *Journal of Asian Studies* 38 (1979): 689–706.

Rimer, J. Thomas. *Modern Japanese Fiction and Its Traditions: An Introduction.* Princeton: Princeton University Press, 1978.

Rodd, Laurel Rasplica. *Nichiren: Selected Writings.* Asian Studies at Hawaii, no. 26. Honolulu: University of Hawaii Press, 1980.

Rolf, Robert. *Masamune Hakuchō.* N.p.: Twayne, 1979.

Rothman, Sheila. *Woman's Proper Place.* New York: Basic Books, 1978.

Rubin, Jay. *Injurious to Public Morals: Writers and the Meiji State.* Seattle: University of Washington Press, 1984.

Rucker, Egbert Darnell. *The Chicago Pragmatists.* Minneapolis: University of Minnesota Press, 1969.

Sanday, Peggy Reeves. "Cultural and Structural Pluralism in the United States." In Sanday, ed., *Anthropology and the Public Interest.* New York: Academic Press, 1976.

Sansom, Sir George. *The Western World and Japan: A Study in the Interaction of European and Asiatic Cultures.* New York: Knopf, 1950.

Sansom, Katharine. *Sir George Sansom and Japan: A Memoir.* Tallahassee, Florida: The Diplomatic Press, 1972.

Saxonhouse, Gary R. "Country Girls and Communication among Competitors in the Japanese Cotton-Spinning Industry." In Hugh T. Patrick, ed., *Japanese Industrialization and Its Social Consequences.* Berkeley and Los Angeles: University of California Press, 1976.

Scheiner, Irwin. "Benevolent Lords and Honorable Peasants: Rebellion and Peasant Consciousness in Tokugawa Japan." In Tetsuo Najita and Scheiner, eds., *Japanese Thought in the Tokugawa Period, 1600–1868.* Chicago: University of Chicago Press, 1978.

————. *Christian Converts and Social Protest in Meiji Japan.* Berkeley and Los Angeles: University of California Press, 1970.

Schilpp, Paul A., ed. *The Philosophy of John Dewey.* Evanston: Northwestern University Press, 1939.

Schonberger, Howard. "The Japan Lobby in American Diplomacy, 1947–1952." *Pacific Historical Review* 46 (1977): 327–59.

Seidensticker, Edward. *Kafū the Scribbler: The Life and Writings of Nagai Kafū, 1879–1959.* Stanford: Stanford University Press, 1965.

Shillony, Ben-Ami. *Politics and Culture in Wartime Japan.* Oxford: Clarendon Press, 1981.

————. *Revolt in Japan: The Young Officers and the February 26, 1936 Incident.* Princeton: Princeton University Press, 1973.

Shimazaki, Tōson. *The Family,* trans. Cecilia Segawa Seigle. Tokyo: Tokyo University Press, 1976.

Sibley, William F. "Naturalism in Japanese Literature." *Harvard Journal of Asiatic Studies* 28 (1968): 157–67.

Sievers, Sharon L. "Feminist Criticism in Japanese Politics in the 1880s." *Signs* 6 (1981): 602–09.

Silberman, Bernard S. "The Bureaucracy as a Political Force, 1920–1945." In James W. Morley, ed., *Dilemmas of Growth in Prewar Japan*. Princeton: Princeton University Press, 1971.

————. "The Bureaucratic State in Japan: The Problem of Authority and Legitimacy." In Tetsuo Najita and J. Victor Koschmann, eds., *Conflict in Modern Japanese History: The Neglected Tradition*. Princeton: Princeton University Press, 1982.

————. "The Democracy Movement in Japan." Ph.D. diss., University of Michigan, 1956.

Silberman, Bernard, and H. D. Harootunian, eds. *Japan in Crisis: Essays on Taishō Democracy*. Princeton: Princeton University Press, 1974.

Smith, Robert J., and Ella Lury Wiswell. *The Women of Suye Mura*. Chicago: University of Chicago Press, 1982.

Spaulding, Robert M. "The Intent of the Charter Oath." In Richard M. Beardsley, ed., *Studies in Japanese History and Politics*. Occasional Papers, no. 10. Ann Arbor: Center for Japanese Studies, University of Michigan, 1967.

Staggs, Kathleen M. " 'Defend the Nation and Love the Truth': Inoue Enryō and the Revival of Meiji Buddhism." *Monumenta Nipponica* 38 (1983): 251–82.

Stevens, R. P. G. "Hybrid Constitutionalism in Prewar Japan." *Journal of Japanese Studies* 3 (1977): 99–133.

Straelin, H. von. *The Japanese Woman Looking Forward*. Tokyo: Kyo Bun, 1940.

Stuart, Henry W. "Dewey's Ethical Theory." In Paul A. Schilpp, ed., *The Philosophy of John Dewey*. Evanston: Northwestern University Press, 1939.

Sudermann, Hermann. *The Old Home*, trans. Charles Winslow Homer. New York: French, 1895.

Taira, Koji. *Economic Development and the Labor Market in Japan*. New York: Columbia University Press, 1970.

Takanashi, Taka (Tanaka Takako). "The Change in the Status of Women under the Modern Conditions of Japanese Life." M.A. thesis, University of Chicago, 1918.

Takeda, Kiyoko. "Japanese Christianity: Between Orthodoxy and Heterodoxy." In J. Victor Koschmann, ed., *Authority and the Individual in Japan: Citizen Protest in Historical Perspective*. Tokyo: Tokyo University Press, 1978.

Takemoto, Toru. *Failure of Liberalism in Japan: Shidehara Kijūrō's Encounter with Anti-Liberals.* Washington, D.C.: University Press of America, 1978.

Takenobu, Y. *The Japan Yearbook, 1930.* Tokyo: Japan Yearbook, 1930.

Tayama, Katai. *The Quilt and Other Stories,* trans. Kenneth G. Henshall. Tokyo: Tokyo University Press, 1981.

Tiedemann, Arthur E. "Big Business and Politics in Prewar Japan." In James W. Morley, ed., *Dilemmas of Growth in Prewar Japan.* Princeton: Princeton University Press, 1971.

Tipton, Elise. "The Civil Police in the Suppression of the Prewar Japanese Left." Ph.D. diss., Indiana University, 1977.

Titus, David. *Palace and Politics in Prewar Japan.* New York: Columbia University Press, 1974.

————. "Political Parties and Nonissues in Taishō Democracy." In Harry Wray and Hilary Conroy, eds., *Japan Examined: Perspectives on Modern Japanese History.* Honolulu: University of Hawaii Press, 1983.

Tsunoda, Ryusaku, Wm. Theodore de Bary, and Donald Keene, eds. *Sources of Japanese Tradition.* 2 vols. New York: Columbia University Press, 1958.

Tsurumi, Kazuko. *Women in Japan: A Paradox in Modernization.* Tokyo: Institute of International Relations, 1977.

Uchimura, Kanzō. "Ninomiya Sontoku—A Peasant Saint." In Ishiguro Tadaatsu, ed., *Ninomiya Sontoku.* Tokyo: Kenkyū, 1955.

Vogel, Suzanne H. "The Professional Housewife." International Group for the Study of Women, *Proceedings of the Tokyo Symposium on Women.* Tokyo: International Group for the Study of Women, 1978.

————. "Professional Housewife: The Career of Urban Middle-Class Japanese Women." *Japan Interpreter* 12 (1978): 17–43.

Walthall, Anne. "The Ethics of Protest by Commoners in Late Eighteenth-Century Japan." Ph.D. diss., University of Chicago, 1979.

Waswo, Ann. "In Search of Equity: Japanese Tenant Unions in the 1920s." In Tetsuo Najita and J. Victor Koschmann, eds., *Conflict in Modern Japanese History: The Neglected Tradition.* Princeton: Princeton University Press, 1982.

Watanuki, Jōji. *Politics in Postwar Japanese Society.* Tokyo: Tokyo University Press, 1977.

White, James W. "Internal Migration in Prewar Japan." *Journal of Japanese Studies* 4 (1978): 82–123.

Wildes, Harry Emerson. *Typhoon in Tokyo: The Occupation and Its Aftermath*. New York: Macmillan, 1954,

Wilkinson, Thomas O. *The Urbanization of Japanese Labor, 1868–1955*. Amherst: University of Massachusetts Press, 1965.

Williams, Justin. *Japan's Political Revolution under MacArthur: A Participant's Account*. Tokyo: Tokyo University, 1979.

Williams, Raymond. *The Sociology of Culture*. New York: Schocken, 1981.

Yamamura, Kozo. *Economic Policy in Postwar Japan: Growth vs. Economic Democracy*. Berkeley and Los Angeles: University of California Press, 1967.

————. "The Japanese Economy, 1911–1930: Concentration, Conflicts and Crises." In Bernard S. Silberman and H. D. Harootunian, eds., *Japan in Crisis: Essays on Taishō Democracy*. Princeton: Princeton University Press, 1974.

Yoshida, Shigeru. *The Yoshida Memoirs*, trans. Kenichi Yoshida. Boston: Houghton Mifflin, 1962.

Young, Arthur Morgan. *The Socialist and Labour Movement in Japan*. Kobe: Japan Chronicle, 1922.

Index

Designer: Betty Gee
Compositor: Auto-Graphics
Text: 11/13 Baskerville
Display: Baskerville
Printer: Braun-Brumfield
Binder: Braun-Brumfield